SECOND EDITION

CREATING A FLEXIBLE WORKPLACE

CREATING A FLEXIBLE WORKPLACE

SECOND EDITION

HOW TO SELECT & MANAGE ALTERNATIVE WORK OPTIONS

BARNEY OLMSTED • SUZANNE SMITH

amacom
American Management Association

New York • Atlanta • Boston • Chicago • Kansas City • San Francisco • Washington, D.C.
Brussels • Mexico City • Tokyo • Toronto

This book is available at a special
discount when ordered in bulk quantities.
For information, contact Special Sales Department,
AMACOM, a division of American Management Association,
135 West 50th Street, New York, NY 10020.

This publication is designed to provide accurate and authoritative information in regard to the subject matter covered. It is sold with the understanding that the publisher is not engaged in rendering legal, accounting, or other professional service. If legal advice or other expert assistance is required, the services of a competent professional person should be sought.

Library of Congress Cataloging-in-Publication Data

Olmsted, Barney.
    Creating a flexible workplace : how to select & manage alternative
work options / Barney Olmsted. Suzanne Smith.—2nd ed.
        p.   cm.
    Includes bibliographical references and index.
    ISBN 0-8144-0214-3
    1. Hours of labor, Flexible—United States.   2. Compressed work
week—United States.   3. Part-time employment—United States.
4. Job sharing—United States.   5. Work sharing—United States.
I. Smith, Suzanne.   II. Title.
HD5109.2.U5046   1994   (.2)
331.25'72'0973—dc20
                                                                94-28096
                                                                CIP

Printing number

10   9   8   7   6   5   4   3   2   1

Contents

Acknowledgments

Although a book revision doesn't require quite the amount of effort that writing the initial publication does, trying to capture five years of change in workplace attitudes and practice and show how they relate to flexibility has been challenging. As with the first edition, we had a lot of help from our friends and colleagues.

Of particular help were Helen Axel, who combed her extensive files for pertinent information; Stan Nollen, whose insights on the growing complexity of contingent employment convinced us that this kind of flexibility had moved beyond the purlieu of this book; Mary Holt, who shared her thoughts on corporate culture change; and Gil Gordon, whose phone calls, faxes, and newsletter keep us up to date on that fast-growing field of telecommuting.

Our thanks to the various people who helped us develop new profiles on current organizational practice, particularly Paul Hackleman, Norma Tombari, Rosemary Mans, Bob Silverforb, Barbara Katersky, Peter Jeff, Michelle Carpenter, Emily Bassman, Andreas Hoff, and Sue Hutchinson.

Once again our editor Adrienne Hickey at AMACOM was fully supportive of the changes we wanted to make and editors Kate Pferdner and Barbara Horowitz made sure that the second edition was as polished as the first.

And of course, the staff of New Ways to Work provided ongoing support, information, and encouragement as they have for more than twenty years.

Preface to The Second Edition

In the Preface to the first edition of *Creating a Flexible Workplace*, we noted that a not-so-quiet revolution was taking place in U.S. organizations and suggested that human resources management was at a crossroads. In retrospect, this was an accurate forecast and a good analogy, and today we have a clearer view of where the two roads—contingent employment and flexible work arrangements—lead.

The Reinventing of America

Since the mid-1980s, corporate America has been engaged in restructuring, reengineering, and reinventing the American workplace. Flexible staffing, or the "core/ring configuration," a human resources strategy that began to attract attention in the mid-1980s, has continued to grow in use. With this method, employers define a core group of primarily full-time employees, and their activities are supplemented by the use of full- and part-time temporaries, consultants, and contractual workers. These "flexible staff," who receive little or no training, collect few if any benefits, and may or may not have possibilities for upward mobility, appear to produce reduced labor costs and presumably act as a buffer for the core during downturns in the economy. The intent is to provide the organization with the flexibility it needs during changing economic cycles.

For many companies, the first stage of taking the core/ring fork in the road is deciding to "downsize." When business improves and "staffing up" begins, rather than rebuilding the regular work-force, management hires contingent workers. The result has been a profound restructuring of the American workplace. In the process, American society is being reengineered as well. A two-tiered labor force is rapidly evolving with little discussion about its long-term impact on the workplace or its ramifications for the larger society.

When the first edition of *CFW* was written, flexible staffing was only one of several tools for managers seeking more flexibility in the way they allocated labor. It has since become a road of its own. Its attraction lies to a great extent in expediency and in unexamined short-term cost savings. At its worst, the organizational traits that become dominant are dependency on the ease of management (a contingent employee can be terminated immediately, at will) and a culture that conveys, subconsciously perhaps, a belief that people are interchangeable, like widgets, and implies that there is no profit to be had from relationships that require mutual commitment. The core/ring configuration today reflects a decade of thinking "lean and mean," rather than working toward "win-win." What its long-term effects will be are unknown, but if "people are our most important assets," we may be poisoning our own well.

Seeking Balance in a Chaotic World

Although contingent employment has received more media atten-tion because it has shattered traditional social contract values in many workplaces and had dramatic effects on the lives of those who have been "downsized" and "de-cored," another flexibility scenario has continued to develop along parallel lines in most organizations. Flexibility as a human resources strategy has made extensive in-roads in a growing number of organizations. In the first edition we described its effects as "a three-way stretch": That is, it makes possible a context in which flexibility for the organization, the individuals within it, and the society at large can interrelate and reinforce each other. Unlike contingent employment, the objectives of this human resources management scenario are long-range and proactive. Its goal is to build a totally flexible workplace through a combination of mutually beneficial tactics. These include:

- Introducing a wide variety of integrated work schedules, many of which are offered on an optional basis
- Using both on- and off-site space arrangements
- Training, retraining, and cross-training employees

Flexibility is seen as a way to:

1. Help each employee achieve his or her full potential
2. Help managers reallocate labor supply as necessary
3. Build employee commitment to the organization, recognizing that this is an important cornerstone of growth and profitability

For a society that wants to operate at the top end of a global economy, these objectives are critical. This revised edition provides an update of the same basic "how to" information as the first. Statistics, resource materials, and some case histories have been emended in order to provide current information and "best practice" models. Much of what is new in this volume, however, relates to the way some leading organizations have begun to take flexibility out of a program mode and integrate it systemwide.

As we move closer to the end of this century, the concept of creating a flexible workplace continues to find adherents who see it as an important aspect of the workplace of the future. This book is intended to provide a tool to that end.

Introduction:
Win-Lose or Win-Win?

In the five years since the first edition of *Creating a Flexible Workplace* was published, there has been an acceptance in concept of the value, to both people and organizations, of workplace flexibility. However, as we noted in the Preface to this edition, there is still great disagreement about how flexibility should be achieved and what the long-term social and economic ramifications of the push-pull between contingent and core flexibility will be. In other words, the verdict is still out on what kind of a workplace and what kind of a society we will have in the decades to come.

A 1993 report from the Wyatt Company, *Best Practices in Corporate Restructuring,* concludes that many practices of the last few years have not achieved their objectives of increasing productivity and profitability. It suggests that it is time to move from corporate restructuring to corporate renewal. This is a notion that seems to recognize that we are at the end of one era and in need of a more long-term, visionary approach for the next. The concept of a continuous process of "redefining one's understanding of the company's key constituencies and their needs" and learning how best to meet these needs, as opposed to viewing change as an event, is the way the report contrasts restructuring with renewal.[1] Such a context would certainly provide more fertile ground for win-win flexibility than the last five years has.

The workplace of the future is one that will need new energy and vision. It is generally characterized as one in which companies will be smaller, hierarchies will give way to flatter organizations in which workers have more responsibility and the vertical division of

1

labor will become horizontal, constant learning and retraining will be necessary, and the economy will be primarily service-oriented.[2] Cross-trained work teams, "virtual organizations," and fluid systems that can react to changing conditions quickly and efficiently are depicted as the coming norm.

If this is true, then win-win workplace flexibility—and worker-friendly management strategies—will be even more important in the future. The smaller the workplace, the more important the contribution and commitment of each individual worker. The flatter the organization and the more team and cell organization within it, the less efficient a two-tier labor force becomes. And the more responsibility and flexibility that is demanded of workers, the more they will ask in return. If current employee polls are any indication, one of the things they will ask for is more flexibility of the kind that suits *their* needs. In the workplace of the future, flexibility must be viewed as a way to facilitate retention and renewal of employees, including cross-training, retraining, and continuing education. It must be used to support and manage a workforce that will be ever more diverse and empowered.

For the employer, the essence of flexibility is the ability to match the firm's labor needs with its labor supply—or put another way, it is the ability to quickly reshape the existing supply in terms of configuration, deployment, and cost. A workforce that consists of employees working a variety of schedules offers more possibilities for expansion or contraction of hours. The more skills each employee has, the more scheduling and site arrangements are possible; and the more dedicated and committed the workforce, the more flexible the organizational response can be.

Workplace flexibility consists of a variety of components, including concepts of:

■ *Numerical, or operational, flexibility.* This aspect of an organization used to be assessed exclusively in terms of the total number of employees in a company. Head count was the tool by which managers were expected to control and manage their work units. As the use of part-time employees has grown, and a mix of full-time and part-time regular employees is seen as a benefit to both employees and the staffing of the organization, the concept of full-time equivalency has been introduced in many firms. This facilitates more operational flexibility. Flexible working arrangements are the means by which some employers have been seeking more operational flexibility, and it is this facet of an organization's ability to respond flexibly that is the primary focus of this book.

■ *Job, or functional, flexibility.* Job flexibility involves skills development, cross-training, job enlargement, and redeployment of staff. Since job restructuring often accompanies the restructuring or reorganizing of work time, it relates to numerical flexibility but is basically a separate consideration.

■ *Financial flexibility.* Financial flexibility can be enhanced by cost-saving strategies related to new staffing and scheduling options for regular employees.

■ *Structural flexibility.* As new kinds of work-time and workspace arrangements are introduced and relationships within the workforce become more team-based, participative, and responsible, structure and systems must become more flexible as well in order to support the change.

Within all four of the categories relating to organizational flexibility, there are possibilities for expanding opportunities for employees as well as achieving business objectives. It is a belief in the power and efficacy of this win-win approach that is the basic tenet of this book.

From the employees' perspective, flexibility is generally defined as having more control over where and when they work. They are seeking better ways to manage their work and their time and to reduce conflicts between work and their personal goals and responsibilities. Companies that formulate policies that allow employees to do this build employee commitment to the organization. Some experts contend that workplace flexibility offers a powerful way to address the new and varied needs of both employees and employers. They argue that "recognizing transitions and conflicts between employees' work and their personal lives—and helping them manage these conflicts—actually increases their psychological availability for work," and that "companies that do not foresee the competitive advantage of managing their human resources more strategically risk being lulled by a false sense of security."[3]

One of the important lessons learned in recent years, however, is that if an organization wishes to move beyond ad hoc accommodation or the program stage and use workplace flexibility strategically, its culture and systems must support this kind of change. Companies trying to introduce flexible work arrangements too often find that these new concepts conflict with a philosophy of increasing productivity by working harder and faster rather than working smarter and better.

Culture, Systems, and Change

As Dr. Stanley Nollen, an early expert in the flexible work arrangements field, observes, "new work patterns are not just minor changes in work schedules. They are an adjustment in the sociotechnical system of the company."[4] As such, they entail a significant culture shift for most organizations.

Workplace flexibility to date has generally been implemented in stages. Typically, the first three stages are (1) small-scale, or ad hoc, experiments, (2) expanding the experience more broadly to other parts of the organization or increasing the number of options, and (3) integrating the initiatives into HR management policy. Policy by itself, however, does not change culture. Many of the firms that have gotten to the policy stage find themselves wondering why usage is low.

Because many of the components of flexibility were originally introduced as employee accommodations, rather than as parts of an overall strategy with management support, they are only rarely perceived as parts of a larger plan. Too often, managers view them as being of little benefit, and employees wonder whether requesting a nonstandard work arrangement will have a negative effect on their career paths. This kind of mindset must change if workplace flexibility is to become a reality. Managers at all levels must understand the business reasons for flexibility. They are the gatekeepers of change in any organization, and they must be encouraged to think in terms of developing flexible management styles and systems that support the goal of a flexible workplace. Employees must feel comfortable in requesting flexible work arrangements, secure in the knowledge that it will not be held against them. In order for these changes to occur, the culture of the corporation must support the concept of workplace flexibility.

What Is Organizational Culture?

At a 1993 national conference on workplace flexibility, Mary Holt, regional vice president, ARC International, Ltd., defined organizational culture as:

> the constellation of beliefs, values, habits, and norms of behavior which actually operate inside an organization. It's the way work

gets done around here, how people choose to relate to each other, how problems get resolved, what gets celebrated. It's not necessarily what people say/claim are the beliefs/values . . . but what actually are. You come to understand a culture much the way an ethnographer works . . . by listening, observing, living with people inside the culture over a long period of time. You don't understand it by just reading vision statements or listening to executive speeches.[5]

Needless to say, most organizations' cultures have not yet embraced the concept of a flexible workplace. As Holt pointed out,

There has been what I call incremental change . . . the changes have been programmatic, or even systemic, in nature. But they have not been transformational—change at the level of beliefs. I suggest to you that it will have to be at the level of beliefs that we will have to work if we are to really transform the workplace.[6]

No matter what the vision statements and policy options say, most organizations' cultures still support the belief that those who work the longest hours are the most productive employees—what Gil Gordon, a leading international expert on telecommuting and other flexible work arrangements, calls the "face time/60-hour monster." He quotes an anonymous manager on the subject of flexibility:

"Sure we have flextime around here. You can come in as early as you want, and stay as late as you have to."[7]

Gordon's suggestions to management seeking to change this pervasive value include:

- ■ Stop colluding with unreasonable expectations.
- ■ The new mantra must be: It's the product, not the process.
- ■ Painful as it may be, we must remember that we are "they."

And finally:

- ■ Long hours correlate with long hours—not necessarily with higher output, efficiency, quality, or customer service.[8]

It is important not to underestimate the degree of change—not just of culture and systems, but of attitude and expectation—that it takes to create a workplace in which people and organizations can function more flexibly. The change is profound and affects all aspects of an organization, from vision statements to payroll systems to labor contract language. It cannot be conceived as a single task, but should instead be considered both an overall objective and a component of a long-range, comprehensive organizational plan. Many of the tenets and underlying policies that promote flexibility run counter not just to organizational culture but also to long-held management assumptions: Using a variety of work-time options violates the principle of standardized scheduling; telecommuting and flexplace (working at home or off-site) arrangements are at variance with the belief that employees should be in sight and on-site; supervising and evaluating performance based on how well an employee produces or meets objectives requires attitudes and skills different from those appropriate for paternalistic over-the-shoulder managing. Real change in attitudes and management style will be needed in conjunction with changes in policy in order to achieve a flexible workplace.

In deciding how to proceed when starting to redefine the culture and the systems so that they will support flexibility, it is first helpful to define some of the problems in the organization that have created the need for more flexibility. For example:

- Fluctuations in product or service supply and demand can result in changes in labor force needs. An organization may want to expand its use of regular voluntary part-time employment or develop a work-sharing capacity.
- Changes in the company's demographics—the graying of the workforce or an increase in the number of employees with family responsibilities—may warrant a new look at phased retirement or flexible and reduced work-time policies.
- Technological innovation that necessitates widespread continuing training or education may encourage experimentation with sabbaticals or regular part-time employment or job sharing to allow employees the time and opportunity to expand their current skills.

Eight Steps to Creating Flexibility

The first edition of *Creating a Flexible Workplace* recommended an eight-step implementation process when introducing one or more new scheduling or staffing options. These steps also provide a framework for managing the comprehensive change that transforming an organization from a "face time," top-down culture to a flexible one demands.

1. *Gain support for the program.* As Jamison and O'Mara point out in *Managing Workforce 2000,*[9] introducing one or several flexible work arrangements entails managing basic change. The introduction of new, flexible systems needs to be systematically diagnosed, designed, and implemented. It needs to be recognized that flexibility alters all aspects of the existing systems, policies, and practices. A change management structure is required, and the best way to build support for this kind of basic change in an organization is to form a cross-function management task force, with representation from top management and all segments of the company that will be affected by the particular options under consideration. Part of the task force's charge should be to:

- *Define the organization's diversity.* Know the composition of the workforce—its age, gender, ethnicity, education, and disabilities. Having individualized information such as marital and parental status and longevity in the workforce is also important. Projecting the composition of the future workforce may provide critical incentives.

- *Understand the organization's workforce values and needs.* This kind of information is more complex than simple demographics. It can be obtained through the use of surveys, focus groups comprising simple or mixed segments of the workforce (ethnic groups, management levels, organizational components, etc.), individual interviews, or advisory or task force groups.

- *Describe the desired future state.* What does the workforce want the organization to look and be like in five years? What will the workplace be doing to (1) better match people and jobs, (2) manage and reward performance, (3) inform and involve people, and (4) support lifestyle and life needs?

- *Analyze the present state.* Are any of the desired changes possible now? Are there policy, systems, or practice barriers that must be addressed first? How do the day-to-day practices of managers contribute to or impede the process? By looking at "where we are" relative to "where we want to be," a plan for change can be developed and implemented.

- *Plan and manage transitions.* The task force should be charged with developing a comprehensive task plan and timeline, developing strategies for building commitment, managing the politics of the organization, highlighting successes, and managing and adapting the implementation steps, sequences, and timing.[10]

In addition, the task force's responsibility will be to:

■ Investigate what similar organizations have done in regard to these options. Having information about other companies' experience can avoid the need to reinvent the wheel and can provide helpful hints on successful implementation as well as competitive incentives.

■ Inventory existing experience in your own organization. In the last five years, most organizations have greatly increased their level of ad hoc experimentation with a variety of flexible work arrangements. Existing experience can provide models and "how to" information on how new options work best within the company culture.

■ Conduct research among employees to determine their wants and needs.

■ Define objectives and desired results.

■ Develop a draft policy statement for review.

■ Develop an action plan and a timeline for evaluating the new program.

■ Set up a system for gathering input into the planning and implementation process and generating feedback during the initial phases of the program. Encouraging suggestions and reactions from all levels of the workforce will help identify problem areas, involving both attitude and process, that must be addressed. It will also begin to enlarge the base of support for the overall program.

■ Revise the policy and action plan as appropriate.

■ Determine the initial scope of the program (that is, whether it will be tested in a pilot project and then expanded to other units, instituted companywide, or introduced incrementally).

■ Set up some kind of process to provide ongoing support for those charged with implementing the change and reiterate top management's commitment to increasing flexibility. As James Taylor, of Socio-Technical Designs, Inc., noted, "In organizational change where there hasn't been the time spent for all members to buy in, middle management says, 'I'm uncertain and anxious and the only way I know to be comfortable is to get in control, to shift back to that old model of defining jobs and work.'"[11]

2. *Set up the program's administration.* The administrators will be charged with implementing the specifics of the program devised by the task force. Responsibility for overall coordination and the devel-

opment of technical assistance for supervisors and employees should be assigned to a particular person. Additional project staff may be needed, depending on the scope of the program.

3. *Design the program.* Designing the specifics of a particular component of the flexibility project may be the responsibility of the task force or of a subgroup designated by the task force. In designing the program, current policy must be reviewed to determine its compatibility with the new objectives, and new policy must be framed where necessary. Process issues such as eligibility, an application process, effect on employee status, and reversibility must be addressed.

4. *Develop resource materials.* Both employees and supervisors will require resource materials. In addition to a program description, educational and technical assistance materials and, in some instances, training will be needed to explain the new options and policies and also provide support and guidance in implementing them. Good resource materials will save supervisors time, since they will be well informed and won't need to go over the same issues again and again with individual employees. Access to detailed information also facilitates planning for both managers and their employees. According to a 1993 Catalyst study, 60 percent of companies had formal policies or guidelines pertaining to flexible work arrangements and felt that clear guidelines ensured success.[12]

5. *Announce the program.* Although this seems an obvious step, some companies have developed an alternative work-time policy and then taken a passive stance, waiting for employees to request the kind of arrangement that the policy already authorizes.

6. *Promote the program.* Several studies have indicated that fewer than 2 percent of employees avail themselves of programs that would allow them to work at home or work part-time.[13] In many cases programs are underutilized because employees do not know about them or are afraid that participating will negatively affect their career paths. If an organization and its employees are to take full advantage of any of the new work arrangements, the program must be promoted on an ongoing basis. The concepts involved are unfamiliar. Even employees who want options like job sharing, leave time, or phased retirement need to be reassured that participating in these programs will not have a negative impact on their career hopes or earning potential. From management's perspective, the benefits associated with most of the options reviewed in this

book come from a "multiplier effect"; that is, the more employees who use the program on a voluntary basis, the greater the benefits.

Although employers frequently worry that too many people will want to work part-time or will "flex" their schedules to such an extent that it is disruptive, experience has shown that this does not often occur. Furthermore, management can and should "fine-tune" the use of these options to suit the needs of the organization, as discussed below.

7. *Evaluate the program.* An evaluation process should be built into the program's design. What was the desired effect? And has the program had that desired effect? If not, why not? What are the financial ramifications? What are the problem areas? Unexpected benefits? How have the organization's employees reacted? What needs to be done?

8. *Fine-tune the program.* Information gained during the evaluation process should be used by the task force to recommend the next steps needed to fine-tune parts of the program that require adjustment. In addition, a process for obtaining feedback from supervisors and employees should be an ongoing component of the flexibility project.

These are the basic steps outlined in each chapter as a model implementation process to be followed when introducing new scheduling or off-site arrangements. Not all steps may apply to every organization or to the introduction or expansion of every option. The more extensive the change in current practice that is sought, however, the more important an in-depth, thoughtful change process becomes. Major shifts in work-time policy require longer-term, companywide efforts.

As with any new tool, implementing the flexible work options we describe in this book will take some effort, time, and commitment. The organization can expect at the outset to experience some difficulties with supervision because of problems in such areas as scheduling and coverage, along with increased complications involving internal and external communications.

However, as Jerome Rosow, president of the Work in America Institute, asserts, the rewards can be great: "New work schedules, when carefully chosen, designed, and executed, are among the best investments an employer can make. The cost is small, the risk is low, and the potential return is high. Best of all, they benefit all parties involved."[14] In short, the benefits of the new scheduling alternatives should warrant the developing of more sophisticated skills and solutions to deal with the problems that will inevitably arise.

The Structure of This Book

The succeeding three chapters deal with restructured full-time and off-site arrangements; the next six chapters describe various reduced work-time options, including leave time and work sharing; and the final chapter looks at future trends affecting the growth of workplace flexibility. Each chapter describes the particular option in several overview sections, followed by an implementation section that outlines the eight-step process for introducing the option within an organization. Questionnaires and worksheets are provided to help managers identify the potential benefits of the option to their organization and outline the pros and cons of introducing it. Checklists summarizing key program design issues and information on the types of resources and training that have begun to emerge are also included to help managers better understand and use these options.

Although these various flexible work arrangements interrelate, they can be implemented either separately or together. Some require extensive and complicated change at all levels within an organization; others are follow-on stages that expand on a shift away from standardized schedules that has already begun.

We hope that the information contained in the following chapters will smooth the way for those managers who want to adopt new work patterns and learn to manage time and space more effectively in their organizations.

Flexible, Restructured, And Off-Site Work

In his 1976 book, *The Future of the Workplace*, Paul Dickson writes:

> There are few facets to the Western way of work which are more depressing and unimaginative than the way in which work time is arranged for us. Our jobs generally demand 40 hours of service in five consecutive eight-hour clips, during which we obediently come and go at rush hours appointed by others. Except for layoffs or prolonged periods of illness, a work life is laid out in front of a person: five-day, 40-hour pieces stretch out like a seemingly endless passing train terminating abruptly at age 65 at a chicken à la king banquet, where a gold watch is presented and the boss picks up the tab for the drinks.[1]

Almost two decades after Dickson wrote those words, things have changed dramatically. The rush hours are still with us, but the gold watch has in most cases been replaced by a "golden handshake," and more and more members of the workforce are employed on flexible, compressed, or reduced work schedules. The first challenge to 9–5 came in the form of flexible schedules, which for the first time gave employees some say in when they might come to and leave work. The next round of innovation restructured the forty-hour week into fewer than five days, giving employees longer workdays but larger blocks of personal time. And more recently, flexplace/telecommuting has been challenging the notion that work is best done in an office environment.

Part I of this book describes the emergence of flextime, the compressed workweek, and flexplace/telecommuting; discusses what employers have identified as the pros and cons of these scheduling arrangements; and looks at the experience of some of the organizations that have used them.

CHAPTER 1

Flextime

*F*lextime is the generic term for flexible scheduling programs—work schedules that permit flexible starting and quitting times within limits set by management. The flexible periods are at either end of the day, with a "core time" set in the middle, during which all employees must be present. Flextime requires employees to work a standard number of hours within a given time period (usually forty during a five-day week). The employer can adapt flextime to the organization's unique needs through the decisions it makes about such issues as (1) whether flexibility is a daily or periodic choice, (2) how core time is defined (see Figure 1-1), and (3) whether credit and debit hours and "banking" of hours are allowed. Some of the possible variations in the use of flextime are:

■ *Fixed starting and quitting times that are selected periodically.* With this option, employees choose their starting and quitting times for a specified period (such as twelve months) and work eight hours daily, following the agreed-upon schedule.

■ *Starting and quitting times that can vary daily.* With this option, employees are free to come to work and leave at a different time each day, provided they work a total of eight hours every day.

■ *Variations in the length of the day (for instance, a six-hour day followed by a ten-hour day), with mandatory core time.* With this option, credit and debit hours are allowed, as long as employees are present during the core time each day and work a specified number of hours by the end of a specified period (such as forty hours a week or

Figure 1-1.   Flextime variations: company flextime programs with core periods.

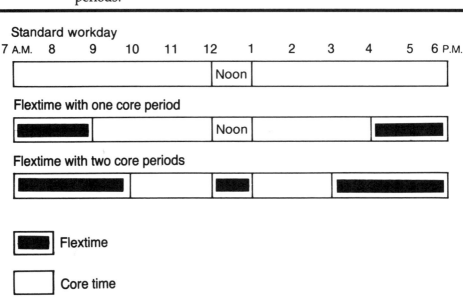

eighty hours during two weeks). For an example of this type of variable-day schedule, see Figure 1-2.

■ *Variations in the length of the day, without mandatory core time.* With this option, credit and debit hours are allowed, and employees need not be present during a core period each day. Employees may also bank time rather than having to work a specified number of hours during a specified time period. Figure 1-3 shows an example of this type of "maxiflex" schedule.

The amount of actual flexibility available to U.S. workers with flexible scheduling options has been estimated as varying from as little as thirty minutes to three hours or more.[1]

Origins of Flextime

Flextime was the first major divergence from the standardized forty-hour, 9–5 workweek. The concept of allowing employees some individual choice in their starting and quitting times was first introduced in Germany in 1967. At that time, it was seen as a means of relieving transit and commuting time problems. Shortly thereaf-

Figure 1-2.   Individual employee's variable-day schedule.

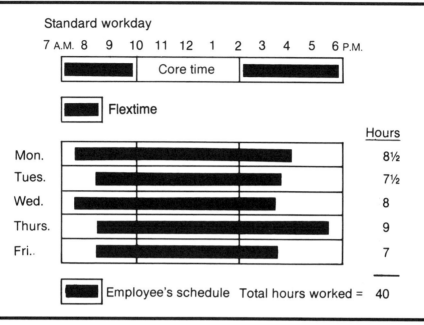

ter, flextime began to gain adherents in Switzerland as a way to attract women with family responsibilities into the labor force. The Hewlett-Packard Company is generally credited with introducing flextime in the United States, using it in its Waltham, Massachusetts, plant in 1972 after having tried it first in a German division. Hewlett-Packard's rationale at the time was that since employees appeared to like having more choice in their starting and quitting times, and since flextime appeared to have few or no adverse effects, this would be a low-cost, effective employee benefit. The primary reason for flextime's emergence would seem to have been a growing recognition that a standardized work schedule was not as appropriate as it had once been, because of both the changing demographics and attitudes of the workforce and changing management problems.

Who Uses Flextime?

According to a report released in 1993 by the Bureau of Labor Statistics, by 1991, the proportion of full-time workers with flexible schedules had increased to 15.1 percent from 12.3 percent in 1985.[2] This BLS survey indicates that the availability of flextime varies

Figure 1-3. Individual employee's maxiflex schedule with banked time.

Standard workday

7 A.M. 8   9   10   11   12   1   2   3   4   5   6 P.M.

| | Core time | |

▮▮▮ Flextime

Week 1		Hours
Mon.		8
Tues.		9
Wed.		10
Thurs.		10
Fri.		6

Week 2		Hours
Mon.		0
Tues.		8
Wed.		11
Thurs.		11
Fri.		10

▮▮▮ Employee's schedule

Total hours worked	83
Two-week required hours	80
Banked hours	3

widely among occupational groups. More than 20 percent of managers, professionals, technicians, and sales workers had flexibility, but only 10 percent or less of blue-collar and service workers said they could vary their work hours. Occupations with the highest proportion of workers on flexible schedules were natural scientists (45 percent), mathematicians and computer scientists (44 percent), and college and university teachers (38 percent).[3]

A 1989 Conference Board/New Ways to Work survey of U.S.

corporations showed that 235 of the 521 respondents used flextime in some part of their organization.[4] In 1991 Louis Harris & Associates surveyed more than 400 senior human resources executives in Conference Board member organizations. Flextime was provided by 77 percent of the firms, and another 13 percent expected to be offering it within five years.[5] A 1992 Society of Human Resources Management survey of its 80,000 members indicated that 57 percent of U.S. businesses have implemented flextime, up from 38 percent four years earlier.[6] And a 1993 Hewitt Associates survey reported that 73 percent of the 839 respondents offered flextime.[7]

Even when flextime is included in personnel policy, however, it is not necessarily available in all departments or to all employees.

When Is Flextime Most Appropriate?

Most employers find that flextime is a low-cost employee benefit that raises morale while enabling the organization to improve coverage, extend service hours, and reduce or eliminate tardiness.

■ *Improving coverage or extending service hours.* Since some employees will undoubtedly want to begin their workday earlier than the usual starting time and others will want to come in later and stay beyond the usual closing time, flextime can enable the organization to improve its coverage or extend its service hours. This, in turn, often reduces the need for overtime.

■ *Providing a low-cost employee benefit.* Flextime is a popular response to changing labor force needs and is particularly effective as a low-cost employee benefit. The demographics of an organization's workforce may dictate the extent of the advantage that is gained by using flextime. It is, for example, greatly valued by working parents as a way to better manage work and family time.

■ *Enhancing employee morale.* There is no doubt that flextime boosts employee morale generally. Other positive results, such as retention of valued employees and improved recruitment, derive from this.

■ *Reducing or eliminating tardiness.* Most employers find that if tardiness is a problem, flextime may be the answer. The reported reduction or elimination of tardiness has been attributed to several causes: In some cases, flextime enables employees to resolve scheduling conflicts or last-minute crises (getting children off to school before leaving for work, fixing a car that won't start, finding care for a sick child) or eases transit problems (with employees coming to work before or after the main commuting crunch).

Pros and Cons of Flextime

■ *Productivity and quality of work.* In an article for the *Harvard Business Review*, Dr. Stanley Nollen, of Georgetown University's School of Business Administration, cites eight surveys and thirty case histories that suggest numerous reasons for flextime's positive impact on productivity. They include:

- Reductions in paid absences (personal business, sick leave) and idle time on the job, which result in more actual labor from the same number of hours worked
- Better organization of work, because meetings, telephone calls, and visits are concentrated into core hours, leaving work that requires thinking and concentration to be done at the beginning and end of the workday, when there are fewer distractions
- People's ability to schedule work according to their own "biological clocks"
- Improved employee morale and job satisfaction, which lead to the outcome known as "a happy worker is a productive worker"
- Better managerial practices, including a shift from a controlling to a facilitating management style and more worker self-management[8]

In a survey of three industries offering flextime to clerical employees, significant numbers of respondents reported a higher quality of work (banks, 54.6 percent; insurance companies, 34.6 percent; and utilities, 29.2 percent), with the remainder reporting no change.[9]

■ *Absenteeism, tardiness, and turnover.* Because employees need or prefer flexible scheduling, reductions in tardiness and turnover, in addition to the reductions in paid absences mentioned above, have been observed in companies that use flextime. These reductions in absenteeism, tardiness, and turnover are in fact the most widely cited cost savings associated with the use of this scheduling option.

Other users of flextime have indicated that it offers advantages in such areas as workplace coverage, overtime costs, employee skills, and recruitment.

■ *Extended organizational workday.* Since some workers generally choose to come in earlier or leave later than the norm, hours of work or service can be expanded and telephone communication with other time zones may be improved. But extending the organizational workday may in some cases also mean extra costs for building security, heating and lighting, and other overhead expenses.

■ *Overtime costs.* Many organizations note a reduction in the use of overtime when a flextime program is in effect. The three-industry survey mentioned earlier cited significantly lower levels of overtime, with 57.6 percent of the banks, 33.9 percent of the insurance companies, and 16.7 percent of the utilities reporting decreased overtime.[10]

■ *Employee skills.* Since in organizations using flextime, employees often cover for co-workers on a different schedule, some employers have observed a cross-training effect that expands employee skills.

■ *Recruitment.* Organizations that advertise scheduling flexibility find that their recruitment pool is generally expanded and improved.

■ *Employee morale, commitment, and productivity.* There seems to be little doubt that flextime's most unassailable asset is its popularity among employees. (Even those workers who choose to retain a 9–5 schedule like the idea that they could change it if they wanted or needed to.) The popularity of this scheduling option in turn enhances employee morale and commitment. And such intangibles as employee morale and commitment are often cited as factors that have a direct impact on productivity. The ability to shift schedules to accommodate individual "biological clocks," mentioned earlier, is also regarded as a way to improve productivity.

The main problems that employers cite with flexible schedules relate to:

■ Inadequate staffing during some hours.
■ Difficulties associated with employee communication, scheduling meetings, and coordinating work among employees on different schedules.
■ Supervisors' concerns about their inability to supervise during the full range of work hours. Many supervisors are uncomfortable with anything but "line of sight" supervision and feel that with flextime, they will have to extend their hours of work in order to be able to properly supervise employees on a variety of schedules.

Additional problems reported with the use of flextime are accommodating employees whose output is the input for other employees, keeping track of hours worked or accumulated, and finding key people unavailable at certain times.[11]

■ *Electronic monitoring equipment.* One disadvantage of the use of flextime can be the one-time expense of purchasing electronic monitoring equipment. However, few companies in the United States seem interested in using electronic monitoring equipment to track employee hours. Such monitoring devices tend to be unpopular with workers because they resemble time clocks. They are primarily used in programs that allow banking of hours.

■ *Concerns about employee abuse of flextime.* Even employers who report experiencing a small amount of abuse do not seem to consider it a major drawback. Flextime is a means of empowering employees and helping them be more accountable and effective in their jobs. Supervisors should be discouraged from "policing" flexible schedules and encouraged to concentrate on coaching and supporting employees who have difficulty self-managing their schedules.

■ *Union attitudes.* Unions remain somewhat skeptical about flextime. There is lingering concern about whether or not it is voluntary and how it affects both overtime and the length of the workday. On the other hand, labor leaders recognize flextime's popularity with workers and hence tend to concentrate on developing equitable ground rules for utilizing this scheduling option.

Should Your Organization Try Flextime?

The tools provided in this section can help you determine whether flextime would be an effective response to your organization's unique staffing and scheduling needs.

Let's start by taking a look at the accompanying group of profiles entitled Organizational Experience with Flextime. These profiles show how and why a flextime program was implemented in two organizations and with what results. As you review these profiles, pay special attention to aspects of the companies' experience that seem particularly relevant to your own organization's situation.

Now turn to the questionnaire shown in Table 1-1, which lists the primary concerns that lead organizations to adopt flextime programs. The more yes answers you have on this questionnaire,

Table 1-1. Flextime questionnaire.

Would Flextime Benefit Your Organization?	Yes	No
Do some employees prefer to come to work early while others prefer to work after regular closing hours?		
If your organization has to communicate with clients or employees in different time zones, would expanding the range of hours that employees are working facilitate this?		
Is tardiness or absenteeism a problem in your organization?		
Are the modes of transportation, particularly during commuting hours, congested in your community?		
Does your organization have a significant number of employees with family responsibilities?		
Would you like to offer your employees a benefit that is known to be popular but costs nothing?		

the greater the chances that flextime is an option you should be seriously considering.

If your questionnaire results indicate that flextime would indeed benefit your organization, you can use the worksheet shown in Figure 1-4 to identify your specific concerns and what you regard as the potential benefits and drawbacks of this approach.

Introducing Flextime

The process of introducing a flextime program starts with the appointment of a planning group to lay the groundwork for the program, followed by the appointment of a project director. In the design phase, decisions are made regarding a number of key issues. Resource materials are then developed, and the program is announced and promoted to the organization's employees. After flextime has been in effect for a period of time, its impact is evaluated and the program is modified as necessary. In the following subsections, we will take a closer look at each of these steps.

Gain Support for the Program

In order to generate support for broad-based use of a flextime program, your first step is to appoint a top-level planning group. The group, or task force, should have representation from all

Figure 1-4.   Flextime worksheet.

Assessing the Need for Flextime

List the main reasons why you are considering flextime:

1. _____

_____

_____

2. _____

_____

_____

3. _____

_____

_____

4. _____

_____

_____

List what you see as the advantages and disadvantages of flextime:

Pros: _____

_____

_____

_____

_____

```
_____

_____

Cons: _____

_____

_____

_____

_____

_____
```

segments of the company that will be affected by a flextime program. Its responsibility will be to:

- Investigate what similar organizations have done with regard to flexible hours.
- Develop a tentative policy statement.
- Develop an action plan. Surveys indicate that the way a flextime plan is implemented determines whether or not it will be successful (see Table 1-2).
- Consult with labor representatives and employees.
- Set up a process for obtaining supervisors' input into the planning and implementation process as well as their feedback during the initial phases of the new program.
- Revise the policy and plan as appropriate.
- Determine the initial scope of the program (that is, whether it will be tested in a pilot project and then expanded to other units, instituted companywide, or introduced incrementally).

Set Up the Program's Administration

Appoint a project director. In order to assure equity and consistent application of flextime guidelines, responsibility for overseeing the implementation of flextime should be assigned to someone in the

Table 1-2. Summary of implementation steps that alleviate flextime problem areas.

	Implementation Step			
Problem Area Alleviated	Appointed Internal Project Director	Held Meetings with Managers, Supervisors	Held Meetings with Employees	Instituted First on Trial Basis
Coverage of work situations		x		
Employee scheduling	x	x	x	
Work scheduling	x		x	
Difficulty of management job	x			
Internal communication	x	x		x

SOURCE: Stanley D. Nollen and Virginia H. Martin, *Alternative Work Schedules*, Part 1; AMA Survey Report (New York: AMACOM, 1978), 38.

human resources management or personnel area. Although departmental supervisors are generally responsible for applying the flextime guidelines to the particular circumstances of their work unit and implementing the program there, a personnel administrator should be available to act as a resource for the supervisors and to monitor the development of the program within individual departments.

Design the Program

Some of the decisions that must be made when designing a flextime program have to do with the parameters of flexibility. Questions must be resolved regarding the following issues:

■ *State and federal labor laws.* What effect will existing legislation have on the proposed flextime program?

■ *Length of company workday and workweek.* What are the organization's operating hours? What are its normal workdays?

■ *Core time.* What hours of the workday or shift will be considered "core," when everyone is expected to be on the job?

■ *Allowable starting and quitting times.* What is the earliest time that an employee can start the workday, and how late can a regular, albeit flexible, schedule go? The most common span extends from 7:00 A.M. to 6:00 P.M. (In a twenty-four-hour, continuously operating plant, these questions may have to be answered in terms of a flexible shift schedule rather than in terms of flexibility within a specified range of day-shift hours.)

■ *Eligibility*. Who will be eligible for flextime? Will it be a companywide option, a pilot project, or a departmental option? If one of the reasons for introducing flextime is to enhance employee morale and commitment, then eligibility should be as broad as possible. Companies should not exclude employees from participation on the basis of occupation. The key question should be function.

Some organizations have worked out special applications to ensure that some kind of increased flexibility is available to all employees. For example, Hewlett-Packard is one of a small percentage of manufacturing firms that allows flexible scheduling for production workers. In its fabrication unit, which is a continuous-shift process, individual flextime is not possible, but group flextime is. The workers together decide what the shift changeover hours will be, subject only to the requirement that there be a fifteen-minute overlap between shifts.

■ *Degree of individual flexibility*. Within the established parameters, how much choice will employees have? Can they vary their hours day to day? Week to week? How much notice must they give their supervisor? If schedules are expected to remain constant for an extended period, how long a commitment must employees make to a particular schedule? What process is there for changing the schedule if it proves inappropriate?

■ *Length of individual workday*. Some companies (primarily those that allow "banking" of time, discussed later in this subsection) do not require employees to work an eight-hour day. In such cases, the core time may constitute the minimum workday period. Four states and two territories mandate eight hours as the maximum length of a workday; they are Alaska, California, Nevada, Puerto Rico, the Virgin Islands, and Wyoming.

■ *Length of individual workweek*. If banking is allowed, can hours be carried over into another workweek? Are there minimum and maximum numbers of hours that an employee can work within a seven-day period? (State legislation may already establish this, and federal forty-hour legislation applies to all nonexempt employees.)

■ *Lunch hour*. Is a lunch hour required each day? Of what duration? Is there any flexibility possible midday?

■ *Personal time off.* How will flextime affect existing provisions for personal time off?

■ *Carryover hours.* If your state does not have legislation prohibiting workdays longer than eight hours, will employees be allowed to bank hours? Within what time limits (a week, a pay period, other)?

■ *Overtime.* How will banking affect overtime? (In the General Motors Corporation flextime policy statement, it is noted that employees electing a banking option must sign a waiver stating that premium pay and overtime will not be applied to hours that the employee has chosen to work in excess of eight hours per day in order to utilize flextime. Some union contracts also contain language that recognizes the difference between employer-mandated overtime work and employee-chosen flexible hours that result in occasional longer-than-normal workdays.)

■ *Coverage and work flow.* How will you ensure that regular coverage continues and, if possible, is enhanced? How much latitude will supervisors have to adjust schedules? In introducing the program, it should be clearly indicated that flextime is a benefit—that the employees' prime responsibility is to get the work done and that flexibility is secondary to the work requirements. In functions such as telephone coverage, interoffice mail, and other central communications tasks, or for employees involved in sequential work flow, the design objective is to maintain coverage while adopting flextime.

■ *Accountability.* How will employee performance be monitored? Will regular performance evaluations be considered sufficient? If banking of time is allowed, what kinds of records will be kept and how? The answers to the monitoring question range from electronic "time accumulators" to "memo ledgers" to honor systems. Unfortunately, there are always some employees who abuse any system. When an otherwise eligible employee has abused the privilege of flextime, the easiest and most effective disciplinary tool is to deny access to the option and require that the employee work standard hours.

■ *Enrollment process.* Who will sign employees up and manage the program in the individual departments? Most flextime programs assign the responsibility for implementing the program to departmental supervisors.

■ *Evaluation process.* How will you evaluate the effects of flexible scheduling? The program should be reviewed periodically so that adjustments to existing schedules can be made if necessary.

Table 1-3 presents a program design checklist that you can use to keep track of your progress in addressing the key design issues associated with introducing flextime.

Once the flextime program has been designed, the next step is to work with your managers to identify a site for a flextime pilot project. When introducing any flexible work arrangement, a pilot project is recommended. This can provide an excellent opportunity for testing the way the program is working, then evaluating and fine-tuning it before expanding its use. Choose a manager or department that wants to use flextime so it will have the best chance for success.

Develop Resource Materials

A printed *program description,* outlining the organization's objectives and detailing the program's terms and conditions, should be made available to all employees who will be affected by flextime. (A sample program description is shown in Figure 1-5.)

As will be discussed later in the chapter, introducing flextime can have a significant impact on how the first-line supervisor carries out his or her responsibilities, particularly in organizations where the participatory style of supervision is not the norm. In general, the greater the change in supervisory style that is needed in order to implement flextime, the more important resource materials will be in making the implementation successful.

Guidelines for managers and supervisors should reinforce a sense of concern and support for supervisors by reassuring them that they are not expected to be available or on site during the entire time range when their employees may be working (this range is called a bandwidth). They can also be used to remind supervisors that time management is now a shared responsibility and that their role should emphasize coaching and facilitating rather than over-the-shoulder supervising. Topics covered in the guidelines might include:

■ The business reasons for introducing the program
■ Legal considerations to be aware of
■ References to relevant personnel policy sections
■ Questions employees are most likely to ask, and answers to them

(Text continues on page 34.)

Table 1-3.   Program design checklist: flextime.

Key Design Issues	Notes
☐ State and federal labor laws	
☐ Company workday and workweek	
☐ Core time	
☐ Allowable starting and quitting times	
☐ Eligibility	
☐ Degree of individual flexibility	
☐ Length of individual workday	
☐ Length of individual workweek	
☐ Lunch hour	
☐ Personal time off	
☐ Carryover hours	
☐ Overtime	
☐ Coverage and work flow	
☐ Accountability	
☐ Enrollment process	
☐ Evaluation process	

Figure 1-5. Sample flextime program description.

PERSONNEL POLICY MANUAL   FEDERAL RESERVE BANK OF SAN FRANCISCO

SECTION: 400   SUBJECT: 412   FLEXTIME WORK SCHEDULE

Effective June 1, 1993
Supersedes April 1, 1991

1. Objective

The flextime work schedule allows employees latitude in scheduling their working hours within the specified limits set forth in this subject.

2. Policy

Individual departments may use a flextime work schedule, subject to the following conditions:

■ The implementation, continuance, discontinuance, or modification of flextime is at the discretion of the management committee in consultation with the senior officer in charge of division/branch and the personnel officer/manager.
■ Adequate staff coverage sufficient to meet the operating requirements of the department shall be maintained at all times.
■ The normal workweek of 40 hours and five days shall be retained.
■ Departments wanting to implement flextime must first pilot a program (typically for three to nine months).

3. Definitions

Flextime is a schedule by which an employee may—on a daily basis and within specific limits dictated by the needs of the job—start work at a time of his/her discretion as long as the employee completes eight hours of work per day. Time limits are placed on the amount of "flex" an employee has by establishing "core hours" and a "bandwidth."

■ *Core hours* are the hours during which all employees must be on the job (excluding regular lunch and break periods).
■ *Bandwidth* is the span of time beginning at the earliest time an employee may start work and ending at the latest time an employee may stop work.

Exempt personnel may, with management approval and as a result of business necessity, work more than eight hours in one day. This option, however, still requires that an individual work a 40-hour, five-day workweek.

The normal lunch break is 45 minutes. An employee may, however, extend his/her lunch break period within the limits of the flexible lunch period as long as

(Continued)

Figure 1-5. *(continued)*

management approval is obtained and the operations of the department are not disrupted.

4. Responsibilities

The personnel officer/manager ensures that flextime is administered in a consistent and equitable manner throughout the bank. The personnel officer/manager also ensures that flextime schedules conform to appropriate state laws and bank policy.

Department management ensures that flextime is administered in a consistent and equitable manner within the department and that flextime arrangements conform to bank policy. Department management also ensures that staffing is available at all times to meet the operational requirements of the department.

The supervisor plans and schedules job assignments, ensuring that there is sufficient staff to meet the schedule.

The employee plans and organizes his/her time to meet the job requirements as established by the supervisor. One or more employees may assume coverage responsibility with the supervisor's concurrence. If a change in schedule is required, the responsible employee must find substitute coverage and inform the supervisor.

5. Procedures

Piloting Flextime

The supervising officer in charge of the department wanting to pilot a program shall receive approval for piloting the program from the senior officer in charge of the branch/division.

During the pilot program, the management of the piloting department maintains statistical data to facilitate evaluation of any significant effects resulting from flextime. The information shall include data regarding:

- Absenteeism
- Turnover
- Overtime for non-exempt employees
- Production statistics, if relevant

Upon completion of the pilot program, the data collected above will be evaluated by the supervising officer in charge of the department piloting the program to determine the feasibility of continuing with flextime.

After completion of the pilot, the supervising officer in charge of the department prepares a short report that includes statistics on absenteeism, turnover, personal business days taken, and non-exempt overtime. This report is submitted to the senior officer in charge of the branch/division for review/approval for continuing with the flextime program.

Work Schedule Coverage Requirements

The following format should be used for the work schedule coverage plan. One copy of the plan should be returned to the supervising officer; the other is to be used in discussions with employees subsequent to employee briefing meetings.

Example:

Work Unit	Function	Total Employees	Employees Needed for Coverage		
			8:00–9:30	11:30–1:30	3:30–4:45

Time Management and Administration

Flextime involves employees as well as supervisors in the dynamic process of time planning and organization.

Each participant should organize his/her work schedule to ensure that the policy and operating requirements for the department are met; that each individual's responsibilities for maintaining adequate work coverage are understood; and that proper time-keeping records are maintained.

Experience and Evaluation Phase

Each supervisor assures that policy and operating requirements are understood and are being met within the work unit.

Computation of Vacation, Overtime, and Sick Leave

The computation of these benefits is the same for employees working flextime as for those working a standard schedule.

Shift Differential

Employees who would normally (i.e., without flextime) complete their workday during the bank's full-status business day and who elect to start or end their workday during the midnight or swing shift are not paid shift differential.

6. Guidelines*
   Bandwidth: The time during which employees *may* be on the job. 6:00 A.M.–7:00 P.M.
   Standard service day: The time during which normal service and functional operations must be available. 8:00 A.M.–4:45 P.M.

(Continued)

Figure 1-5. *(continued)*

Core time:	The time when all employees are to be on the job, unless specifically excused: 9:30 A.M.–11:30 A.M. 1:30 P.M.–3:30 P.M.
Flexible time:	Designated time when employees may or may not be present: 6:00 A.M.–9:30 A.M. 11:30 A.M.–1:30 P.M. 3:30 P.M.–7:00 P.M.
Contracted hours:	The total number of hours that must be accounted for during the time period—e.g., 40 hours.
Accounting period:	Time period over which contracted hours can be accumulated—e.g., one week.
Lunch break:	The time an employee is off the job during the midday flex period—e.g., minimum ½ hour, maximum two hours.
Daily hours:	The number of hours that must be worked daily by non-exempt employees—e.g., eight hours.
Maximum weekly hours:	The number of hours that may be worked by non-exempt employees without requiring overtime pay—e.g., 40 hours.

*These guidelines are illustrated for the standard day shift.

■ A problem/solution matrix (Table 1-4)
■ Checklists of implementation steps
■ Sample forms and timesheets

Figure 1-6 is a worksheet that suggests the steps department managers should go through to introduce a flextime program successfully.

Guidelines for employees should include information on:

■ Eligibility
■ Proposal development
■ How to ensure appropriate backup during flex hours
■ Keeping communication lines open with supervisor and co-workers

Announce the Program

Once the program is in place, it should be announced and information meetings held for employees who will be affected. This will

(Text continues on page 38.)

Table 1-4. Examples of flextime problems and their solutions.

Problem	Solution
Management or supervision problems	
First-line supervisors reluctant.	Training/education—"try it, you'll like it."
Role of first-line supervisor.	Reeducation in job.
Scheduling of meetings was made more difficult.	Earlier scheduling; most problems resolved with minor rearrangements of our own attitudes; i.e., willingness to alter inflexible habits we had gotten comfortable with.
Employees who work as a team cannot agree on a work schedule.	Company "business hours" prevail.
Coffee breaks—we had used a set time for each department, but dropped it with flexible hours. The first day everyone went to coffee at the same time and we had standing room only.	We did nothing—the next day the problem went away. Moral: treat people as adults and they'll act as adults.
Departmental scheduling—allowing too many to use flextime at the same time.	Require at least ⅓ staffing at all times.
Supervisors not having same degree of flexibility, sometimes required to work longer hours to cover entire workday.	Supervisors decide who will come in early and stay late; they then rotate.
Supervisory resistance—they were suspicious, insecure; doubted that employees would produce.	Launch pilot demonstration project, keep circulating testimonials.
Resistance from senior supervisors who felt loss of status and loss of control, and were unable to internalize the "Theory Y" philosophy that must accompany flextime.	After ten to twelve months they had adjusted.
Involvement of first-level supervisors in planning phase.	Extensive meetings on work scheduling processes and employee control procedures.
Coverage problems	
Telephone coverage by secretaries.	They established their own rotating schedule so that at least one person was available to cover phones.
Lack of agreement as to start/stop time between interfacing work groups.	Brought groups together, identified problem, and had it solved by agreement.

SOURCE: Stanley D. Nollen and Virginia H. Martin, *Alternative Work Schedules, Part 1; AMA Survey Report* (New York: AMACOM, 1978), 42–43.

(Continued)

Table 1-4.   *(continued)*

Problem	Solution
Coverage problems *(continued)*	
Small groups unable to cover some positions if flextime adopted.	Did not allow these small groups to participate.
Receptionist does not arrive until 9:00 A.M.	Another employee had to become familiar with telephone answering and receiving visitors.
Staffing switchboard to closing time on Fridays.	Told department employees to solve it; they did.
Coverage of key desks for inside and outside contacts.	Had to ask a few people to reduce their flextime opportunities.
Communication and coordination problems	
Coordinating two-shift operations.	Had day and evening shift make recommendations themselves, and if they couldn't solve it we just put people back on regular shift.
Had an immediate shift to an earlier workday, 7:30 A.M. to 3:30 P.M., which cut down on communication with the West Coast.	Met with department heads and employees to discuss problem and work out coverage to 5:00 P.M.
Interaction with other departments still on an 8:00 to 5:00 schedule.	Personnel from other departments had to adjust their thinking and communications to the core period.
Timekeeping problems and employee abuse of flextime	
Minor number of abuses.	Individuals involved put on standard hours.
Employees abusing the honor system of timekeeping.	Staff meetings, constructive administration of discipline.
Not observing core hours requirement.	Talked to all employees; closer supervision.
Honor system not reliable.	Time recording devices a must.
Flextime accumulators too expensive.	Implemented honor system.
Many employees felt no need to keep time records.	We reiterated our instructions and conducted an audit to assure compliance.
Cheating on time cards.	Peer pressure; employee taken off flextime if necessary. The employees tend to "police" each other because they don't want to lose flextime for all.

Figure 1-6.   Manager's flextime worksheet.

Once the parameters of the flextime program have been determined, department managers should:

1. *Analyze their department's staffing and work-flow* configuration to determine critical aspects of introducing flextime in their department. The aspects to be considered are:

   Peak service or demand times: A.M.   P.M.

   Daily:
   Weekly:
   Monthly:
   Quarterly:

   Regularly scheduled meeting times:

   Current standard workday: _____

   Ideal work schedule coverage (extended hours with gap period; contracted with overlap or any other **daily, weekly, or quarterly** configuration that would improve the match between labor force availability and work-flow demand): _____
   _____
   _____

   Bandwidth available to _____**employees** (core hours plus beginning and ending flexible options)

   Coverage if scheduling changes are approved as requested: _____
   _____

   Adjustments to be made:

2. *Next, hold meetings with managers* to discuss concept, answer questions, and get their input on procedures and scheduling approaches.

3. *Design guidelines* for your department.

4. *Schedule meetings with employees* to review guidelines and procedures for selecting schedules.

5. Accept employee applications, review them, and announce final approval of schedules.

give employees an opportunity to ask questions and enable managers to clarify the specifics of the flextime option.

Promote the Program

Since flextime is so popular with employees, it is generally not necessary to promote its use—only to inform employees that it is available and let them know what process exists in their work unit for utilizing it. Any promotion is usually conducted as part of external recruitment or public relations efforts.

Evaluate the Program

Much of a full-time program's success involves relatively intangible factors, such as employee morale and the potential for motivating workers and enhancing their commitment. There are more concrete business objectives that can be accomplished as well, however. Once a flextime program has been implemented, a feedback process should be set up so that "glitches" can be identified. Surveys and focus groups of managers and employees can be helpful in gathering evaluation information. Outcomes to review, particularly in terms of their cost impact, should include improved recruitment, impact on overtime, improved customer service as a result of expanded hours of operation, retention of valued employees, reduced absenteeism, and employee satisfaction.

Fine-Tune the Program

With a flextime program, the most frequent problem areas involve management or supervision and work coverage. These problems, which can be identified through the type of ongoing evaluation process discussed in the preceding subsection, are amenable to management intervention.

Table 1-4 presents a detailed listing of problems that commonly occur with flextime programs, together with solutions that actual users have found effective.

Special Considerations for Supervisors and Managers

The role of first-line supervisors is radically affected by the introduction of flextime. As Simcha Ronen observes in his book *Flexible Working Hours:*

> A critical factor in the success or failure of a flexible work hours system is the attitude of first-line supervisors toward the pro-

gram. Flexitime, by its nature, requires a supervisory style which focuses on planning and coordination as opposed to monitoring. . . . With flexitime, supervisors should be less concerned with time-keeping functions, and should be willing to spend more time on planning, scheduling, and coordinating functions; they will have to place less emphasis on employee control and develop a more participatory style of supervision. Since this may not be an easy adjustment for some first-line supervisors, the organization must be prepared to facilitate the process through orientation beginning as soon as the decision is made to implement flexitime.[12]

As noted earlier, it is critical that supervisors be included in the initial design phases of the flextime program. How much training the supervisors will require and how much resource material must be developed for them will depend to a great extent on the organization's culture and existing supervisory norms.

Companies that have a generally participative style of supervision as opposed to a primarily monitoring style will probably find that their supervisors adapt with only a minimum of retraining. If a radical change in supervisory style is necessary in order for the organization to implement a flextime program, then consideration should be given to holding a training session dealing with indirect supervisory techniques and evaluating on the basis of results rather than process.

In all cases, however, educating supervisors and managers about the logistics of the flextime system and its potential advantages before the program is implemented or during its initial phases will help pave the way for a smooth introduction of the system.

Summary

Flextime, a work-scheduling approach in which starting and quitting times vary within a range established by management, was the first of the nontraditional scheduling options to gain acceptance. It was a response to both changing workforce demographics and management problems in enforcing the standard inflexible 9–5.

While surveys have indicated acceptance of flextime by a growing number of organizations, they have also revealed that many of those organizations limit the job classifications or departments that are eligible to participate in the flextime program.

Flextime seems best suited to situations where management wishes to expand coverage or service hours, offer a low-cost employee benefit that will not only boost morale but also improve recruitment efforts and help the organization retain its valued employees, and reduce or even eliminate tardiness.

In assessing the advantages and disadvantages of flextime, the key considerations are as follows: Flextime is highly popular with employees. It enhances productivity, employee skills, and quality of work and facilitates recruitment while reducing absenteeism, tardiness, turnover, and overtime costs. The extension of the organizational workday that comes with a flextime program permits an expansion of coverage and service, although this benefit can be partly offset by a corresponding rise in overhead costs resulting from keeping the facility open for longer hours.

Problems with flextime primarily involve maintaining adequate coverage, establishing effective channels of communication, keeping track of time worked, and correctly determining which employees and job functions should be eligible for flextime. Unions are concerned about flextime's impact on overtime and the length of the workday and about whether this option is truly voluntary. But given flextime's popularity with workers, unions tend to concentrate on seeing that flextime is implemented fairly rather than opposing the program altogether.

Introducing flextime in the organization involves the basic eight-step process that was presented in the Introduction. However, this work-scheduling approach does have a significant impact on the functions of first-line supervisors. Since flextime is most likely to succeed in an atmosphere of participative management, steps must be taken to ensure that first-line supervisors are adequately prepared (through training and resource materials) to utilize this management style.

ORGANIZATIONAL EXPERIENCE WITH FLEXTIME

American Express Travel Related Services

Description: American Express TRS is a worldwide supplier of financial and travel services. It employs 29,000 people in its domestic operations and is headquartered at the World Financial Center, New York City.

Reason for Using Flextime: The TRS vision is to be "known around the world" as the Best Place To Work. A 1989 employee survey identified flexibility as an employee need. Strategic goals were established in order to become the employer of choice and to invest in building a competitive edge to attract/retain quality people. Out of this came initiatives that encouraged greater use of flexibility, including flextime, job sharing, part-time with benefits, and split shifts.

Implementation Process: Workplace flexibility arrangements vary among locations because of businesses and schedules within TRS. A brochure describes the various possibilities, and employees are encouraged to consult their department managers for information about current options.

In 1993, flexible time was increased from 6 A.M. to 6 P.M. in order to allow for even greater flexibility. Most facilities are twenty-four-hour operations and offer the flexibility for employees to opt for their preferred hours.

Impact to Date: Employee tenure has lengthened, and the ability to attract/retain good employees has been strengthened. Flexibility is itself a form of empowerment and complements TRS' semiautonomous work teams' ability to manage their own schedules and absences (absence rates have been reduced significantly).

SOURCE: American Express brochure; presentation by Doug Schlegel, TRS Human Resources, Phoenix, Ariz. (Sept. 21, 1993); conversation with Barbara Katersky, American Express TRS, New York.

Pitney Bowes Inc.

Description: A manufacturer of office equipment, headquartered in Stamford, Connecticut, with approximately 6,000 employees at headquarters.

Reason for Using Flextime: The program was designed to provide a greater degree of flexibility to clerical employees. The attitude is: "You're adults, so we'll treat you like adults." The program helps with recruiting; job candidates with school-age children find it especially attractive. It also helps alleviate problems of absenteeism and lost time. If an organization has flextime, its employees are not expected to use a lot of sick days.

Implementation Process: Approximately 1,100 nonexempt clerical employees at corporate headquarters are eligible for the flextime option. Although banking time is not permitted except within a given week, if an employee works 37½ hours in less than five days, then he or she is entitled to a half-day off.

The program is implemented by department, with the department head determining what core hours will be. Supervisors must ensure that phones are being covered.

Impact to Date: The program, which was instituted in the late 1970s, takes cooperation between employer and employee and requires more supervisory time. People who use flextime like it very much, however. They seem willing to put in the extra effort to make the program work.

It's a real punishment when the option has to be taken away for disciplinary reasons. Employees fight to get back in the program. Flextime is now an integral part of the organization.

SOURCE: Telephone interview with the manager of personnel, Pitney Bowes corporate headquarters (June 1988). Conversation with Linda Higueras, Director, Diversity Employee Relations, April 1994.

CHAPTER 2

Compressed Workweek

Compressed workweek refers to a workweek (usually forty hours long) that is condensed into fewer than five days. The most common formulas are 4/10 (four ten-hour days, as shown in Figure 2-1), 3/12 (three twelve-hour days, as shown in Figure 2-2), and 9/80 (a week of four nine-hour days and one eight-hour day followed by a week of four nine-hour days). The 9/80 in Figure 2-3 is designed to show how to designate the hours for payroll purposes.

The first type of compressed schedule to be introduced was the four-day workweek, and until the 1990s, it was the most widely used. Recently the most growth has been in the use of the 9/80 format because of its popularity with employees.

As organizational development experts Herman Cadon and Allan Cohen note:

> The compressed work week can be utilized in two differing ways: most commonly, the unit operates for five to seven days, more than eight hours a day (up to and including around-the-clock), but the individual employees only work three to four and one half days per week; or an entire firm or unit can operate only four days per week, with all (or most) employees in attendance for all of the four days. Under the first arrangement, days off will vary among individuals in such a way that the optimum number of employees are at work on the busiest days or at busiest periods of the day.[1]

Figure 2-1.   4/10 compressed workweek schedule.

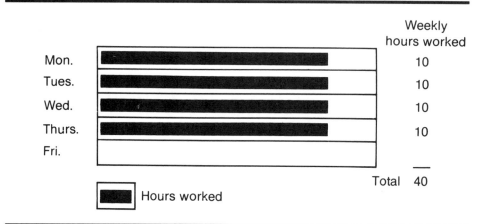

Figure 2-2.   3/12 compressed workweek schedule.

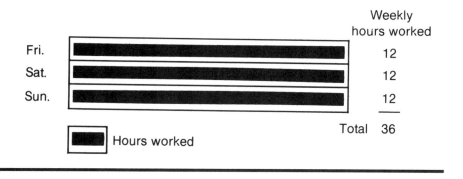

Origins of the Compressed Workweek

Introduced in the early 1970s, the compressed workweek, along with flextime, was an effort to create alternatives to the standard five-day, forty-hour workweek by reallocating the same number of hours to fewer days. From the employer's perspective, this allowed plant facilities to be used for longer periods with fewer startups and shutdowns, and it gave employees longer blocks of personal time and cut down on commuting time.

The compressed workweek used to be a controversial form of alternative scheduling. Since the mid-1970s, its popularity has peaked and waned and picked up again. While interest in it fell in

Figure 2-3. 9/80 compressed workweek schedule.

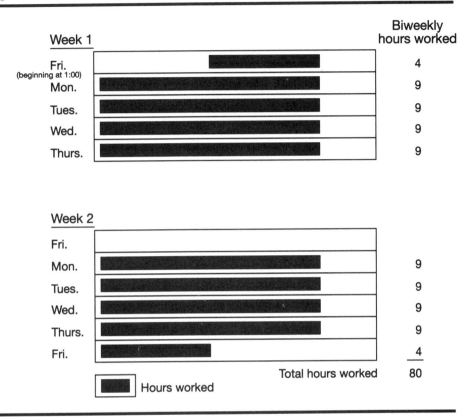

the late 1970s, the Bureau of Labor Statistics noted that between 1979 and 1985, the use of compressed workweeks grew four times as fast as overall employment growth.[2] Although some employers have implemented a compressed schedule companywide, most use a combination of several different versions or integrate it with other arrangements like flextime. Increasingly it is being offered to exempt employees as an individual option.

Who Uses a Compressed Workweek?

A survey conducted in the mid-1980s indicated that 15 percent of the respondents used some kind of compressed workweek schedule somewhere in the organization, but not necessarily companywide. At that time these schedules were most common in three industries:

government (29 percent in this category reported using it), health care (31 percent), and entertainment or recreation (42 percent).[3] The 1989 national survey of corporate use of flexible work arrangements conducted by New Ways to Work and The Conference Board reported that 36 percent of the 521 respondents were presently using this kind of schedule. The study indicated that the manufacturing sector was only slightly more likely to use compressed workweeks than firms in the service, financial, or insurance industries.[4] A 1993 Hewitt Associates survey reported that 21 percent of the respondents used this kind of schedule.[5] Compressed workweeks are also used extensively in public agencies, especially police and fire departments, and in small manufacturing companies. Unfortunately, there has been little research in recent years to indicate what the national trends are in terms of using compressed workweeks.

When Is a Compressed Workweek Most Appropriate?

Compressed workweeks are used most often in situations where employers are attempting to improve the allocation of labor time or decrease the cost of overtime or of operating capital equipment.

If the company's labor force favors such a schedule, it is a way to offer a low-cost employee benefit at the same time. Some employers have used a compressed schedule during the summer months to provide employees with longer weekends. These "summer hours" schedules are very popular. Providing exempt employees who need full-time work with a schedule that allows them an extra day off has become another reason for using compressed schedules.

In 1990 passage of federal legislation and introduction of a growing number of local and regional clean air and transportation regulations gave new impetus to the use of compressed workweeks. The Federal Clean Air Act of 1990 requires employers with 100 or more employees in ten badly polluted regions of the country to design "trip reduction programs" in order to reduce solo commuting to work. The states that are affected are California, Connecticut, Delaware, Illinois, Indiana, Maryland, New Jersey, New York, Pennsylvania, Texas, and Wisconsin. (Two programs in Southern California were underway by 1992 as a result of similar local legislation already in force.) Use of compressed workweek schedules and/or flexplace/telecommuting programs (see page 65) is becoming a popular means of compliance with the ride reduction provisions of the legislation.

Pros and Cons of a Compressed Workweek

■ *Legal considerations.* In the following states and territories, the law requires that overtime premiums be paid for hours worked in excess of eight a day: Alaska, California, Nevada, Puerto Rico, the Virgin Islands, and Wyoming. This wage and hours legislation creates a barrier to the use of compressed schedules, unless an industry or group of employees has been exempted in some way or unless an organization has established a compressed workweek under conditions specified in a particular state's regulations. For example, compressed schedules of forty hours a week are authorized in some states if an organization's nonexempt employees have been polled and two-thirds are in favor of such a change and if the affected employees receive two consecutive days off within each workweek. Compensatory time in lieu of overtime is also allowed in some cases if it is used during the same pay period. In all states the federal forty-hour-a-week rule applies, and in order to comply, companies wishing to use a 9/80 schedule must consider systems changes (see Bechtel case history, page 64).

■ *Employee morale.* A compressed workweek can affect employee morale either positively or negatively. In general, compressed workweeks get mixed reviews from employees; some like to work longer days in return for longer weekends, while others don't like such schedules at all.

■ *Family time.* Those employees who do like the compressed workweek often cite the opportunity for more family time as one of the reasons. On the other hand, there are working parents who cite fatigue and child care problems as negative results. The type of schedule used is an important variable in this case.

■ *Recruitment.* Most employers using a compressed workweek report improved recruitment as a result of employee interest in having more and longer blocks of personal time.

■ *Absenteeism, tardiness, and turnover.* Modest improvements in these rates have been reported.

■ *Staffing.* Because the compressed workweek permits employees to have more concentrated time off, they become more willing to accept shift work and weekend assignments and work during peak periods of activity. The compressed workweek has allowed some employers to attract skilled employees to undesirable shifts.

■ *Supervision.* Because of problems with scheduling and coverage and increased complications involving internal and external communications, supervision is perceived to be more difficult with the compressed workweek. However, as noted in the Introduction, this is the case when an organization first adopts any of the new scheduling arrangements discussed in this book. Such difficulties tend to taper off as the organization gains management expertise with the particular work-time alternative.

■ *Fatigue.* Since the compressed workweek increases the length of the workday, some employees are quite tired by quitting time. This makes compressed schedules unpopular with some workers, particularly older employees and some working parents. Using a 9/80 schedule often mitigates this factor.

■ *Productivity.* Related to the issue of fatigue is the issue of productivity. The impact of the compressed workweek on productivity gets mixed reviews, with some employers reporting an improvement and others complaining about a drop-off in productivity toward the end of long shifts—a drop-off that they attribute to fatigue.

■ *Commuting.* Many employees cite an improvement in commuting as a benefit of the compressed workweek because they are often arriving and leaving at times other than rush hours and have to travel to work one fewer day per week.

■ *Scheduling.* In a study of alternative work time conducted by Stanley Nollen and Virginia Martin, more than a third of the compressed workweek users reported rearranging shifts to improve scheduling. The report noted the following:

> The shift changes were of many varieties. For the four-day week combined with five-day operation, the simplest change is dividing the workforce into two teams, each working four days—a Monday–Thursday team and a Tuesday–Friday team. This staggering of workers keeps all functions at least partially covered during all five days. In four-day operations with two shifts, hours may be rearranged; for example, if the old hours were 7:00 A.M. to 3:30 P.M. and 4:00 P.M. to 12:30 A.M. the new hours might be 6:00 A.M. to 4:00 P.M. and 4:00 P.M. to 2:00 A.M. In computer operations two 12-hour shifts a day for two teams of workers each working three days (one on Monday–Wednesday and the other on Thursday–Saturday) is a way to achieve six-day coverage 24 hours a day. Peak workloads during one part of the day or week can also be managed through certain shift arrangements. In police work, for example, ten-hour shifts can be overlapped: a 7:00 A.M. to 5:00 P.M. shift, a 5:00 P.M. to 3:00 A.M.

and a third 9:00 P.M. to 7:00 A.M. shift overlapping the busy night hours. Overloaded areas in a firm's operation can be eased by adding a Friday–Sunday team in those areas, thus adding weekend hours, or a weekend team can replace a third weekday shift. Compressed workweeks that are four and a half days long are often accomplished by adding an hour a day to Monday–Thursday operations to permit Friday afternoons off.[6]

■ *Utilization of plants and equipment.* Extended operating times mean that facilities and capital equipment can be used more efficiently. If, for instance, capital equipment must be operated continuously because of the nature of the production process, longer and fewer shifts are generally most cost-effective, since this reduces the expense associated with startups and shutdowns.

■ *Labor cost per unit.* The reduction in startups and shutdowns that accompanies the compressed workweek translates into a corresponding reduction in the labor hours required to perform these functions. In the case of units whose employees are assigned to distant work sites, the cost of travel to and from the work site is cut when the employees work a greater number of hours per trip. The use of a compressed workweek may also result in a better match between staffing levels and peak-period activity, which may in turn reduce overtime costs.

■ *Utility costs.* If the organization is able to schedule all or part of its operations within hours when special discounts are given by utility companies, there may be a significant reduction in utility costs associated with use of the compressed workweek.

■ *Union attitudes.* Unions are generally skeptical about compressed schedules. They are concerned about the fatigue factor and the long-term effects on employee health. They are also sensitive to any encroachment on overtime or the protections embodied in the Federal Fair Labor Standards Act, particularly the forty-hour workweek. Some union contracts specify both an eight-hour day and a forty-hour week. As with other alternative work time schedules, however, some unions whose members feel the need for such options have supported, or taken the lead in negotiating, a compressed workweek schedule.

■ *Failure rate.* It should be noted that the compressed workweek used to be known for its high failure rate. The survey by Stanley Nollen and Virginia Martin, cited in Nollen's *New York Schedules in Practice,* indicated that "28 percent of one time users had abandoned it."[7] According to Nollen, "[T]hese failures occurred quite quickly when they happened and were usually caused by trouble with fatigue, coverage, scheduling, productivity and supervision. They were also caused in some cases by employee discontent."[8] Planning that includes employee input on the type of compressed schedule that is preferable would certainly improve the success rate. With good planning, many long-term users report no difficulty with the arrangement and perceive a number of benefits that have held up over a period of time.

Should Your Organization Try A Compressed Workweek?

This section provides some tools that can help you decide whether a compressed workweek would aid in solving your organization's staffing and scheduling problems.

The accompanying material entitled Organizational Experience with the Compressed Workweek profiles several different examples of compressed workweek usage. Reading this should help you focus on the major issues associated with the use of a compressed work-week.

The questionnaire shown in Table 2-1 lists the primary concerns that lead companies to try compressed workweeks. The more yes answers you have on this questionnaire, the greater the chances

Table 2-1.   Compressed workweek questionnaire.

Would a Compressed Workweek Benefit Your Organization?

	Yes	No
Do you have problems with recruitment or turnover for weekend coverage or for some shifts?		
Would you like to expand the use of some of your more expensive equipment?		
Do some of the workers in your work units have to travel long distances to and from work sites?		
Would it be more cost-effective to combine three shifts into two?		
Would your employees like more three-day blocks of personal time?		
Is commuting during rush hour a problem for many of your employees?		

that you should be taking a serious look at this scheduling arrangement for your organization.

If your questionnaire results point to the adoption of a compressed workweek, you can use the worksheet shown in Figure 2-4 to list your specific concerns and outline what you see as the advantages and disadvantages of a compressed schedule.

Introducing a Compressed Workweek

To introduce a compressed workweek in your organization, begin by appointing a planning group to build support for the proposed program by addressing at the outset the problems that have sometimes caused such programs to fail. Depending on how complex and extensive the program is expected to be, it is often necessary to appoint a project administrator to oversee the program's implementation. As you move into the design phase, you will work out the details of a variety of critical issues. Supporting resource materials should then be created and the program announced to employees. If the compressed workweek is not optional, promotion will be necessary only in the planning stages. If it is to be an individual option for exempt employees, promotion may be appropriate. As with other flexible work arrangements, you will want to evaluate the program's progress and make adjustments based on your company's experience with it. The following subsections discuss this introduction process in greater depth.

Gain Support for the Program

A compressed workweek retains the forty-hour-a-week mode and the standard that everyone reports to work and leaves at the same time. Consequently, for many managers it requires less of a change in supervisory style than flextime does. The most common reasons for introducing a compressed workweek are (1) to improve production scheduling and the use of facilities and capital equipment and (2) to improve employee morale and relations.

Unless a companywide application is planned immediately, a full-blown task force approach may not be necessary. At a minimum, however, a planning group should be appointed.

Holding meetings with managers, supervisors, and employees and, where all or part of the workforce is unionized, with labor groups is the most effective means of gaining support for this

Figure 2-4. Compressed workweek worksheet.

Assessing the Need for a Compressed Workweek

List the main reasons why you are considering a compressed workweek:

1. _____

   _____

   _____

2. _____

   _____

   _____

3. _____

   _____

   _____

4. _____

   _____

   _____

List what you see as the advantages and disadvantages of a compressed workweek:

Pros: _____

   _____

   _____

   _____

   _____

_____

_____

Cons: _____

_____

_____

_____

_____

_____

scheduling arrangement. The meetings have two purposes: (1) to articulate organizational objectives and (2) to solicit suggestions. Since the reasons most often reported for failure of a compressed workweek have been scheduling and communications problems, fatigue, and employee dissatisfaction, it should come as no surprise that organizations that include managers, supervisors, and employees in the planning process appear to have a higher success rate than those that do not. Stanley Nollen and Virginia Martin observe that "In particular, holding meetings with managers and supervisors was associated with better productivity and work scheduling experiences, with a lower frequency of management problems."[9]

Set Up the Program's Administration

If the compressed workweek will be used in more than one form and in more than one work unit, a project administrator should be appointed to work with the planning group to coordinate the planning meetings, gather information about other organizations' experience with a compressed workweek, plan the program, act as a resource for supervisors and employees during its initial phases, and monitor the program as it is implemented, evaluated, and revised.

Design the Program

The following are some of the issues that you will have to deal with in designing a compressed workweek:

■ *State and federal labor laws.* Your first step is to review federal and state labor laws to determine what kinds of compressed scheduling options are possible. As we've noted, federal law limits to forty the number of hours in a week that can be worked by nonexempt employees without paying overtime, and some states impose a daily maximum (usually eight hours). Employers interested in using the 9/80 model must change their systems in order to comply with the Fair Labor Standards Act's forty-hour rule (see Bechtel profile, page 64).

■ *Labor contracts.* Existing labor agreements should also be reviewed to see whether their provisions conflict with the use of a compressed work schedule.

Once the legal parameters have been established, some of the remaining design questions that must be answered are:

■ *Extent of the program.* In which areas or departments of the organization will you have a compressed schedule? Will it be an individual option for exempt employees? If so, what eligibility criteria will be established? Will a standard workweek still be an option for employees who would prefer it?

■ *Compressed workweek model(s).* What model(s) of compressed scheduling will best suit the objectives that you identified?

■ *Operating and shift schedules.* Must operating schedules be changed? (Will the organization operate fewer days? More days?) What kinds of shift changes will be necessary? (Will some shifts be combined? Will new shifts be added, perhaps on weekends or during peak periods of activity?)

■ *Workforce allocations.* Will it be necessary to reallocate personnel in order to keep the organization functioning at maximum efficiency with a compressed workweek?

■ *Holidays and paid time off.* Will changes in paid holidays be made? Some companies that use the 4/10 format, for example, alter their previous holiday plan of ten paid holidays of eight hours each to eight paid holidays of ten hours each.

■ *Duration of the program.* Will the compressed schedule be in effect year-round or only during part of the year (for example, summer)?

The program design checklist shown in Table 2-2 can help you chart your progress in addressing the design issues we've just considered.

Develop Resource Materials

Developing resource materials and training programs related to the introduction of a compressed workweek helps eliminate the problems experienced by some of the organizations that encountered employee resistance or communication and scheduling problems when they introduced a compressed workweek.

An information sheet detailing any changes (such as in operating schedules or holidays) occurring as a result of the introduction of a compressed workweek or the availability of a compressed workweek as an individual option should be made available to all affected employees.

Figure 2-5 shows the guidelines that one large manufacturing company developed for the use of twelve-hour shifts in its plants, together with an assessment of what the organization regarded as the benefits and drawbacks of this type of scheduling. Information

Table 2-2.   Program design checklist: compressed workweek.

Key Design Issues	Notes
☐ State and federal labor laws	
☐ Existing labor contracts	
☐ Extent of the program (in terms of departments, production units, areas, and so on)	
☐ Scheduling model(s)	
☐ Operating and shift schedules	
☐ Workforce allocations	
☐ Holidays	
☐ Duration of the program	

Figure 2-5. A manufacturer's materials on the use of a twelve-hour shift.

12-Hour Shift Guidelines

Guidelines plants have typically elected to adopt in establishing 12-hour shift schedules are:

1. No additional cost to the site (may require some adjustment in wage premiums).
2. Must not liberalize intent of current policies covering pay and benefits.
3. Comply with applicable federal (Fair Labor Standards Act and possibly Walsh-
   Healey) and state laws.
4. Improve employee relations (employees need prior understanding of effects).
5. Must not adversely affect safety, productivity, or attendance.
6. Preserve management's right to reestablish 8-hour system.

Typical 12-Hour Shift Schedule

Rotation:

	Mon.	Tues.	Wed.	Thurs.	Fri.	Sat.	Sun.	Hours per Week
Week 1	D	D	D	D	off	off	off	48*
Week 2	off	off	off	off	N	N	N	36
Week 3	N	off	off	off	D	D	D	48*
Week 4	off	N	N	N	off	off	off	36

D = 6 A.M. to 6 P.M.   N = 6 P.M. to 6 A.M.

A Plant's Evaluation of a Compressed Workweek Schedule

Advantages	Disadvantages
• Employees view as a positive response to request of employees working a rotating shift schedule. • Improved production-mechanical relationships. Same operating crew shuts down and starts up equipment, minimizing outages and improving safety. • Wives generally in favor. • Employee is off every other weekend.	• Brought pressure for some form of added recognition of day employees. • Some initial problem in adapting for communications. • An adjustment period was required for adapting to 12 hours of work. • Overtime scheduling is more of a problem, since the plant permits 4 hours' holdover (16-hour maximum per day).

*Federal law requires overtime rates to be paid for hours worked over 40 in a
workweek. State laws may have some application.

• Has resulted in mechanics volunteering for shift assignments. • Use of gloves, overalls, tags, etc., reduced by one third. Also, one third less shift business paperwork. • Shift exchange time reduced. • Trips to the plant (safety, cost, energy) reduced by one third. • Same employees relieve each other, improving communications and relationships.	• Use of day employees to relieve shift employees is complicated. • Now have difficulty getting volunteers to fill day assignments from shift crews.

of this sort would be helpful in preparing managerial and supervisory personnel for an upcoming switch to a compressed workweek.

Announce the Program

Whether the compressed workweek program is confined to particular work units or departments, is offered as an individual option for exempt employees, or is instituted companywide, a general announcement should be made when it is adopted.

Promote the Program

Company- or work-unit-wide programs in states that require an employee election before a compressed schedule is adopted greatly benefit from promotion strategies that explain the reasons for the program and the benefits to affected employees. If adopted as a companywide or departmental schedule, these scheduling arrangements are not an employee option and do not require internal promotion. Increasingly, however, employers are allowing employees who would prefer a standard schedule to remain on one. Promotion in many cases may be valuable as part of a recruitment effort or a public relations program.

Evaluate the Program

According to the Nollen-Martin study cited earlier, about one in four users of the compressed workweek changes the way in which the organization originally used it.[10] With any new scheduling arrangement, it is important to detect problems early, and this can be done only if some kind of evaluative mechanism is built into the initial implementation process. Baseline data should be obtained and feedback from both supervisors and employees should be solicited so that the impact of the program can be assessed in terms of both business results and employee reaction. In addition to the compressed workweek's effects on job performance and on the workers themselves, the effect on three cost areas (overtime, unit labor costs, and utilities) is often measured.

Fine-Tune the Program

Once the results of the evaluation are in, you will probably find that some changes are called for. Table 2-3 provides examples of some of the problems that employers have encountered in using a compressed schedule and the ways in which they have dealt with these problems.

Summary

The compressed workweek consists of a variety of scheduling options in which the standard forty-hour workweek is condensed into fewer than the standard five days. The popularity of this alternative has had its ups and downs since it was first introduced in the early 1970s, but its use seems to be growing since the introduction of the 9/80 model and its availability as an individual option for exempt employees.

Studies indicate that compressed workweeks tend to be more common in certain industries and that employers tend to institute the practice in selected departments rather than companywide. This may be changing, however, as clean air legislation and individual employee requests encourage wider use of compressed workweeks. Many employers adapt the compressed workweek concept to their unique needs by using different scheduling models in different departments or areas, depending on the nature of the work or the workers involved.

Employers who decide to institute a compressed workweek usually do so in order to better allocate their labor time or use their facilities and capital equipment more effectively. And since some employees—particularly those who want more personal time or who have other demands on their time but cannot afford to reduce their income—like the compressed workweek, it can also serve as a low-cost employee benefit.

The compressed workweek has been reported to offer the following advantages: Absenteeism, tardiness, and turnover decrease somewhat. Employee morale may be enhanced (but only if the employees favor the compressed scheduling option), and recruit-

Table 2-3. Examples of problems with compressed workweeks and their solutions.

Problem	Solution
Work scheduling problems	
Poor supervisory coverage.	Asked supervisors to work five days.
Coverage in all departments was necessary at all times.	Maintained skeleton crews and compensatory time off was granted.
Telephone coverage, Friday billing.	Cross-training; some people work five days (eight hours a day).
Customer service coverage on Friday afternoons.	Group established its own rotating coverage so a person would be present.
Customer service calls.	Rearranged shifts.
Incoming freight.	Notified local delivering carriers.
Maintaining contact with distributors, salesmen on Fridays.	Scheduled necessary contact employees on a Tuesday-Friday workweek.
Problem of service to policyholders.	Assigned 7 percent of four-day work-week force to a Tuesday–Friday schedule with 93 percent working Monday–Thursday.
Supervisors did not like to work Friday afternoon.	We found that neither policyowners nor agents came in or called on Friday, so we use an answering service for all closed hours.
Communication from one team to another.	We developed a one-hour overlap.
Communications with employees much more complex.	Required added management time.
Employee scheduling problems	
Starting times for employees under flextime schedule were not acceptable when the ten-hour workday was instituted.	Employees were permitted to select a new flextime schedule; lunch hours were cut to thirty minutes to shorten the day.
Office employees who contact customers also wanted a four-day week.	We staggered their workweek; that is, half had Monday off, half Friday.
Too many wanted Mondays or Fridays off.	Each department's management simply spelled out the minimum staff required for those days and it was left up to work groups to decide who would be there.

SOURCE: Stanley D. Nollen and Virginia H. Martin, *Alternative Work Schedules*, parts 2 and 3 (New York: AMACOM, 1978), 58–60.

(Continued)

Table 2-3. *(continued)*

Employee scheduling problems *(continued)*	
Adverse effect on nonparticipating employees' morale.	Not solved.
Some married women with children find it inconvenient to arrive home late.	Solved by putting only those people who want the four-day week in that department.
Changing of daily shift hours.	Employees had to adjust and in some cases change their transportation.
Train schedules for departing employees require up to 1½ hr. wait on Friday afternoon.	Called Burlington Railroad—they are adding a train.
Babysitting and transportation.	Allowed flexibility in reporting and quitting times.
Fringe benefit reallocation problems	
How to pay for benefits such as days of vacation, holidays, funeral pay, sick days.	Generally we divided by "4" instead of "5." Everyone involved gets "1" less, but the same number of hours.
Sick days.	Had to change "sick days" to "sick hours" because of longer working day in four-day week. Now give forty-eight hours per year instead of six days.

ment often improves. Employees become more willing to accept traditionally undesirable assignments (shifts, weekends), since longer blocks of personal time compensate them for the inconvenience. While an improvement in productivity is cited by only some employers, an improvement in commuting is commonly reported. Employers under mandate from federal or local air quality and transportation agencies to reduce employee ridership have found this scheduling arrangement effective in doing so. The compressed workweek can be used to tailor shifts in a way that improves scheduling. And this work-time alternative permits more effective use of plants, equipment, and labor and may result in decreased utility costs.

On the negative side are potential problems with employee morale involving those workers who don't favor the adoption of the compressed workweek and problems with supervision. Longer workdays can result in employee fatigue and a negative impact on productivity. Restrictions imposed by state legislation can sometimes make the compressed workweek a less attractive option for employers, as can the concerns of some unions and the provisions of some union contracts.

The basic eight-step process for implementing a new work-time alternative that was presented in the Introduction applies to the compressed workweek, although, if the program is mandatory, it may not need to be promoted to employees once it is in place. But care should be taken at the outset to gain the understanding and support of all who will be involved in the program and to provide resource materials and training that address (and may help prevent) some of the potential problems.

ORGANIZATIONAL EXPERIENCE WITH
THE COMPRESSED WORKWEEK

Shell Canada Limited

Description: The Shell Canada chemical plant at Sarnia, Ontario, makes polypropylene and isopropyl alcohol. It is a continuous-process facility, operating seven days a week, twenty-four hours a day.

Reason for Using a Compressed Workweek: When the plant was built, a primary goal was to maximize both economic and human performance and quality of work life. The latter was defined, in part, as the creation of a learning environment, which necessitated a redesign of shift work. Another reason for reexamining existing procedures was the attrition associated with shift work. Shift scheduling was becoming increasingly unpopular with the plant's labor force because of the social dislocation it entails. The resulting costs of turnover, recruitment, and training needed to be addressed.

Implementation Process: The first step was converting from eight-hour to twelve-hour shifts. This solved some problems (workers liked it better because it gave them three days off a week and more daytime work) but created new ones. For example, covering absences was more difficult with a compressed workweek, overtime issues had to be resolved, and paid leave time had to be recalculated.

The next stage of implementation entailed a major overhaul of work schedules, training, and management style. The objective was to obtain multiskilled workers and reduce the amount of shift work. To achieve this, the plant basically redesigned the organization. Shift work was combined with nonshift work, and training time is now part of the regular schedule.

Impact to Date: Workers have fewer nonstandard hours and are more self-managing; shift workers are multiskilled and continually trained. Both union representatives and management have collaborated to achieve the program's success.

SOURCE: Stanley D. Nollen, *New Work Schedules in Practice: Managing Time in a Changing Society,* Work in America Institute Series (New York: Van Nostrand Reinhold, 1982), 83–93; conversations with Shell staff (Dec. 1993).

Royal Bank of Canada

Description: The Royal Bank of Canada is headquartered in Montreal. It is the largest financial services institution in Canada and employs 52,000.

Reason for Using a Compressed Workweek: In order to respond to the changes in workplace demographics and worker expectations in ways that would enable the bank to recruit, retain, and motivate a quality workforce, in 1989 Royal Bank conducted an extensive review of human resources findings and workforce trends, both internal and external to the organization. The result was the implementation of a comprehensive Work and Family Program composed of five major categories, including leave policies and benefits, dependent care programs, flexible work arrangements, work- and family-related management training, and Work and Family Resource Libraries.

Implementation Process: Since 1990, employees of Royal Bank of Canada have had a variety of flexible work arrangements to choose from—including Part-Time, Job Sharing, Flextime, Flexiplace, and Compressed or Modified Workweeks. Staff of Montreal's Materials Distribution Centre now work the standard 37½-hour work week in four 9½-hour days. Staff who prefer to retain the five day a week schedule may request to do so.

Impact to Date at Materials Distribution Centre: Under the previous standard five-day week, shipments generally were made on Friday afternoon. This was too late to make transit connections until Monday morning. With the compressed schedule, materials arrive at their destination in a much more timely fashion. Since the Centre supplies all the branches' and departments' materials and supplies, from stationery forms to promotional materials, this has had a beneficial effect on Royal Bank's operations nationally. Employees enjoy their three-day weekends and ability to commute on off-peak hours. The few who preferred a standard workweek staff the warehouse and office on Fridays, receiving shipments and handling rush orders.

SOURCE: Royal Bank of Canada company magazine; conversations with Norma Tombari, Manager Work and Family Program (Jan. 1994).

Bechtel Corporation

Description: Large construction-and-engineering firm employing 30,900 worldwide and 4,000 in the San Francisco home office.

Reason for Using a Compressed Workweek: Originally piloted in southern California in conjunction with that region's Clean Air Initiative. Introduced in San Francisco office as a quality of life issue plus being an asset in recruiting and retaining top engineering talent.

Implementation Process: Successful pilots in Los Angeles and Houston led to a decision that the San Francisco office consider using a compressed schedule. A task force was formed that included representation from HR, Legal, Payroll, Public Relations, Engineering, and Business Lines. Clients were consulted on their reaction to the change in schedule. Management proposed a 9/80 schedule with half the company's staff receiving a day off on alternate Fridays. Staff prefering a standard 40/week schedule are allowed to do so. Because of California's eight-hour rule, company elections were mandated in order to implement the Compressed Workweek. Bechtel chose to make the election companywide, including exempt, as well as the required nonexempt, employees in the process. Extensive information meetings for employees were held to explain the program, and promotional materials were distributed. A large transportation fair was held to assist employees with changes in commuting requirements due to a longer workday. More than 90 percent of the employees voted for the program.

Impact to Date: In order to comply with Fair Labor Standards Act (FLSA) overtime requirements, the standard pay period start was changed from Monday to midday Friday. Commute time has been reduced by 10 percent. Employee absences have decreased, and the program is very popular. At the end of the first year and second year of the 9/80 program, data were collected through a survey of employees and managers. It showed that 9/80 does not detract from the overall effectiveness of business operations. With 9/80, Bechtel continues to sustain the company's high level of productivity and employees' quality of life has improved.

SOURCE: Bechtel materials; Jeff Pelline, "S.F. Bechtel Workers Begin New Schedule," *San Francisco Chronicle* (Jan. 2, 1991); conversations with R. I. Silverforb, Corporate Human Resources (Jan. 1994).

CHAPTER 3

Flexplace

Increasingly, employers are finding that allowing regular employees to work at home during a part of their scheduled hours both accommodates the needs of some employees and benefits the organization. In some communities, a positive effect on the environment is also cited. Whether the term used to describe the arrangement is *flexplace, working at home* or from a *satellite* office, *telecommuting*, or *telework*, the practice is growing. Some employees working at home are full-timers; others are on part-time schedules. Some are professionals; others, managers, clerical workers, and, in some instances, production workers.

Origins of Flexplace

Although flexplace was among the kinds of flexible and reduced work-time options suggested by proponents of greater workplace flexibility in the early 1970s, it was not until the 1980s, with the astounding growth of personal computer use, that the arrangement received much attention as an option for regular employees. A 1984 report entitled *Telecommuting: The State of the Art and Market Trends*, issued by Electronic Services Unlimited, a New York–based consulting group, suggested two reasons for telecommuting's rapid expansion: the "growth of the information society and the explosion of chip technology." The report also noted that "telecommuting is highly compatible with current life-style trends."[1]

The forces driving employee interest in flexplace options stem from the same social, demographic, and attitudinal changes that have stimulated the need for other nonstandard work arrangements discussed in this book. With two-paycheck families the new norm and commuter-hour traffic jams common in more and more communities, working at home, either temporarily or regularly, during part of the workweek is seen by some employees as an attractive option.

Who Uses Flexplace?

In 1981, Frank Schiff, then vice president and chief economist for the Committee for Economic Development, gave a talk entitled *Flexiplace: An Idea Whose Time Has Come* before the Engineering Management Society's Institute of Electrical and Electronics Engineers. In it, he commented:

> Some of the best immediate possibilities for use of flexiplace exist for engineers, computer programmers and analysts, architects and designers. The concept also has considerable applicability to various kinds of white-collar and clerical jobs that already rely importantly on use of computer terminals and that frequently involve "batch" work, such as word processing, accounting, insurance analysis, processing of insurance claims, etc. Work at home also has special potential for activities that call for output at odd hours—for example, overnight typing and checking of medical reports first prepared by doctors in rough form. Eventually even various production activities in manufacturing may become candidates for "flexiplace." After all, any work that involves remote control devices could in theory be guided at a considerable distance from the place where the actual production activities take place.[2]

At the time, Schiff's comments bordered on the visionary, but much of what he projected has occurred in the intervening years. Although we still do not know the real extent of the change in terms of the status of flexplace options for regular employees, LINK Resources has conducted an annual work-at-home survey since the mid-1980s, and its data shows a continuous growth trend. In 1993 LINK reported that there were 41.1 million homeworkers (defined as people who do at least eight hours of job-related work at home each week). This is an increase of 5.4 percent from 1992. Telecommuters number 7.6 million, or 6 percent of the U.S. labor force, and what LINK calls "pure corporate telecommuters," corporate salaried employees working during normal business hours, number 5.09 million, up 21.5 percent from 1992.[3]

Only 11 percent of telecommuters work thirty-five or more hours a week at home; 36 percent average one day a week at home. Demographically, 54 percent of telecommuters are male, and 49 percent have children under eighteen; 55 percent of telecommuters own a PC, but only 13 percent had the PC provided by or reimbursed by the employer.[4]

A study sponsored by the Small Business Administration (SBA) on the characteristics of home business owners and telecommuters sheds some light on who these workers are and concludes that they have a great deal in common with their colleagues in the office. Conclusions include the fact that:

- Work patterns of telecommuting and nontelecommuting employees are similar.
- Home-based work is not associated with employees who have a young child. Employees do *not* themselves provide care for their children on telecommuting days.
- Telecommuters receive promotions at a greater rate than nontelecommuters. This may be due to their holding management jobs.[5]

When Is Flexplace Most Appropriate?

Flexplace not only is a popular option among employees but also is appropriate for employers who feel a need to save on office-space costs, expand their recruitment pool, perform certain types of tasks more efficiently, improve continuity of services, extend coverage, and employ individuals who might find standard on-site, 9–5 working arrangements prohibitively difficult.

■ *Space.* In most urban areas, the cost of office space has been rising for some time. With financial management and cost containment a priority for all employers, for certain organizations having some employees work off-site has proved to be an effective way to trim the cost of office space.

■ *Popularity with employees.* Employees regard flexplace as offering many benefits. In addition to family considerations, these benefits include not having to "dress for success"; a saving in time, since the employee does not have to spend a portion of each workday commuting, as well as increased flexibility and control when it comes to the use of time; and access to employment for those who are homebound because of a disability or some other factor.

Increasingly, in urban areas, the expense of housing and commuting are also major employee considerations. Studies by Runzheimer International, a consulting organization specializing in relocation costs, have indicated that the housing and commuting costs in and around New York City are getting to the point where "[I]t may not pay to be a commuter."[6] Estimated costs of living for a family of four in major cities are Washington, D.C., $71,622; Boston, $68,750; Chicago, $65,812; and Los Angeles, $75,975.[7] To offset these costs, employers have in the past paid higher salaries or provided specialized "perks" such as commuting subsidies to attract good applicants or encourage current employees to relocate. Employees who work under flexplace arrangements, on the other hand, can reduce or eliminate commuting costs and live in less expensive areas, farther from the employer's place of business.

Taken as a whole, these advantages of flexplace from the employees' perspective make the arrangement a low-cost employee morale booster.

■ *Compliance with environmental legislation.* In 1990 passage of federal legislation and introduction of a growing number of local and regional air and transportation regulations gave new impetus to the use of flexplace. The Federal Clean Air Act of 1990 requires employers with 100 or more employees in ten badly polluted regions of the country to design "trip reduction programs" in order to reduce solo commuting to work. The states that are affected are California, Connecticut, Delaware, Illinois, Indiana, Maryland, New Jersey, New York, Pennsylvania, Texas, and Wisconsin. In a growing number of areas, state and regional regulatory mandates are also being passed. As noted in Chapter 2, "Compressed Workweek," flexplace is becoming a popular way to comply with the reduction in ridership component of this type of legislation.

■ *Labor force availability.* Finding an adequate supply of job candidates is a problem in some areas, and flexplace and telecommuting options allow employers to recruit from an expanded, geographically dispersed labor pool. In many areas, a related issue is lack of transit facilities, which makes working at home attractive.

■ *Nature of the work.* Flexplace arrangements can be a more efficient way of performing some types of tasks—for example, data entry or form processing—because the work can be done at odd hours with less distraction than usually occurs in an office setting. This is true with many professional-level jobs as well, particularly those that benefit from quiet, undisturbed thinking time.

■ *Continuity of services.* In some parts of the country, incentives for flexplace have included the possibility of maintaining services during inclement weather, such as winter blizzards. Under such circumstances, flexplace employees have an edge on those who must commute, in terms of both getting to the job and productivity on the job.

■ *Extended coverage.* Expanding the hours of service is also possible with flexplace. This is particularly helpful if the organization has service operations that cover several time zones or wants to conduct an activity or offer a service that does not need to be office-based (for example, catalog shopping) during a larger portion of the workday.

■ *Employing the hard to employ.* Some applications of flexplace or telecommuting arrangements have been aimed at bringing employment opportunities to workers with disabilities that make it difficult for them to work full time in an office or as a means of economic development in rural settings where job opportunities are scarce.

Pros and Cons of Flexplace

The advantages and disadvantages of flexplace involve such issues as cost versus savings, the impact of this arrangement on productivity, how to supervise and evaluate off-site workers, the need to maintain adequate contact with off-site workers, security of proprietary information, and union attitudes.

■ *Cost considerations.* Cost efficiency has been a major factor in employer receptivity to telecommuting and flexplace arrangements. At the top of the list of incentives has been a desire to cut the rising cost of office space and overhead. In addition to rent, this includes the cost of insurance, parking, and security. Flexplace options reduce this type of expense even when satellite offices are added, since these may be located in outlying areas where space is cheaper. According to leading international telecommuting expert Gil Gordon, "the real estate issue will be the hot telecommuting topic to watch in the next few years."

One result of employer concern about space costs has been the emergence of the concept of the "virtual office." This type of space usage is sometimes described as "nonterritorial." AT&T has established a virtual office for its account executives (AEs) in a number of its branch sales offices. It has space for fifty core staff plus drop-in space for from 65 to 100 telecommuters. The ratio of desks to "visiting" staff is one to eight. Each AE is given a laptop PC with software, a cellular phone, voice mail, and electronic mail. In addition to reducing space costs (72,000 square feet reduced to 26,500), this kind of office environment emphasizes the need for AEs to be out in the field relating to the customers rather than sitting at a desk. IBM uses a nonterritorial office for some of its sales and service personnel, and Digital Equipment is using this approach for sales staff in some of its locations.[8] Employee reaction to this kind of involuntary telecommuting is unknown at this writing. However, at least one ex-employee of Perkin-Elmer didn't like it. An eight-year sales and service representative in Alaska didn't mind working from home but felt that the company wasn't "acknowledging that this was an inconvenience for me and a huge benefit for them." The two sides were not able to come to terms.[9]

As noted earlier, employees do like the idea of voluntary flex-place arrangements. When this option is available, the organization will find that it can recruit from an expanded labor pool that will include individuals who for one reason or another could not accept an on-site position, and that it can more effectively retain its existing employees, some of whom might leave the company if an off-site opportunity were not offered. By minimizing turnover, the organization saves on new-hire costs. Some companies have even been able to reduce or eliminate relocation costs by allowing employees to telecommute or work off-site when the office moves or when the employees are offered a transfer to another company location and prefer not to move.

On the expense side are the costs of purchasing and maintaining equipment for employees who are working off-site. Providing insurance for the equipment and concerns about liability and job-related employee injuries have been deterrents to the use of flexplace arrangements in some cases. However, employers using telecommuters seem to feel that these costs can be minimized and are offset by the savings on space and overhead and the gains in productivity (discussed below).

■ *Productivity*. Employers that have evaluated their off-site projects report productivity gains of from 15 to 20 percent. Some show even higher gains, and the worst case seems to be to break even. These employers credit such gains to employees' having fewer distractions, being able to work at personal "peak" times, experiencing increased motivation because they have the desired flexibility, and working on a more continuous basis because meetings and other such duties that tend to interrupt the normal flow of work are scheduled together.[10] The possibility of expanding use of expensive equipment and of extending coverage or service hours are additional factors that can increase productivity.

The scheduling flexibility made possible by employee use of personal computers in their homes can also boost productivity. After-hours work on home-based personal computers is growing and is more common than full-time telecommuting in most organizations. According to a survey of forty-eight companies in the Pittsburgh area conducted by Professor Paul Goodman of Carnegie-Mellon University, the practice nets companies extra time from workers. It also allows employees greater flexibility in allocating their time and enables them to work when creative insights strike.[11] For telecommuting employees who are working with data supplied by a central computer, the ability to access the information source during less busy time periods can speed the response rate considerably.

■ *Supervision and evaluation.* A major concern for some employers has been supervising and evaluating off-site employees. Many worry about how to tell whether an employee is working when he or she is off-site and out of sight. Managing by objectives rather than by monitoring is necessary, and this requires a change in attitude and style for many managers and supervisors. The temptation for some supervisors of employees working at home with electronic equipment is to track their output by electronic monitoring. This can result in considerable stress for the employees and has become an increasingly controversial issue as more and more workers become telecommuters.

When it comes to evaluating an off-site employee's work, most employers recommend that two of the primary criteria be (1) quality of work and (2) completion of projects. For many managers, the perception that it is hard to measure these factors for telecommuters is a significant attitudinal barrier with respect to off-site, computer-assisted options. However, as more managers gain access to appropriate resources and training, there seems to be less trouble evaluating performance.

■ *Maintaining contact with off-site employees.* Retaining the connectedness of off-site workers and minimizing their sense of isolation is another issue that must be addressed. Even employees who are temperamentally suited for working on their own at home sometimes feel lonely and out of the mainstream. This problem can be addressed by scheduling regular office contact, either at the main plant or at satellite offices, and by making good use of communications vehicles such as the telephone or electronic mail.

Regular contact is important, too, in terms of retaining employee loyalty and commitment. Concerns about an erosion in employees' sense of being part of an organization have kept some employers from developing flexplace options. However, the opposite effect seems to be true, with most companies reporting enhanced commitment as a result of their having accommodated employees' needs for flexibility, particularly when contact with the office is maintained, at least on a minimal level.

■ *Security.* Many data-processing managers worry about telecommuting employees having unsupervised access to company data. Whether at home or in the office, all employees must comply with operating procedures aimed at protecting information privacy. If there is a need to access a special system, the employee should discuss this with appropriate supervisory staff. If necessary, it is generally possible to limit work with confidential data to days when the employee is scheduled to be in the office. Since regular employees are often able to take home software for use in their personal computers, employers should not regard the security issue as being applicable only to those employees who do most of their work off-site.

■ *Union attitudes.* Labor representatives have expressed a variety of opinions and concerns regarding flexplace and telecommuting. They have been particularly apprehensive about the potential for changing an employee's status from regular to "independent contractor" as a condition of working from the home. The AFL-CIO has opposed telecommuting on the grounds that when workers are based at home, it is difficult or impossible to enforce labor standards designed to protect them. The Communications Workers of America (CWA) has resisted attempts to establish flexplace programs for workers in the telecommunications industry. In 1992, however, the CWA developed guidelines for pilot projects that stipulate:

■ Pay and benefits for telecommuters must be equal to those of other employees performing the same work.

■ Telecommuters must work from the office a minimum of two days each week.

■ Managers should visit a telecommuter's home no more than twice a month with a minimum of twenty-four hours' notice.

■ The company should furnish equipment and supplies (including telephone equipment) and reimburse employees for additional utilities and insurance costs paid by the employee. The union also should have the right to inspect equipment at home to ensure that it is safe and ergonomically sound.

■ Telecommuters should be routinely advised of job openings and advancement opportunities. The union has a right of access to communicate with telecommuters.

■ Excessive monitoring should be prohibited, and employees should be given notice of monitoring.

■ There should be no preferential scheduling for telecommuters.

■ Training should be provided for telecommuters to keep them up to date.

■ Employees must not be hired directly into a telecommuting position, and employees must have the option to terminate the agreement.

The CWA also wants to be involved in the planning process for telecommuting pilot projects and wants assurances that subcontracting will be abolished in any job area where telecommuting is used.[12]

Should Your Organization Try Flexplace?

In this section, you will be considering the use of flexplace from the perspective of your own organization. Could some of the problems it faces be effectively addressed through the introduction of off-site options?

Start by referring to the accompanying group of profiles entitled Organizational Experience with Flexplace. In it are described the flexplace programs offered by two companies. As you read about why these programs were started, how they were implemented, and what effect they have had, consider whether the issues and strategies discussed there might be relevant to your company's situation.

Table 3-1 is a questionnaire that lists some concerns that lead

Table 3-1. Flexplace questionnaire.

Would Flexplace Benefit Your Organization?

	Yes	No
Is the amount or cost of office space of concern in your company?		
Can you identify specific types of jobs that could be performed more efficiently off-site than on-site?		
Have some of your organization's employees requested more flexible schedules because of family responsibilities or other needs?		
Are your operations in the process of becoming decentralized?		
If decentralization is planned or underway, might some valued employees leave the company rather than relocate?		
Is the community you operate in concerned about the negative impact of heavy rush-hour traffic?		
Does your firm have a data processing backlog?		
Does your organization have trouble attracting qualified job applicants?		

employers to try flexplace. If, in reviewing the questions, you find yourself repeatedly agreeing that your organization does indeed face these conditions, then off-site arrangements might be worth a try. Figure 3-1 is a worksheet that can be used to examine flexplace in greater detail, including the specific reasons why this option seems called for and its potential pluses and minuses.

Introducing Flexplace

The process of introducing a program of flexplace options starts with gaining broad-based support for this move. The program's administrative staff is then appointed, and the entire array of program design issues are addressed. The organization not only develops resource materials for both managers and employees who will be involved in the flexplace program but also trains these people in order to minimize the problems that can be associated with this arrangement and maximize its benefits. After a period of time, the program's progress is assessed, and its provisions are modified as necessary. We'll take a closer look at these steps in the following subsections.

Gain Support for the Program

Management and labor both have concerns about flexplace and/or telecommuting that must be addressed in order to gain support for

Figure 3-1. Flexplace worksheet.

Assessing the Need for Flexplace

List the main reasons why you are considering flexplace:

1. _____

   _____

   _____

2. _____

   _____

   _____

3. _____

   _____

   _____

4. _____

   _____

   _____

List what you see as the advantages and disadvantages of flexplace:

Pros: _____

_____

_____

_____

(Continued)

Figure 3-1. *(continued)*

```
_____

_____

_____


Cons: _____

_____

_____

_____

_____

_____
```

this kind of option. Forming a cross-disciplinary project team is a good way to solicit input from various functions of the organization, for example, Human Resources, Benefits, Corporate Communications, and other affected departments. In a unionized environment, a joint labor-management group with balanced representation is desirable.

Set Up the Program's Administration

The program's scope and its technical ramifications will determine the type and extent of the administrative staff that will be needed. At a minimum, a project administrator should be appointed to work with the project team. Other support groups might include subgroups for technical implementation and human resources implementation.

Design the Program

Before decisions can be made regarding policy and process, the primary intent and business objectives of the program must be defined and articulated. Is this going to be a telecommuting program that will focus on tasks, space configuration, and cost factors? A companywide human resources management program that will respond to employees' needs while giving the organization new options as well? A combination of the two?

Whatever the decisions regarding the program's objectives, once those decisions are made, the following issues, which are common to any kind of off-site arrangements, must be addressed:

■ *Scope.* A fundamental question is that of the program's initial size. Does a pilot project make sense as a way to test the new program and its processes? If not, will the option be offered companywide or restricted to particular job classifications or departments? Will certain jobs be excluded?

■ *Eligibility.* Related to the question of scope is that of eligibility. Two factors should be considered when establishing policy in this area: (1) who is able to work effectively in an off-site environment and (2) the employee's relationship to the company. The consensus of most employers that offer flexplace options is that the arrangement should be restricted to current employees who are familiar with the company's culture and committed to its goals rather than new hires.

Experience also suggests that voluntary in-house applicants should be carefully screened. Not everyone is able to work off-site. Some people cannot deal with the distractions; others are overwhelmed by the isolation. Workaholics who can't set limits tend to burn out, and "fast-trackers" worry about their careers plateauing if they are not visible in the office. Consequently, in addition to task-related functions, the psychological makeup of the employee should be considered, including such factors as the need for self-discipline and motivation and the ability to work on his or her own, without regular supervision or the social support of co-workers.

■ *Legal and tax considerations.* The company's tax experts, accounting advisers, and legal counsel should be consulted regarding any potential problems with zoning regulations covering at-home work, insurance considerations, and questions about employee status. The following are some tips for avoiding problems in the area of liability when an organization sets up a flexplace program:

■ If work is to be performed at home, it should take place in a dedicated area that is open to inspection by the employer.
■ The best defense against liability problems is good education and preventive steps to identify and reduce risks.

■ The company should get the facts on its state's workers' compensation statutes and look for remote-work precedents.

■ A "telecommuter's agreement" should be used to spell out rights and responsibilities.

■ The company should make sure that any equipment provided for the remote site is safe and working well.[13]

■ *Compensation and benefits.* Some special considerations in the area of compensation and benefits to which the organization should be sensitive are:

■ Existing options regarding types of employment status, pay levels, and benefits coverage should be carefully examined to make sure telecommuters are treated fairly and equitably.

■ The company should avoid taking a short-term view on salary and benefits cost control, since it may lose in the long run if it skimps in these areas.

■ Creative ways should be sought to apply pay-for-performance approaches to telecommuters.

■ If the company has a flexible benefits or "cafeteria compensation" plan, an attempt should be made to use it to the telecommuters' advantage or, if need be, change it to their advantage.[14]

■ *Off-site scheduling.* Regular employees who work off-site part of the time may be employed on either a full- or a part-time basis. It is important, however, that they not be scheduled to work 100 percent of their hours off-site. Some regularly scheduled time in either the main office or a satellite office should be required. Experts generally recommend that a minimum of 20 percent of employees' regularly scheduled time be on-site. It is this mandatory contact that ensures the employees' continued identification with the company's culture and community and with its overall objectives.

■ *Establishing common-space work areas or satellite or neighborhood work centers.* A variety of techniques have been developed to ensure that telecommuters and other off-site employees have some office "territory" to come to. Some companies provide "common-space work areas." When off-site employees return to the office, they don't have their own desk, but they do have shared desks and space in which to work among their office-based co-workers and with their home-based colleagues.

Using satellite offices, where off-site employees can work part of the time, is another way in which companies can combat the isolation factor associated with flexplace. If the company's own program is not large enough to warrant that approach, neighborhood work centers, shared by several organizations, have begun to emerge to address the need for telecommuters' supply and support services. Both types of facility are generally less expensive than space at the main plant. Satellite offices or neighborhood work centers should be placed where they will both minimize the need for travel and accommodate the need that many off-site workers have for occasional access to an office environment.

■ *Length of commitment and reversibility.* Rather than leave a flexplace arrangement open-ended, some employers ask for a specific time commitment—for example, six months or a year—after which the initial provisions of the flexplace agreement are reviewed and reaffirmed or renegotiated. If telecommuting is involved, with a commitment in equipment from the employer, this ensures that the employee will give it a good try. As we've noted, flexplace is not for everyone. When valued employees find that they are unable, for whatever reason, to continue the arrangement, a process should exist for them to return to the on-site work environment.

■ *Application process.* The kind of application process that a company establishes for employees interested in a flexplace option will depend on who is eligible to participate in this type of arrangement and what the primary objective of the program is. If the option is to be generally available within certain parameters, then a request to the immediate supervisor may be the most appropriate kind of application. In this case, the organization should develop guidelines for supervisors, similar to those recommended for other new work arrangements, detailing how to respond to requests for off-site work. If the program is to be primarily a technically oriented telecommuting option, then a more generalized application process will be needed—for example, posting telecommuting openings along with other job listings.

Once program and policy have been developed by the project team, the policy segments should be reviewed by internal experts on safety, computer security, legal issues, etc. This not only improves the document but also helps build buy-in for the program.

Table 3-2 is a checklist that summarizes the major program design issues we have covered in this subsection. You can use it as a handy review of these issues and to record your progress in dealing with them.

Table 3-2.   Program design checklist: flexplace.

Key Design Issues	Notes
☐ Intent and business objectives	
☐ Scope	
☐ Eligibility	
☐ Legal and tax considerations	
☐ Compensation and benefits	
☐ Off-site scheduling	
☐ Establishing common-space work areas or satellite or neighborhood work centers	
☐ Length of commitment and reversibility	
☐ Application process	

Develop Resource Materials

As is the case with most of the new employment alternatives, if optimum benefits for individual employees as well as for the organization are to be achieved, information resources for both employees and managers must be developed. Ideally, these resource materials should be used in conjunction with a training program for employees and managers.

Resource Materials for Employees.   Employees will need resource materials that address such issues as the following:

■ Loss of living space
■ Setting up a home office
■ Combatting isolation
■ Support services (machine repair, photocopying, and so on)
■ Personal financial ramifications, such as increased home costs (electricity) versus savings (commuting, lunch, clothing) and tax implications, if any

■ Dealing with distractions at home
■ The importance of setting objectives and meeting deadlines

Some companies, such as the Travelers Insurance Company, have developed addendums to their corporate employee handbook for telecommuters that reinforce their status as "Travelers employees first and telecommuters second."

Resources for Managers.   Managers will need guidelines on how to assess (1) the suitability of telecommuting for the potential telecommuter, (2) the particular job, and (3) various aspects of the off-site environment.

1. When evaluating the *potential of the employee* to work off-site, points to consider are:

   ■ Is he or she self-motivated, self-disciplined, and highly skilled and experienced in the job? Does he or she have good time management skills? What was his or her last performance evaluation? If there were problem areas, how would telework affect them?
   ■ Has he or she been with the organization long enough to be familiar with its culture and its policies and procedures? A minimum of one year's tenure is suggested.
   ■ Is he or she aware of his or her own operating style and strengths and weaknesses? (A self-analysis tool can be very helpful in teaching the employee to define things like job satisfiers, work style, degree of independence, and other related factors. It can also provide a basis for the employee's business case for participating in the telecommuting program.)
   ■ Does his or her job require some creative thinking time?
   ■ Is he or she able to work with a minimum of office social interaction?
   ■ Will the employee have enough days scheduled in the office to ensure that he or she will not feel isolated or separated from the organization?
   ■ Does the employee understand the importance of regular interaction with the office or work group? Does he or she have good enough communication skills to sustain it?
   ■ Does he or she have a strong desire to make the telecommuting arrangement work?

2. When reviewing the *characteristics of the job*, points to consider
   are whether it:

   ■ Has tasks that are clearly defined with measurable output.
   ■ Requires daily interaction with the work group or face-to-
     face contact with clients.
   ■ Requires a high amount of concentration or has aspects
     like writing, data entry, or phone contact that can be done
     as well or better off-site.
   ■ Is a management position. If so, does that manager really
     have to be on site all the time, or is there already a lot of
     long-distance management because of travel or off-site
     meetings?
   ■ Requires the use of electronic equipment. If so, what kind?

3. *Off-site environment* issues include:

   ■ Is there a safe, dedicated work space that can be inspected
     if necessary?
   ■ Are there small children or dependent adults in the house-
     hold? Who will be supervising them while the employee
     works?
   ■ Does the employee have the necessary equipment to do
     the job? If not, what arrangements would need to be
     made?

Other management issues that can be covered are multiple
teleworkers in a department, dealing with employees who are not
suitable for telework, supervising and providing feedback to an off-
site employee, performance tracking, helping off-site employees set
goals and timetables, helping off-site employees stay "in the loop,"
and establishing and maintaining appropriate levels of communication, with regular times to review goals and progress.

Policy guidelines relating to electronic monitoring should be
developed for supervisors. Both the Computer and Business Equipment Manufacturers Association (CBEMA) and 9 to 5, an affiliate of
the Service Employees International Union (SEIU), have issued
guidelines expressing different perspectives on the issue, but with
overlapping concerns.

CBEMA suggests that:

■ Employees should know how, why, and when their work is
  being monitored.
■ They should have access to their records.

- They should be measured only on organizational goals.
- Measurement statistics should be used for problem spotting and early action.
- Individual differences should be acknowledged, and workers should be able to regulate their work as much as possible.
- Rewards should be appropriate.
- Production standards should not be raised repeatedly.[15]

SEIU and 9 to 5 recommend safeguards relating to the following issues:

- *Right to know.* Ban software programs with subliminal messages. Notify workers when monitoring occurs. Give workers complete access to their files and tell them how data is collected, used, and interpreted.
- *Right to due process.* Set up grievance procedures for appeal of unfair or incorrect data and adjust pay accordingly.
- *Employee input.* Set standards or quotas with employee input so that they reflect system problems, quality of service, and workload variability.
- *Meaningful standards.* Collect productivity statistics by work group, not individual worker. Prohibit speedups. Bar use of monitoring results for discipline. Collect only data that is relevant to the work performed. Average worker performance by the month, not the week or the day. Sample periodically rather than continually. Make quantitative measures only one part of evaluations.[16]

Training for Managers and Employees.   In the case of flexplace and telecommuting options, printed resource materials are not enough. Telecommuting experts consider training for telecommuters and other flexplace employees (and their managers) to be critical to the program's success.

For employees, training should cover:

- Technical issues, such as the use of voice mail
- Security
- Office setup
- Time management
- Setting objectives and measuring performance
- Expected procedures
- Psychology of working at home

Training topics for managers might include:

■ How to screen employees to determine who can successfully work off-site
■ How to manage at a distance by controlling results rather than activity levels
■ How to take advantage of telecommuting's flexibility and redesign schedules to increase efficiency
■ How to avoid or minimize co-worker backlash

In their book *Telecommuting*, Gil Gordon and Marcia Kelly present the following four guidelines for manager training:

1. Recognize and acknowledge the natural resistance of many managers to managing from a distance. It's an understandable reaction, but not a legitimate obstacle.
2. Stress the difference between close supervision and good supervision.
3. Stress the difference between observing activity and managing for results.
4. Before managers of telecommuters can learn the specific skills they'll need, help them assess and discuss their general attitudes about remote supervision.[17]

Gordon and Kelly also indicate that managers who will be supervising off-site employees will need basic or refresher training in the following areas and that this training should focus on those aspects of these skills that are peculiar to remote supervision:

■ Planning the work and breaking it into tasks
■ Delegating specific tasks to subordinates
■ Setting timetables for interim progress checks
■ Assessing progress according to time and quality criteria
■ Giving effective performance feedback on positive and negative points[18]

Announce the Program

As with other alternative arrangements, it is important to inform your firm's employees about the flexplace program. Whether or not they will be personally affected, either now or in the future, they can take pride in the fact that their organization is moving in new, innovative directions.

Promote the Program

As we've already noted, not everyone is able to work successfully off-site, at home. Careful screening of voluntary applicants must take place. Promotion efforts should reflect this fact. If a pilot project will be used initially, internal publicity about its progress can serve as a means of promoting awareness of the arrangement and of the constraints related to its availability.

Evaluate the Program

As is the case with the other alternative arrangements we've discussed, your flexplace program should be evaluated after it has been in operation for a number of months to determine whether or not it is meeting its objectives and to identify and correct any problem areas. The scope and intent of the program will determine how extensive an evaluation you should undertake. Some of the issues to look at are:

- Environmental impact—for example, reduced car use
- Improved recruitment/retention
- Reduced turnover
- Savings on training/retraining
- Productivity
- Employee satisfaction/dissatisfaction
- Office space and equipment use

Fine-Tune the Program

After evaluation, the program should be modified as necessary to correct any problems that have been identified. For example:

Problem	*Solution*
Supervisors complain that they feel uncomfortable with employees working off-site.	Hold meetings for supervisory personnel at which they can voice their concerns. Use a facilitator who can provide information about how these problems have been handled in other firms.
Telecommuting employees complain of feeling isolated and separated from their co-workers.	Check to be certain that regular workplace contact is being maintained. Identify on-site events (social, training, and so on) that telecommuters can be encouraged to attend.

Problem	*Solution*
Exit interviews indicate that many employees do not know that flexplace might have been an option for them.	Use employee communication channels to promote wider awareness of the program.

Summary

Flexplace is an option in which regular employees work primarily off-site, either at home or from a satellite office. The practice may or may not require a computer terminal. Two factors have prompted the growing use of this arrangement: (1) the same social, demographic, and attitudinal changes that have increased the overall need for workplace flexibility and (2) technological developments in the computer field that have facilitated off-site work.

Estimates vary with respect to how widespread flexplace is, since some reports lump regular employees working mainly off-site in with home-based entrepreneurs and with regular employees who work at home only on an occasional basis, and other reports focus just on off-site work that involves computer use (telecommuting). The types of work that lend themselves to being performed away from the employer's principal place of business include work that already is heavily computer-dependent, batch work, and work that must be done at odd hours.

An employer usually offers flexplace options in order to:

■ Accommodate employees' needs
■ Comply with clean air legislation
■ Reduce the need for high-cost office space
■ Improve employee retention and broaden the labor pool from which the company is able to recruit
■ Ensure continuity of services
■ Extend coverage
■ Provide employment opportunities for individuals with special needs, such as a disability that makes it difficult to work in an office full-time

In some cases, off-site options are also offered to enhance the performance of certain types of work that are best done at unusual hours, spontaneously (when insight occurs), or without the distractions common in an office setting.

When an employer weighs the advantages and disadvantages of flexplace, the following factors figure importantly in the decision: Flexplace arrangements, as noted above, enable the organization to cut its expenditures for office space and sometimes for relocation, although the organization does incur the cost of purchasing, maintaining, and insuring equipment for off-site workers and must address such concerns as liability and job-related employee accidents. The employer that offers flexplace options will normally see significant productivity gains from these workers. Supervising employees working under flexplace arrangements does require a change in style and attitude that can at first be difficult for those managers and supervisors who are more accustomed to managing by assessing the employee's visible level of activity than to managing by assessing actual results.

Also among the pluses and minuses of off-site work are such considerations as the fact that some system must be established to ensure that the organization maintains regular contact with its off-premises workers, both to combat a potential sense of isolation and to foster loyalty and commitment to the organization. Compromising the security of proprietary information has thus far not proved to be a problem when employees are allowed to work at a distance from the main plant or office. Unions have mixed feelings about flexplace, with some expressing concerns about its impact on the status of participating employees and others pointing out that it is difficult to enforce provisions designed to protect workers when those workers are primarily based at some location other than the employer's main premises.

When it introduces flexplace arrangements, the organization should focus at the outset on addressing management and union concerns about the practice and on making sure that the technical aspects of the implementation process (issues associated with computer use) are well thought out. The program design phase will involve detailed planning around a variety of issues in order to maximize the benefits of off-site arrangements to both the employees and the organization.

Resource materials are directed at addressing the concerns that potential program participants and their supervisors will have about the impact of working outside of the employer's main premises and should be backed by a training program designed to make sure that employees can effectively work off-site and that supervisors can effectively evaluate output without the need to personally monitor input.

A decision to offer a flexplace option would be popular with your employees and could lead to a drop in office space costs and improvements in such areas as productivity, recruitment (which, in turn, can result in an improvement in the affirmative action profile), employee retention, and coverage, while insulating the organization from certain types of interruptions to service. So if there are jobs in your company that would lend themselves to being performed on a flexplace basis or valued employees you might lose without such an option, this type of arrangement can be an attractive alternative to traditional 100 percent on-site work patterns.

ORGANIZATIONAL EXPERIENCE WITH FLEXPLACE

Pacific Bell

Description: Pacific Bell, a telecommunications company, is part of Pacific Telesis, which is based in San Francisco. Pacific Bell provides telecommunications services to business and residence customers in California.

Reason for Using Flexplace: When the first telecommuting trials began in 1984, the objective was to alleviate traffic congestion. In 1985, the trials were expanded to accommodate employees' requests for alternative work arrangements, and to utilize the company's own experience with the program to enable other companies to develop telecommuting programs that utilize the capacity of the public network more effectively. In the 1990s the focus of telecommuting has again expanded to include experimenting with employees working out of "virtual offices" in order to reduce the amount of office space used and therefore cut real estate costs.

Implementation Process: All salaried employees are eligible to participate in the program with their supervisor's concurrence.

Prospective telecommuters and their supervising manager are expected to become familiar with the company's telecommuting policy and to complete a short "telecommuting agreement" that both sign. This agreement defines the telecommuting relationship in terms of frequency of telecommuting, telecommuter's schedule, company equipment (if any) that the telecommuter uses off-site, and so forth. Telecommuters and their supervisors are expected to sign this agreement and keep it in the telecommuter's personnel file.

A training course is available, although not required, for telecommuters and their supervising managers. Depending on the nature of the job, the company may provide a business line in the employee's home, specifically for telecommuting, and other equipment as needed.

Impact to Date: The company began tracking the incidence of telecommuting by use of a special payroll code in 1991. When employees telecommute, this special code is entered for the day that the telecommuting occurred. The sole purpose of this code is to enable the company to track the frequency of telecommuting. Since that time, the number of employees telecommuting has increased slowly but steadily. Currently, the numbers show that approximately 14 percent of eligible employees telecommute each month. Telecommuters and their supervisors have been supportive of the program, citing increased productivity and flexibility, reduction of time spent commuting, and contributing to better air quality.

SOURCE: Emily Bassman, Director, Virtual Office Development, Pacific Bell (March 1994).

J. C. Penney

Description: J. C. Penney is a national retail store chain headquartered in Dallas. Its large catalog telemarketing division employs approximately 10,000 people.

Reason for Using Flexplace: Having a trained group of customer service representatives on-line at home enables J. C. Penney to deal with sudden "spikes" in its catalog business. The company now has a national network operations center in Brookfield, Wisconsin, so that if, for example, Richmond receives more calls than it can handle, the overflow can be transferred to Pittsburgh.

Using telecommuters also allows the company to add to its base of "associates," as J. C. Penney refers to its customer service representatives. Expanding this employee group is important, since it tends to have a high rate of turnover.

From the telecommuter's point of view, working at home can offer such advantages as saving on the cost of a second car or, for disabled individuals, the opportunity to hold down a job at all.

Implementation Process: Only employees who have already worked in a J. C. Penney catalog center for a year are entitled to convert to working on an at-home basis. The pay and benefits for off-site employees are the same as those for employees who work on the company's premises. In considering applications to work off-site, management looks for people who don't need a lot of supervision and are self-motivated. The key to the program's success is picking the right participants.

Before the flexplace agreement is finalized, a management representative visits the employee's residence to ensure that adequate space (about 45 square feet) is available and that it has proper lighting and is off the major traffic pattern of the home. If the work site is acceptable, the company supplies the computer equipment and communicates daily with the telecommuter on his or her home screen.

Impact to Date: The program, instituted in 1981, has been quite successful from both the employer's and the employees' points of view. The goal is to expand the program so that there will be twenty-four to forty-eight telecommuters in each of J. C. Penney's fourteen catalog centers.

SOURCE: Telephone conversation with J. C. Penney's planning and programs manager for telemarketing (June 1988).

Reduced Work Time

Surprisingly, although most 19 million Americans, or one-fifth of the U.S. labor force, work less than full-time, there is no agreed-upon definition of part-time employment. Employers tend to view part-time very broadly as far as hours worked are concerned. It is an umbrella term referring to anything less than the standard full-time schedule for a particular profession or industry. Thus, part-time for lawyers, teachers, federal employees, and corporate managers may each be very different in terms of hours worked per day, week, month, or year.

Until the late 1970s, anyone on a part-time schedule was regarded as belonging to a peripheral workforce rather than the regular workforce. As the economy has shifted from a production to a service orientation, however, the way in which work is scheduled, from both a service delivery and a human resources management perspective, has become increasingly important. The traditional 9–5, five-day–week schedule is not necessarily the most efficient format for either one, and various new kinds of part-time schedules have begun to emerge, originally in response to employee pressures and more recently because of organizational ones.

A major barrier to learning how to use less than full-time schedules efficiently has been management's attitudes about regular part-time employees. In commenting on this at a national conference on part-time employment, Dr. Stanley Nollen—a professor at the Georgetown University School of Business Administration, a leading authority on alternative work time, and co-author of *Perma-*

nent Part-Time Employment: The Manager's Perspective—noted the following:

> My last point [is] about part-time employment: We have here really a cultural or attitudinal stereotype situation as to how managers think about part-time employment. It is not that part-time employees are less productive; no, they are probably more productive. It is not that they are less committed, less loyal; you have heard reports stating the opposite is true. Employers do not doubt those kinds of reports; you do not get any argument from employers about loyalty, commitment, dedication, quality of work, all of that is okay.
>
> The difference is that part-time employees are different. . . . [E]mployers believe that part-time employees are not career-oriented. They are not going to be there forever. They are not looking forward to the same kind of future in the company as full-time employees are looking forward to.[1]

Although there may once have been some basis for this stereotype of part-timers as not being career-oriented, as the workforce has changed, so, too, has the composition of the part-time segment of the labor force. By 1986, according to Bureau of Labor Statistics figures, almost 2 million voluntary part-timers were managerial and professional employees.[2] Part-time is now a transition strategy for many workers; it is a way to retain partial attachment to the labor force while education is completed, children grow older, or new skills are acquired. This is particularly true of women; they currently make up almost two-thirds of the part-time labor force, and most of them are very career-oriented.

Management is now beginning to realize that most voluntary part-timers will at some point want to return to full-time employment, which is why many organizations have begun to experiment with new kinds of voluntary reduced work time and to devise processes by which employees may return to full-time employment at a later date. The emergence of regular part-time employment and its subsets—job sharing, phased or partial retirement, voluntary reduced work-time programs (V-time), leave time, and work-sharing programs—has come about largely because employers want to retain good employees. There has also been a growing understanding that employees perform better if work schedules can be constructed to meet the needs of both the job and the worker.

Part II focuses on the various forms of regular part-time employment that employers have begun to use in order to create more flexibility for the organization and its employees. So that their special applications and uses can be explored in detail, a separate chapter will be devoted to each of these options, including regular part-time (discussed in Chapter 4) and its subsets of job sharing (Chapter 5), phased or partial retirement (Chapter 6), V-time (Chapter 7), leave time (Chapter 8), and work sharing (Chapter 9).

CHAPTER 4

Regular Part-Time Employment

Regular part-time, a term that came into common use between the mid-1970s and 1982, is part-time employment that includes job security and all other rights and benefits available to an organization's regular full-time workers.

According to the Bureau of Labor Statistics, 18 percent of all nonagricultural wage and salary workers were working part-time in 1990, 13.6 percent of them voluntarily and 4.5 percent involuntarily.[1]

From the mid-1970s until the 1982 recession, voluntary part-time was the fastest-growing segment of the labor force. According to the Bureau of Labor Statistics, while the total number of people employed increased by 27 percent between 1970 and 1982, the number of part-time workers rose by 58 percent.[2] At the same time, the nature and structure of voluntary part-time work began to change. In 1982, the Bureau of Labor Statistics reported that there were 2.5 million professional-level part-time jobs, a number that reflected four times the rate of increase for all part-time jobs during the 1970–1982 period.

Unfortunately, since the mid-1980s, (1) involuntary part-time employment has steadily increased and (2) there has been little research relating to the need for, or the extent and nature of, voluntary reduced work time.

Origins of Regular Part-Time Employment

Three of the reasons why part-time employment has begun to move into the mainstream are:

1. *Changes in workforce demographics.* Women have entered the workforce in unprecedented numbers since the late 1970s. It is estimated that by the year 2000, approximately 47 percent of the workforce will be composed of women and that they will account for almost two thirds of the labor force growth for the previous decade.[3] Many women workers have small children, and most must work for economic reasons, whether they are married or not. This radical change in women's employment needs and expectations has been a major driving force behind the change in the dynamic of the part-time labor force and the expanded use of flexible and regular part-time schedules.

2. *The shift from a production-based to a service-industry-based economy.* Less than full-time schedules are much more prevalent in service industries than they are in production-oriented organizations. In large part this is because of the peaks and valleys of activity that are common in client-driven operations.

3. *The increasing need that workers are feeling for more personal time.* Full-time workers today are under increasing stress and find difficulty in managing the other responsibilities in their lives, such as family, recurrent education or training, and community work.

These trends are interrelated, because not only do women currently make up two-thirds of the voluntary part-time labor force, but many are in service-oriented jobs and carry the burden of "the second shift" of family. The ramifications of these factors have combined to make reduced work time, or the lack of it, a bottom-line issue for many employers.

Traditionally, employers used part-time as an appropriate response to a staffing problem—an arrangement that would improve operations. According to Dr. Stanley Nollen:

> If absenteeism among women manufacturing employees is high because of pre-school children then job sharing is a solution to that problem. If a bank has peak loads on Monday mornings, Friday afternoons, and every mid-day then, of course, part-time tellers are a solution to that peak load problem. If creative work is the kind of work that is best done in random spurts, flexibly, then perhaps flexibly scheduled part-time employment is the answer to that kind of employment problem. That is why firms hire part-time employees in most cases I think. They have a problem to solve.[4]

The conditions of regular part-time employment began to change for the better in the late 1970s as employers discovered organizational reasons such as those cited above to use part-time employees and began to consider part-time a valuable scheduling option. Figure 4-1 illustrates how part-timers can be used to achieve various types of coverage, in contrast to the traditional full-time schedule. Unfortunately, employer interest in part-time became a two-edged sword in the late 1980s as organizations also began to use more hourly, nonbenefited, often involuntary part-time employees in order to reduce labor costs.

Even the growth of hourly part-time has not mitigated the interest in reduced work time, however. Chris Tilly, author of *Short Hours, Short Shift: Causes and Consequences of Part-Time Work*, estimates that there are "three million full-time workers who would prefer to work part-time but are blocked by employers' unwillingness to grant them schedule flexibility."[5]

Who Uses Regular Part-Time Employees?

A 1989 Conference Board/New Ways to Work national survey of U.S. corporations showed that 90 percent of the 521 respondents used regular part-time employees in their organization.[6]

In 1991, Louis Harris & Associates surveyed over 400 senior human resources executives whose firms were members of The Conference Board. Eighty-five percent said their firms provided regular part-time opportunities for nonexempt employees, and 53 percent had managers and professionals working part-time; 17 percent expected to have professional-level part-time in five years.[7]

A 1993 Hewitt Associates survey of 1,034 major employers reported that 67 percent offered opportunities for part-time employment.[8]

Health service providers, banking and other financial services institutions, insurance companies, and the legal profession have all experienced an increase in the use of regular part-time employment. A 1986 New Ways to Work survey of work-time options in the legal profession showed that of 141 law firms, corporate legal offices, public-interest organizations, and government entities questioned, 20 percent had a policy allowing attorneys to work part-time.[9]

Figure 4-1. Sample part-time schedules for flexible coverage.

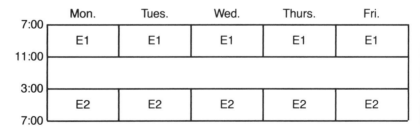

Traditional Full-Time Schedule

	Mon.	Tues.	Wed.	Thurs.	Fri.
9:00					
	E1	E1	E1	E1	E1
12:00					
	** ———————————Lunch——————————— **
12:30					
	E1	E1	E1	E1	E1
5:00					

One employee (E1) works 7.5 hours/day, 5 days/week
Total Hours/Week = 37.5

Shared Schedules

Coverage during the lunch hour

	Mon.	Tues.	Wed.	Thurs.	Fri.
9:00					
	E1	E1	E1	E1	E1
1:00					
	E2	E2	E2	E2	E2
5:00					

Two employees (E1 and E2) work 4 hours/day, 5 days/week
Total Hours/Week = 40; Each Employee's Hours/Week = 20

Coverage at both ends of the day

	Mon.	Tues.	Wed.	Thurs.	Fri.
7:00					
	E1	E1	E1	E1	E1
11:00					
3:00					
	E2	E2	E2	E2	E2
7:00					

Two employees (E1 and E2) work 4 hours/day, 5 days/week
Total Hours/Week = 40; Each Employee's Hours/Week = 20

(Continued)

Figure 4-1. *(continued)*

Double coverage during the lunch hour

	Mon.	Tues.	Wed.	Thurs.	Fri.
9:00 – 11:00	E1	E1	E1	E1	E1
11:00 – 1:00	E1 & E2	E1 & E2	E1 & E2	E1 & E2	E1 & E2
1:00 – 3:00	E2	E2	E2	E2	E2

Two employees (E1 and E2) work 4 hours/day, 5 days/week
Total Hours/Week = 40; Each Employee's Hours/Week = 20

Double coverage needed

	Mon.	Tues.	Wed.	Thurs.	Fri.
9:00 – 1:00	E1 & E2	E1 & E2	E1 & E2	E1 & E2	E1 & E2

Two employees (E1 and E2) work 4 hours/day, 5 days/week
Total Hours/Week = 40; Each Employee's Hours/Week = 20

Peak-time coverage

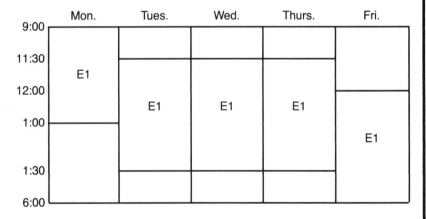

Peak-time employee (E1) works 16 hours/week
Total Hours/Week = 16

When Is Regular Part-Time Most Appropriate?

Regular part-time employment has a number of organizational uses, including retention of valued employees, improved scheduling, cost reductions in some instances, and improved recruitment.

■ *Retention of valued employees.* Most managers initially choose to use part-timers in order to keep a good worker who might otherwise have had to leave the organization. Retaining a trained employee who has performed well but who must work part-time is usually more cost-effective than replacing that employee with a new hire.

■ *Improved scheduling.* Standard 9–5 schedules are not always appropriate in terms of accomplishing the tasks that must be done. Some facilities or services are more effectively managed by using split shifts or operating on an extended basis; others must respond to peak periods that occur daily, weekly, seasonally, or on a fluctuating basis. Supplementing the full-time workforce with regular part-timers can give the organization the flexibility it needs to match its labor supply to the demands of the work.

■ *Cost savings.* The use of regular part-timers can result in cost savings in several areas. If an employee wants to reduce his or her work time and the extra hours are not replaced, payroll costs are cut. If the extra hours are replaced but are worked by a less-experienced and less-costly new hire, the organization still comes out ahead in terms of payroll costs.

Costs associated with absenteeism and turnover have been positively affected by the availability of regular part-time options—and these costs can be significant. A 1993 study by Commerce Clearing House of Chicago reported an increase of 36 to 38 percent in unscheduled absences in the U.S. workplace. Employers' estimates of these costs ranged from $247 to $534 per worker.[10] Turnover expense includes the recruitment, training, and learning curve time for the new employee. A popular rule of thumb estimates that to be an additional cost of 93 percent of the first-year salary of any new hire.[11]

Scheduling flexibility can be another area of savings. If an organization's regular part-timers are able to take on a few more hours during peak periods, the organization may be able to cut back on involuntary overtime.

■ *Improved recruitment.* Although some companies report mixed results in recruiting part-timers, this may be because the conditions of employment (such as salary scale and benefits) that they are offering these employees are not sufficiently attractive. Many employers have cited significant improvements in both the number and quality of applicants when they add a regular part-time option to their full-time recruitment campaign.

Pros and Cons of Regular Part-Time

As we've seen in the preceding section, for managers, the primary benefits of being able to provide employees with reduced work-time options are the potential for retaining trained and committed workers, a better match between workload and worker availability, improved recruitment, and cost savings resulting from reduced absenteeism and turnover.

Costs are a major factor in an organization's decision about the feasibility of using part-timers. Although, as noted earlier, the use of part-timers can result in cost savings in certain areas, managers worry that costs may be increased in other areas, such as fringe benefits. It is important to perform a detailed analysis of costs versus benefits in considering any voluntary reduced work-time option, and the costs of *not* offering such an option should be given serious consideration. When Aetna Life & Casualty analyzed the human resource reports for 1989 voluntary turnover, it discovered that the cost associated with losing administrative (nonexempt) personnel had been $46.5 million and the cost for technical (exempt) turnover had been $55.0 million.[12] (See Table 4-1.) This information led to the development of programs designed to respond to the needs of workers who needed more flexibility; included among the new options were regular part-time, job sharing, and a gradual, or phased, retirement program. One result was a decrease in turnover of employees returning from maternity leave from 23 percent to 12 percent. (See Aetna profile, page 144.)

Management must also consider the impact of public and private policy and the attitudes of management, unions, and employees toward the concept of voluntary part-time employment.

In the following subsections, we will take a closer look at each of these factors that significantly affect an organization's decision on whether—and how—to use part-timers. Concerns about the complications of supervising part-timers are another major consid-

Table 4-1. Reasons and costs for voluntary terminations at Aetna Life & Casualty.

1989 Voluntary Terminations: Administrative Level Expenses Annualized

Reason for Leaving	Annual Salaries of Employees Who Voluntarily Terminated in Business Division/Business Unit										
	A	B	C	D	E	F	G	H	I	J	K
Return to school	$3,585,280	$3,061,542	$2,166,120	$189,387	$212,058	$384,880	$74,375	$110,592	$123,402	$26,994	$15,425
Workload	131,976	428,232	179,850			7,571	55,300				
More money	1,248,160	1,836,476	636,064				134,172				
Advancement	1,951,272	1,912,806	1,810,480	104,496	32,784	34,950	74,262		14,500		
Job content	612,122	1,280,901	471,240	40,000	13,500	13,500	107,832				
Job challenge	226,740	193,544	206,687		13,500	12,800	15,200				17,500
Sick leave/no return	281,181	574,018	187,560			28,750	13,200				
Geographic location	592,572	781,344	961,285	30,100	15,285	40,299	13,000				
Health	269,787	310,540	194,599	15,500		26,848	25,800	15,000	31,570		
Company benefits	16,350		18,618								
Enter new field	1,231,110	2,303,028	1,260,369		33,590	87,486	136,213	17,500	34,000		
Conflict w/supervisor	376,298	106,078	210,345	19,570			14,500	21,000			
Conflict w/co-workers	127,170	31,692	54,240								
Travel demands	39,549		34,000		17,000	14,070					
Commute	143,055	184,142	83,424			13,085					
Overtime			13,600								
Unknown	1,819,512	1,693,948	1,194,952	119,142	69,960	172,907	234,960	13,600		5,928	
Spouse relocated	562,178	978,300	439,350			60,876					
Family obligations	2,016,195	2,196,172	1,406,300	81,220	16,600	148,272	57,415				
Military service	84,138	3,900	25,990				12,500				
Working conditions	170,764	186,153	109,347				17,443				
Dissatisfied w/job training	48,051										
Would not move	146,796										
Other	58,385	973,980	69,415					16,000			
TOTAL SALARIES	$15,738,641	$19,058,828	$11,733,835	$599,415	$424,277	$1,046,294	$986,172	$193,692	$203,472	$32,922	$32,925
× 93% (Turnover Exp. Factor)	$14,636,936	$17,724,710	$10,912,467	$557,456	$394,578	$973,053	$917,140	$180,134	$189,229	$30,617	$30,620

TOTAL ADMINISTRATIVE TURNOVER EXPENSE $46,546,940

(Continued)

Table 4-1. *(continued)*

1989 Voluntary Terminations: Technical Level Expenses Annualized

Reason for Leaving	Annual Salaries of Employees Who Voluntarily Terminated in Business Division/Business Unit										
	A	B	C	D	E	F	G	H	I	J	K
Return to school	$ 836,517	$ 844,688	$ 427,880	$ 198,048	$ 57,270		$ 19,889		$98,625	$144,150	
Workload	462,656	244,387	462,213								
More money	2,228,776	1,176,428	1,136,834	80,451	67,500		24,000	53,000			
Advancement	6,257,705	3,207,344	4,404,450	656,700	155,200	$171,948	475,124	$198,384	193,500	128,400	$ 69,682
Job content	1,147,230	1,166,560	845,002	248,297						44,000	
Job challenge	468,720	494,224	132,030	55,000				45,000			
Sick leave/no return	122,710	96,376	195,888								
Geographic location	998,676	1,005,516	1,033,524	89,151	28,000		102,201	47,200		47,400	
Health	264,240	104,144	129,835	37,046			25,000	28,000			
Company benefits											
Enter new field	2,507,842	2,100,215	2,738,892	218,897	91,299	22,800	86,001	81,800	125,915		
Conflict w/supervisor	359,856	261,600	234,352								
Conflict w/co-workers	18,221	25,000		22,000							
Travel demands	78,501	166,650	103,704								
Commute	175,182	129,410	92,852	15,852							
Overtime	24,000										
Unknown	712,536	682,500	715,288	29,500	41,504		95,400				
Spouse relocated	1,328,880	1,020,870	685,944	300,504			35,000	40,600	110,976		
Family obligations	1,700,439	2,358,136	1,621,620	480,828	176,752	68,800	84,999	23,100	27,560	73,101	39,000
Military service											
Working conditions	308,550	161,958	120,670								
Dissatisfied w/job training	20,500	71,499									
Would not move	85,209		38,800								
Other	105,276	2,407,887	76,500	35,500	21,001			22,000	41,500	53,000	
TOTAL SALARIES	$20,212,222	$17,725,392	$15,196,278	$2,467,774	$638,526	$263,548	$947,614	$486,084	$651,076	$490,051	$108,682
× 93% (Turnover Exp. Factor)	$18,797,366	$16,484,615	$14,132,539	$2,295,030	$593,829	$245,100	$881,281	$452,058	$605,501	$455,747	$101,074
TOTAL ADMINISTRATIVE TURNOVER EXPENSE											$55,044,140

SOURCE: Excerpted from Sherry Herchenroether, "Retain or Replace? Not So Rhetorical a Question," *Looking Ahead* XIII, nos. 1/2 (Washington, D.C.: National Planning Association, 1991), 41–42.

eration, one that will be discussed in a separate section later in the chapter.

Employee Retention

Losing trained personnel who are an integral part of a company's culture can be a significant expense, particularly if you add up all the relevant factors, such as the investment already made in the employee in terms of training and experience; downtime, if the position is not filled right away; recruitment and interviewing costs; and the initial adjustment/learning curve period for the new employee. (See Tables 4-1 and 4-2.) It therefore makes good sense to accommodate the trained employee who, for reasons of health or conflicting responsibilities, must work part-time, at least for a while. At all levels of responsibility and in all industries, this need to retain valued employees has provided the primary impetus for the expansion of regular part-time employment.

Common byproducts of accommodating employees' needs for reduced work-time options are:

■ Improved job performance
■ Increased energy
■ Increased motivation and commitment to the organization

Scheduling

The ability to tailor the workforce to meet the precise needs of the work to be performed (which often calls for uneven and/or fluctuating coverage) is, as mentioned earlier, another primary advantage of part-time employment.

Some managers have begun to use a combination of part- and full-time employees to improve scheduling in particular areas. Transamerica Occidental Life Insurance Company uses students to staff a four-hour night shift that supplements the work of its regular clerical personnel. Employers that work with the general public— such as motor vehicle licensing departments, banks, and ticketing agencies—usually have peak hours of client demand. Many have successfully integrated part-time employees with their regular full-timers during these periods.

If flexible scheduling, geared to current demand, is the objective, Noyes Publications, a small publishing company in New Jersey, provides a good model:

> Four regular part-time employees [out of twenty-four total] handle the billing and typing invoices. Full-time employees are

Table 4-2. Cost of losing employees.

Hiring Recruitment	Unfilled Position	Search Firms	Interviewing by everyone = Salary dollars	Resumé review/decisions after interviewing = Salary dollars
Costs	$	$	$	$

Training	Initial required training, tuition/salary	Developmental training, tuition & salary dollars	Other
Costs	$	$	$

Experience and Development	Expertise in PR/other areas	Expertise in Telecommunications	Other
Costs	$	$	$

Termination	ERO costs	Savings Plan	Other
Costs	$	$	$

SOURCE: Developed by Pacific Bell, 1992.

never hired for these positions because the volume of the firm's incoming mail orders fluctuates throughout the year.

While part-time employees generally work four to five hours a day, they are free to skip a day or two if they have an outside commitment, or if they or their manager see that there is too little work for them to do. Unlike their full-time colleagues, they are also free to report to work anytime from 8:00 A.M. to 9:30 A.M., so their flexible hours are one of the chief benefits they receive, along with the same fringe benefits as the full-time employees. Neither turnover or last-minute cancellations have been a problem, reports Griffin [the office manager].[13]

As more employers recognize the value of part-time work as a management tool, some organizations have begun to create special pools designed to rehire the organization's own former employees (either retirees or workers who have left because of the pressure of family responsibilities) on a part-time, on-call basis. This practice has provided an additional resource for managers faced with sporadic or seasonal staffing needs and is very popular with the employees involved.

Recruitment

In the previous section, we mentioned the significant improvement in the number and quality of job applicants that many employers report once they broaden their recruitment campaign to actively solicit part-timers, not just full-timers. The inclusion of part-timers not only expands the pool of potential applicants but also sends a signal to applicants for full-time positions that the organization is a supportive, innovative employer—one that they would like to work for.

Recruitment campaigns focusing on part-time can also target particular segments of the labor force, such as reentry women, seniors, students, and people with health limitations for whom full-time work would be difficult or impossible. An advertisement for secretaries run by the Walgreen Company's corporate office in suburban Deerfield, Illinois, produced so many qualified applicants that the company was able to fill the open positions and set up a substitute pool as well.

Cost Implications

In order to justify expanding the availability of part-time work, managers and supervisors need detailed information about costs.

The expense associated with any position can be broken down into direct costs (base salary and employee benefits), indirect costs (administrative overhead, training, supervision, and facilities), and program costs (those associated with absenteeism, turnover, coverage, recruitment, and productivity).

Table 4-3 shows a breakdown of the costs in each of these three categories. It can be used to compare the costs associated with a regular full-time position and the costs associated with one or more part-time options that might be used to perform the same work. (Table 4-4 is a blank copy of this form that you may wish to use to do your own cost analysis.) An item-by-item analysis such as this enables managers and supervisors to pinpoint the cost impact of using part-timers for any given position and, if necessary, adjust the conditions of employment in ways that will make the use of part-timers more cost-effective for the organization.

(Text continues on page 111.)

Table 4-3. Cost analysis by position: example.

		Half-Time		
	Current Cost of the Position	Current Employee	New Hire	New, Less Experienced
I. Direct costs				
A. Base salary	$30,000.00	$15,000.00	$15,000.00	$10,500.00
B. Employee benefits				
1. Statutory				
• Social Security (6.2% of first $60,600)	1,860.00	930.00	930.00	651.00
• Medicare 1.45%	435.00	217.50	217.50	152.25
• Unemployment insurance (2.3% of first $7,000)	161.00	161.00	161.00	161.00
• Worker's compensation ($.85 per $100 of compensation)	255.00	127.50	127.50	89.25
2. Compensatory				
• Sick leave (2 weeks)	1,153.85	576.92	576.92	403.85
• Vacation (3 weeks—current employee; 2 weeks—new hire)	1,730.77	865.38	576.92	403.85

| | Current Cost of the Position | Half-Time | | |
		Current Employee	New Hire	New, Less Experienced
• Holidays (10 days)	1,153.85	576.92	576.92	403.85
• Other				
3. Supplementary				
• Insurance				
Prorated life ($10,000)	50.00	25.00	25.00	25.00
Medical/dental ($125 deductible)	1,500.00	750.00	750.00	750.00
Long-term disability	250.00	125.00	125.00	85.00
• Pension (13% salary)	3,900.00	1,950.00	1,195.00	1,365.00
• Profit sharing (5%)	150.00	75.00	75.00	52.50
• Stock purchase options				
• Tax shelter annuities				
• Tuition payments				
• Discount purchase plans				
• Other				
Total direct costs	$42,599.47	$21,380.22	$20,336.76	$15,042.55
II. Indirect costs				
A. New hire administration			$ 150.00	$ 150.00
B. Training			500.00	500.00
C. Supervision	$2,000.00	$1,000.00	1,000.00	1,200.00
D. Square footage (80 square feet)	480.00	240.00	240.00	240.00
Total indirect costs	$2,480.00	$1,240.00	$1,890.00	$2,090.00
III. Program costs				
A. Absenteeism				
B. Turnover				
C. Coverage				
D. Recruitment				
E. Production rates				
Total program costs	$0.00	$0.00	$0.00	$0.00
TOTAL COSTS	$45,079.47	$22,620.22	$22,226.76	$17,132.55

Table 4-4. Cost analysis by position: worksheet.

	Current Cost: Full-Timer	Part-Time __ Hours	__ Hours	__ Hours
I. Direct costs				
A. Base salary				
B. Employee benefits				
1. Statutory				
• Social security (___% of first $_____)				
• Medicare (___%)				
• Unemployment insurance (___% of first $_____)				
• Worker's compensation (___ per $100 of compensation)				
2. Compensatory				
• Sick leave (___ weeks)				
• Vacation (___ weeks— current employee; ___ weeks—new hire)				
• Holidays (___ days)				
• Other				
3. Supplementary				
• Insurance Prorated life ($_____) Medical/dental ($____ deductible) Long-term disability				
• Pension (___% salary)				
• Profit sharing (___%)				
• Stock purchase options				
• Tax shelter annuities				
• Tuition payments				
• Discount purchase plans				
• Other	_____	_____	_____	_____
Total direct costs				
II. Indirect costs				
A. New hire administration				
B. Training				
C. Supervision				
D. Square footage (_____ square feet)	_____	_____	_____	_____
Total indirect costs				

	Current Cost:	Part-Time		
	Full-Timer	__ Hours	__ Hours	__ Hours
III. Program costs				
A. Absenteeism				
B. Turnover				
C. Coverage				
D. Recruitment				
E. Production rates	_____	_____	_____	_____
Total program costs	_____	_____	_____	_____
TOTAL COSTS				

The following subsections analyze each of the three major cost areas listed in Table 4-3 in terms of its ramifications for part-time work and suggest ways to formulate a fair but cost-effective policy on the use of part-timers. This discussion will emphasize the cost implications that are of greatest concern to managers and supervisors: fringe benefits, administrative overhead, training, supervision, space and equipment use, absenteeism and turnover, and productivity.

Direct Costs. The category of direct costs includes base salary (which involves not only the relatively simple issue of pay for regular hours worked by part-timers but also the more complicated issue of pay for overtime hours that they work) and fringe benefits.

Base Salary. Regular part-timers should be paid a pro rata of what a full-timer with the same qualifications would make. This establishes an equitable foundation on which to build a program of integrated full- and part-time employment options.

The growing use of overtime has become a cause for concern in many organizations today. Employers use overtime as a cost-containment tool that allows them to expand operations without expanding the labor force. Unions often defend this practice because many of their members want premium overtime pay. Even though other employees may not want the extra hours, they, too, must work these hours if the organization regularly uses overtime in this manner. As companies downsize their workforce significantly without downsizing the work itself, employee burnout is often a result.

Overtime becomes a particularly sensitive issue for part-timers when management's expectation is that part-time employees will regularly work overtime at straight pay. When this is a "hidden agenda," it undermines the working relationship of part-timers and their employer. The scheduling requirements of the position should be spelled out in the basic contract. If the requirements change and a full-time schedule (or more than a full-time schedule) is really needed, then perhaps the part-time schedule should be expanded to more hours (say, thirty to forty) to include a second part-timer or converted into a shared arrangement. This is fairer than expecting the incumbent employee to regularly work more hours than were originally contracted for.

Employee Benefits. As part-time workers have become a more important segment of the labor force, renewed attention has been paid to the conditions of work for regular part-timers. In particular, the issue of providing fringe benefits for less than full-time employees lies at the core of the debate about how to achieve flexibility in the workplace. Although such practices as compensating part-timers at a lower rate of pay than full-timers, laying them off ahead of full-timers, and denying them benefits have not disappeared, since the late 1970s there has been a slow trend toward improving the conditions of part-time work. These improvements include providing pro rata compensation (mentioned above) and giving part-time employees the same fringe benefits that full-timers receive.

In 1993 the BLS reported for the first time on benefits for part-time employees in organizations with 100 or more employees. (See Figure 4-2.) About half of these employees received paid vacations and paid holidays, and over one-fourth had health care and defined-benefit pensions available to them.[14]

Mark Manin, a Massachusetts-based benefits consultant, suggests that organizations examining the issue of benefits for part-timers should keep three basic considerations in mind:

1. The question of whether to include or exclude part-time employees when it comes to a benefits program should be considered a strategic-planning issue and reflect the organization's economic environment, relevant demographic factors, and labor force needs.
2. It should be recognized that there has been increased pressure to include part-timers in benefits programs because these workers are becoming an increasingly important force in the workplace.

Figure 4-2. Comparison of benefits for part-time and full-time employees.

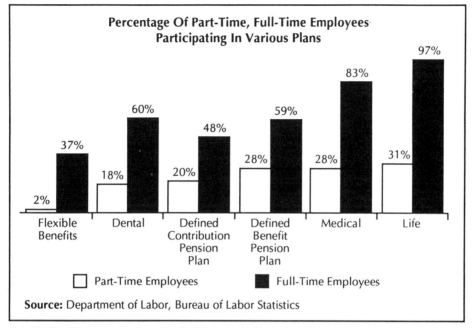

SOURCE: Department of Labor, Bureau of Labor Statistics.

3. The overall trend in federal legislation is toward mandated and portable benefits, and it is reasonable to believe that legislation in this area will be forthcoming in the future.[15]

Howard Schultz, the CEO of Starbucks Coffee, believes his business could not achieve profitable growth without providing competitive benefits. Fifty percent of his 1,800 employees are part-timers who receive a benefits package that includes stock options, medical and dental insurance, and a free pound of coffee each week.[16]

Since the cost of fixed benefits has been climbing for years, employers today are clearly concerned about containing this cost, eliminating duplication of coverage, and providing benefits that are really needed rather than frills. When it comes to part-timers, they are looking for ways to offer fringe benefits that are both equitable and cost-effective. One way to provide benefits for less than full-time workers is to prorate those benefits, in terms of the cost. This can be done either by asking the part-time employee to share in the extra cost or by offering less costly coverage, e.g., coverage that is paid for the employee but fee-based for dependents. Another approach is to include these employees in flexible benefits plans. Flexible benefits plans, sometimes referred to as cafeteria plans, are benefits programs that give employees a choice of which benefits they will receive, within a certain value range.

Flexible benefits formulas have the potential for individualizing both the types of benefits an employee receives and the cost of those benefits. While growing interest in flexible benefits has encouraged those who advocate extending access to benefits coverage to all regular part-time employees, as of the late 1980s, the trend has not been in the direction of inclusion. The reasons are unclear, but between 60 and 90 percent of flexible benefits programs exclude all part-timers.[17] It may be that the shift to flexible benefits is coming at the same time as increased awareness of the need for cost containment and that the inclusion of an extra class of employee will most certainly cost more.

In the long run, however, exclusion may have a negative impact on other cost areas, such as recruitment, turnover, productivity, and the organization's ability to be sufficiently flexible. As Manin and others suggest,[18] a comprehensive analysis of how a benefits strategy fits in with overall organizational objectives should be used as the basis for decisions in this area, and the current and future role of regular part-timers should be among the considerations.

In 1988 Representative Pat Schroeder introduced the Part-Time and Temporary Employees Protection Act, which called for inclusion of all employees on a pro rata basis in whatever pension and health benefits are offered to regular full-time workers. It was reintroduced in 1992 and 1993 with additional clauses that call for improving data collection on part-time and contingent workers and enabling unemployed part-timers to collect unemployment insurance if they are willing and able to seek part-time work (not just full-time, as is currently required).

Various states, concerned about the growing number of people without health insurance, have also undertaken initiatives in this area. In April 1988, Massachusetts Governor Michael Dukakis signed the country's first law guaranteeing health insurance to all residents of a state. The law will gradually introduce health coverage for residents of Massachusetts who are currently uninsured, both those who are working and those who are unemployed. Michigan, Maine, and Denver County, Colorado, are offering subsidies or other financial incentives to encourage small employers to begin providing health insurance. Oregon offers tax credits to small employers that start providing coverage to previously uninsured employees, and a New Hampshire law now prohibits insurers from barring group insurance coverage to persons working fifteen hours or half the normal workweek on a regular basis.

At this writing it is unclear what shape the Clinton Administration's health plan will eventually take. Clearly, however, if universal health coverage is the result, this will resolve many of the questions raised in the paragraphs above.

In analyzing the cost implications to an organization of using regular part-time employees, it is helpful to look at the costs associated with a single position, as was illustrated in Table 4-3. For an employer, however, the cumulative, or multiplier, effect will be the most important factor. Only a few companies (see Aetna example, p. 144) have conducted detailed cost-benefit analyses in which they add up the costs of absenteeism or turnover and recruitment for particular positions and balance these costs against productivity gains resulting from better scheduling or improved employee morale. Managers need to be trained to discard outdated attitudes about regular part-time employment and think beyond the extra administrative expense or resist the temptation to reduce costs by dropping a few employees from the insurance rolls. Such considerations as protecting the investment already made in current employees, avoiding the costs of recruitment, and determining the future potential of employees who may need temporary accommodation should be given equal weight in managers' assessment.

Fringe benefits differ from one company to another, but they always fall into three categories: statutory, compensatory, and supplementary. Using the cost analysis in Table 4-3 as an outline, let's consider some of the factors in each area as they relate to part-timers.

Statutory Benefits. For part-timers, these benefits include Social Security, unemployment insurance, and workers' compensation insurance:

■ *Social Security.* This benefit is currently computed, for each employee, at 6.2 percent of income up to $60,600 a year (1994 ceiling). Employers incur extra expense only if they hire a new employee to fill the vacated hours and the total position pays more than the current ceiling.

■ *Medicare.* This is computed for each employee at 1.45 percent of income with no ceiling, so there is no extra expense.

■ *Unemployment insurance.* Although rates and limits vary from state to state within the framework of federal legislation, unemployment insurance is also computed on a per capita basis. Since rates are affected by layoffs, if voluntary part-time options are available to enable the employer to achieve cutbacks in payroll cost and minimize layoffs, this may help to keep the organization's "experience rating" low.

■ *Workers' compensation insurance.* While this insurance is mandated, its cost is determined by the particular policy carried by the employer. It is usually based on a percentage of payroll, which means that part-timers do not cost more than full-time employees.

Compensatory Benefits.   Wages paid for time not worked, such as sick leave, holidays, and vacation, fall into this category. They are generally prorated for part-timers so that the cost is comparable to the cost for full-time employees. In some cases, employers have reported savings in this benefit area as a result of offering part-time options.

Supplementary Benefits.   This benefit area is more complex and less standardized than the others. These benefits supplement an employee's income by providing some or all of the following: insurance (medical, dental, life, long-term disability), pension, profit sharing, stock purchase options, tax-sheltered annuities, tuition payments, and discount purchase plans. From an employer's standpoint, the most important, and most costly, of these benefits are medical and dental insurance and pensions.

■ *Medical and dental insurance.* These two types of insurance coverage are major considerations for both the employer and the employee. Employees need access to group coverage in order to afford health insurance. For the employer, this coverage is one of the most costly fringe benefits. In order to include regular part-time employees in health insurance plans without doubling their premiums, many employers prorate the cost of health benefits according to hours worked. This kind of approach is equitable to all parties and is compatible with the concept of flexible benefits.

■ *Pension plan.* After medical and dental insurance, an organization's pension plan is the most important supplementary benefit. Pensions are computed as a percentage of salary, and the cost can be automatically prorated.

Indirect Costs. With respect to regular positions, indirect costs include administrative costs (both ongoing and for new hires), training, supervision, and space and equipment use.

■ *Administrative overhead.* The cost of ongoing administrative overhead is slightly higher per labor hour for part-time employees than it is for full-timers. On the other hand, the record-keeping associated with adding new hires to the payroll and removing employees who have left the organization is minimized by retaining employees who would have resigned to seek part-time work elsewhere. These savings should be included in the organization's overall assessment of the impact of part-time on administrative costs.

■ *Training.* Although many employers expect training costs to be higher for part-time employees, actual experience reveals mixed results. A 1978 study of private-sector use of permanent part-time employment reported the following: "[I]n a majority of cases, employers' training experiences with part-time workers are the same as with full-time workers in terms of administrative cost of effort. When there are differences, costs are as likely to be lower for part-time workers as higher."[19] Another source indicates that "Twenty to thirty percent of all users have marginally higher training costs."[20] Some employers feel that it takes longer to recover their training costs because part-timers are on the job fewer hours. On the other hand, one reason for offering part-time options is to retain good employees so that training costs will not be lost permanently.

■ *Supervision.* Supervision of part-timers can be complicated by special communications needs, since these employees are not always available, and extra attention must be paid to the design of work schedules. Furthermore, if the hours originally worked by a single full-time employee are split between two part-timers, then the number of employees requiring supervision will also increase. Since most managers have had only limited experience with supervising and evaluating part-timers, many express concerns about increased demands on supervisors. Widespread use of regular part-time at all levels is still too new to assess how valid these concerns are, what the cost ramifications might be, or whether the problems will disappear as more managers and supervisors become comfortable with supervising employees on a variety of schedules and learn more about what kinds of part-time schedules are most appropriate to particular staffing needs.

■ *Space and equipment.* Whether or not space and equipment are properly used when regular part-time employment is expanded depends on management's willingness to analyze the needs of the tasks and schedule employees' use of space and equipment accordingly. Some employers fear that having more employees automatically means using more equipment and more space. In reality, space and equipment can be shared, and the use of both can be extended through the proper integration of a variety of schedules.

Program Costs. The costs in this category that will be of greatest interest to most employers are those associated with retaining valued employees and reducing absenteeism and turnover and the effect of part-time employment on productivity.

■ *Retention of valued employees.* As Table 4-2 and the Aetna charts remind us, there can be a considerable investment lost whenever a good employee is forced to leave because of a lack of flexible work options.

■ *Absenteeism and turnover.* The occurrence of absenteeism and turnover tend to decline when regular part-time options are available. If a particular job classification has exceptionally high rates of either absenteeism or turnover, it may be precisely because employees holding that position have difficulty with a full-time schedule (because of heavy pressure, tedium, or a conflict with other responsibilities), making the availability of regular part-time positions an ideal solution.

■ *Productivity.* Part-time's impact on productivity is a human resources management cost variable. Whether or not having the option of working part-time affects a company's productivity positively is hard to prove or disprove. Part of the problem lies in the difficulty of defining productivity, particularly in the service industries.

Where managers and supervisors have been surveyed, their subjective opinions and anecdotal evidence seem to weigh on the positive side. Most agree that absenteeism is reduced by proper use of part-time and that part-timers are generally task-oriented and have a high level of energy and commitment. It is common to hear such comments as "I sacrifice some convenience. I have to be a little more organized, but I get a lot more productivity"; "[B]ecause working part-time is important to her, I get an unusual person for a bargain price"; and "I see part-time work as a management tool that makes people more efficient—both the part-timers and their supervisors. I use part-time to raise the quality of work in this office."[21]

With respect to the entire range of cost factors associated with the use of part-time employment, the grand total of each employer's "balance sheet" will be determined by a multitude of factors specific to the individual organization's pattern of use. With support from top management, careful planning and policy development, and effective training of supervisory personnel, the savings side should begin to expand as the organization's experience with less than full-time options grows.

Public and Private Policy Barriers

Sometimes existing policy (both the organization's own internal policies and those of federal or state government) can constitute a barrier to new forms of part-time employment. This type of barrier tends to pose a problem in cases where an employer offers part-time options for older workers or even develops an on-call, part-time pool of its own retirees or other ex-employees, as Bankers Life and Casualty Company, Continental Bank, The Travelers Corporation, Corning Glass Works, Atlantic Richfield Company, and other companies have done. These pools are used for peak-period coverage, as a source of substitutes for vacationing or sick workers, or in job classifications that have high turnover or absenteeism.

For older workers, the barriers to working part-time are financial. Most pension plans today contain two types of provisions that discourage senior employees' working part-time either as a way of phasing in to retirement or after retirement. First, pension benefits are generally tied not only to an employee's length of service but also to the pay level reached during the last few years of employment. It is this latter criterion that adversely affects the employee who might want to reduce work time—and pay—during the final years of a career. Employees who work fewer hours in the last several years of their work life are penalized by a reduction in their retirement income. Second, the pension provisions of some organizations prohibit the company from making both salary and pension payments to the same employee at the same time.

Employers must eliminate these barriers if they want to facilitate phased retirement or offer attractive part-time options to their senior employees. For example, The Travelers Corporation changed its pension plan to permit retirees to work 960 hours annually instead of 480 hours. Chapter 6 includes two excellent models that show

how senior employees can be allowed to reduce their hours and work part-time before retirement without diminishing their pensions.

In addition to the barriers so often established by the provisions of an organization's own pension plan, the federal government erects its own barrier to part-time employment for seniors in the form of the Social Security "earnings test." The earnings test now in effect places unduly restrictive limitations on the amount that retirees can earn without having their Social Security benefits taxed. For some time there has been discussion in Congress and in the Department of Health and Human Services about repealing this law. It is expected that in the near future, it will be removed as a barrier to the employment of older workers.

Management Attitudes

Some of management's negative attitudes about part-time employees have already been discussed. It should be stressed, however, that on the whole, managers who have had experience with part-timers are enthusiastic. In a study of part-time employment conducted by New York State, 214 supervisors and personnel officers were sent survey forms. Responses from 115 indicated that 65 percent of the personnel officers viewed part-time favorably, as did 71 percent of the supervisors with part-time staff and 57 percent of those without part-timers. Supervisors also reported either no difference in job performance or better job performance when part-time employees were compared to full-time employees.[22]

A very important question for department heads and supervisors is whether using part-timers will adversely affect department budgets and personnel allocations. If part-time is to be successfully integrated with full-time employment, managers should have the authority to allocate the necessary number of hours among both full- and part-time employees as they see fit, without worrying that the use of part-time will result in a diminished allocation.

Concerns about communication with part-time employees and having to spend extra supervisory time are also commonly expressed. These topics are discussed later, in the section entitled Special Considerations for Supervisors and Managers.

When asked what kinds of help they would like in expanding the use of part-time, managers and supervisors express a desire for top-level support, information on where and how part-time has been used successfully in other places, and supervisory training.

Union Attitudes

Until very recently, unions had a consistently negative view of part-time employment. It was perceived as being exploitive and undermining full-time employment. When job sharing emerged in the mid-1970s, a few unions recognized it as an exception to traditional forms of part-time, in that it retained the definition of the position as being full-time and extended the benefits of full-time employment to part-time personnel. Since the mid-1970s, one labor group, Service Employees International Union (SEIU), has taken the lead in negotiating policies for part-timers and developing program approaches that protect the working conditions of part-time employees. The objective is to expand opportunities for voluntary part-time employment and to integrate part-time and full-time staff. In general, unions whose membership expresses a need for good part-time work have begun to support that demand. Those whose membership does not express such a need continue to view part-time with suspicion.

Employee Attitudes

The few public polls that have dealt with the issue of part-time as an employee option have indicated that whether they currently want to work part-time or not, most employees recognize that some of their co-workers do need this option and that at some future date, they themselves may, too. Consequently, they support the development of policies that offer opportunities for voluntary, equitable part-time employment. In a New York State poll of 13,812 workers in 200 agencies, over two-thirds of the 2,947 responding employees approved the development of more part-time jobs.[23] A 1991 national poll of over 1,000 working adults indicated that 70 percent of all respondents would trade pay for more personal time.[24] Internal company surveys have been another source of information confirming the need for more flexibility, including less than full-time options. This continuing interest in opportunities for reduced work-time arrangements has been the driving force behind the evolution of new forms of regular part-time work such as job sharing, phased retirement, and V-Time programs, which will be discussed in detail in subsequent chapters.

Should Your Organization Try Regular Part-Time?

The tools provided in this section can help you analyze your organization's staffing and scheduling needs and determine whether, in light of those needs, you should begin a program of regular part-time employment or expand regular part-time options if part-time is already used sporadically within your organization.

The accompanying group of profiles entitled Organizational Experience with Regular Part-Time shows how and why a program of regular part-time employment was implemented in three organizations and what impact the use of this work-time option has had. As you read these profiles, notice whether and how the experience of these companies with regular part-time might be relevant to the needs of your own organization.

Table 4-5 is a questionnaire that lists the most significant problems that organizations are usually trying to solve when they introduce or expand regular part-time options. If you answer yes

Table 4-5. Regular part-time questionnaire.

Would Regular Part-Time Benefit Your Organization?

	Yes	No
Have good employees left the organization because part-time is not an option?		
Are some departments or job classifications experiencing above-average turnover or absenteeism?		
In order to handle the normal work load, have you had to overstaff in some areas or use an excessive number of substitutes?		
Must your organization's schedules conform to work demand rather than having all tasks performed according to a standardized schedule?		
Is 50 percent of any department or job classification comprised of women of childbearing age?		
Is expanding coverage or extending your company's hours of operation an objective?		
If expanding coverage or extending hours of operation is an objective, would a part-time shift or the addition of some part-time personnel facilitate achieving this objective?		
Is upward mobility to the point of "plateauing" a problem in your company?		
If you are concerned about plateauing, would it help any if some of your mid- or upper-level people wanted to cut back their hours?		
Is burnout a problem for any of your company's employees?		
Would some senior employees prefer a part-time schedule?		
Are there positions for which it is difficult to recruit good applicants?		

repeatedly on this questionnaire, chances are that your company would benefit from supplementing its program of full-time employment with a program of carefully selected part-time options designed to better meet its scheduling and staffing needs and the needs of its employees.

Assuming that the use of regular part-timers does appear warranted, you can complete the worksheet shown in Figure 4-3. It will help you pinpoint the specific problems you wish to solve by introducing or expanding the use of regular part-time and weigh the pros and cons of such a move.

Introducing or Expanding the Use of Regular Part-Time Employment

The steps for introducing or expanding the use of any new work-time option are basically the same. In the case of regular part-time, in addition to developing a policy and a program, management must often remove barriers in current policy and find ways to deal with attitudinal inhibitors. This latter is particularly important because of the widespread bias against part-time work and part-time workers. But even companies that ostensibly have a policy against using regular part-time employees have generally made some exceptions to that rule or authorized ad hoc part-time arrangements. At some point, however, this becomes an unsatisfactory way of contracting with employees, and the development of enabling policy is the logical next move.

Gain Support for the Program

The first and most important step in this process is to gain the support of top management for making the change. It is important that the move toward using regular part-time be viewed as a positive action with business benefits rather than a reactive one, since policy language relating to regular part-time employment will provide the basis later on for the use of more specialized forms of regular part-time, such as job sharing, V-Time programs, and phased retirement. Researching other organizations' reasons for using regular part-time, establishing demographic data, surveying employees, and/or holding focus groups to assess internal business needs for regular part-time are ways to build a case for this option. Since most organizations have some ad hoc experience with reduced work-time options (often more than they realize), it is also important to identify

Figure 4-3.   Regular part-time worksheet.

Assessing the Need for Regular Part-Time

List the main reasons why you are considering using or expanding the use of regular part-time employment:

1. _____

   _____

   _____

2. _____

   _____

   _____

3. _____

   _____

   _____

4. _____

   _____

   _____

List what you see as the advantages and disadvantages of regular part-time:

Pros: _____

_____

_____

_____

Cons: _____

the successes that already exist and use the managers and employees involved as resources.

Bringing middle managers and labor representatives into the design process is a way to gain their support as well. This will be critical once the policy is developed because it will largely be implemented by middle managers and supervisors.

Set Up the Program's Administration

If this is to be an active, successful program, forming a cross-disciplinary task force and appointing a coordinator to provide information and technical assistance to managers and interested employees should be part of the process. It is essential in the initial stages to have someone responsible for seeing that the pieces fall into place. Utilizing regular part-time in a proactive way requires systemwide change and broad-based support no matter how supportive the company culture is expected to be. Since most cultures have a built-in resistance to anything but minimal use of regular part-time, the task force can provide a critical function by soliciting input and building support for the change from various areas of the organization in addition to doing the strategic planning for the introduction and use of regular part-time.

Design the Program

Designing a program for the use of regular part-time employment is a two-step process, involving the removal of barriers in existing policies and union contracts and the creation of an effective new supporting policy on regular part-time. We will now consider each of these steps, together with the policy issues that must be addressed in each one.

Eliminate Current Barriers.   The first step in designing the program should be to review current personnel policies and union contracts to identify and eliminate any internal constraints on the use of regular part-time schedules. The following policy issues often create obstacles and must be addressed in order to enable the organization to use regular part-time arrangements:

■ *Head count.* This system, which requires counting each part-time employee the same as a full-timer against personnel authorizations, hampers supervisors who want to use regular part-time assignments. A system of full-time equivalency (FTE) allows for more flexibility; it expresses department allocations in terms of the number of hours worked rather than the number of persons doing the work. An increasing number of companies have reexamined their head count policy, authorizing the use of full-time equivalency in order to manage current staffing and scheduling needs.

■ *Compensation.* In general, a policy that calls for disparate levels of compensation between part-timers and full-timers in the same job classification and with the same level of skill and experience presents an obstacle to using regular part-time as an employment option. (See the earlier subsection entitled Direct Costs for a detailed analysis of how fringe benefits can be handled equitably for regular part-time employees.)

■ *Reductions in force.* In many organizations, policy still dictates that during a workforce reduction, all part-timers must be laid off first, regardless of length of service, special qualifications, or other considerations. If an organization wants to encourage the use of reduced work-time options, this policy should be changed so that part-timers are laid off according to the same formula used for reducing the number of full-time employees.

■ *Impact on retirement income.* As noted earlier in the chapter, in order for part-time to be a viable option for current senior employees, policy should be developed to ensure that retirement income will not be negatively affected if employees reduce their work time before retirement.

Barriers to working part-time after retirement (for example, provisions that prohibit a company from making both salary and pension payments to the same employee at the same time) should also be examined to eliminate potential problems in setting up a part-time pool of the organization's retirees.

Create New Policy. The second step in designing the program is to formulate new policy that supports the use of regular part-time as an employment option. The following are some of the issues that must be addressed:

■ *Voluntary nature of part-time employment.* Policy and procedure language should clearly state that part-time is not mandatory and that full-timers are protected against involuntary conversion of their jobs to part-time.

■ *Budget policy.* Developing policy that details how an expanded use of part-time will affect supervisors' budgets is a critical question. This relates to the issue of head count but also includes such questions as whether caps will be set on the number of positions that can be restructured and what will happen to percentages of work hours left over if employees work more than half-time but less than full-time.

■ *Eligibility.* The issue of who and how many is one of the important questions that employers raise about regular part-time. For example, should the option of reducing work time be limited to top performers? Probably not. Although supervisors are generally more inclined to support a valued employee's request for a change in status, managers should remember that if an employee's weak performance is due to stress, burnout, or conflicting personal obligations, a reduced work schedule may improve the quality of his or her work. Scheduling options like regular part-time are not just a new kind of employee benefit. They are management tools that when properly used can help employees function better.

If regular part-time is an option in all departments and for all job classifications, how should supervisory positions be handled? Many organizations still retain the stereotype of part-time employment as an appropriate mode for low-level or peripheral employees, and make it a rule that supervisory positions cannot be worked on a part-time basis. They cling to the idea that managerial, professional, and highly trained technical employees should make a commitment of more than full-time. The debate rages: Should exempt personnel, particularly those in supervisory capacities, be allowed to work on less than a full-time basis?

As experience grows, attitudes change, and the trend today is in favor of options and flexibility. In New York State, where various kinds of regular part-time work have been pioneered since the mid-1970s, as many as one-fourth of the part-time employees have supervisory responsibilities. Other employers, too, have used both part-time and job sharing successfully in supervisory positions.

An early Massachusetts study of part-time employment concerned specifically with the performance of part-time supervisors defines three models of part-time supervision:

1. The "consultant" model, in which supervisors advise and coach their employees instead of keeping a close watch on them
2. Part-time supervisors of part-time personnel, where the work group often functions as a specialized unit tangential to the primary function of the organization
3. First-line supervisors of full-time personnel

The study concluded that part-time supervisors functioned well where the first two models were used, but that job sharing was probably a better arrangement for first-line supervisors whose subordinates were on full-time schedules.[25] Recognizing the need for part-time options in higher-level jobs, some employers, such as the Federal Reserve Bank and US West, have developed job sharing and part-time options specifically for their managerial and professional staff.

■ *Probationary period.* If the part-timer is a new hire, either the probationary period can be the same as for a full-timer or, if there would appear to be insufficient time to evaluate the employee's ability because of fewer hours on the job, a longer period may be stipulated.

■ *Seniority.* A formula for accrual of seniority by part-timers needs to be defined.

■ *Reversibility* and other changes in work schedule. As we've noted, most employees who request a reduction from a full- to a part-time schedule, as well as many applicants who are only interested in part-time when they first start working for an organization, want a less than full-time job because of a temporary need, such as caring for young children, the desire to gain new skills or finish their education, illness, or burnout. A procedure for returning to or moving toward full-time should be established. If the arrangement is short term—for example, during a summer—a day for returning to full-time may be specified in the proposal. It may take more time to return to full-time from a longer-term part-time arrangement. It probably will not be possible for employees to make such a change in status "on demand," but establishing a preferred list and an application process will assure employees that they are viewed as being full-fledged workers on a part-time schedule, not as a different category of worker.

Supervisors may feel that the department needs more work hours than the part-time arrangement provides. Rather than authorizing supervisors to arbitrarily require part-timers to work more hours or return to full-time, some organizations define a process that attempts to accommodate the part-time arrangement either through job sharing or by filling the hours some other way. Justification of the need for increased hours from a program standpoint is another way of ensuring that there is a legitimate reason for the proposed increase.

Refer to Table 4-6, which is a program design checklist. It provides an overview of the key design issues associated with the introduction or expansion of part-time options and can be used to record your progress in dealing with each of these issues.

Develop Resource Materials
The organization needs to develop one set of resource materials targeted toward managers and supervisors and another targeted toward the company's employees and applicants.

Guidelines for Managers and Supervisors. Because of long-held negative stereotypes about part-timers, it is particularly important that the guidelines developed for managers and supervisors reflect top management's support for and encouragement of part-time options—hopefully at all levels. Explicit, written guidelines provide a valuable resource for middle-level management. (Sample policy language is shown in Figure 4-4.)

Guidelines for managers and supervisors should include an introduction that gives an overview of standard part-time employ-

Table 4-6. Program design checklist: regular part-time.

Key Design Issues	Notes
Eliminating current barriers	
☐ Head count	
☐ Compensation	
☐ Reductions in force	
☐ Impact on retirement income	
Creating new policy	
☐ Voluntary nature of part-time employment	
☐ Budget policy	
☐ Eligibility	
☐ Probationary period	
☐ Seniority	
☐ Reversibility and other changes in work schedule	

ment and whatever variations (job sharing, phased or partial retirement, V-Time, leave time, and work sharing) the organization is authorizing. The guidelines should include information on the business advantages that accrue to the organization from widening the types of available work schedules (such as increased flexibility and improved cost-effectiveness) and the benefits that managers and supervisors can expect (such as a recruitment edge, retention of good employees, improved scheduling, and decreased absenteeism).

Managers' and supervisors' rights and responsibilities should be clearly articulated. They should be reassured that using part-time employees will not adversely affect their department's personnel allocations or budget. Their rights in terms of approving or disapproving a request, terminating or reversing the arrangement if it is unsatisfactory, and increasing hours if the agreed-upon ar-

Figure 4-4. Sample policy on regular part-time employment.

Full-Time Employees

Full-time employees:

- Are hired to fill a position that requires at least 40 hours' work per week.
- Receive a weekly salary, subject to withholding, according to company policy and the current salary structure and ranges.
- Are eligible for benefits and for participation in company plans, as outlined in the ''Key to Employee Benefits'' booklet and the benefits policies.

Part-Time Employees

Part-time employees:

- Are hired to fill a position that requires 20 or more hours but less than 40 hours work per week (accumulating at least 1,000 hours worked per year).
- Receive a prorated salary, based on the number of hours worked and subject to withholding, according to company policy and the current salary structure and ranges.
- Are eligible for benefits and for participation in company plans, as outlined in the ''Key to Employee Benefits'' booklet and the benefits policies.

SOURCE: *Survey of Private Sector Work and Family Policy* (San Francisco: New Ways to Work, 1986), 28–29.

rangement is insufficient should be described in detail. Employee rights should also be discussed. It should be stressed that these workers are regular employees on a part-time schedule; they should not be viewed as second-class employees because of their reduced hours. Reinforce the fact that although a part-time schedule does affect salary, leave, and other kinds of employment conditions that relate to the number of hours worked, it does not affect status and tenure-related issues.

A step-by-step procedure for responding to requests for a reduced schedule should be provided. The example that follows is not intended to be specific to a particular organization's needs but is presented for guideline purposes only.

1. *Request information from personnel.* The personnel department should be able to provide policies and procedures relating to regular part-time employment.

2. *Ask the employee to submit the request in writing.* The request should include a suggested beginning date, an estimate of how long

the employee would like to work part-time, and a suggested scheduling arrangement. If the employee is interested in job sharing, this information should be included.

3. *Meet with the employee and discuss the request.* Try to bring to the surface any potential problem areas; for example, if the employee is a supervisor, what does the record show about supervisory problems that might be even worse with a reduced schedule? Or can the employee's strengths overcome possible difficulties associated with supervising on a part-time basis? Discuss the time frame for the decision and any next steps.

4. *Decide.* Proceed as follows in making the decision:

■ Talk with other supervisors of part-time employees and current part-timers. They will be able to offer practical advice that may be of considerable help. Remember that the single most important factor in the successful use of any form of part-time is the support of the immediate supervisor.

■ Determine whether there is a well-defined job description. Is the suggested time frame adequate for getting the work done? Would the needs of the position in question be better served by having one or more part-timers working independently or by a job-sharing arrangement?

■ Consider the potential for success in terms of the employee's past performance (experience indicates that employees who are effective workers as full-timers are also effective as part-timers) and his or her reasons for wanting to reduce work time (if the reasons are work related—for example, a poor match between skills and job requirements or a personality problem—reducing the schedule may not have the desired effect; if the reason is stress, outside pressures, illness, or a need to branch out, part-time may well alleviate the difficulty).

■ Review the results once the new schedule is in operation. Managers should be cautioned to be aware of "workload creep." Reduced work schedules need to be evaluated in terms of establishing an appropriate workload. Monitoring the actual workload, perhaps by having the employee keep a log of his or her work hours during the pilot period, can be helpful.

Information Materials for Employees and Applicants. Resource materials must also be developed for employees and applicants interested in working less than full-time. They will be interested in such issues as:

■ *Eligibility.* Who is eligible to request a part-time schedule?

■ *Financial impact.* Can the employee afford to work part-time? Financial impact worksheets—including information on compensation, fringe benefits, and retirement benefits—can help employees make this assessment and help managers promote the program. One employer's resource materials provide a breakdown of how various time reductions would affect an employee's gross and net pay. It covers such fine points as the fact that because an employee's taxes would drop with a 10 percent time reduction, a 10 percent cut in gross pay would result in less than a 10 percent reduction in net pay. (Sample financial impact worksheets are presented in Chapter 7.)

■ *Job-related impact.* What effect, if any, will the reduced schedule have on the worker's employment status and chances for advancement?

■ *Process.* How does a full-time employee apply for or request a reduced schedule? A proposal checklist detailing the issues that should be covered when approaching the appropriate supervisor can be very helpful. Topics generally included are a description of the desired option; the suggested number of hours to be worked and a proposed schedule; how the new arrangement will affect co-workers, customers, and the communication process; suggested evaluation process; trial period; and any other pertinent information.

An information sheet, brochure, or booklet outlining the questions and answers relating to these issues is a particularly helpful tool if part-time is going to be actively promoted as an employment option.

Announce the Program

Management should open channels of communication as soon as policy has been established. Many good policies on regular part-time are seldom used because employees don't know about them or fear there is risk in requesting a nonstandard schedule. If regular part-time is to serve as a means of enabling an organization to respond flexibly to changing conditions, it must be perceived as an integral component of the organization's human resources policy.

An announcement is also essential to forestall employee apprehensions about why the policy is being introduced. Management will have to stress that this is a voluntary employee option, designed to respond to the changing needs of the workforce as well as the changing needs of the organization.

Promote the Program

Traditional management attitudes about part-time employment have a mirror image in employees' perceptions of working part-time. Even those workers who would prefer a part-time schedule are often skeptical about the possible negative effects that reducing work time temporarily may have on their career advancement and job security. Most accept the fact that they will probably be "on hold," or slowed down in their advancement within the organization, while they are working fewer hours, but they need assurance that they will not be shelved for good or targeted for the next downsizing. Middle managers and supervisors must be encouraged to provide this assurance, and it must be stressed in promotional materials.

If the company has an employee newsletter, it can be used to describe success stories and promote the regular part-time program on an ongoing basis.

Evaluate the Program

Although few organizations have bothered to conduct an evaluation of their reduced work-time programs, this can be very helpful in identifying what is effective and what isn't, where the cost savings are and how they can be enhanced, how supervisors and employees feel about regular part-time and what improvements they might suggest, and so forth.

The evaluation should reflect the business reasons for introducing the program. When reviewing the impact of a reduced work-time program, points to consider are reductions in turnover, impact on recruiting, improvements in scheduling, employee morale, reduced absenteeism, and impact on benefits costs.

Fine-Tune the Program

Any human resources program has glitches when it is new. As these become apparent, either through the evaluation process or from day-to-day observation, they must be dealt with. A process for fine-tuning should be agreed upon at the outset.

Table 4-7 lists some typical problems that arise when an organi-

Table 4-7. Examples of problems with regular part-time and their solutions.

Problem Indicators	Possible Solutions
Coverage is inadequate during peak hours, mornings, or late afternoons.	Arrange for coverage by a co-worker or subordinate; consider filling the remainder of the job; change the employee's schedule.
Coverage is too heavy during slow periods.	Review work scheduling; determine whether work flow patterns should or can be changed. Revise employee schedules, taking the unit's peak work load into consideration.
There is not enough time to meet with the staff as a group.	Set a core time each week when all staff members are on the job.
A co-worker resents that the part-time employee leaves "early."	Be sure that the schedule is not leaving the work unit short of staff during busy hours; make necessary schedule adjustments. Explain that the employee is following the approved schedule. Remind co-workers that part-time employees receive only a percentage of full-time pay and accruals.
Co-workers complain that when answering the employee's telephone, they never know when to say he or she will be in.	Post the part-time employee's schedule in a convenient location (near the telephone) so co-workers can tell callers when the employee will be in.
The employee feels left out of the mainstream of the unit's functions. The employee feels that he or she is uninformed on agency or office policy, procedures, or happenings that full-time employees take for granted.	Be sure that the employee works with other employees on projects or assignments. Look for patterns in meeting schedules, office communications, and informal networks that isolate the employee. Make sure that the part-time employee is properly oriented to the job, agency, and people.
A co-worker complains about handling calls and problems when the part-time employee is out.	Review the co-worker's decisions about what needs to be handled immediately and what can wait for the part-time employee. Set guidelines in this area. Determine whether the schedule arrangement (such as two workdays followed by three days off) is causing problems. Consider ways to distribute urgent matters more equitably. Consider that the

SOURCE: Adapted with permission from *Part-Time Schedules: A Guide for NYS Supervisors and Managers* (Albany: New York State Department of Civil Service, 1985), 31–32.

Table 4-7.   *(continued)*

Problem Indicators	Possible Solutions
	absence of full-time employees from the office might be contributing to the problem. Change the part-time employee's schedule.
The part-time employee isn't taken seriously.	Convey by attitude, words, and assignments that the employee is a valuable and respected part of the unit. Be sure that people deal with the part-time employee on matters under his or her jurisdiction; don't let people go around the employee. See whether anything in the employee's behavior is contributing to the image.

zation uses part-timers, together with the solutions that have been found to be effective.

Special Considerations for Supervisors and Managers

The key to successful use of regular part-time is the manager. A New York State Department of Civil Service publication on part-time employment notes:

> As fiscal resources diminish and pressures for productivity and quality of worklife increase, managers must find better ways to manage two of their most valuable resources: people and time. One way that production and workforce satisfaction can be increased is by increasing the options for linking people and time.[26]

For managers and supervisors, this means learning more about redesigning work schedules, supervising a work unit that encompasses a variety of full and reduced schedules, and evaluating workers based on how they are performing within this context. For most managers today, this is a new and relatively untapped area of expertise, but one that it is vital for them to master if their organizations are to become truly flexible.

Managers and supervisors will require training to develop this sort of expertise. Most of them, as noted, have little experience in using part-time schedules or supervising part-time employees in anything other than low-level positions. Those who have not had direct experience with part-timers generally have negative attitudes about part-time work and part-time workers and seldom think of reduced work-time schedules as a potentially powerful management tool.

Because the role of the supervisor is critical to the successful use of part-time employment, resource development and training in this area can be absolutely essential to integrating full- and part-time scheduling arrangements, especially if long-range plans include using specialized forms of regular part-time such as job sharing, phased retirement, work sharing, or V-Time. Areas in which training is particularly important are:

- Management's objectives in expanding the use of reduced work time
- Previous experience with part-time in other similar companies or in other departments within the organization
- Redesigning work schedules and channels of communication
- Personnel policy issues relating to part-timers
- Fiscal policies relating to the use of part-timers
- Supervising and evaluating part-timers

The balance of this section examines several of these key issues in greater detail.

■ *Analyzing job task and work flow.* Setting up a work schedule properly from the start based on an analysis of job/task and work flow is critical to being able to manage a part-time employee and evaluate his or her performance, particularly if the part-time employee was previously a full-timer. Too often, employers have authorized a reduction in schedule hoping that the same amount of work could be accomplished in fewer hours. The result is generally failure—or a totally burned-out employee. For their part, in their desire for a reduced schedule, employees sometimes bite off more than they can chew, promising to accomplish in twenty hours what can only be done in thirty. Work schedules should be carefully discussed before a part-time arrangement is agreed upon or failure will have been built in from the outset.

Even if a schedule is initially successful, it may have to be redesigned at some point because of changes in the workload or work flow. What started out as a part-time schedule might come to make more sense as a full-time shared position. Or twenty-five hours a week might become more appropriate than twenty or thirty.

A supervisor considering a request that would leave part of a job title vacant must make a variety of decisions: what percentage of full-time is appropriate to the needs of the employee and those of the department; how the new schedule will fit with other employees' work flow; which tasks will be given priority in the new schedule, which can be completed by someone else, and which will not be done or will be postponed or rescheduled; and what kind of part-time schedule would work best. Part-timers can be scheduled in various ways, including a slight reduction in each workday; a half-day every day, covering mornings, afternoons, peak hours, or a combination of these; two and a half days each week; two full days one week and three full days the next; one week on and one week off; two weeks on and two weeks off. Whatever schedule is initially agreed upon, it should be evaluated at the end of a trial period and rearranged if necessary.

■ *Designing good channels of communication.* Not only designing but using good channels of communication is another important aspect of managing a mix of part- and full-time employees. With expanded use of flexible full- and part-time schedules, opportunities for communication between co-workers and between supervisor and subordinates are less frequent. Communication is also the key to successful coordination of activities and must be actively encouraged. Posting daily schedules can be very helpful, particularly if employees do a lot of off-site work or if schedules vary from week to week. Setting meeting dates well in advance so that notices of them do not fall through the cracks can also be important. Part-time employees often find that it is helpful to their job performance for their co-workers or supervisor to be able to contact them during nonwork hours if the situation demands it. This should be defined as a privilege, however, and it is one that should not be abused by those at the workplace.

■ *The "hours" issue.* Part-time employees work a pro rata of an organization's full-time schedule. In organizations where employees work long days and weeks, finding an appropriate way to delineate part-time for exempt employees can be a problem. If the reality of the company culture dictates fifty hours of work a week for exempt full-time employees, part-timers in exempt categories will be expected to work a pro rata of that schedule. What appears to some managers and part-timers to be the simplest means to deal with this issue, keeping track of the actual number of hours worked, can create more problems than it solves. It can lead to the unintentional reclassification of an employee from exempt to hourly. Since 1990, the U.S. Department of Labor has interpreted the 1938 Fair Labor Standards Act to mean that policies that pay exempt employees on the basis of hours, or allow exempt employees to take unpaid leave in part-day increments, constitute a basis for reclassifying them as hourly employees. This means that the employee is subject to overtime requirements; all similar employees in the organization may be reclassified as well.

■ *Helping the part-timer stay in the mainstream.* Often part-time employees feel left out or "second-class." Their supervisors can help them feel connected by looking for and correcting patterns in the work or the schedule that isolate them unnecessarily, making sure that meetings are scheduled at times they can attend, and providing positive feedback on good work. It is important to keep part-timers aware of important developments through memos, voice messaging, etc. It is also important to make sure that they are able to participate in training opportunities and remain eligible for promotion.

■ *Evaluating part-time employees.* Evaluation of part-timers should take the same form as evaluation of full-timers. Their accomplishments should not be compared to those of a full-timer in the same position, however, but should instead be assessed in light of the way tasks and objectives were quantified at the beginning. If this was done correctly, then evaluation should flow easily from that projection; if not, the projection can be adjusted.

The evaluation of part-timers not only will involve an assessment of their activities and accomplishments but also will require greater emphasis on their ability to communicate and coordinate with co-workers than would be the case with the evaluation of full-time employees.

Summary

Regular, part-time employment is a reduced work-time arrangement in which the part-time worker is regarded as a full-fledged employee of the organization, entitled to job security and other rights and benefits available to full-timers.

The sharp increase in the interest in voluntary regular part-time since the mid-1970s can be attributed to the economy's shift from a production orientation to a service orientation, to the radical change in the employment needs of women, many of whom work in service industries, and to the growing recognition that an organization's ability to be flexible is increasingly important in a global economy. Offering a program of voluntary regular part-time options is one way for employers to respond to the needs of employees, who might otherwise be forced to leave the organization or who might not seek employment with the organization in the first place because they require a less than full-time schedule. It is also a way to enhance an employer's ability to respond flexibly to staffing and scheduling problems, such as peak-time workloads.

The increase in the use of part-timers, particularly in the retail and service sectors of the economy, has included an increase in the number of managerial and professional-level employees who choose reduced work-time options. This is in contrast to the traditional perception of part-time as a scheduling alternative appropriate only for low-level job classifications.

An organization's decision to use regular part-time workers is generally prompted by several considerations. Offering voluntary part-time schedules can enable the organization to attract a higher quality of job applicants and retain trained employees who might otherwise leave the organization in search of reduced hours. Part-time can give the company the flexibility it needs to respond to the demands of its work without over- or understaffing. And in some situations the move toward part-time can reduce costs.

In assessing the advantages and disadvantages of permitting the use of part-time schedules, an organization must weigh a variety of factors. Part-time, as noted, normally results in the retention of valued employees and provides the organization with an effective tool for tailoring its labor supply to meet staffing and scheduling demands. Part-time also normally results in an improvement in the quality and quantity of job applicants, although some employers have reported little success in this area.

The costs of a move toward part-time will vary according to the decisions that each individual employer makes in structuring its program of reduced work-time options. The employer will have to carefully analyze direct and indirect costs and program costs to determine the impact of converting selected positions to a part-time schedule. Once the cost impact has been determined, it may then be necessary for the employer to adjust various aspects of the conditions of employment in order to design a program for using part-time that meets the needs of employees at a cost that is attractive to the organization.

The company considering regular part-time will have to investigate and deal with whatever barriers to this form of employment may exist both within the organization's own policies and in the regulations of government agencies. The attitudes of the major parties affected by the decision on part-time (management, unions, and employees) must also be taken into account.

The standard eight-step process for introducing a change in work-time practices applies to the introduction of regular part-time, with special emphasis on the following areas: Since part-time employees have traditionally been regarded as second-class workers, care must be taken to gain support from all levels of management for the concept of part-timers as full-status workers on a less than full-time schedule. (Resource materials directed both toward managers and supervisors and toward employees and applicants are an essential component of the effort to gain broad-based support for the use of regular part-time.) Failure to achieve this fundamental consensus could doom the program at the outset. Designing a program for regular part-time will involve the elimination of internal constraints on the use of this option, followed by the development of a comprehensive new policy that addresses the entire range of issues associated with regular part-time.

It is important that supervisors and managers be adequately prepared to cope with the special demands of supervising and managing part-timers. Training should particularly emphasize such areas as how to analyze the requirements of a position and design a part-time work schedule (or a combination of part-time schedules) that will enable those requirements to be met, and how managers and supervisors can establish good channels of communication between themselves and their part-timers and between the full- and part-time employees who report to them.

In short, provided the employer has "done its homework" by carefully analyzing the cost implications and other key issues and developing widespread support for the program, offering reduced work-time alternatives on a regular basis can be a cost-effective move that brings a number of benefits for both employer and employees.

ORGANIZATIONAL EXPERIENCE WITH REGULAR PART-TIME

Bank of America

Description: Bank of America is a large commercial bank headquartered in San Francisco. It employs 98,000 people and has lending operations around the world.

Reason for Using Part-Time: Staffing is challenging in banking operations because of the dynamic work environment. In addition, some of the work has to be done outside of regular business hours and deadlines are unforgiving. Processing a fluctuating workload is a daily problem that requires creative staffing and scheduling solutions in order to adjust the size of the workforce to the size of the workload, hour-by-hour in some operations. In order to achieve the required flexibility in scheduling, Bank of America has developed staffing models that consist of a mix of full-time, part-time, and hourly employees.

Implementation Process: Part-time employees are hired to work regular schedules that are twenty or more hours a week and are eligible for benefits. Hourly employees are hired to work varying schedules that are nineteen hours or less a week. All employees can be asked to work overtime.

Impact to Date: Having a mix of part-time, full-time, and hourly staff has proven to be very effective in helping the bank to deal with fluctuating workloads—both in the branches and in operations work. Research was conducted in 1991 to evaluate the performance and productivity of the different categories of worker in two proof centers. The productivity of part-time employees was notable.

In this study, performance was measured by quantity of output (in this case, checks processed). In one center, a comparison of the three groups showed that the average output rate of full-time employees was 1,200 to 1,300 items per hour compared to 1,400 to 1,500 items per hour for hourly employees and 1,500 to 1,650 items per hour for part-time employees.

Turnover and its relationship to training cost recovery was also studied. Approximately two-thirds of the part-time employees had been with the bank from three to five years so training costs were fully recovered. This was not the case with hourly employees, whose turnover rate was higher.

SOURCE: Unpublished research by Dr. Stanley Nollen, Georgetown University School of Business Administration; phone conversations with Bank of America HR staff; Bank of America brochure (February 1994).

Harbor Sweets

Description: Harbor Sweets is a chocolate-making company, located in Salem, Massachusetts, with approximately 150 employees.

Reason for Using Regular Part-Time: To attract and retain committed employees and to accommodate employees' needs for flexible and reduced working arrangements. Most of the employees work a twenty- to forty-hour schedule.

Implementation Process: There is no formal process for requesting part-time. A schedule is arranged and responsibilities agreed upon when a new employee is hired. All workers receive paid vacation, and those working thirty-two hours or more receive full benefits. Employee meetings are held four or five times a year to discuss company business, and employee suggestions for improvements are encouraged and acted upon.

Impact to Date: Hiring emphasis has been on recruiting the hard-to-employ, the elderly, the handicapped, and non-English-speaking applicants and advising work schedules to meet their needs as well as those of the company. The result has been the formation of an effective, committed workforce. Employees suggested work sharing and postponement of a bonus during an unprofitable year. The next year sales were up, and profits were shared.

President Ben Strohecker says, "Through total trust, choosing to allow people to stretch to their potential, and by letting them know it's O.K. to make a mistake, you get unbelievable results."

SOURCE: Anne Driscoll, "Candy Maker in Massachusetts Asks Even Part-Timers for Work Advice," *New York Times* (Mar. 20, 1988): 30; conversation with Harbor Sweets (Dec. 1993).

Aetna Life & Casualty

Description: Aetna Life & Casualty Company is the nation's largest publicly held insurance and financial services company. It is based in Hartford, Connecticut, and employs 43,000.

Reason for Using Regular Part-Time: Aetna's workforce is more than 70 percent female. Regular part-time was suggested as one of several flexible work options that would help the company retain highly trained and qualified employees. This was reinforced by college recruiters, who reported that college graduates were interested in whether or not companies offered flexible work arrangements. Other options the company offers are job sharing, work-at-home, and phased retirement.

Implementation Process: Aetna created a task force in response to the Hudson Institute's *Workforce 2000* report to review policies, procedures, and benefits appropriate to "the new workforce." Recommendations of this group were that programs must be national in scope; Aetna must realize that families come in many shapes and sizes; and there was need for child care and elder care support, family leave, and support for workplace flexibility. One result was formation of a unit called Work/Family Strategies to act on the task force's recommendations. The next year a separate task force was formed to address the need for corporate support for workplace flexibility. Head count was identified as a barrier, and a full-time equivalency system was eventually adopted. Resource materials were developed for managers and supervisors, and a training workshop on alternative work time was developed.

Impact to Date: Approximately 13 percent of Aetna's employees work part-time, share a job, work at home, or work a compressed workweek. Aetna estimates that it saves over $2 million a year by retaining trained workers, many of whom return from family leave and utilize a flexible work arrangement as a transition back to a full-time schedule. Although it has only anecdotal data to support this, the company believes that productivity, retention, recruitment, and loyalty have improved as a result of offering these new scheduling options. Publicity from national recognition of the flexible work arrangements program has brought calls from all over the country as well as applications from talented individuals who want more flexibility.

SOURCE: Aetna Life & Casualty resource materials; conversations with Aetna HR staff (Dec. 1993).

CHAPTER 5

Job Sharing

Job sharing is a form of regular part-time work in which two people voluntarily share the responsibilities of one full-time position, with salary and benefits prorated. The term covers a spectrum of shared responsibility ranging from jobs that are essentially *split* between two people, requiring no, or very little, interaction, to jobs that must be *shared* collaboratively in all aspects. Where a job falls on this continuum depends upon the nature of the tasks to be performed and the degree of proposed interaction. At one end are job sharing receptionists or production-line workers, where the amount of sharing may be limited to discussing the coordination of their schedules. At the other extreme are executive assistants, engineers, or marketing directors who often need to be interchangeable. Their sharing is ongoing.

Origins of Job Sharing

The term *job sharing* was first coined in the mid-1960s. This option was devised as a way to create more part-time opportunities in career-oriented job categories in which the positions could not be reduced in hours or split into two part-time jobs. It represents an attempt to bring regular part-time into parity with regular full-time employment. When a position is defined as a full-time job that is temporarily being filled by two people instead of one, it is assumed that the conditions of employment (such as rate of pay, fringe benefits, and seniority) remain the same as for other positions in the same classification. As more employees express an interest in reducing work time at some point in their careers and as employers become interested in offering reduced work time as an employee option or benefit, the issue of improving the conditions of part-time employment has assumed increasing importance. Job sharing has played a significant role in making part-time work more equitable by emphasizing that it is the employees who are part-time, not the job.

Who Uses Job Sharing?

Relatively unheard of in the private sector until the late 1970s, job sharing has been growing on a case-by-case basis for the last decade. By 1986, several independent surveys of private-sector organizations showed that between 11 and 18 percent of the respondents reported having job sharers.[1]

A 1989 Conference Board/New Ways to Work survey, which was the first national survey of flexible scheduling and staffing in U.S. corporations, showed that 98 of the 521 respondents had job sharers in their organization.[2] In 1991 Louis Harris & Associates surveyed over 400 senior human resources executives in Conference Board member organizations. Job sharing was provided by 47 percent of the firms, and another 22 percent expected to be offering it within five years.[3] A 1993 Hewitt Associates survey indicated that 32 percent of the 839 respondents offered job sharing.[4]

A 1983 survey of 260 health care organizations conducted by New Ways to Work (NWW) indicated that 52 percent of the respondents were using job sharing. A total of twenty-eight different health care classifications have been restructured this way, including those of registered nurse, emergency room nurse, epidemiologist, and nurse anesthetist. Another NWW survey of the legal profession indicated a growing use of job sharing in both public and private law firms and agencies.[5]

In the public sector, the federal government was an early user of job sharing. Congress passed legislation in 1978 that authorized professional-level part-time and specifically encouraged job sharing. This led to replacement of the "head count" system with one based on full-time equivalency, and all federal agencies were instructed to set up programs and procedures designed to facilitate wider use of part-time and job sharing. After a hiatus of interest in the mid-1980s, in 1990 Congress and the Office of Personnel Management

(OPM) renewed their efforts to support federal employees who wanted to work part-time and job share. Agencies were asked to publicize the fact that this was an option, and an electronic registration system, "The OPM Connection," was established to help would-be sharers find partners. A handbook was also developed to help sharers and managers understand the concept and work out mutually agreeable arrangements.

The fifty states have also been interested in this new form of part-time for a number of years. A phone survey of the fifty states' personnel offices conducted by New Ways to Work in 1986 indicated that thirty-five states allowed state employees to share jobs. At that time, eighteen states had written policies, and twelve had authorizing legislation.[6]

When Is Job Sharing Most Appropriate?

Job sharing, like other forms of reduced work time, permits an organization to retain valued employees. From a manager's perspective, job sharing has some additional aspects that make it particularly effective in terms of enhancing opportunities for flexibility. These include creating part-time opportunities in job classifications that are not easily reducible or divisible, new kinds of scheduling options that are possible only if a job is shared by two people, the potential for increasing the breadth of skills and experience in a single position, and special kinds of pairings that facilitate the achievement of human resources management objectives.

■ *Retention of valued employees.* Job sharing's unique attribute is that it is a way of allowing employees to work part-time in positions that cannot be either reduced in hours or split into two discrete part-time jobs. This is especially true in higher-level positions. For instance, when incumbents in such positions as the human resources manager at Excelan, Inc., the deputy director for legislation in the state of California's Employment Development Department, and the head of the Travelers Insurance Company's retiree job bank wanted to work part-time, job sharing was the arrangement agreed upon. Job sharing has also proved very useful in positions where continuity is necessary, but, for one reason or another, turnover has been a problem. Receptionists and various types of clerical support personnel have been allowed to share jobs for this reason at Alza Corporation, Hewlett-Packard, Steelcase Inc., Quaker Oats Company, and many other companies.

By offering job sharing options, the organization can retain the services of good workers in these types of positions who might otherwise leave in search of a suitable part-time schedule.

■ *Improving coverage and continuity.* Having a position covered by two employees rather than one permits the employees and their supervisors to develop a variety of creative work schedules tailor-made to satisfy the requirements of both the workers and the work. Since job sharers usually cover for each other, the organization gains needed continuity while the employees gain a built-in substitute for those times—both planned and unplanned—when they must be away from their jobs.

■ *Increasing the breadth of skills and experience.* This feature of job sharing reflects the old adage "Two heads are better than one." And in fact, pooling the skills and experience of two employees usually enhances the range of capabilities that can be applied to the work.

■ *Achieving human resources management objectives.* Job sharing offers the possibility of creatively pairing workers in ways that will enable the organization to accomplish very specific human resources objectives in such areas as training, phased retirement, and upward mobility.

Pros and Cons of Job Sharing

The advantages of job sharing, as noted above, are associated with retention of good workers who need a less than full-time schedule, improvements in scheduling and continuity, expansion of the talents available within a single position, and achievement of human resources management objectives.

As we observed in Chapter 4, the adoption of any part-time scheduling arrangement requires careful management analysis of costs versus benefits. This is particularly true in the case of job sharing. Because there are so many possible permutations, the fiscal implications of job sharing are complicated and warrant more consideration. In examining the costs and savings associated with converting one or more individual positions to a job sharing basis, the employer must look at the entire range of cost factors. In addition to the impact on administrative costs that comes from having more employees, such cost considerations as rates of turnover and absenteeism, recruitment, training, fringe benefits, and, of course, the potential for increased flexibility should all be taken into account. As with other forms of regular part-time employment, there can also be significant costs in *not* offering these options.

While it is essential to examine the ramifications of job sharing for individual positions, the cumulative effect can also be important: What kinds of costs or savings might be expected if a number of positions in either the same job classification or a variety of job classifications are restructured? An analysis of job sharing's costs and benefits should include both the impact of restructuring individual positions and the impact of developing a program designed to encourage the restructuring of a range of positions. In each case, the bottom line will be defined by why and how a particular organization uses job sharing.

The balance of this section examines the positive or negative ramifications of each of these factors. The later section entitled Special Considerations for Supervisors and Managers addresses another problem often cited in connection with job sharing—the inconvenience of introducing a work arrangement that entails managing additional employees in a new way.

Scheduling and Continuity

The possibilities for designing more effective schedules and addressing continuity problems are one of job sharing's exciting features. The standard schedule, 9–5, five days a week, is not necessarily an appropriate time arrangement for all jobs any more than for all workers. As Figure 5-1 shows, job sharers and their supervisors have redesigned work schedules in various innovative ways that take advantage of the fact that two people rather than one are filling the job. In positions where there are regular peak periods of heightened activity, where extended coverage would be an advantage, or where clients regularly require off-site meetings, having two employees who can overlap, be in two different places at the same time, or work a split shift can be a distinct advantage.

Time lost to vacations, accidents, or illness and turnover periodically interrupts an organization's work flow. When job sharers are given the responsibility for scheduling and allowed to trade time, they are able to fill in for each other, and time and services are not lost; neither does the organization incur the cost of a substitute or temporary worker.

The possibility of sharers' trading work time, one of the unique

(Text continues on page 152.)

Figure 5-1.   Sample job sharing schedules.

Traditional Full-Time Schedule

	Mon.	Tues.	Wed.	Thurs.	Fri.
Week 1	E1	E1	E1	E1	E1

One employee (E1) works 8 hours/day, 5 days/week
TOTAL HOURS/WEEK = 40;
TOTAL HOURS FOR 2 WEEKS = 80

Job Sharing Schedules

One week on/one week off

	Mon.	Tues.	Wed.	Thurs.	Fri.
Week 1	E1	E1	E1	E1	E1
Week 2	E2	E2	E2	E2	E2

Two employees (E1 and E2) work 8 hours/day for 5 days one week
and are off the next week
Total Hours/Week = 40; Total Hours for 2 Weeks = 80; Each
Employee's Hours for 2 Weeks = 40

One week on/one week off over a weekend

	Mon.	Tues.	Wed.	Thurs.	Fri.
Week 1	E1	E1	E1	E2	E2
Week 2	E2	E2	E2	E1	E1

Two employees (E1 and E2) work 8 hours/day for 5 consecutive
workdays and are off the next 5 consecutive workdays, with each 5-
day period interrupted by a weekend
Total Hours/Week = 40; Total Hours for 2 Weeks = 80; Each
Employee's Hours for 2 Weeks = 40

Half-day on/half-day off

	Mon.	Tues.	Wed.	Thurs.	Fri.
9:00 Week 1 1:00	E1	E1	E1	E1	E1
5:00	E2	E2	E2	E2	E2

Two employees (E1 and E2) work 4 hours/day, 5 days/week
TOTAL HOURS/WEEK = 40;
EACH EMPLOYEE'S HOURS/WEEK = 20

Shared job with half-day overlap on Wednesday

	Mon.	Tues.	Wed.	Thurs.	Fri.
Week 1	E1	E1	E1 & E2	E2	E2
Week 2	E2	E2	E1 & E2	E1	E1

Two employees (E1 and E2) work 2½ days/week with a Wednesday
overlap
Total Hours/Week = 40; Total Hours for 2 Weeks = 80; Each
Employee's Hours for 2 Weeks = 40

Shared job with half-day overlap on Friday

	Mon.	Tues.	Wed.	Thurs.	Fri.
Week 1	E1	E1	E1	E1	E1 & E2
Week 2	E2	E2	E2	E2	E1 & E2

Two employees (E1 and E2) work 4½ days one week with a Friday
overlap and ½ day the next week on the Friday overlap
Total Hours/Week = 40; Total Hours for 2 Weeks = 80; Each
Employee's Hours for 2 Weeks = 40

aspects of job sharing, has several important ramifications for both the manager and the employees. Organizational benefits are significant. Continuity can be greatly enhanced if there is agreement initially that sharers will substitute for each other whenever possible. If they are also allowed to trade time and self-schedule for personal reasons as well, employees are generally very receptive to assuming this kind of responsibility. The result can be a significant reduction in the amount of work time lost because of accidents, illness, or an employee's need for more personal time. If one partner leaves the position, the other can provide 50 percent coverage, and often more, until a new sharer is hired.

From the employees' perspective, the ability to trade work time and arrange their own schedules allows them to respond to personal needs as well as work-related ones. If there is an illness in the family or a transportation problem, job sharing may enable the employee to cope without the organization's losing work time. Sharers are also able to take advantage of special opportunities, such as attending a short course or seminar or traveling with a spouse.

The concept of trading work time raises the question of the obligation of partners to substitute for each other. In practice, sharers who are allowed to self-schedule for personal reasons generally are expected to fill in during each other's absences insofar as is feasible. Increasingly companies are developing language that addresses these issues, such as "sharers will substitute for each other whenever possible." Sometimes time limits are stipulated regarding how long, and to what extent, one partner will be expected to fill in for another who is absent for an extended period of time or who leaves the company's employ. Other policies permit this aspect of job sharing to be negotiated between the sharers and their direct supervisor, with the caveat that the issue of trading time and substituting must be discussed and agreed upon before the arrangement begins.

Skills and Experience

In addition to creating opportunities for fine-tuning schedules, allowing two people to fill one job can greatly expand the number of skills and the types of experience available in a single job title. In many fields, work is becoming increasingly complex, and an individual in one position is often expected to demonstrate competence in a variety of areas. When two people team up to share a position, they generally offer a wider range of skills than a single incumbent.

Human Resources Management Objectives

By offering the possibility of creating "special teams," job sharing can facilitate the achievement of an assortment of objectives in the area of human resources management. The following are some examples of the types of employees who can be paired and the types of objectives that such pairings can accomplish:

- Two senior employees may share a job as a way of phasing in to retirement.
- A senior employee may job share with a younger employee, thereby enabling the older worker to train his or her replacement while phasing in to retirement.
- An employee ready for promotion can share a job half-time at a higher grade level and remain half-time at his or her current position. This option can permit an employee to advance in situations where there is no full-time opening at the higher grade level.
- An entry-level employee can share a position half-time while completing his or her education or training half-time. This way, the organization not only retains the services of the employee during the learning process but also ends up with a more qualified employee.

Job sharing's potential for creating openings and permitting movement in a relatively static workforce situation may become increasingly important as employers strive for stability along with flexibility.

Cost Implications—The Position Approach

To evaluate the overall costs—and savings—the organization must establish its objectives and define its reasons for instituting job sharing. Is job sharing being considered in response to one employee's request, because of recruitment difficulties, as an alternative to layoffs, or as a way to manage several of these problems at once? And in what areas can savings, both current and future, be projected if job sharing is instituted?

Drafting a balance sheet that shows the entire range of cost factors (direct and indirect costs and program costs) can help an employer identify all the considerations that should be included in the final equation. Tables 5-1, 5-2, and 5-3 are sample worksheets that show a comparison between the costs associated with a current full-time position and the costs associated with various types of job sharing arrangements that might be used to accomplish the same

Table 5-1. Cost analysis by position: example of job being shared by current employee and new hire.

		Current Cost of the Position	Job Sharing		
			Current Employee	New Hire	Total
I.	Direct costs				
	A. Base salary	$30,000.00	$15,000.00	$15,000.00	$30,000.00
	B. Employee benefits				
	1. Statutory				
	• Social Security (6.2% of first $60,600)	1,860.00	930.00	930.00	1,860.00
	• Medicare (1.45%)	435.00	217.50	217.50	435.00
	• Unemployment insurance (2.3% of first $7,000)	161.00	161.00	161.00	322.00
	• Workers compensation ($.85 per $100 of compensation)	255.00	127.50	127.50	255.00
	2. Compensatory				
	• Sick leave (2 weeks)	1,153,85	576.92	576.92	1,153.84
	• Vacation (3 weeks—current employee; 2 weeks—new hire)	1,730,77	865.38	576.92	1,442.30
	• Holidays (10 days)	1,153,85	576.92	576.92	1,153.84
	• Other				
	3. Supplementary				
	• Insurance				
	Prorated life ($10,000)	50.00	25.00	25.00	50.00
	Medical/dental ($125 deductible)	1,500.00	750.00	750.00	1,500.00
	Long-term disability	250.00	125.00	125.00	250.00
	• Pension (13% salary)	3,900.00	1,950.00	1,950.00	3,900.00
	• Profit sharing (.5%)	150.00	75.00	75.00	150.00
	• Stock purchase options				
	• Tax shelter annuities				
	• Tuition payments				
	• Discount purchase plans				

	Current Cost of the Position	Job Sharing		
		Current Employee	New Hire	Total
• Other				
Total direct costs	$42,599.47	$21,380.22	$21,091.76	$42,471.98
II. Indirect costs				
A. New hire administration			$ 150.00	$ 150.00
B. Training			500.00	500.00
C. Supervision	$2,000.00	$1,000.00	1,000.00	2,000.00
D. Square footage (80 square feet)	480.00	240.00	240.0	480.00
Total indirect costs	$2,480.00	$1,240.00	$1,890.00	$3,130.00
III. Program costs				
A. Absenteeism				
B. Turnover				
C. Coverage				
D. Recruitment				
E. Production rates				
Total program costs	$0.00	$0.00	$0.00	$0.00
TOTAL COSTS	$45,079.47	$22,620.22	$22,981.76	$45,601.98
DIFFERENCE				+$522.51

work. Table 5-4 is a blank copy of this worksheet that managers may wish to use in performing their own cost analysis.

The remainder of this subsection examines the cost implications of restructuring individual jobs to a shared mode—the position approach. It covers direct costs (which comprise base salary, including overtime, and a variety of fringe benefits and are usually the most significant expenses that will be incurred) and indirect costs (which comprise costs in such areas as new-hire administration, training, and the use of space and equipment and are usually a less significant expense for most employers). You may refer to Chapter 4 for a discussion of program costs (those associated with the rates of absenteeism and turnover, coverage, recruitment, and production rates), which can also be a factor.

After we consider the costs of converting individual positions to job sharing, we will turn our attention in the following subsection to some of the fiscal multiplier effects that organizations have achieved by using the program approach—that is, instituting job sharing on a broader basis by restructuring one or more groups of positions.

Table 5-2. Cost analysis by position: example of job being shared by two current employees.

		Job Sharing		
	Current Cost of the Position	Current Employee	Current Employee	Total
I. Direct costs				
A. Base salary	$30,000.00	$15,000.00	$15,000.00	$30,000.00
B. Employee benefits				
1. Statutory				
• Social Security (6.2% of first $60,600)	1,860.00	930.00	930.00	1,860.00
• Medicare (1.45%)	435.00	217.50	217.50	435.00
• Unemployment insurance (2.3% of first $7,000)	161.00	161.00	161.00	322.00
• Workers compensation ($.85 per $100 of compensation)	255.00	127.50	127.50	255.00
2. Compensatory				
• Sick leave (2 weeks)	1,153.85	576.92	576.92	1,153.84
• Vacation (3 weeks)	1,730.77	865.38	865.38	1,730.76
• Holidays (10 days)	1,153.85	576.92	576.92	1,153.84
• Other				
3. Supplementary				
• Insurance				
Prorated life ($10,000)	50.00	25.00	25.00	50.00
Medical/dental ($125 deductible)	1,500.00	750.00	750.00	1,500.00
Long-term disability	250.00	125.00	125.00	250.00
• Pension (13% salary)	3,900.00	1,950.00	1,950.00	3,900.00
• Profit sharing (5%)	150.00	75.00	75.00	150.00
• Stock purchase options				
• Tax shelter annuities				
• Tuition payments				
• Discount purchase plans				
• Other				
Total direct costs	$42,599.47	$21,380.22	$21,380.22	$42,760.44

	Current Cost of the Position	Job Sharing		
		Current Employee	Current Employee	Total
II. Indirect costs				
A. New hire administration				
B. Training				
C. Supervision	$2,000.00	$1,000.00	$1,000.00	$2,000.00
D. Square footage (80 square feet)	480.00	240.00	240.00	480.00
Total indirect costs	$2,480.00	$1,240.00	$1,240.00	$2,480.00
III. Program costs				
A. Absenteeism				
B. Turnover				
C. Coverage				
D. Recruitment				
E. Production rates				
Total program costs	$0.00	$0.00	$0.00	$0.00
TOTAL COSTS	$45,079.47	$22,620.22	$22,620.22	$45,240.44
DIFFERENCE				+ $160.97

Direct Costs. The cost factors in this category are base salary and any overtime that may be incurred plus fringe benefits.

Base Salary. It might seem that sharing a job would have no salary-related implications. However, partners in job sharing teams may or may not have the same level of skills and experience, so they may or may not qualify for the same salary range. Sharers' salaries should be based both on their time arrangement (such as 50-50 or 60-40) and on their individual skills and experience.

This often results in savings on the salary costs of a particular position. For example, the salary of a full-time personnel analyst with five years' experience on the job might be $35,000. If this person wishes to reduce hours and can be paired with a less-experienced new hire (who would earn $20,000 if he or she were hired full-time), the total base salary of the shared position would be only $27,500 ($17,500 [half of $35,000] + $10,000 [half of $20,000]) instead of $35,000 for the full-time services of the more-experienced employee, saving the organization $7,500. Similarly, if a senior-level teacher (who would earn $30,000 full-time) is paired with an entry-level teacher (who would earn $18,000 full-time), the combined

Table 5-3. Cost analysis by position: example of job being shared by current senior employee and less-experienced new hire.

	Current Cost of the Position	Job Sharing		
		Older, Experienced Current Employee	Less-Experienced New Hire	Total
I. Direct costs				
A. Base salary	$30,000.00	$15,000.00	$10,500.00	$25,500.00
B. Employee benefits				
1. Statutory				
• Social Security (6.2% of first $60,600)	1,860.00	930.00	651.00	1,581.00
• Medicare (1.45%)	435.00	217.50	153.30	370.80
• Unemployment insurance (2.3% of first $7,000)	161.00	161.00	161.00	322.00
• Workers compensation ($85 per $100 of compensation)	255.00	127.50	89.25	216.75
2. Compensatory				
• Sick leave (2 weeks)	1,153.85	576.92	403.85	980.77
• Vacation (3 weeks—current employee; 2 weeks—new hire)	1,730.77	865.38	403.85	1,269.23
• Holidays (10 days)	1,153,85	576.92	403.85	980.77
• Other				
3. Supplementary				
• Insurance				
Prorated life ($10,000)	50.00	25.00	25.00	50.00
Medical/dental ($125 deductible)	1,500.00	750.00	750.00	1,500.00
Long-term disability	250.00	125.00	85.00	210.00
• Pension (13% salary)	3,900.00	1,950.00	1,365.00	3,315.00
• Profit sharing (.5%)	150.00	75.00	52.50	127.50
• Stock purchase options				

	Current Cost of the Position	Job Sharing Older, Experienced Current Employee	Less-Experienced New Hire	Total
• Tax shelter annuities				
• Tuition payments				
• Discount purchase plans				
• Other				
Total direct costs	$42,599.47	$21,380.22	$15,043.60	$36,423.82
II. Indirect costs				
A. New hire administration			$ 150.00	$ 150.00
B. Training			500.00	500.00
C. Supervision	$2,000.00	$1,000.00	1,200.00	2,200.00
D. Square footage (80 square feet)	480.00	240.00	240.00	480.00
Total indirect costs	$2,480.00	$1,240.00	$2,090.00	$3,330.00
III. Program costs				
A. Absenteeism				
B. Turnover				
C. Coverage				
D. Recruitment				
E. Production rates				
Total program costs	$0.00	$0.00	$0.00	$0.00
TOTAL COSTS	$45,079.47	$22,620.22	$17,133.60	$39,753.82
DIFFERENCE				−$5,325.65

position would cost a school district $24,000 ($15,000 + $9,000) instead of $30,000, for a savings of $6,000.

Employers are often surprised at the idea of paying job sharing partners at different rates. Paying at the rate that each of the job sharers would receive if he or she were employed full-time in the same job classification is the most common policy, however, and one that sharers perceive as equitable.

Related to the issue of base salary is the issue of overtime. As was discussed in Chapter 4, because of growing fixed costs per employee, many employers have increased their use of overtime

Table 5-4. Cost analysis by position: worksheet.

	Current Cost: Full-Timer	Job sharing		
		Employee A	Employee B	Total
I. Direct costs				
A. Base salary				
B. Employee benefits				
1. Statutory				
• Social Security (____% of first $_____)				
• Medicare (____%)				
• Unemployment insurance (____% of first $_____)				
• Workers compensation (____ per $100 of compensation)				
2. Compensatory				
• Sick leave (____ weeks)				
• Vacation (____ weeks—current employee; ____ weeks—new hire)				
• Holidays (____ days)				
• Other				
3. Supplementary				
• Insurance Prorated life ($_____) Medical/dental ($____ deductible) Long-term disability				
• Pension (____% salary)				
• Profit sharing (____%)				
• Stock purchase options				
• Tax shelter annuities				
• Tuition payments				
• Discount purchase plans				
• Other	_____	_____	_____	____
Total direct costs				
II. Indirect costs				
A. New hire administration				
B. Training				
C. Supervision				
D. Square footage (_____ square feet)	_____	_____	_____	____
Total indirect costs				

	Current Cost:	Job sharing		
	Full-Timer	Employee A	Employee B	Total
III. Program costs				
A. Absenteeism				
B. Turnover				
C. Coverage				
D. Recruitment				
E. Production rates	_____	_____	_____	____
Total program costs	_____	_____	_____	____
TOTAL COSTS				
DIFFERENCE				

instead of expanding their permanent workforce. Such extensive use of overtime can be quite costly for the employer and can result in increased pressure on the organization's employees, sometimes leading to burnout. Employers of job sharers, on the other hand, are often able to reduce or eliminate the need for overtime by improving the scheduling in particular positions. Job sharers can be scheduled to work together during periods of peak demand, or the supervisor can arrange a gap period that extends service hours without either employee's having to work more than an eight-hour day. If an employer allows sharers to trade time freely, the organization achieves increased scheduling flexibility and maximum coverage at no extra cost.

In instances where overtime is still necessary, the question arises of when job sharers should receive premium pay. The formula preferred by advocates of job sharing is derived from the concept of treating a shared job the same as any other full-time position in the same job classification. Using this rule of thumb, overtime is paid when the nonexempt sharers' combined hours total more than forty a week. The premium pay is divided equally between them if both have worked the same number of hours in that pay period or distributed proportionally on the basis of extra hours worked if they have not.

Employee Benefits. Fringe benefits differ from one company to another and, as noted in Chapter 4, fall into three categories: statutory, compensatory, and supplementary. The following material does not repeat the detailed discussion contained in Chapter 4 but instead focuses on the benefits considerations that most directly affect job sharing.

Statutory Benefits. This benefits category includes Social Security, unemployment insurance, and workers' compensation insurance.

■ *Social Security*. Employers incur extra expense for job sharers only when two employees share a position that pays more than $60,600. Most jobs pay less than that. For positions at or above the ceiling, the employer must contribute 6.2 percent, up to a maximum ceiling of $121,200 (double the $60,600). Job sharers in a position paying $65,000, for instance, would cost an employer $272.80 (.062 × $4,400 [the amount by which the combined salary exceeds the $60,600 ceiling]) more per year in Social Security than one full-time employee who held the same job.

■ *Medicare*. Medicare costs are computed for each employee at 1.45 percent of income with no ceiling, so there is no extra expense.

■ *Unemployment insurance*. It is difficult to generalize about unemployment insurance costs associated with job sharing because the rates and limits vary from state to state. For example, on a $7,000 ceiling, an employer with a 2.3 percent rating pays $161 for a full-time employee making $30,000. If the position is shared, the employer pays double the cost—$322. It should be pointed out, however, that as with other forms of regular part-time, employers that institute job sharing or expand the practice in order to avoid layoffs may save money in the long run, because by retaining current workers, the organization minimizes unemployment insurance claims, thereby keeping its "experience rating" lower than it otherwise would be.

■ *Workers' compensation insurance*. This cost is usually based on a percentage of payroll, which means that no additional expense is incurred if a position is shared.

Compensatory Benefits. Such fringe benefits as sick leave, vacation, and holidays are generally prorated according to the amount of time worked by each sharer, so job sharing does not automatically increase the organization's costs in this category. In fact, some employers have found that a job sharing arrangement may cut the expense associated with illness, absence, or vacation, because the sharers can cover for each other when one partner is away from the job, reducing the need to utilize expensive substitutes or temporary agency personnel.

Supplementary Benefits. As is the case with other regular part-timers, it is important for employers to extend supplementary benefits, particularly medical and dental insurance, to job sharers. In order to do this without doubling the cost they incur, some employers pay half the health insurance amount for each job-sharer that they would normally pay for a part-time employee. The sharers are then given the option of paying the remainder. This approach often results in cost savings if sharers are covered under a spouse's policy and elect not to receive (and pay for half the cost of) this benefit from the employer. It also ensures equitable treatment if the employee has no other access to group health insurance and must avail himself or herself of the opportunity to obtain coverage in this manner.

Indirect Costs. Before restructuring a full-time position so that two people can share it, employers should review the administrative overhead costs associated with new hires as well as the costs associated with training and the use of space and equipment.

■ *Administrative overhead.* In addition to the ongoing costs of administrative overhead, the costs associated with a new hire could include recruitment of a replacement if a current full-time employee leaves. But no new-hire costs are incurred if the job sharing team consists of two current full-timers who want to cut back their hours.

■ *Training.* If one or both sharers require specialized training that cannot be imparted by an incumbent partner, the employer will incur the cost of having both partners trained by someone else within the organization. If one partner is a current full-timer who is able to train his or her partner, the cost is limited to the time spent by both partners in the training process. If the team comprises two people currently working full-time in the same job classification as the position to be shared, then no initial training costs will be incurred.

■ *Space and equipment.* If the team members need to work together at the same time, extra space and equipment may be required. Most pairs, however, schedule their time so that they can share space and equipment.

An often-overlooked cost saving in this area stems from the fact that job sharing cuts down on absenteeism and turnover. When a full-time employee is away from his or her job, the employer is paying for equipment, space, heat and lights, insurance, and even a stall in the company parking lot for someone who isn't there. Whether the absence results in an empty office desk, a vacant production-line work station, or an unstaffed factory punch press, the cost to the organization is considerable. In addition to the reduction in the overall rates of absenteeism and turnover, the fact that job sharers can fill in for each other in the event that one does become sick or resign also enables the employer to better recoup its investment in space and equipment.

Cost Implications—The Program Approach

Employers that have had successful experience with a few shared positions often consider expanding the use of job sharing. They can do this either one job at a time, by focusing on a group of positions or employees, or by targeting a particular company problem. For example, an employer may decide to make a priority of job sharing requests from employees with young children or older employees nearing retirement age. Another employer may designate certain positions, such as computer programmer or market researcher, as open to job sharing. Yet another may use the idea of two people's sharing one full-time job as a recruitment device or as a means of attempting to reduce absenteeism.

The main reason for taking a group, or program, approach rather than continuing to restructure one job at a time is to solve a problem and/or to compound the savings achieved in previous, smaller job-sharing experiments. This subsection explains some of the reasons why employers have formulated job sharing programs and presents guidelines for doing so.

■ *To reduce absenteeism.* When employees have nonwork responsibilities that conflict with their jobs, the result at the workplace may be chronic or intermittent absenteeism. When the problem is generic rather than individual, it becomes an organizational concern. At least that's what Pella Corporation, a Midwestern manufacturer, thought when it realized that absenteeism on its production line was appreciably higher than the company average. An employee with good skills but a poor attendance record suggested job sharing as an option for production-line employees, almost all of whom were working mothers with young children. The company thoroughly reviewed her suggestion and then let her share her job as a pilot project. Four years later, there were thirty job sharing teams, absenteeism had dropped from 5.8 percent to 1.2 percent, and the company had eliminated the need to overstaff the production line. (The following section of this chapter presents a detailed profile of Pella's experience with job sharing.)

■ *To improve recruitment.* Advertising a job as open to either one full-time or two job sharing applicants can both expand and enhance an organization's recruitment efforts. By offering job sharing, Fireman's Fund Insurance Companies was able to attract better applicants for hard-to-fill positions (see Figure 5-2); Walgreen's used job sharing successfully to recruit in a locale whose labor force had a high percentage of homemakers; and New York Life Insurance Company advertised shared positions in an effort to stabilize a segment of the company's activities where there was high turnover. A Minneapolis law firm recently reported a "deluge" of qualified respondents when it advertised for an HR support person on a job shared basis.[7] The Oklahoma State University brochure in Figure 5-3 is an example of a job sharing promotional tool.

■ *To provide new options for senior employees.* Varian Associates in Silicon Valley and The Travelers Insurance Company are two firms that offer job sharing as an option for senior employees. Varian does it in conjunction with its phased retirement program; The Travelers Insurance Company, as an option within its program of part-time employment for annuitants.

■ *To provide released time for training.* McKesson Corporation in San Francisco has been using job sharing in conjunction with its efforts to provide work experience for high school–age youth in ways that expand opportunities for its current employees as well. Each student works two hours a day, five days a week, in various departments, including office services, the mail room, documentation services, and personnel. He or she is assigned a work supervisor and trained on the job by that person. After the student is trained, the full-time employee who had been performing the tasks is free to cross-train in other departments in order to expand his or her skills and potential for advancement during the two hours that the student replacement is working.

■ *To supplement a work-sharing strategy.* If a company decides to cut back on paid hours of work during an economic downturn in

(Text continues on page 169.)

Figure 5-2. Advertisement featuring job sharing as a recruitment tool.

SOURCE: *San Francisco Sunday Examiner and Chronicle* (Jan. 31, 1982), 40.

Figure 5-3.   Brochure for job candidates explaining a job sharing program.

Job-Sharing, A Team Approach

Team Approach

A Job-Sharing Plan Which Works!

Office of University Personnel
407 Whitehurst Hall
Oklahoma State University

SOURCE: Oklahoma State University, Stillwater, Okla.

Job-sharing, the *new* way to work, is proving feasible and effective on the Oklahoma State University Campus.

Job-sharing involves two persons accepting the responsibility for one full-time position, thus giving each person that much desired commodity—*time*; time for travel, family or recreation, while still utilizing skills and knowledge of the work world.

These part-time positions are particularly beneficial for women during child-bearing years, older women not yet ready for retirement, or those who just want to keep their hand on the pulse of the work world.

Cooperation, Compatibility and *Communication* are the key factors for a successful and effective team. Job-sharers find that the flexibility of hours far out weighs the disadvantages of the lower salary.

Job-sharing is an ideal solution for many campus positions such as receptionist, file/clerk, clerk/typist and many others. Employers are seldom left stranded, as team workers cooperate when personal emergency situations arise, and they equalize staff pressure during peak activity periods.

It has been proven that not only are two heads better than one, but two persons sharing the same job can give an extension of service and often an increase in productivity of 25% or more. There is less absenteeism, tardiness and more pride in work done well. Reasons for this higher quality of work efficiency can be attributed to higher energy, enthusiasm and motivation. Together, job-sharers can frequently offer a lot more than a single employee.

Director of University Personnel Services Gene Turner says, "I'm a great believer in this program because it has worked so well for us. There are a lot of talented people who want to work less than an eight hour day. Given the options of tailoring their schedules to meet their own needs, these people are most productive, dependable and highly motivated."

(Continued)

Figure 5-3. *(continued)*

OKLAHOMA STATE UNIVERSITY

Marita Johnson who shares receptionist duties in the Office of University Personnel Services, says "Job-sharing in the Personnel Office has provided a way to re-enter the work world which I left to raise my family and yet it provides the flexibility for my partner and me to adjust our work schedules to accomodate our interests and to meet the needs of our families. It has also brought my family closer together, because we each assume responsibility to help make each other's day a little bit better."

Marita's partner, Sandy Barth concurs by saying, "I love it. What else can I say? I have been so happy since I came to work for Personnel Services in November of 1979. My life has been so full. I loved being at home when my children were there, but when they were all in school I felt the need to be around people and to grow mentally. I wasn't sure I could work, I had been away from it for so long. The people I work with have given me a great deal of support and confidence in my self. Having a friend as a partner is another advantage. We work together setting up our schedule and we are very flexible when one of us wants to change. I feel as though I have the best of both worlds."

Potential job-sharers are encouraged to find a partner, perhaps a neighbor, bridge partner, or just a friend with whom they feel they could work successfully. However, the Office of University Personnel Services maintains a list of names of those wishing to be paired for a position on a part-time basis.

Brush-Up Programs

Brush-up programs for those wishing to re-enter the job market are available. An open-end clerical program is now being offered by Oklahoma State University and area vocational schools offer complete clerical programs as well as some adult education classes in this locale.

Those persons employed in a permanent half-time position are now eligible for sick leave and annual leave at a proportionate rate.

For more detailed information, please contact:

Employment Interviewer
Office of University Personnel
Whitehurst Hall, Room 407
Oklahoma State University
Stillwater, Oklahoma 74078
(405) 624-5373

order to save jobs and retain employees, voluntary job sharing is one option that may be offered. Several airlines have authorized job sharing for flight attendants and ticket personnel for this reason. (Chapter 9 discusses work sharing in detail.)

■ *To retain valued employees.* Retention of trained workers is probably the most prevalent factor in persuading employers to try job sharing for the first time. Levi Strauss, Quaker Oats, Steelcase, and others have cited the need to accommodate employees who had to reduce their work time for a while and whose positions could not be handled on a part-time basis as the reason for initially experimenting with job sharing and then formulating policy or guidelines expanding its use.

Supervisors' Attitudes

Job sharing is still a new idea in many companies, and supervisors' reactions to it vary widely. Those who have had experience with job sharing generally support it enthusiastically as an option, although they may feel that the attributes of the particular pair they supervised were the primary factor in making this scheduling alternative successful. Those lacking experience with job sharing tend to be skeptical about allowing two people to share one position.

Union Attitudes

Labor leaders tend to view job sharing more favorably than they do other forms of part-time work. This is largely because of their perception that job sharing retains the form of a full-time position and so is a way to upgrade part-time employment. As with other forms of reduced work time, unions are concerned that it be voluntary, that base salary scale and fringe benefits be maintained, that protections against speedup be instituted, and that layoffs occur according to some kind of seniority process rather than part-timers automatically being laid off first.

Employee Attitudes

Employees in general are enthusiastic about the introduction of flexible and reduced work-time options such as job sharing. Whether or not they are interested in working that way themselves, they recognize these policies as representing the company's willingness to innovate and be supportive of employee needs. Negative attitudes may arise, however, if a particular job sharing team does not communicate well with co-workers (a special concern in terms of scheduling arrangements) or if the option is perceived as being used in a way that reflects favoritism.

Should Your Organization Try Job Sharing?

The purpose of this section is to help you analyze job sharing in light of your organization's staffing and scheduling needs and decide whether adopting this technique would be advantageous.

First, the accompanying group of profiles ("Organizational Experience with Job Sharing") describes how and why job sharing was used in two organizations and what effect it has had. Consider the ways in which the experience of these organizations might parallel the circumstances that your own company faces. Table 5-5 raises a series of issues that are of primary concern to organizations that institute job sharing. The more yes answers you have on this questionnaire, the greater the chances that job sharing would benefit your company.

If, based on your questionnaire results, it appears that job sharing is the direction in which your organization should move, you can complete the worksheet shown in Figure 5-4. It can be used

Table 5-5. Job sharing questionnaire.

Would Job Sharing Benefit Your Organization?

	Yes	No
Have you had to turn down employee requests for a reduced schedule because the jobs in question could not be done on a part-time basis?		
Have some of the employees whose request for a reduced schedule was turned down left your organization as a result?		
Are some departments or job classifications experiencing above-average turnover or absenteeism?		
Have you had to overstaff in some areas or use an excessive number of substitutes to compensate for turnover or absenteeism?		
Do many of your employees who have been on parental leave decide against returning to full-time work?		
If your organization's schedules must conform to work demand, could work flow be improved by having a team of job sharers overlap during a peak period or extended coverage by creating a gap?		
Is upward mobility difficult in some departments or job classifications?		
Would some of your organization's senior employees prefer a part-time option?		

Figure 5-4. Job sharing worksheet.

Assessing the Need for Job Sharing

List the main reasons why you are considering job sharing:

1. _____

_____

_____

2. _____

_____

_____

3. _____

_____

_____

4. _____

_____

_____

List what you see as the advantages and disadvantages of job sharing:

Pros: _____

_____

_____

_____

_____

(Continued)

Figure 5-4. *(continued)*

Cons: _____

---

to list the specific concerns that have prompted you to consider job sharing and examine the positive and negative effects that the use of this alternative work-time approach might have.

Introducing Job Sharing

In practice, job sharing has generally been introduced in an organization in an incremental way, often starting with one position that is restructured in response to a particular situation, as an exception to the general rule. If this first experience is successful, the use of job sharing is expanded—either on a case-by-case basis, to address a particular issue, or as a pilot project of some sort—and is finally incorporated as a general option. Once an organization has gotten beyond the first stage of experience, it should consider developing regulations and a set of procedures or management guidelines that will govern the use of job sharing.

Gain Support for the Program

Even if regular part-time is an accepted work mode, the introduction of job sharing as an employee option will need the support of top management, middle management, and labor representatives. Forming a task force to gather information about job sharing and why it would be a good management tool for your firm can be a way to both organize support and make the business case for your organization. Because it is a new kind of working arrangement in many organizations, job sharing is often viewed skeptically even by supervisors who have successfully used part-time employees. This makes support from top management at the outset particularly important. If an organization has had several positive experiences with individually negotiated job-sharing arrangements or has conducted a successful pilot project to test job sharing at a number of different levels, this support will be easier to gain.

Set Up the Program's Administration
The task force should also identify a coordinator of the job sharing initiative, one who will continue in that role after the work of the task force has been completed in order to be a resource and provide backup support for managers and sharers after job sharing has become an option.

One of the first responsibilities of the task force should be to review and assess any ad hoc or pilot project experience your company has had, identify what worked and what didn't, and research the experience of other organizations. Information about opportunities that were lost because the organization did *not* have a job sharing option can also be helpful.

Design the Program
Whatever the scope of the program that the task force decides on, this subsection provides guidelines and suggestions for (1) which areas of existing policy should be reviewed and revised if they constitute barriers to the use of job sharing and (2) how to develop new policy that will facilitate the successful introduction of job sharing as an employment option.

Eliminate Current Barriers. The first step toward eliminating current barriers is to review your organization's existing personnel policies and union contracts as they relate to job sharing and address any internal constraints that may be found. If your company now uses regular part-time employees in responsible positions, policy language may already be in place and will need only slight adaptation to encompass job sharing.

The balance of this subsection discusses some of the major

barriers to the use of job sharing that you may discover in your review of current policies and contracts.

■ *Head count.* Just as with regular part-time, the head count system is a barrier to job sharing. When organizations require each part-time employee to be counted the same as each full-time employee against personnel authorizations, the use of part-time is discouraged. For the purpose of facilitating job sharing, some employers define each partner as "half a head"; others reassess the appropriateness of the head count system and move toward a system of full-time equivalency.

■ *Compensation.* All forms of compensation normally attached to a particular position when it is held by one full-time employee should be maintained and divided between the sharers in a way that is equitable both to the employer and to the job sharing employees. Salary scale should remain the same, and fringe benefits should be prorated based on the amount of time worked by each barrier. (A detailed analysis of the compensation and benefits issue can be found in the Pros and Cons of Job Sharing section earlier in this chapter; see the subsection there entitled Cost Implications— The Position Approach.)

■ *Reductions in force.* As is the case with other forms of less than full-time work, policy dictating that during a labor force reduction, all part-timers must be laid off first—regardless of length of service, special qualifications, or other considerations—makes job sharing and other types of part-time unattractive. A problem particular to job sharing occurs when the partners have different seniority status; policy must be devised that addresses the effect of layoffs not only on each of the individual sharers but also on the future of the job sharing team.

■ *Impact on retirement income.* Job sharing has often been discussed as a way to implement phased retirement for older workers and is generally included in policy language describing possible options for senior employees who want to work fewer hours in the period leading up to their retirement. The same problems occur as with other forms of regular part-time, however, if provision is not made to ensure that the reduced-time arrangement does not negatively affect retirement income. (For a more detailed discussion of this issue, refer to the subsection on Public and Private Policy Barriers in the section of Chapter 4 entitled Pros and Cons of Regular Part-Time.)

Create New Policy. The organization needs to establish personnel policies and processes that ensure uniform treatment of job sharers. These will support managers who are interested in experimenting with a new kind of work arrangement, assure consistent handling of different cases, and create for these employees a sense of fairness and integration into the organization's overall workforce. The issues that you will need to address include:

■ *Eligibility.* Which and how many employees will you allow to job share? Will you accept outside applications for all or part of a position? Or will you limit the option to current full-time employees? Will you exclude any job classifications from the program?

■ *Application process.* Where can an employee obtain a set of regulations governing the employment of job sharers? Whom does the employee talk to first? What kind of preparatory work should the employee have done (such as partner identification, proposed schedule, or task analysis)? Is there a particular form to fill out? Where can it be obtained?

■ *Compensation.* How will salary be apportioned? What kinds of fringe benefits will sharers receive, and what will they cost the company? What constitutes overtime? (See the earlier subsection entitled Cost Implications—The Position Approach for a detailed analysis of compensation and suggestions for various ways to deal with these issues.)

■ *Effect on employee status.* The way compensation, fringe benefits, and other conditions of employment are handled is critical to how employees on less than full-time schedules perceive the company's fairness and their status as it relates to that of other workers. Prorating compensation and benefits according to hours worked is generally a good rule of thumb. Additional areas that should be addressed are seniority and service credit, order of layoff, probationary period, promotional opportunities, and vesting in retirement programs.

■ *Pair formation.* Must employees find their own partners and present themselves as a team? If so, must a partner be from the ranks of current employees, or can the partner who is already employed propose someone from outside the organization? Will the company help in the process (by setting up a partner-finding box in the personnel department or allowing E-mail to be used for a search, for example)?

■ *Scheduling.* How much trading off of work time will you allow partners? Are there any constraints that you wish to impose on the types of schedules that can be constructed? Some questions about scheduling involve policy issues that are best decided by top management; others involve decisions that may best be left to the supervisor. For instance, one reason for limiting certain types of schedules might be that your company's bookkeeping or payroll scheduling systems rule them out. In general, however, employers have found that the most effective organizational policy is one that encourages the widest possible flexibility, allowing the sharers and their supervisor to work out the details of a particular schedule within the context of company regulations.

■ *Replacement of partners.* What happens if one partner is incompetent, or the partners prove to be incompatible, or one wants to terminate the job sharing arrangement, either to return to a full-time position within the company or to leave the company altogether? To what extent will the remaining sharer be expected to fill in until a new partner is found? Provisions must be made in advance for dealing with such problems. (The section entitled Special Considerations for Supervisors and Managers later in this chapter discusses this issue more fully.)

■ *Conditions for reversibility.* How does a job sharer apply to return to full-time work? Will an application from a current sharer receive priority attention when the organization fills full-time openings? If so, to what extent?

New forms should be designed and current ones altered as appropriate. For example, a line might be added to the personnel request form allowing a supervisor to indicate a willingness to consider applications from job sharing teams.

The program design checklist presented in Table 5-6 will serve as a handy reference for the main issues related to job sharing that you will have to address during the program design phase of the implementation process.

Develop Resource Materials
Managers and supervisors will require resources outlining a step-by-step process for handling job sharing requests, and employees will require resources covering such major issues as eligibility, application procedures, and reversibility.

Guidelines for Managers and Supervisors. The organization should provide its managerial and supervisory personnel with detailed

Table 5-6.   Program design checklist: job sharing.

Key Design Issues	Notes
Eliminating current barriers	
☐ Head count	
☐ Compensation	
☐ Reductions in force	
☐ Impact on retirement income	
Creating new policy	
☐ Eligibility	
☐ Application process	
☐ Compensation	
☐ Effect on employee status	
☐ Pair formation	
☐ Scheduling	
☐ Replacement of partners	
☐ Conditions for reversibility	

information on how to respond to employee requests to job share. If guidelines covering requests to reduce a full-time position to regular part-time already exist, a section on job sharing can be added. New York State, which has a very dynamic program designed to facilitate voluntary part-time and job sharing, developed an excellent booklet for its managers, from which many of the points in this subsection are drawn.[8] Other organizations have begun to develop booklets for managers and employees with detailed information on the "menu" of flexible work arrangements the organization offers.

In general, the process of responding to an employee request to job share follows the steps listed below (which will, of course, be modified based on the requirements of your particular company).

1. *Request information from personnel.* Policies and procedures from the personnel department covering part-time and job sharing should be reviewed.

2. *Ask the employee to submit the request in writing.* Such a request should include a proposed schedule, a proposal for how the job will be shared, the name of a potential partner, a suggested beginning date for the job sharing arrangement, and, if possible, an estimate of how long the employee would like to job share. At the time the employee is asked to submit a written request, provide him or her with a checklist (such as the one shown in Table 5-7) indicating what the proposal should cover. (A checklist should be included in whatever type of resource materials are developed.)

3. *Meet with the employee(s).* Discuss the request, a time frame for the decision, and what the next steps might be. Open communication among all parties is important.

4. *Decide.* The following steps are suggested in making a decision to approve or turn down a job sharing request:

■ Talk with other supervisors and employees in the company who have had experience either with part-time or with job sharing, particularly if this is the supervisor's first experience with job sharing. These contacts can offer practical advice and raise issues that should be discussed and agreed upon before the new work arrangement begins.

■ Determine whether the proposal takes advantage of the partners' individual strengths or accommodates their differing levels of skills and experience. Could this aspect of the proposal be strengthened? Table 5-8 offers an example of how the tasks within a single position might best be allocated between partners having (1) similar types and levels of skills, (2) dissimilar skills at approximately the same level, and (3) significantly different levels of skills and experience. Figure 5-5 then illustrates how a schedule could be arranged to make the best use of the talents of these three combinations of partners.

■ Consider the request's chances for success in terms of the following factors: Are one or both of the proposed job sharers current employees? Does their previous work record indicate that they could be successful in a job sharing arrangement? Look for compatible performance records. Since these employees will need

Table 5-7.   Sample checklist for a job sharing proposal.

Checklist for a Job Sharing Proposal	
Key Issues to be Covered in the Proposal	Notes
☐ *Advantages to the employer if the job is restructured:* for example, improved scheduling, better coverage, retention of a trained employee.	
☐ *Strengths of the particular team:* for example, combined experience, additional skills, complementary personalities.	
☐ *Proposed work plan:* how tasks and responsibilities will be divided.	
☐ *Proposed schedule:* how work time will be divided.	
☐ *Communication techniques:* how the partners will communicate with each other, with their supervisor, and with co-workers (such as a notebook, a posted schedule, or taped messages).	
☐ *Responsibilities for continuity:* for example, exchanging time, coverage during partner absence or illness, partner turnover.	
☐ *Other issues:* any cost benefits that you can identify, responses to particular concerns that your supervisor might have, examples of similar or comparable companies where job sharing has been used. Supporting information may be attached.	

to work together as a team, they should have demonstrated good interpersonal and communications skills. Does their proposal look as if they have thought through the problems of sharing this job? Have they put together a good plan for scheduling, communication, cooperation, and so forth? Are they willing to be flexible and responsible in terms of their time commitments so that the conti-

(Text continues on page 182.)

Table 5-8. Media specialist position restructured by task.

Task Analysis	1. Interchangeable structure for partners with similar skills		2. Equal division of responsibilities for partners with dissimilar skills		3. Unequal division of responsibilities for partners with significantly different levels of skills and experience	
	Person A	Person B	Person A	Person B	Person A	Person B
Physical						
Drafting	x	x	x		x	
Layout	x	x		x	x	
Maintaining audiovisual equipment	x	x	x			x
Maintaining media resource file	x	x		x		x
Mental	Person A	Person B	Person A	Person B	Person A	Person B
Responsibility for completion of tasks	x	x	x	x	x	
Developing and implementing annual media budget	x	x		x	x	
Designing and editing media tools	x	x	x		x	
Writing articles, news releases	x	x		x	x	x
Designing ads for community publications	x	x	x			x
Interpersonal	Person A	Person B	Person A	Person B	Person A	Person B
Arranging appearances of guests on media, public affairs programs	x	x	x		x	
Training and supervising media interns	x	x		x	x	
Organizing press conferences	x	x	x		x	
Submitting weekly reports to program manager	x	x		x		x

SOURCE: Adapted from *Incorporating Sharers* (San Francisco: New Ways to Work, 1981), 14–15.

Figure 5-5. Sample scheduling options for media specialist position restructured by task.

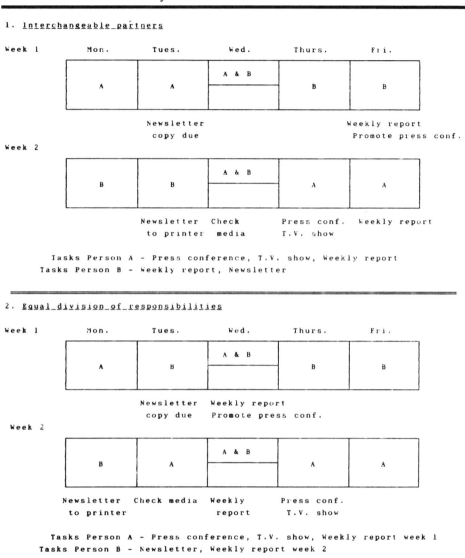

1. Interchangeable partners

Week 1

	Mon.	Tues.	Wed.	Thurs.	Fri.
	A	A	A & B	B	B

Newsletter copy due   Weekly report Promote press conf.

Week 2

	Mon.	Tues.	Wed.	Thurs.	Fri.
	B	B	A & B	A	A

Newsletter Check   Press conf. Weekly report
to printer media   T.V. show

Tasks Person A - Press conference, T.V. show, Weekly report
Tasks Person B - Weekly report, Newsletter

2. Equal division of responsibilities

Week 1

	Mon.	Tues.	Wed.	Thurs.	Fri.
	A	B	A & B	B	B

Newsletter Weekly report
copy due   Promote press conf.

Week 2

	Mon.	Tues.	Wed.	Thurs.	Fri.
	B	A	A & B	A	A

Newsletter Check media Weekly   Press conf.
to printer   report   T.V. show

Tasks Person A - Press conference, T.V. show, Weekly report week 1
Tasks Person B - Newsletter, Weekly report week 2

SOURCE: Adapted from *Incorporating Sharers* (San Francisco: New Ways to Work, 1981), 17.

(Continued)

Figure 5-5.   *(continued)*

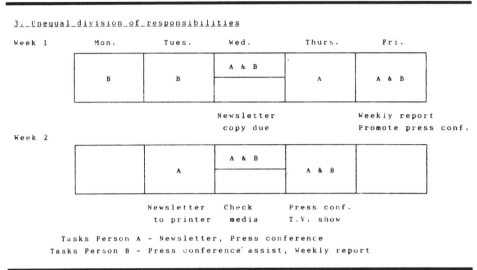

nuity of the job will be ensured? Does this arrangement offer advantages to the organization (such as improved scheduling, retention of good employees, implementation of affirmative action goals, cost reduction resulting from differences in salary scale, or availability of a greater range of skills)? Are there ways in which the proposal could be improved?

If the request is one you feel disposed to authorize, but there are changes you would like to make in some part of the proposed arrangement, meet with the employee(s) to discuss modifying the request.

Once you have made a decision to approve or disapprove the request, notify the employee(s) and other appropriate parties (supervisor, union representative, personnel department), stating your recommendation and your reasons for arriving at the decision. If the request to job share has been denied, possible alternatives might be suggested.

Information Materials for Employees.   Potential sharers must have guidelines on the following issues:

■ *Eligibility.* Are there limitations on who can job share? Can outside applicants be considered as partners? Are any job classifications excluded?

■ *Process*. What must an interested employee do to participate in the program? Information about application procedures, proposal development (see Table 5-7), forming partnerships, and so forth should be readily available to employees. What, if any, process has the organization developed for helping employees find job sharing partners internally? (Some employers simply set up a file box in the personnel office where prospective sharers fill out information and can self-refer to potential partners. Others have developed computerized referral systems.)

■ *Contingency planning*. Under this heading come such questions as: How can a job sharing arrangement be reversed? How can schedules be renegotiated? Can partners trade time, and to what extent?

Figure 5-6 is a sample description of a job sharing program. A program description such as this can serve as a useful resource for managers and supervisors as well as for interested employees.

Announce the Program

Once the program has been designed and the policy approved, the job sharing option should be announced to managers, supervisors, and employees.

Promote the Program

If the job sharing program is to be used, however, and not just gather dust in the company's policy and procedure manual, it must be actively promoted. And because this working arrangement is new, its use must be promoted both to employees and to managerial and supervisory personnel. This can be done in a variety of ways— for example, through newsletter stories about successful teams, in management directives, or on company bulletin boards.

The need to promote the program actively is one reason why the company should name a coordinator with ongoing responsibility for supervising the job sharing program and encouraging its use.

Evaluate the Program

After the program has been in place for from six to twelve months, it should be evaluated. This can be done by surveying, or holding focus groups with, all or some of the job sharers' supervisors and the job sharing employees themselves to obtain their reactions to the existing program and suggestions for improvements. Some key

(*Text continues on page 186.*)

Figure 5-6.   Sample program description: job sharing.

POLICY & PROCEDURE MANUAL

PAGE: 5270
INDEX TITLE   Human Resources

SUBJECT: Job Sharing
DATE: February 1987

Policy

Recognizing the potential positive impact on recruiting, retention, attendance, productivity, and morale job sharing can offer, Presbyterian-University Hospital encourages
its application where appropriate. This policy describes the characteristics of "job
sharing" and the effect on benefits of those employed in this manner.

Definition

Job sharing involves two employees who would otherwise be classified as regular
part-time in policy #5320, who each work at least "half time" in the same position,
and who agree to combine their hours of employment to total those of a regular full-
time employee (80 hours per pay period). The agreement, in writing, on Form 1083-
4240-1186, which is attached to and part of this policy, indicates that these employees will arrange their own work schedule and will cover for each other's nonwork
days whenever possible, even on short notice, in order to staff a regularly scheduled
full-time position. (However, job sharing partners are not required to work full-time to
cover for an absence that exceeds three weeks.) Job sharing partners may choose
to work portions of a day, such as A.M. and P.M., or may work alternating days,
weeks, or months, as approved by the department head.

Selection

The job sharing position, when vacant, will be posted and filled in accordance with
Selection Policy #5200. However, candidates will additionally be evaluated for their
compatibility to function as a team.

Two part-time positions, totaling 80 hours per pay period, that are occupied may be
combined to a full-time shared position, without posting, at the discretion of the
department head. These situations should be reviewed by the Senior Vice President,
Employee Relations, approved by the Administrative Representative, and follow the
other provisions of this policy.

SOURCE: Roland Rogers, Director, Division of Human Resources, Presbyterian-
University Hospital (Dec. 1986). Used by permission.

Pay and Benefit Differences

Both job sharing partners will be paid in accordance with the pay grade and salary ranges established for the position they share, even though duties may vary slightly.

Each job sharing partner will receive an individual rate of pay and performance evaluation based on experience and performance in accordance with policy #5420, Compensation Program.

As defined in policy #5320, a regular part-time employee is one who is employed on a basis of 16 or more hours, but less than 40 hours, per week. Policy #5700, Benefit Programs, indicates that *not* all benefit programs are available to regular part-time employees. Those employed on a job sharing basis are eligible for the following additional benefits at half the level available to full-time employees:

> Paid holidays (at 4 hours' pay), including personal holidays (16 hours total)
> Life insurance (1,040 hours times hourly base rate; $7,500 minimum)
> Health insurance, including major medical (employee pays 50% of premium)
> Dental insurance (employee pays 50% of individual premium)

JOB SHARING AGREEMENT

The undersigned employees and department head agree to enter into a job sharing arrangement for the position of _____ in _____ department under the following conditions:

1. The scheduled hours (shift) and days of the week of the position are: _____

_____

2. These employees will arrange their own work schedule to provide continuous coverage for the position. Should either employee require time off for paid or unpaid absence—such as sick leave, personal holiday, or vacation—the other employee will cover for that absence, even upon short notice, whenever possible. However, coverage is not required for absence beyond three weeks.

3. a. Methods of communication to be used by participants to coordinate the duties of the position: _____

_____

_____

b. Initial schedule arrangements: _____

_____

_____

(Continued)

Figure 5-6. *(continued)*

---

   c. Accommodations expected on short-term notice: _____

      _____

      _____

4. This agreement may be terminated by either employee or by the department head on four weeks' written notice to all parties. Reasons would include termination of employment, scheduling difficulties, inflexible partner, etc.

   Should a suitable replacement not be found for a terminating partner within a reasonable period (four or more weeks of active recruitment), the remaining partner may choose to work on a regular full-time basis, may resign the job shared position, or may transfer to regular part-time status if suitable vacancies exist at that time.

Employee [*signature*]	Date	Employee [*signature*]	Date
Senior Vice President Employee Relations	Date	Department Head	Date

Form 1083-4240-1186

---

questions might be: How are the processes working? What kinds of problems have been identified? What additional resources are needed?

Fine-Tune the Program

The information obtained during the evaluation should be used to fine-tune the job sharing program. This is a process that should be repeated periodically during the first five years of the program in order to apply generally what individual managers, supervisors, and sharers have learned.

Table 5-9 will give you an idea of some of the problems you can expect to find after a job sharing program has been in effect for a period of time and what types of solutions have proved effective. A number of the problem indicators and possible solutions shown in Table 4-7 for regular part-time employees are also applicable to the job sharing experience.

Table 5-9. Examples of job sharing problems and their solutions.

Problem indicators	Possible solutions
Coverage is too heavy during slow periods and insufficient during peak activity.	Review work scheduling; determine whether work flow patterns should or can be changed. Revise employee schedules, taking the unit's peak work load into consideration.
Job sharers don't have time to coordinate.	Arrange the schedule so job sharers have overlapping time. Consider increasing emphasis on logs, memos, and other written communication.
It is hard to know who is in. Job sharers have been informally swapping time.	Maintain a calendar with the employees' schedules. Have employees swap times only with your knowledge and approval.
One job sharer appears to be pulling more weight than the other.	Adjust assignments if one job sharer is getting higher-priority assignments. Review job responsibilities with each job sharer; summarize responsibilities in writing. See whether changes would improve the less-dominant job sharer's skills in handling the assignments.
One job sharer appears to complete assignments too slowly.	Handle as for a full-time employee. Discuss assignments and establish reasonable deadlines. Review what part of the assignment each job sharer is responsible for. See whether one job sharer's delays are causing the other to miss deadlines. Distribute the work differently.
One job sharer spends time chatting with co-workers and socializing. The other job sharer is resentful.	Discuss behavior standards and expectations. Sometimes schedule arrangements cause unequal time for socializing. For example, if one job sharer works full days and has a lunch break while the other works half-days with no lunch break, the socializing time is inequitable. Meet with the job sharing team to work out differences.
One job sharer feels that the other is getting the choice, more interesting assignments.	Considering each person's strengths and weaknesses, balance work assignments fairly. Reward or praise job sharers equally for equal performance. Ask the job sharers to talk over their differences and recommend their own solution.

SOURCE: Adapted with permission from *Part-Time Schedules: A Guide for NYS Supervisors and Managers* (Albany: N.Y. State Dept. of Civil Service, 1985), 31–32.

Special Considerations for Supervisors and Managers

Job sharing is still a new employment option in most organizations. For supervisors, it generally represents a departure from normal procedures and requires the development of some new attitudes and management skills in the following key areas:

■ *Supervisory support.* The most critical factor in the successful use of job sharing is the support of the immediate supervisor. If the supervisor has been involved in, or was responsible for, the decision to authorize the job sharing arrangement, then initial support can be assumed, and positive experience with job sharing will increase the supervisor's support for future shared arrangements.

■ *Communication.* During the first three months of the job sharing arrangement, establishing good habits of communication (between the sharers, between the sharers and their supervisor, and between the sharers and their co-workers) will be a primary objective and is an area that the supervisor should be sensitive to. Logs and posted schedules are essential tools. If problems arise, they should be dealt with immediately, before negative feelings—particularly on the part of co-workers, clients, or other departments—develop.

■ *The balance in the sharers' partnership.* The potential for an imbalance in the sharers' partnership is another important issue to which the supervisor must be sensitive. One partner may start to become dominant, especially if the sharing was initiated by an employee who formerly held the job full-time. This kind of imbalance is easier to correct at the outset than if it becomes an established way of relating.

■ *Duplication of effort.* Excessive overlap is something to watch out for. Some job sharing employees, anxious to share equally and enjoying each other's company and support, experience difficulty in letting go of the need to be at every meeting and to participate in all major functions associated with the position. They lose sight of the fact that such overlapping coverage will limit what they are able to accomplish.

■ *Division of work.* When two people share the responsibilities of one full-time job, the tasks can be split between the two of them in several different ways (as was illustrated earlier in Table 5-8 and Figure 5-5):

- The sharers can be jointly responsible for the entire job. In this case, the employees are considered interchangeable, and there is no division of any of the components of the work. Production-line workers and stenographers are examples of the types of employees who are expected to handle every part of the job while they are there.
- The sharers can be independently responsible for portions of the job. The sharers may cover phone calls and handle urgent situations for each other, but basically their responsibilities are autonomous. This model works well if the job can be divided by caseload or client base, function, or project assignments.
- The sharers can have some independent and some joint responsibilities. In a secretarial team, one partner may have stronger numerical skills, while the other is a better writer. Ideally, the division of work should reflect particular strengths or differences of experience.

- *Evaluating sharers.* Whatever the basis for the division of tasks, however, evaluations usually take place on two levels: individual performance and the ability to work as a member of a job sharing team. Since no two people are alike, supervisors should recognize that sharers may progress at different rates. One partner may merit a salary increase while the other partner does not. As with the case of prorated salary scales, the inherent fairness of evaluating the sharers individually is generally evident and should not be considered a problem in itself. If the team has become unbalanced, an effective and perceptive evaluation may provide an incentive to improve the sharing dynamic.

- *Replacement of partners when a sharer wishes to end the job-sharing arrangement.* Many supervisors worry about the complications that could result from incompatibility of job sharing partners or a decision by one sharer to end the partnership because he or she wants to go back to a full-time position within the company or even leave the company. As noted earlier, procedures for such contingencies should be discussed and decided upon in advance wherever possible. For example, many employers negotiate an agreement that if one partner decides to withdraw from the arrangement, the remaining partner will fill in to the extent possible until a replacement can be found. This ensures continuity and is one of the organizational advantages of job sharing that employers report. The same principle holds true if one partner proves to be incompetent or if the two partners prove to be incompatible.

Most employers have found that replacing partners is not difficult and that employees who want to job share can work with a variety of types of partners. Some organizations encourage the remaining employee to find a new partner, while others prefer to use regular recruitment channels. In the latter case, it is very important, at some stage, to involve the remaining sharer in the process of interviewing for a new partner.

■ *Developing familiarity with existing job sharing arrangements.* If a supervisor is moved into a job where job sharers are included among his or her subordinates, the situation may require some special attention, particularly if the supervisor has had no previous experience with managing job sharers. It will be important for the new supervisor to familiarize himself or herself with the background and current status of the arrangement. This should include such activities as reviewing the organization's policy on job sharing; looking at any written records covering each job sharing pair, such as the initial job sharing proposals or letters of understanding from the previous supervisor; and clarifying the current schedule (fixed hours, seasonal schedule changes, holiday arrangements, and so on) of each member of the job sharing team.

It will be important, too, for the supervisor to talk with each of the teams about the strengths and shortcomings of the arrangement as well as expectations and previous agreements; in his or her initial meetings with the teams, the supervisor should also clarify assignments and performance criteria and discuss ways to keep the channels of communication open.

Summary

The use of job sharing, in which a single full-time position is jointly held by two part-timers, has increased steadily as a means of permitting less than full-time work in positions that cannot be handled on a part-time basis. The essence of the concept is that the job itself in fact requires a full-time commitment, with the associated conditions of employment (salary, fringe benefits, and so on) remaining the same as for a full-timer but divided between the two holders of the position. Job sharing is considered a useful tool if an organization wants to stem the loss of valued employees, improve scheduling, ensure continuity, and broaden the range of skills and experience in a particular position. By carefully selecting the members of certain job sharing teams, an organization can also achieve objectives in the area of human resources management.

Improvements in scheduling and continuity are regarded as a major advantage of job sharing. Having two employees rather than one permits the organization to set up creative schedules in which the employees work overlapping hours, work simultaneously at two different sites, or work a wide span of hours broken by a gap—schedules that respond to the needs of the work itself rather than being dictated by the constraints of a rigid 9–5 schedule. The presence of two employees also provides the organization with a built-in, trained substitute who can maintain the work flow during the absence of either job sharer.

Occasionally, differences in experience, temperament, and the nature and level of skills will become evident when two employees share a single position. Rather than regarding such differences as a drawback of job sharing, the savvy supervisor will take maximum advantage of them by helping the sharers divide up the work and the schedule in ways that focus on each job sharer's strengths and abilities. By pooling the talents of two employees, each of whom is working in the areas of his or her primary capabilities, the organization often finds itself getting more, and better quality, work for its money than it can from a single employee.

Job sharing's role in the achievement of human resources objectives is, as noted, another positive feature of this arrangement. Many companies set up job sharing teams with a certain very specific outcome in mind. The two part-timers sharing the position may both be phasing in to retirement; one may be training his or her replacement, perhaps in preparation for retirement or in preparation for advancement to a higher-level position; one may be training half-time at a higher level at which a full-time job opening has not yet become available. The possibilities in this area are limited only by the imagination of the company's management.

In weighing the advantages and disadvantages of using job sharing, the employer will have to take a detailed look at the costs associated with this option. Some surprises may be in store, since the organization often finds that savings in base salary result when part of a position is filled by an employee who qualifies for a lower salary range, and the use of overtime may drop sharply. When the cost of group health insurance is shared by the company and the part-time employees and other benefits are prorated, job sharing will not double, or even substantially increase, the organization's

benefits costs. In fact, the organization sometimes reduces its benefit outlay when part-timers covered by a spouse's policy decline
health insurance coverage. Job sharing will increase the costs associated with administrative overhead somewhat because the number
of employees will rise, but the cost of new-hire administration and
training will increase only if the implementation of this arrangement
requires hiring new employees or training one or both job sharers.
If the job sharers' schedules are set up to enable them both to use
the same space and equipment, no extra expense in this area is
incurred. And in fact, the decrease in absenteeism and turnover
generally associated with the use of job sharing often offsets whatever moderate cost increases may be involved.

The employer would do well to look beyond the (often considerable) advantages of restructuring individual positions to a job
sharing mode and examine the broader potential advantages to the
organization of adopting a program approach—offering the option
in categories of positions or companywide. Employers that opt for
a more widespread use of job sharing usually do so because this
approach will enable them to multiply the savings that can be
achieved when individual positions are shared and/or solve chronic
problems (such as reducing absenteeism in certain job categories,
improving recruitment efforts, retaining valued employees, facilitating continuing education, and allowing senior employees to cut
back their work hours prior to retirement).

The attitudes of unions, supervisors, and employees play a
significant role in an employer's decision about the use of job
sharing. Since shared jobs are regarded as full-status positions that
happen to be worked by part-time employees, unions are usually
more receptive to this scheduling alternative than they are to other
forms of part-time, provided the sharers are protected against
inequities that could creep into the arrangement. Supervisors may
initially be skeptical about job sharing but tend to support the
option once they have had successful experience with it. Most
employees regard the introduction of job sharing favorably, but care
must be taken to see that the practice is handled both efficiently
and equitably. If certain job sharing teams fail to communicate well
with co-workers or the sharers appear to be receiving favored
treatment, the organization could lose employee support for job
sharing.

In implementing job sharing, a company must focus on generating understanding of, and support for, this work-time alternative;
removing any organizational barriers that may discourage the use

of job sharing; defining a comprehensive new policy on its use; developing resource materials that can help both supervisors and employees systematically consider the entire range of relevant factors before they enter into a job-sharing arrangement; promoting the use of job sharing once the program is in place; and modifying the program on an ongoing basis to eliminate problems that have been noted by the involved parties and incorporate suggested improvements.

Successful implementation of a job sharing program will require the knowledgeable and skilled participation of an organization's supervisory personnel. Supervisors have to be particularly sensitive to the following types of issues: Sharers must communicate effectively, both with each other and with their fellow employees, including the supervisor; one sharer should not become dominant, throwing the partnership out of balance; the two partners must not duplicate each other's efforts; the sharers' responsibilities should be allocated so as to focus on their respective strengths; they have to be evaluated both on their individual accomplishments and on their ability to function as part of a job sharing team; and provisions must be in place to guarantee continuity of work when an employee leaves a shared position.

The organizational advantages of permitting job sharing as a companywide option can be considerable for the employer that has examined this scheduling arrangement closely, selected it for the right reasons, and planned its use with care.

ORGANIZATIONAL EXPERIENCE WITH JOB SHARING

Pella Corporation

Description: Pella Corporation, a Midwestern manufacturer of Pella windows and patio doors, employs approximately 2,500 people. In addition to its job sharing program, the company offers a compressed workweek and has used work sharing as an alternative to layoffs.

Reason for Using Job Sharing: Job sharing was originally tried in 1977 in response to an employee's request. Management was interested in its potential for reducing absenteeism and overstaffing on the production line.

Implementation Process: The job sharing program is open only to current full-time employees in three of the company's production-line and clerical job classifications. Eligible employees are responsible for finding their own partners; the company serves a clearinghouse function by providing a mechanism for potential job sharers to list their names and self-refer to possible partners. The sharers work out their own schedules; partial days are not allowed, however, because of the disruption they would cause in a production-line setting. Sharers are responsible for covering their own absences. Anyone joining the program must remain in it for six months; anyone dropping from the program cannot rejoin for one year.

Impact to Date: According to the company, absenteeism immediately improved by 81 percent in test group A and 31 percent in test group B. (The latter included a six-month stretch of full-time work.) The need to overstaff in order to compensate for absenteeism was eliminated, and overtime was reduced. Also, the supervisor no longer had to take responsibility for finding replacements for absent production-line workers.

Health and dental insurance costs were doubled because the company chose to provide full benefits to job sharers.

The program is very popular with both employees and supervisors.

SOURCE: Materials developed by the Pella Corporation (formerly Rolscreen Company), Pella, Iowa, to describe the organization's job sharing program

(1982); *Analyzing the Cost* (San Francisco: New Ways to Work, 1981), 8; conversation with Pella Corporation personnel staff (1993).

Northeast Utilities

Description: A utilities company headquartered in Hartford, Connecticut, with 10,000 employees.

Reason for Using Job Sharing: The organization initially used job sharing as a way to attract and retain applicants for positions as customer representatives. Later, its use was expanded in order to retain current employees who were leaving because of conflicts between forty-hour jobs and family responsibilities.

Implementation Process: The management committee authorized a job sharing pilot project in December 1986. A maximum of fifty pairs were set up for testing purposes. All Northeast Utilities employees are eligible to apply, with the exception of workers covered by union contracts and employees in supervisory or managerial positions requiring work leadership.

Jobs may be split in any way agreed upon by the sharers and their supervisor. A common schedule has been three days on and two off one week, followed by two days on and three off the next. Other possible arrangements include two and one half days weekly; alternate days, weeks, or months; or half-days. Employees are encouraged to find their own partners, but if they cannot, the job is posted. If no in-house applicant can be found, the company advertises outside the organization.

Sharers working twenty hours a week or more receive full health insurance benefits for themselves but not for their dependents. They may purchase dependent coverage at group rates, however. Other benefits are prorated.

Impact to Date: By offering job sharing, the company succeeded in attracting a large pool of applicants who were interested in part-time employment. In addition, the company cites increased productivity, reduced use of sick leave and personal time, reduced turnover, and improved employee morale.

Northeast Utilities also notes that job sharing cuts down on the need for temporary help, since sharers may choose to work full-time when their partners are sick or on vacation. It has also reduced the need for overtime.

Northeast Utilities' management development analyst, Louise Klaber, credits the support of the CEO and the human resources manager for the program's inception. Initial acceptance was difficult and took a long time. She also noted that having a written contract is important because it reassures supervisors that they will not lose control of the situation.

SOURCE: "Benefits of Job Sharing," *Human Resource Management News* (July 25, 1987): 2; *The National Report on Work and Family,* special report no. 5 (Washington, D.C.: Buraff Publications, May 1988), 23.

Steelcase

Description: Steelcase is located in Grand Rapids, Michigan, and is the world's largest manufacturer of office furniture and equipment. It employs 14,000 people in the United States.

Reason for Using Job Sharing: Job sharing was first tried at Steelcase when two full-time pricers asked to reduce their hours. After six months the experiment was evaluated. Benefits to Steelcase were lowered absenteeism and turnover, positive impact on affirmative action, possibilities for peak period coverage, ability to retain valued employees, the availability of a wider range of skills in the position, higher morale and more energy from "fresher" employees, the ability to offer new options to older employees, and full-time job coverage even during vacations and illnesses.

Implementation Process: Job sharers must have at least one year of full-time service before they can submit a request to reduce their workload. Positions with supervisory and/or budgetary responsibilities are not eligible for job sharing. Prospective job sharers must first get their department management's permission to apply for job sharing. The personnel office then helps arrange a team by posting the matching half of the position. The sharer's schedule is worked out with the position's supervisor, along with plans for communication between the partners and agreements about backup and days off. Sharers are expected to cover for each other during vacations and, when possible, during absences for illness. Although there is a great deal of flexibility about what kind of schedule is acceptable, hourly workers are not allowed to work half days but any combination of full days is permissible. One of the most popular is seven days on and seven days off, with the first day being a Wednesday. This eliminates the problem of Monday holidays going primarily to one partner. Another widely used schedule is to alternate two days one week, three days the next.

Impact to Date: Initially, most of the job sharers at Steelcase were exempt employees in clerical positions. In 1988, Steelcase expanded job sharing to all its employees, including 6,500 production personnel.

In order to reconcile the extra cost of providing full fringe benefits for each sharer, Steelcase decided to prorate the cost of fringe benefits for sharers, with one exception—sharers would receive two-thirds of the educational benefits that full-time employees receive.

The company believes that these programs provide many benefits for both the employees and the organization. The employees have the freedom to pursue personal/family goals and the ability to remain in the workforce, continue earning income, continue to have access to company-provided benefits on a modified basis, and maintain the social aspects of work. Steelcase benefits from improved employee morale, decreased absenteeism, increased productivity, and better job coverage.

SOURCE: Marti O'Brien and Peter Jeff of Steelcase, Inc., Grand Rapids, Michigan. *Business Link,* 4, no. 2. *Working Mothers Magazine,* October 1990. Conversation with Steelcase HR staff, January 1994.

CHAPTER 6

Phased and Partial Retirement

Phased retirement is a way for individuals to retire gradually by reducing their full-time employment commitment over a set period of years. Partial retirement is a part-time employment arrangement for senior employees in which salary may or may not be combined with partial retirement income. It has no defined time limitation.

In 1978, management expert Peter Drucker described phased and partial retirement as "the central social issue in the United States." His was a voice expressing early concern that we develop policies that "encourage people to stay on the job and remain economically productive, rather than encourage them to retire early so that there is more room at the top."[1]

Several issues continue to make Drucker's words relevant today. The first is the cost of recent downsizing programs that focus on promoting the early retirement of senior employees. Providing pensions and health insurance for retirees has been described as a "time bomb" for many companies. The second compelling reason is the specter of employee shortages by the year 2000. Older workers, who often have difficult-to-replace skills and experience, may become a sought-after human resource in the next decade. Making room for young and mid-career workers continues to be a problem in many companies. Allowing seniors to reduce work time can create more options for younger employees, too.

Several related trends make phased and partial employment of seniors an attractive management option. They include:

■ *The trend toward earlier and earlier retirement.* In 1986, 84 percent of all employees who retired from large companies with pension plans did so before they were 65, compared to only 62 percent in 1978.[2] As the baby-boomers age, encouraging older workers to retain at least a partial attachment to the labor force broadens both the employers' and the workers' options as economic and social factors change.

■ *Projected skills shortages.* In the next decade U.S. employers will face not only a shrinking labor force but also one that is deficient in both basic and specialized skills. Retaining the skills and experience of senior employees can mitigate the impact of these shortages.

■ *Older workers' interest in staying in the workforce longer and in working part-time.* A poll by The Travelers Insurance Company showed that 43 percent of that organization's sixty-two- to sixty-five-year-old employees planned to continue working past age 65, and 85 percent of the survey respondents who were 55 or older wanted part-time jobs.[3] A 1989 Louis Harris survey of men 55–64 and women 50–59 estimated that "significant numbers of persons that age would like to continue working, provided the jobs were tailored to their needs."[4]

■ *The steady decrease in the ratio of employed workers to retirees and their dependents.* In 1935, when Social Security was initiated, the ratio was nine to one. In 1978, it was four to one. Current employment policies that encourage earlier and earlier retirement are narrowing the gap even further. It is projected that by 2025, the ratio will be close to three to one.[5] A shift to later or partial retirement would ease the increasing demands on both private and public pension funds. Current Social Security regulations already are poised for a shift to older retirement. By 2022 they will have raised the retirement age for receiving full benefits to 67. In addition, congressional discussions about constraining entitlements may lead to even speedier change in this area.[6]

Origins of Phased and Partial Retirement Programs

In the early 1970s, the idea of phased retirement began to be discussed and then initiated in Europe. For the most part, the impetus for these programs in Great Britain, Germany, France, and Belgium came from top-level management within individual companies. The notable exception to this pattern is Sweden, where legislation allows eligible workers nationwide to reduce their schedule in the years preceding their eligibility for retirement and to receive a stipend that offsets the wages lost through cutting back on paid work time. The reasons for the emergence of phased retirement in Europe are complex, having to do with such factors as demographics, the introduction of new technology, and changes in attitudes about work and leisure. They were, however, basically grounded in a concern for the welfare of older workers and a desire to alleviate the negative impact of abrupt, full retirement.

In the United States, private-sector phased retirement began to attract employers' attention for some of the same reasons, but interest in it was slower to take hold. In 1978, amendments to the Age Discrimination in Employment Act made most compulsory retirement before age 70 illegal. In 1987, new legislation outlawed mandatory retirement and, effective in 1988, compelled employers to continue contributing to pension plans for workers over age 65.

With the baby-boom generation moving into the workforce and women working in unprecedented numbers, some companies began to experiment with new part-time and phased retirement options for their senior employees. (Table 6-1 shows some of the alternatives that are now available to older workers.) While the primary objective in most cases was to improve possibilities for the advancement of younger workers, accommodating the needs of senior employees was also a goal.

Who Uses Phased and Partial Retirement?

An early user of phased retirement was the state of California. In 1974, it passed legislation enacting the "Reduced Work Load Program" for the members of the State Teachers' Retirement System. This program allows certain teachers nearing retirement age the option of reducing their hours of employment as a means of phasing in their retirement. In order to protect the teachers' retirement income and fund the program, the legislation stipulated that "although the program involves a salary reduction corresponding to the reduced employment, it allows participants to continue earning credits for retirement benefits at the same rate as full-time employees." Teachers can choose to continue paying into the retirement fund as though they were working full-time, and the district employing them contributes on the same basis. The objectives of this innovative California program are twofold: (1) to ease the financial

Table 6-1. Work options available to employees 50–64 years of age and 65 years or older, by size of employer.

Working Patterns	250–300		301–500		501–1,000		1,000+		Total	
	50–64	65+	50–64	65+	50–64	65+	50–64	65+	50–64	65+
Flexible schedule of less than 40 hrs/wk	30.5%	41.1%	37.0%	45.8%	38.7%	41.7%	36.4%	38.8%	36.0%	42.2%
Regularly scheduled part-time	51.7	50.7	53.3	59.5	64.1	68.7	64.2	61.1	58.1	60.5
Seasonal or part year	33.6	21.2	35.1	36.2	32.4	30.6	41.8	40.2	35.9	33.3
Gradual retirement	25.8	24.3	19.5	18.4	17.2	14.9	19.4	19.0	20.2	18.8
Possibility of full-time	a*	94.4	a	95.8	a	89.8	a	97.1	a	94.5
Job sharing	14.6	15.7	13.6	16.9	12.4	13.6	22.4	20.5	15.7	16.9
Job transfers	67.7	59.4	78.9	75.7	78.4	67.8	87.1	77.5	78.6	71.5
Consulting	28.7	33.3	37.9	39.2	35.6	34.5	56.2	56.3	40.1	41.6
Flextime	33.6	a	33.5	a	27.6	a	39.0	a	33.6	a

*Question not asked.

SOURCE: Malcolm J. Morrison, *The Transition to Retirement: The Employee's Perspective* (Bureau of Social Science Research, Inc., 1985).

and psychological trauma of retirement for senior teachers and (2) to permit the earlier employment of new teachers.[7] A later section of this chapter includes a profile providing further details about the "Reduced Work Load Program."

In 1980 the faculty members of the state's university system were offered a phased retirement option. This program, in addition to offering university employees sixty years or older who have twenty or more years of university service the option of working part-time and phasing into retirement, also allows its participants to supplement their reduced salary base with outside earned income and/or with payments from the University of California Retirement System.

In 1984, a third program, the Partial Service Retirement program, became effective. Employees who are eligible for participation include all state miscellaneous employees sixty-two years or older who have a minimum of five years of credit in the Public Employees' Retirement System (PERS). Workers must reduce their work time by at least 20 percent but not more than 60 percent. Participants may elect to receive a partial retirement allowance while they are working on a reduced schedule. Unlike most phased retirement programs, they may also opt to return to a full-time schedule at a future date. If they do withdraw from the program, however, they may not reapply for partial retirement for five years. (A brochure describing this program in more detail is shown in Figure 6-4.)

More recently, private-sector companies have also begun to introduce alternative employment options for their older workers—some in response to employee needs, others in reaction to *Workforce 2000* projections of worker shortages that are expected to make themselves felt by the end of the 1990s. Aetna's "Graduate Retirement" plan allows employees to change from full-time to part-time status in the two or three years preceding retirement. Levi Strauss uses job sharing to help senior employees work part-time and has developed a phased retirement alternative as well. Polaroid Corporation announced a pioneering "Tapering-Off" program years ago in which older employees could reduce the number of their work hours gradually, cutting back on a daily, weekly, or monthly basis. Varian, a California Silicon Valley electronics company, set up a phased retirement program for employees who planned to retire within three years, were fifty-five years of age or older, and had five years of service with the organization.

Unfortunately, these programs are often underutilized because for several years, companies have concentrated on downsizing and proffering "golden handshakes" to senior employees. Renewed interest in phased retirement may result, however, from some of the negative experiences of companies that used aggressive early retirement programs. Many employers found that by selectively offering expensive retirement bonuses, they not only lost those employees they would have preferred to keep but also aroused resentment among workers who had to be content with the basic retirement plan. In addition to the morale issue, many companies are finding early retirement incentives overly expensive in the long run.

When Are Phased and Partial Retirement Most Appropriate?

Demographic trends indicate that by the year 2000, phased and partial retirement will be options that are increasingly important to all employers. The baby-boomers are aging and the number of young people coming into the labor market is decreasing. The median age of the workforce is expected to reach 39 by the year 2000, and the overall population growth will be the slowest in the country's history. Between 1990 and 2000 the number of 45- to 54-year-olds will increase 46 percent.[8]

Phased and partial retirement options are appropriate ways to encourage employees with hard-to-replace skills or experience to extend their work life. They are also ways to introduce more management options with which to deal with such issues as cost control, upward mobility, and employee burnout.

Pros and Cons of Phased and Partial Retirement

The advantages and disadvantages of phased and partial retirement programs can be asserted in terms of (1) human resources considerations and (2) cost considerations. Although the concepts of phased and partial retirement still represent a radical departure from the current policy of most private-sector organizations and experience with these options has thus far been limited, this section presents what we do know at this point about the reasons for the effects of offering reduced work-time programs for older employees.

A survey of Western European personnel executives, conducted by the International Management Association in the early 1980s, identified a range of problems involving both human resources considerations and cost considerations that were judged to be major obstacles to introducing alternative work patterns, including phased retirement. These obstacles, together with the percentage of respondents identifying each obstacle as a significant problem, are:

- Insufficient thought given to hidden extra costs (31.8 percent)
- Inadequate commitment by top management (31 percent)
- Insufficient thought given to solving production problems (30 percent)
- Union opposition (29.8 percent)
- Insufficient thought given to human problems and reactions (28.3 percent)
- Resistance by lower and middle management (28.1 percent)
- Lack of briefing and/or training to show employees how to take advantage of the greater flexibility (27 percent)
- Lack of support from the workforce (18 percent)

Human Resources Considerations

The introduction of phased and partial retirement options generally helps employers retain workers who have special skills or long-term experience with the company. Unfortunately, trends in recent years have been in the opposite direction. For example, Exxon Corporation lost nine of its top oil spill experts in 1986 as a result of early retirement incentive programs.[9] Incentives aside, if older employees are faced with a take-it-or-leave-it choice between retiring or continuing to work full-time, some would rather retire. Reducing their hours is an attractive alternative that can induce a number of these employees to extend their work life. Phased and partial retirement can also be a way to revitalize older workers who are suffering from burnout.

A program of part-time options for workers nearing retirement age can be a valuable adjunct to an organization's overall recruitment strategy. It enables the organization to attract skilled seniors who can bring greater balance to its pool of talent and experience.

By permitting senior employees to cut back their hours, a company increases the available opportunities for upward mobility and cross-training. Younger full-timers can assume responsibility for the vacated portion of these positions, which lets them phase in to a higher level and, in some instances, be trained by the incumbent.

It can also be a job creation strategy. At Rhone-Poulenc, the French chemicals multinational, a gradual early retirement program was extended as a job creation program. Older workers who volunteer for the program receive 80 percent of their last pay, plus a bonus, when they switch to part-time hours. Social Security payments for employees in the gradual early retirement program are paid based on a full-time salary. The program will allow the company to hire 1,000 young people, long-term unemployed, and workers returning to the job market during the next three years.

When an organization offers attractive part-time work alternatives that meet the needs not only of older workers but often of younger ones as well, the net effect tends to be a rise in employee morale.

Employers considering the feasibility of offering their employees a partial or phased retirement option must also address such issues as administrative and managerial barriers, workforce utilization, future personnel needs, and the social impact that this work-time alternative might have on the organization.

Phased or partial retirement can defuse the possibility of legal challenges to early retirement plans. Most lawsuits arising from early retirement programs are based on questions of age discrimination (were all employees offered the same retirement terms, or were younger ones offered a more lucrative package?) and whether or not the employees were coerced into accepting premature retirement. Not allowing employees enough time to decide about a proposed retirement package has been held to be a form of coercion in some cases. Successful age-discrimination suits result in higher award damages than any other kind of bias suit,[10] so it is worthwhile to examine policies and programs in terms of the kinds of treatment they afford senior employees.

Cost Considerations

As noted at the beginning of the section Pros and Cons of Phased and Partial Retirement, phased and partial retirement are relatively new options that have not yet been used by large numbers of organizations. Yet it is safe to say that these options, when properly introduced, can be very cost-effective. On what do we base this conclusion, given the admittedly limited experience with phased and partial retirement? This conclusion becomes evident when the cost implications of some early retirement programs—the most common alternative to phased or partial retirement—are examined.

From the 1950s until the present, early retirement has been an increasingly sought-after objective for both employers and employees. Most organizations that downsized their operations actively promoted early retirement. But it turns out that pushing employees into early retirement can prove very expensive for an employer. As the cost effects of these early retirement programs come to light, they should provide an incentive for wider use of such alternatives as phased and partial retirement.

The main costs associated with early retirement programs include the prolonged expense of financing various aspects of the program (such as health insurance for younger retirees and an increase in the pension benefits being paid out by the organization) and loss of experienced and talented workers.

Health insurance for retirees is a benefit that is proving to be tremendously costly for many companies. According to a *New York Times* article, "[M]any companies have been studying their situation and finding that their unfunded liabilities for retirees will equal or exceed the complete operating profit for the year. The numbers are generally in the same range as pension liability—but unfunded."[11]

The extent of the problem involving unfunded health insurance liability often corresponds to the age of the company. New organizations often have a more favorable ratio of active employees to retirees. In 1987 Digital Equipment Corporation, for example, had 110,000 active employees and only 1,000 retirees. Bethlehem Steel Corporation, on the other hand, had 37,500 employees and 70,000 retirees. In general, a Fortune 500 company has approximately three active employees to every retired one. For a typical company, the cost of funding health insurance for retirees is estimated at from 1 percent to 3 percent of payroll.[12]

A hidden cost cited by employers is that of providing full health benefits for younger retired workers who are not yet eligible for Medicare and who remain enrolled in the company's health insurance plan.

Other hidden costs include those associated with training junior employees who are unfamiliar with the duties formerly handled by early retirees and, sometimes, the cost of hiring former workers as consultants.

When benefits, pension payments, and incentive payments for early retirement are totaled, and increased expenses for training and consultants are considered, the sum constitutes a major problem for many organizations, even when the savings from payroll reductions are taken into account. In view of the high cost of early retirement programs, it would seem appropriate for employers to ask themselves what are the cost implications of *not* offering a phased and partial retirement alternative that could enable the organization to reduce its payroll without increasing its pension payout or incurring the expense of providing medical insurance to retirees who are no longer productive workers.

And finally, employers considering the advisability of permitting senior workers to reduce their hours should examine the issues of demographics and employee morale as they affect costs. A careful look at the demographics of an organization's labor force can give management an idea of how many employees, and in what job classifications, might take advantage of phased or partial retirement options. An improvement in employee morale and commitment was mentioned in the preceding subsection as a human resources consideration. Although employee morale is difficult to assess as a cost factor, its undeniable effect on productivity should not be overlooked. Phased or partial retirement is an option that many employees value, regardless of whether or not they are nearing retirement age.

Should Your Organization Try Phased Or Partial Retirement?

At this point, you will want to determine whether or not yours is one of the types of organizations mentioned earlier whose needs and characteristics make it a good candidate for trying a program of phased or partial retirement options.

This section contains two profiles (see Organizational Experience with Phased and Partial Retirement) that describe what happened when two employers instituted a program of reduced worktime alternatives for senior employees. These profiles will help you start considering some of the major issues involved in offering phased or partial retirement options and identify which issues are likely to play the biggest role in your own organization's decision about these options.

Now turn to the accompanying questionnaire (Table 6-2) listing the primary concerns that lead organizations to adopt phased or partial retirement programs. If, on this questionnaire, you find yourself repeatedly indicating that your organization does face the situations described, it's a good bet that some of these problems could be resolved through the introduction of less than full-time alternatives for older employees.

Assuming that your questionnaire results indicate that your organization should be seriously considering phased or partial

Table 6-2. Phased and partial retirement questionnaire.

Would Phased or Partial Retirement Benefit Your Organization?

	Yes	No
If your organization has offered early retirement incentives in the past, have there been negative consequences, such as employee resentment or underestimated costs?		
If your company has plans to restructure its workforce in the near future, will senior employees be one of the groups targeted and offered incentives to leave voluntarily?		
If there is a problem with upward mobility in some of your organization's job classifications, would it be alleviated by having some senior employees cut back their hours or share jobs?		
Have any older workers expressed an interest in reducing their schedules or phasing in to retirement?		
Do some of your company's senior employees have skills that would be difficult to replace when they retire?		
Do other organizations in your industry offer phased or partial retirement options?		
Would morale be generally enhanced if your company's employees knew that phased or partial retirement alternatives were available to them?		

retirement, the accompanying worksheet (Figure 6-1) can be used to list the problems you would hope to solve through the introduction of this type of option and what associated benefits and drawbacks might be expected.

Introducing Phased or Partial Retirement Options

The organization that wants to offer part-time alternatives for its older workers starts by gaining top management's support and then appointing both a task force, which will be charged with designing the program and gaining companywide support, and a project administrator. Key issues are explored and policy is established during the program design phase. Once policy is finalized, the organization develops resource materials for employees who are nearing early retirement age and for managers and supervisors. The program announcement must be followed by an active promotion effort, to overcome the existing bias in favor of early retirement.

Figure 6-1. Phased or partial retirement worksheet.

Assessing the Need for Phased or Partial Retirement

List the main reasons why you are considering introducing a phased or partial retirement option:

1. _____

_____

_____

2. _____

_____

_____

3. _____

_____

_____

4. _____

_____

_____

List what you see as the advantages and disadvantages of phased or partial retirement:

Pros: _____

_____

_____

_____

(Continued)

Figure 6-1. *(continued)*

_____

_____

_____

Cons: _____

_____

_____

_____

_____

_____

After the program has been in effect for a period of time, it is evaluated and modified as needed.

In this section, we will take a closer look at each of these steps in the program implementation process.

Gain Support for the Program

Since existing policy in most organizations has actively encouraged early retirement, changing this orientation will require strong support from top management. Long-held attitudes will need to be countered and present policy and processes changed in order to introduce part-time options for senior employees in a way that will elicit significant participation. Establishment of the program will require time, commitment, and leadership from all levels of management.

Once leadership from the top has been secured, a cross-functional task force that incorporates representatives from middle management, the relevant fiscal and administrative areas, and the human resources side of the organization should be established. This is a way to ensure broad input into the change process as well as gain support. The task force should be charged with reviewing current policy, conducting research on other similar companies' programs, developing a rationale for new policy and program objectives, recommending specific policy changes, and devising a process for implementation, evaluation, and fine-tuning.

Set Up the Program's Administration

The task force should appoint a project administrator, both to act as staff during the development of the program and to serve as a resource to managers and employees after its inception.

Design the Program

The process of designing a program of phased or partial retirement includes the following tasks: reviewing existing personnel policies to identify aspects of current policy that can hinder the use of part-time employees (for a discussion of such policy barriers, refer to the subsection entitled Design the Program in the section of Chapter 4 entitled Introducing or Expanding the Use of Regular Part-Time Employment); collecting information about the policies and programs of similar companies, both in the same industry and in other industries; and defining program objectives and developing policy that will support phased or partial retirement options. The definition of program objectives and the development of policy should concentrate on the following issues:

■ *Eligibility.* How many years of employment will be required for eligibility? At what age is an employee eligible? For maximum participation rates, a lower age is preferable, but it should be assumed that some of the younger employees who reduce their hours either will want to return to full-time schedules at some point or will be preparing themselves for a transition to a new employment area. This should be taken into consideration when setting program objectives and making policy decisions about duration of enrollment and reversibility.

■ *Effect on employee status and benefits.* The fringe benefits of major concern to senior employees are medical and dental insurance and pension. Policies that prorate the cost of inclusion in the group insurance plan protect those senior employees on a part-time schedule who are not yet eligible for Medicare.

In order to protect retirement income, some formula should be devised that allows the organization and senior employees on a reduced schedule to continue contributions to the pension fund as

if participants in the program were working full-time so that retirement income is not adversely affected. Such protection exists in the
state of California's "Reduced Work Load Program," described
earlier in the chapter. Teachers who qualify are allowed to cut back
their schedule, but they and their employing school districts continue paying into the retirement fund as though they were still
working full-time. An evaluation of the program by the state's
legislative analyst showed that the program resulted in net savings
to both the districts and the retirement fund.

The remaining status and benefit areas that will be affected are
the same as for other regular part-time employees and are discussed
in Chapter 4 in the sections entitled Pros and Cons of Regular Part-
Time (see the Cost Implications subsection) and Introducing or
Expanding the Use of Regular Part-Time Employment (see the
Design the Program subsection).

■ *Duration of enrollment.* An important question related to the
basic intent of the program is whether the company views it as
essentially a phased retirement or a partial retirement option. If the
intent is to minimize early retirement and encourage workforce
retention, then stipulating an earlier age with no limitations on
length of time in the program and a provision for reversibility may
be most appropriate. If, on the other hand, the program's objective
is to encourage retirement but cushion its impact, then length of
participation should be specified. Most programs limit participation
to one to five years before full retirement.

■ *Minimum and maximum time reductions.* Some programs define
the parameters of reduction; for example, in the California Public
Employees' Retirement System, "Work time may be reduced by at
least 20 percent but not more than 60 percent."[13] Others only
establish the maximum schedule reduction that will be allowed:
"Employees must work a minimum of twenty hours a week."

■ *Arrangements for work-time reduction.* The range of scheduling
choices within the various existing phased retirement programs
includes gradually shortened workdays or workweeks, regular part-
time and job sharing, and extra leave time, which can be taken in a
variety of ways, such as days, weeks, or months off. Ideally, the
supervisor and the participating employee should have as much
latitude as possible to design an appropriate schedule.

■ *Changes in work time.* Most programs allow enrolled employees to change their reduced schedule once a year, with their supervisor's approval. A common practice for employees who are phasing

into retirement is to increase the reduction each year until full retirement is reached.

■ *Reversibility*. Whether or not an employee can withdraw from the program and return to full-time work is a critical question. The answer is determined by what the employer hopes to achieve through the program. One program stipulates that employees who withdraw cannot reenroll for five years.

The program design issues just discussed are summarized in Table 6-3, which you can use to keep track of where you stand in addressing each issue.

Develop Resource Materials

A company that wants to introduce a program of phased or partial retirement options for its senior workers must develop resource materials both for managers and supervisors and for older employees. A program description, such as the one in Figure 6-2, can be a useful aid for managers and supervisors as well as for interested workers.

(Text continues on page 217.)

Table 6-3.   Program design checklist: phased or partial retirement.

Key Design Issues	Notes
Eliminating current barriers	
☐ Impact on retirement income	
Creating new policy	
☐ Eligibility	
☐ Effect on employee status and benefits	
☐ Duration of enrollment	
☐ Minimum and maximum time reductions	
☐ Arrangements for work-time reduction	
☐ Changes in work time	
☐ Reversibility	

Figure 6-2. Sample program description: phased retirement.

RETIREMENT TRANSITION PROGRAM

General

A voluntary Retirement Transition Program has been established for the benefit of regular employees who would like to work a reduced work week during the three year period immediately preceding their planned retirement. The objective of the program is to broaden employment alternatives available to employees and to provide interested employees a gradual transition from full employment to the usual reduced activity of retirement. During this period of reduced work schedule, employees will be permitted to continue their participation in company benefit plans.

Job Assignments

In some cases the reduced work schedule may require a change in job assignment. For example, under normal circumstances it would not be possible for a supervisor to continue in this role when working less than full time. Therefore, a condition of participation will be the availability of a job that can be performed by an employee working less than full time. Participation in the program will be limited to a maximum of three years.

Eligibility Requirements

The program will generally be available to any regular employee with a minimum of 5 years of service who will have attained a minimum age of 55 at the time participation in the program commences, and who plans to retire within three years. There may, however, be some employees occupying positions who, due to the nature of the work requirements, cannot be accommodated by this program.

Requests for Participation

Employees who wish to participate will indicate their interest by initiating a written request for voluntary participation. The request will be sent to the employee's supervisor who, in coordination with his supervisor, will indicate the availability of a suitable job assignment before forwarding the request to Personnel. Since it might take several months in some instances to find replacements and suitable alternative jobs for those volunteering for the program, requests should be initiated at least three months prior to the date the reduced work week is desired. Alternative jobs must be identifiable and meaningful.

Details of the administration of the program are as follows:

A. Work Schedule

Three months prior to the end of the quarter following or coincident with an employee attaining age 55, or any quarter thereafter preceding the date the employee requests entry into the program, an application for the program will be initiated by the interested employee requesting

Varian / 611 Hansen Way
Palo Alto / California 94303-0883 U.S.A.

SOURCE: Varian Associates, Palo Alto, Calif. (1988).

Figure 6-2. *(continued)*

---

a reduced work week. Requests can be made for a 4 day work week or a 3 day work week, but schedules for as little as one-half time (20 hours) can be requested. Twenty hours would be the minimum work schedule allowed.

There may be special work situations when two half-time employees could fill one job, i.e., each employee could work 20 hours. In this event each employee might work 4 hours each day for five days, or one employee might work two full days and then 1/2 day with the second employee completing the work week.

During the course of the program either the employee or the supervisor may request a change in the work schedule if the individual's situation or the company's needs change.

B. Length of the Program

Once an employee has begun participation in the program, he/she will continue in the program until retirement or earlier termination of employment, but in any event the period will not exceed three years.

C. Wage and Salaries

1. Job Classifications

Participants will normally retain the job classification held prior to participating in the program. Changes in job classifications may sometimes be necessary, e.g., supervisors who are given non-supervisory positions in order that they might work a reduced work schedule, employees who accept an assignment in a lower classified position to enable them to participate, etc. The employee's hourly equivalent rate upon entry into the program will continue to be paid unless the employee is assigned to a job in a lower classification.

2. Merit Increases

Employees in the program will continue to be eligible for merit increase consideration based on performance and according to guidelines.

3. Supervisory Positions

Employees who have been in supervisory positions will be relieved of supervisory responsibilities prior to being placed on the reduced work schedule and will be required to apply for the program at least three months in advance so that plans for a replacement may be made.

4. Overtime

While overtime is not generally contemplated under the program, the following will apply if overtime is worked:

(Continued)

Figure 6-2. *(continued)*

RETIREMENT TRANSITION PROGRAM   Page 3

     a. <u>Non-exempt employees</u>: Hours worked in excess of 8 in one day or 40 in one week will be paid at 1½ times the regular rate. Work performed on scheduled days off will not be paid for at premium rates unless it exceeds 8 hours in one day or 40 hours in one week.

     b. <u>Exempt employees</u>: The provisions governing overtime for exempt employees on a full time work schedule will apply to exempt employees in the Retirement Transition Program (i.e., exempt employees must be scheduled to work on the sixth day for four consecutive weeks).

D. <u>Benefit Plan Participation</u>

    1. Employees in this program will continue to be eligible for participation in the following benefit plans on the same basis as regular employees. Where eligible earnings determine the degree of participation, the employee's participation will be based on his reduced income level.

       a. Group medical & dental insurance plan
       b. Group life insurance plan*
       c. Stock purchase plan*
       d. Cash Option Profit-Sharing plan*
       e. Retirement and Profit-Sharing plan*
       f. Service Award program
       g. Tuition refund plan
       h. Travel accident insurance
       i. Holidays (which fall on scheduled work days)
       j. Vacation (accumulation pro rated based on scheduled hours of work. Vacation may be charged on scheduled work days only)
       k. Sick leave (accumulation pro rated based on scheduled hours of work. Sick leave may be used on scheduled work days only)
       l. Leaves of absence with pay* (emergency leaves, jury duty, etc.)
       m. Short-Term Disability insurance*
       n. Long-Term Disability insurance*

E. <u>Termination of the Program</u>

    1. Once an employee begins participation, it is intended that he/she continue for a maximum of three years or until an earlier termination or retirement. However, as with any other employee, a participant will be subject to all conditions affecting other employees, including layoff, leaves of absence, etc.

    2. Should an employee's personal circumstances be substantially changed after entering this program, for example, an unanticipated change which results in economic hardship, etc., return to full time status will be considered upon employee initiated request. There may also be situations when the company may request an employee to return to full time status for a limited period of time until a temporary emergency situation can be resolved.

* Level of participation in these benefits is related to eligible earnings.

6/82

Resource Materials for Managers and Supervisors. Materials designed for use by managers and supervisors should emphasize the organization's reasons for wanting to expand the employment options for senior workers to include phased or partial retirement. Some companies also provide managers and supervisors with materials that outline the major pros and cons of such a program from the employees' perspective. These resource materials should also identify the program coordinator, to whom specific or unusual questions should be directed.

Figure 6-3 and Table 6-4 are examples of the types of information materials that managers and supervisors find helpful. Figure 6-3 is the phased retirement section of Xerox Corporation's "Guide to Flexible Work Systems," a resource booklet for managers and employees. Table 6-4 shows at a glance how various time reductions affect such key issues as total workdays, vacation allowance, holidays, and pension credits.

Resource Materials for Employees. Having resource materials available for senior employees who are approaching early retirement age is extremely important if an organization wants to encourage older workers' maximum participation in a phased or partial retirement program. These information materials should cover such issues as the following:

■ *Voluntary nature of the program.* Does the older employee have to accept a reduced schedule? The voluntary nature of the program should be emphasized, and employees should be encouraged to think about when they want to retire or whether they want to retire at all. If workshops or counseling services are already available for senior employees, the option of phased or partial retirement should be incorporated into the materials and the program format.

■ *Financial implications.* What impact will phased or partial retirement have on Social Security, taxes, and benefits, particularly health insurance and the pension plan? Special resource materials for senior employees should focus on the short- and long-range financial ramifications of cutting back their schedules to various part-time levels. (In Chapter 7 on voluntary reduced work time programs, another regular part-time option, there are some sample resource materials that present the sort of highly detailed information that can let employees know exactly what they are getting into by reducing their schedules to a specified extent.)

(Text continues on page 223.)

Figure 6-3.   A program description for phased retirement.

Phased Retirement

Definition

Phased retirement is a way for employees to retire gradually by *voluntarily* reducing their full-time employment over a defined period of time. The objective of a phased retirement program is to broaden employment alternatives available to employees and to provide interested employees a gradual transition from full employment to the usual reduced activity of retirement.

Policy

The concept of phased retirement is covered under Personnel Policy 202.3, part-time employment. A copy of Policy 202.3 can be found in the Work and Family file drawer available on the Ethernet System.

Benefits of Phased Retirement

Phased retirement is a way to encourage employees with hard to replace skills or experience to extend their careers.

PHASED RETIREMENT GUIDELINES

Eligibility Requirements

The program is available to any regular full-time employee with a minimum 10 years of service, who will have attained a minimum age of 55 at the time participation in the program begins, and who plans to retire within two years. Please note that there may be some employees occupying positions who, by the nature of their assignments, cannot be accommodated by this program.

Requests for Participation

Employees who wish to participate in the phased retirement program should indicate their interest by initiating a written request for *voluntary* participation to their manager with a copy to their Human Resources Manager.

Work Schedule

At least three months prior to the end of the quarter following or coincident with an employee attaining age 55 or any quarter thereafter preceding the date the employee requests entry into the program, a written request should be initiated by the interested employee requesting a reduced work schedule (e.g., phased

SOURCE: "A Guide to Flexible Work Systems," Xerox Corporation, 1991.

---

retirement). Twenty hours per week should be the *minimum* work schedule allowed. Requests can also be made for job sharing arrangements.

Duration of the Program

Once an employee has begun participation in the program, he/she will continue in the program until retirement or separation with the Company, but in any event, the period will not exceed two years.

Job Grade

Participants in the program retain their job grade held prior to participating in the program.

Salary

Participants in the program also retain the same rate of pay they held prior to participating in the program, however, in all cases payment is made based on the number of hours actually worked. Time reporting is required for all part-time positions, including those which are classified as exempt. Refer to the section entitled "Facts about Part-Time Employment" for current pay eligibility.

Benefits

There is a significant difference in the benefits paid to part-time employees, depending upon whether they work less than 30 hours per week or 30 hours or more per week. Refer to the section entitled "Facts about Part-Time Employment" for current benefits eligibility.

Merit Increases

Employees in the program will remain eligible for merit increase consideration (MPP/MIP) based on their performance.

Termination of Participation

Once an employee begins participation in the program, it is intended that he/she will continue for a maximum of two years or until separation from the Company or retirement. However, an unanticipated change in an employee's personal circumstances may warrant return to full-time status. Return to full-time status should be considered upon employee-initiated request. Also, business needs may dictate an employee return to full-time status for a limited period of time.

(Continued)

Figure 6-3.   *(continued)*

Phased Retirement Checklist

Manager Responsibilities	*Employee Responsibilities*
☐ Review Personnel Policy 202.3 on part-time employment, found in the Work and Family file drawer, to understand the benefits and pay changes associated with employee's conversion to part-time status.	☐ Understand benefits and pay changes associated with the conversion to part-time status; review Personnel Policy 202.3 on part-time employment found in the Work and Family file drawer.
☐ Review and discuss request with employee and Human Resources Manager, if appropriate. Assess request for phased retirement in view of employee and business needs.	☐ Develop and submit written request for phased retirement to your manager (include such things as starting date, schedule, etc.).
☐ If requested is approved and the appropriate levels of approval have been obtained, communicate changes in employee status relative to pay and benefits through a memo similar to the one contained in the Appendix (pages 58–59).	☐ Review request for phased retirement with your manager.
	☐ If request is approved, ensure you receive and understand memo regarding conversion to part-time status.
☐ Develop scheduling tool (e.g., Flexforce Timeline™) to keep track of employee's schedule.	☐ Advise internal and external customers about your new work schedule.
☐ Advise internal and external customers of the employee's new work schedule. Make sure schedule is posted in a convenient location.	☐ Post your schedule in a convenient location so customers and co-workers know when you are available.
☐ Monitor the program (e.g., adherence, employee and customer satisfaction, productivity, etc.).	☐ Ensure that you complete a time card weekly and submit to your manager. Refer to Questions and Answers on pages 38–39 and 53–55.
☐ Ensure that employee completes time cards weekly. Refer to Questions and Answers on pages 38–39 and 53–55.	☐ Attend job related training and meetings; adjust schedule if necessary.
☐ Evaluate the impact of the program and identify opportunities for improvement.	☐ Evaluate the impact of phased retirement (take note of problems or concerns that arise).

This form is available electronically in the Work and Family file drawer.

Phased Retirement Design Checklist

Key Design Issues	Notes
☐ Eligibility (55 years old and minimum 10 years)	
☐ Impact on pay and benefits: Personnel Policy 202.3	
☐ Employee and business need for the program	
☐ Impact on customers, business, and work group	
☐ Duration of the program	
☐ Conditions for reversibility (How can an employee revert back to full-time status? When? How?)	
☐ Responsibility for continuity: illness, absence, etc.	
☐ Communication (How will part-time employee stay in contact with manager? With co-workers?)	
☐ Proposed work plan (How will tasks and responsibilities get done?)	
☐ Proposed schedule	
☐ Coverage and workflow	
☐ Scheduling model (e.g., Flexforce Timeline™)	
☐ Evaluation process	

This form is available electronically in the Work and Family file drawer.

Table 6-4. Reduced-time chart.

% Time Worked	Reg. Hrs. on PEP*	Paid Hrs. per Yr.	Work Hrs. per Yr.	Workdays per Yr.	Work Hrs. per Mo.	Vacation Allow.†	Holiday Allow.‡	Pension Credit per Yr.	Head Count Acc't.
100%	40 hrs.	2,080	1,832	229 days	153	160 hrs.	88 hrs.	1.00	1
90%	36 hrs.	1,872	1,649	206 days	137	144 hrs.	79 hrs.	.90	9/10
80%	32 hrs.	1,664	1,466	183 days	122	128 hrs.	71 hrs.	.80	4/5
75%	30 hrs.	1,560	1,374	172 days	114	120 hrs.	66 hrs.	.75	3/4
70%	28 hrs.	1,456	1,282	160 days	107	112 hrs.	62 hrs.	.70	7/10
60%	24 hrs.	1,248	1,099	137 days	91	96 hrs.	53 hrs.	.60	3/5
50%	20 hrs.	1,040	916	114 days	76	80 hrs.	44 hrs.	.50	1/2

NOTE: Used not to baffle and confuse, but to assist in tracking time worked, etc.—basically to keep [*employees*] from cheating *themselves.*

*PEP = Part-time Employment Program.

†Assumes member has earned *10 extra* V-days [*vacation days*] (10 yrs. service).

‡Holiday allowance based on 11 days (full-time).

SOURCE: Polaroid Corporation, Cambridge, Mass., *Corporate Retirement Administrator*, Feb. 1983.

■ *Eligibility*. Who is eligible to participate in the program, at what age, and with what length of service? Are any individuals or job classifications excluded from participation in the program?

■ *Schedule changes and reversibility*. Can an agreed-upon schedule be renegotiated, and on whose authority? How often may the schedule be changed? Is reversibility possible if the senior employee subsequently decides that full-time employment is preferable? If a worker withdraws from the phased or partial retirement program, will there be a specified time period during which he or she cannot reenroll?

■ *Application process*. How can an employee find out about the program and apply to participate? The organization should establish a procedure whereby interested employees can obtain both general information and individualized information about the program and its potential impact on them as well as procedures for submitting and reviewing applications.

Figure 6-4, which describes the Partial Service Retirement program of the state of California's Public Employees' Retirement System, is an example of the type of resource materials that employees find helpful. It provides an overview of all the key issues associated with such a program, focusing particularly on the effect that a schedule reduction will have on the employee's retirement allowance (on which the employee's pension will be based).

Announce the Program

Simply announcing that the company is now offering a phased and/ or partial retirement option will not be enough to ensure participation in this kind of program. Active promotion of both the concept and the program will be needed to counter the many years of emphasis on early retirement.

Promote the Program

Leaving the workforce as soon as possible has been promoted as a positive objective since the early 1950s. It will take sustained encouragement to get senior employees to recognize the benefits to themselves and to the organization of remaining longer in the workforce. At least three areas must be addressed educationally in order to create a new orientation that will result in a successful phased or partial retirement program:

(Text continues on page 229.)

Figure 6-4. Brochure for employees explaining a partial retirement program.

Introduction

The Partial Service Retirement program, which became effective January 1, 1984, allows you to reduce your worktime and receive a partial retirement allowance at the same time. The amount of your partial retirement allowance is based upon the reduction of your worktime.

For example, if you reduced your worktime by 50%, your allowance would equal 50% of what you would be entitled to if you had taken a full service retirement instead of a partial service retirement. A reduction in worktime of 30% (meaning you would work 70% of full time) would entitle you to an allowance equal to 30% of your full service retirement allowance.

Worktime may be reduced by at least 20% but not more than 60%. In other words, you must work at least 40% time but not more than 80% time to participate. **Your agency must approve the reduction in worktime you wish to choose.**

Qualifying and Applying

You must meet all of the following requirements to be eligible for partial service retirement:

- be a full-time State miscellaneous member (this includes State college employees who are PERS members),
- be age 62 or older, and
- have a minimum of five years of PERS service credit. (This includes any PERS-credited service. Service credit with another California public retirement system cannot be used to meet the five-year requirement.)

State industrial, patrol, and safety members, as well as University of California employees, are **not** eligible for this benefit.

Your Personnel Office keeps the necessary application/election form (Partial Service Retirement Application, DPA-062) if you wish to apply. **Remember: You must receive departmental approval before you can apply.**

You should submit your application/election form to PERS at least 45 to 60 days before your effective date of partial retirement. This will insure that your election will be processed in a timely manner. The effective date of your partial retirement can be the first of any pay period.

SOURCE: *Partial Service Retirement* (Sacramento: California Public Employees' Retirement System, June 1984).

Your Allowance

There are three things you need to know to estimate your partial retirement allowance:

Service Credit

The amount of PERS-covered service you've earned. (Refer to your last PERS Annual Member Statement and add any service credit you may have earned since that time.)

Benefit Factor

This is the percent of pay to which you are entitled for each year of service. It is determined by your age at partial retirement.

Your Age	Benefit Factor
62	2.272%
62¼	2.308%
62½	2.346%
62¾	2.382%
63+	2.418%

Final Compensation

Generally, this is your average monthly payrate for the last consecutive 36 months. You may elect another 36-month period if it produces a higher average.

If your PERS service was coordinated with Social Security, you have never contributed on the first $133.33 of your monthly earnings. So when computing your allowance, you must reduce your final compensation by that same $133.33.

Once you've determined these three things, you can begin calculating your estimate. You may also contact your nearest PERS Area or Field Office for an estimate.

Step 1

Determine the highest full service retirement allowance to which you would be entitled. Multiply your:

Service Credit (X) Benefit Factor (X) Final Compensation

Example:

Nancy is applying for partial service retirement. She will be 62½ years old on the effective date of her partial retirement, with 25 years of service credit. Her final compensation is $1,500, and she **is not** coordinated with Social Security. Nancy's estimate would be as follows:

Years of Service Credit		Benefit Factor		Final Compensation		Highest Full Service Retirement Allowance
25	(X)	2.346% (=58.65%)	(X)	$1,500	=	$879.75

(Continued)

Figure 6-4. *(continued)*

Your Allowance

If she **were** coordinated with Social Security, her final compensation must include the $133.33 reduction:

25   (X) 2.346% (=58.65%) (X) $1,366.67   = $801.55
                                                ($1,500 – $133.33)

Your Example:

Determine your highest full service retirement allowance.

Years of Service Credit		Benefit Factor		Final Compensation		Highest Full Service Retirement Allowance
_____	(X)	____% (=____%)	(X)	$_____*	=	$_____

* Do you need to reduce your final compensation for coordination with Social Security? See above.

Step 2

Now, multiply your answer in Step 1 by your reduction in worktime.

Your Highest Full Service Retirement Allowance (From Step 1)	(X)	Your Reduction Of Worktime (Percentage)	=	Your Partial Service Retirement Allowance

Example:

Nancy has been approved to reduce her worktime by 40%. By using the answer in the example in Step 1, she can estimate her partial retirement.

Highest Full Service Retirement Allowance		Reduction Of Worktime		Partial Service Retirement Allowance
$879.75	(X)	40%	=	$351.90

Your Example:

Determine your partial retirement allowance by multiplying your answer in Step 1 by your reduction in worktime.

Your Highest Full Service Retirement Allowance		Your Reduction Of Worktime		Your Partial Service Retirement Allowance
$_____	(X)	____%	=	$_____

Other Considerations

Withdrawal and Subsequent Worktime Changes

You may end your partial service retirement and withdraw from the program, at any time, with your employer's approval. Once you withdraw, however, you cannot reapply for five years.

You must also obtain your employer's approval if you wish to make additional changes with your worktime after your partial retirement begins. Decreases in your (already) reduced worktime are possible once every fiscal year, while increases may be made only once every five years.

Allowance Adjustments

Unlike a full service retirement, there are no provisions which allow for cost-of-living increases. Your partial service retirement allowance will not be recalculated due to increases in age, salary, or service credit as long as you participate in the program. It may change, however, if you increase or decrease your worktime percentage, or if an adjustment to your allowance payable on the date you enter into partial retirement is necessary.

Changing Jobs

You may transfer from one State agency to another and continue your partial retirement as long as you remain a State miscellaneous employee and your new employer approves your continuation in the program.

Separating From Employment

If you decide to permanently separate from PERS-covered employment, you cannot continue your partial retirement. You may instead choose to apply for a full service retirement (see your "PERS State Miscellaneous" member booklet), terminate your PERS membership and receive a refund (a return of your contributions on deposit

with PERS, plus interest), or leave your contributions on deposit with PERS and defer taking your full service retirement.

Entering a Full Service Retirement

You may fully retire at any time while participating in the partial retirement program; however, the duration of your partial retirement may affect the calculation and amount of your full service retirement allowance. If you choose to fully retire before earning one year of PERS service credit while participating in the program, your full service retirement allowance would be calculated differently than if you had earned more than one year's service credit. **You should be aware that it is to your advantage to fully retire after earning at least one year of service credit.** Contact your nearest PERS Area or Field Office for an estimate and explanation of your full service retirement allowance after partial retirement.

Please Note: Because your worktime has been reduced to participate in this program, it will take more than one fiscal year to earn one year of PERS service credit.

Taxes and Payroll Deductions

When you begin your partial retirement, you will receive a letter from PERS showing the amount of your contributions as well as any credited interest which has been set aside to help pay for your partial retirement allowance. You can use this information to receive a determination from either the IRS or any other tax authority as to your tax liability.

Only appropriate income taxes can be deducted from your partial retirement allowance. PERS cannot advise you about the taxability of your partial retirement allowance. You must contact your local IRS or other tax authorities for information in this area.

(Continued)

Figure 6-4. *(continued)*

Other Considerations

All other deductions which you may have (health and life insurance premiums, union dues, credit union payments, deferred compensation plans, purchasing additional PERS service credit, etc.) must be taken from your State salary. If you have any questions regarding payroll deductions, ask your Personnel Office.

Health and Dental Insurance

Your health and dental plans would not be affected by your participation in the program. You should remember, however, that any premium payments will be deducted from your State salary and not your partial retirement allowance.

Social Security

You may draw Social Security benefits while receiving your partial retirement allowance; however, your earnings—the combination of your State salary and your partial retirement allowance—may cause an offset to your Social Security benefits. Contact your local Social Security office for more information.

Injury, Illness, Leaves of Absence

If you become injured or ill—during your participation in the program—and cannot perform your job, you may be eligible for a disability retirement. Obtain a copy of our separate leaflet called "Disability Retirement" for more information. If your injury or illness requires that you take a leave of absence or go on Non-Industrial Disability Insurance, you may continue your partial retirement with your employer's consent. You may remain in the program if you require other types of leave; ask your Personnel Office.

Provisions for Your Beneficiaries

Unlike a full service retirement, there are no provisions which allow you to provide benefits to someone, after your death, by reducing your partial retirement allowance

and selecting a retirement option. Rather, if you should die while in the program, your beneficiaries would be eligible for the same pre-retirement death benefits as the beneficiaries of members who do not participate in the program. All death benefits are explained, in detail, in your "PERS State Miscellaneous" member booklet.

Please Note: Because a portion of your contributions is used to help pay for your partial retirement allowance, any benefit which includes a return of your contributions, plus interest, to your beneficiary will be affected.

☐   ☐   ☐

Important Numbers (Area Code 916)

If you have any questions regarding the status of your partial service retirement—after you have applied—you may call the PERS Benefits Division at 445-5030, or 485-5030 (ATSS).

TDD Interpreter Numbers

Information	445-4900
	485-4900 (ATSS)
Benefits Information	323-4290
	473-4290 (ATSS

1. Managers need to understand what fiscal benefits this reduced work time option for senior employees will bring to
   the organization and to society, and individual workers need
   to understand what ramifications this type of program has
   for their economic well-being.
2. The organization must counter negative myths about the
   capabilities of older workers. Such myths tend to support
   management and employee bias in favor of retiring early
   rather than extending work life.
3. The organization must also counter negative attitudes about
   part-time work and part-time workers.

Evaluate the Program

The program should be evaluated in terms of the guidelines established at the outset by the task force. One objective should be to
look at participation rates; another, to look at cost, especially as it
compares to previous policy initiatives (such as early retirement)
relating to older workers.

Fine-Tune the Program

On the basis of the evaluation results, the program can be modified
to improve its effectiveness. For example:

Problem	*Solution*
Employee participation rates are low.	Promote the program companywide. Hold focus groups with senior employees to have them critique the program.
Evaluation indicates that senior employees are interested, but are concerned about making an irreversible decision to retire.	Consider adjusting program policy to allow a return to full-time employment if desired.
Supervisors are reluctant to approve requests for participation in program.	Require written response to requests, which include a reason for the denial.

Summary

Phased and partial retirement are employment alternatives in which
older workers reduce their time commitment prior to full retirement.

This reduction can take place either gradually over a specific number of years (phased retirement) or for an open-ended period of time (partial retirement). These options provide employees with a middle ground between full-time work and full retirement that can help cushion the shock of retirement while at the same time relieving employers of some of the burden of providing pension payments and health insurance for a steadily growing number of retirees. These less than full-time alternatives not only meet the needs of older employees but also provide a way for younger workers to advance.

Reduced work time options for senior employees were first offered in Europe in the 1970s, primarily by private-sector companies. The concept gained acceptance more slowly in the United States, with phased and partial retirement programs introduced on a limited basis. But many of these programs fell victim to the wave of downsizing in the early 1980s, in which incentives were commonly offered to push older workers into an abrupt early retirement.

However, under legislation enacted in the 1970s and 1980s, employers were prohibited from compelling their older workers to retire, and the maximum pension that a company could pay to early retirees under a corporate defined-benefit pension plan was sharply reduced. These laws tended to discourage early retirement and provided a powerful incentive for both companies and older workers to seek more creative alternatives to full retirement. Coupled with the effect of this legislation was the discovery by employers that the widespread use of early retirement had a variety of negative consequences. Dismissing older workers via the "golden handshake" proved to be a costly move that often resulted in the loss of valued personnel and a drop in employee morale.

Phased and partial retirement are effective strategies for retaining senior workers whose skills and experience will be difficult to replace and for increasing the range of options available to management for coping with such problems as burnout and the need for upward mobility. These reduced work time alternatives are most appropriate in organizations with an aging workforce that have policies or practices discouraging layoffs, in organizations that want to supplement an existing predominantly young workforce by recruiting more seasoned employees, and in organizations whose active use of early retirement brought negative consequences.

In considering the adoption of a program of part-time employment for senior workers, an organization should consider such advantages as the retention of skilled and experienced staff, a broadened recruitment effort, increased opportunities for upward mobility and cross-training, and enhanced employee morale. The organization that offers attractive alternatives to full retirement will also not find itself the target of lawsuits arising from an overly aggressive promotion of early retirement.

Although experience with phased and partial retirement has to date been rather limited, the fact that these options are cost-effective can be deduced by examining the high cost of widespread use of early retirement. As noted above, companies that made it a practice to lure older workers into cutting short their work life quickly found themselves bereft of talent, facing morale problems that threatened to affect productivity, and saddled not only with the one-time expense of retirement incentives but also with the ongoing expense of sharply increased pension payments and unfunded liabilities for retiree health insurance. Such experience revealed the wisdom of offering employment options under which older individuals could continue to function in a part-time capacity as productive workers rather than retiring abruptly to become full-time burdens upon the corporate coffers.

The standard eight-step process for implementing an employment alternative will, in the case of phased and partial retirement, focus particularly on establishing strong support for the program at the outset, developing resource materials that fully explain the advantages of these options, and actively promoting the program's use. In all cases, this emphasis is designed to overcome the firmly entrenched assumption on the part of both managers and workers that early retirement is the only desirable goal for older employees.

A carefully designed and skillfully promoted program of reduced schedules for senior workers is, in short, a strategy whereby an organization can both recoup its investment in trained and experienced employees and combat the rising cost of pensions and retiree health benefits.

ORGANIZATIONAL EXPERIENCE WITH PHASED AND PARTIAL RETIREMENT

Varian Associates

Description: Varian is a high-technology manufacturer of electron tubes, analytical instruments, medical instruments, and semiconductors. It is located in Palo Alto, California, and employs approximately 45,000 in the San Francisco Bay area. Other employment options used by Varian have been work sharing as an alternative to layoffs and, occasionally, job sharing.

Reason for Using Phased Retirement: The "Retirement Transition Program" was announced in 1977 to provide an additional option for senior employees and to enable the company to retain valued workers who might otherwise have retired.

Implementation Process: Interested employees who are age 55 or older, have at least five years' regular service with Varian, and plan to retire within three years complete a Retirement Transition Program Application Form and submit it to their supervisor for approval. In some cases—for example, if the employee's current job includes supervisory responsibilities—approval may require a change in job assignment.

Requests can be made for a four-day workweek, a three-day workweek, or less. The minimum work schedule allowed is twenty hours per week. During the course of the program, either the employee or the supervisor may request a change in the work schedule if the individual's situation or the company's needs change.

Participants normally retain their original job classification, although changes may sometimes be necessary. Employees continue to be eligible for merit increases. Medical and dental coverage remain the same, but some other benefits (life insurance, retirement and profit sharing, paid leaves for such reasons as jury duty, and disability insurance) are prorated.

Participation in the program is limited to three years, at the end of which the employee retires. Return to full-time status will be considered if the employee's personal circumstances change substantially after entering the program and the employee requests it. The company may also ask an employee to return to full-time status for a limited period of time until a temporary emergency situation can be resolved.

Impact to Date: Although the program has not been heavily used, it has on several occasions allowed the company to retain employees with hard-to-recruit skills or experience. However, because of reductions in force in the past few years, the average age of Varian's workforce has risen from the mid-30s to 41–42. This may lead to greater use of the Retirement Transition Program in the future.

SOURCE: Descriptive material from Varian Associates, Palo Alto, Calif.; telephone interview with Varian's corporate human resources staff (Dec. 1993).

State of California Public School Teachers

Description: The state of California has been a pioneer in the field of alternative work time and offers a number of work-time options for state employees. The State Teachers' Retirement System's "Reduced Work Load Program" is available to public school teachers.

Reason for Using Phased Retirement: The option was introduced in order to allow teachers nearing retirement to phase out of their careers. To a lesser extent, it was also intended as a way to phase in new teachers.

Implementation Process: Under the "Reduced Work Load Program," teachers fifty-five years of age or older who are within ten years of retirement, have worked full-time in a district for the immediately preceding five years, and have worked for a total of at least ten years can negotiate to reduce their schedule to half-time. In order to receive full retirement credit, the employee and his or her employer contribute to the retirement fund "the amount that would have been contributed if the member was employed on a full-time basis." The employee retains full health coverage and other rights and benefits, "for which he makes payments that would be required if he remained in full-time employment." Retirement income remains the same as if the employee had continued to work full-time.

Impact to Date: The program was evaluated in 1980 by the state's legislative analyst. At the time, it had been in operation for five years.

Employers indicated that the program had reduced their salary costs because "[t]he salaries of the participants, typically senior employees in or near the top of the salary scale, are usually more than the salaries of new employees hired on a part-time basis to replace the Reduced Work Load Program participants."

SOURCE: *The Reduced Work Load Program of the State Teachers' Retirement System* (Sacramento, Calif.: Office of the Legislative Analyst, Sept. 1980), 1–23.

CHAPTER 7

Voluntary Reduced Work Time Programs

V-Time (short for voluntary reduced work time) programs are a way to offer reduced work time options to a broad base of employees in a way that integrates part-time with full-time employment. V-Time is a time/income trade-off arrangement that allows full-time employees to reduce work hours for a specified period of time with a corresponding reduction in compensation. Although this option can be offered to individual employees on an ad hoc basis, it is most effective when offered as a formal program. V-Time differs from regular part-time employment in that there is usually a time limit on the arrangement, and a process is defined for return to full-time status.

The V-Time program design was originally developed as a way to accommodate employees who needed a temporary alternative to full-time employment. The first V-Time pilot project was implemented, however, as a joint labor-management effort to minimize layoffs. V-Time programs emcompass the concept of regular part-time, including job sharing, but also provide for smaller time reductions than most part-time or job sharing arrangements. Under a typical V-Time program:

- Reductions of work time (and pay) ranging from 2.5 percent to 5 percent, 10 percent, 20 percent, 30 percent, and up to 50 percent are offered.
- The schedule remains in force for a designated period, usually six or twelve months, to allow employees and employer to try out the new arrangement, with the assurance that the

commitment can be either renegotiated or terminated at the end of that period.

■ All employee benefits are maintained, with some being pro-rated.

■ A supervisor must authorize an employee's participation in the program.

■ The time off can be taken either on a regular basis, as a reduced day or week, or in a block of time, such as extra leave or days off from work.

Origins of V-Time

As noted, the original impetus for the development of V-Time programs was employees' need for a reduced work time option that would be available to more people because of the smaller increments of reduction than are offered by traditional part-time or job sharing and that would provide the same conditions of work as full-time employment, coupled with a process for returning to full-time after the need for part-time had passed. As Figure 7-1 shows, the most popular choices of salary reduction in the New York State "Voluntary Reduction in Work Schedule Program" (formerly called the

Figure 7-1. Work/salary reductions selected under New York State's "Voluntary Reduction in Work Schedule" program.

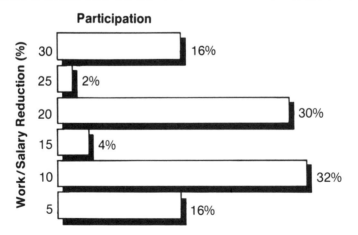

SOURCE: Employee information packet (Albany: New York State Department of Civil Service, Apr. 1984). Used by permission.

"Voluntary Furlough Program"), which was begun in 1984, are the 10 percent and 20 percent options.

Service Employees International Union (SEIU) was the organization that designed the original V-Time program. SEIU and the county administration in Santa Clara, California, had since the early 1970s recognized the growing need for less than full-time work options. Previous negotiations had led to an agreement to expand traditional part-time classifications and to initiate split codes, or job sharing, for county employees. In 1975, SEIU attempted unsuccessfully to introduce a V-Time program within the county because, as Michael Baratz, executive director of the local, said, "Our people wanted more personal time." The following year, when the county announced a budget crisis and forecast a 6.5 percent reduction in staff, the union again introduced its idea of a voluntary reduced work hours program. This time, the board of supervisors lent its support to the concept as a way to minimize layoffs, and the program was begun in December 1976.

Today, more and more employees nationally are expressing a need or desire for a reduced schedule at some point in their careers. The first effort to quantify this need occurred in 1978. Table 7-1 is from *Exchanging Earnings for Leisure: Findings of an Exploratory National Survey on Work Time Preferences*. Although this survey dates from 1978, it is still worth noting, since a number of smaller polls have recently confirmed many of its findings. Although less comprehensive than the Harris survey, it supports the same conclusion—that "prevailing work-time conditions are at variance with the preferences of today's workers."[1]

During the 1980s at least four national surveys of working parents indicated the need for more work time options.[2] The November 1988 *Better Homes and Gardens* magazine, reporting on that year's poll, noted that: "As in past questionnaires, letter writers passionately and repeatedly plead for work arrangements that accommodate your families' needs: 'I would like to see more part-time jobs available for parents whereby they could work 20–30 hours a week, make a decent salary, and still be eligible for benefits. . . .' Other respondents suggest work that can be done primarily at home—maybe going into an office part of the week."[3] And a poll of The Travelers' senior employees indicated a considerable interest in part-time employment from that segment of the population.[4]

More indicative of recent attitudes, however, are the responses of the 1,010 adults who were interviewed for a study conducted for the Hilton Hotels Corporation in 1991. This survey examined peo-

Table 7-1. Stated worker preference toward exchanging portions of current income for alternative forms of free time.

Value of Tradeoff	Shorter Workday vs. Pay	Reduced Workweek vs. Pay	Added Vacation vs. Pay	Sabbatical Leaves vs. Pay	Earlier Retirement vs. Pay
Nothing for time	77.0	73.8	57.8	37.9	64.0
2% of pay for time	8.7	11.6	23.2	24.2	17.6
5% of pay for time	5.8	—	8.5	8.0	8.1
10% of pay for time	—	7.6	6.2	4.8	5.9
12% of pay for time	5.5	—	—	—	—
15% of pay for time	—	—	—	4.8	—
20% of pay for time	—	4.5	2.2	—	4.4
30% of pay for time	1.6	—	—	—	—
33% of pay for time	—	—	2.0	—	—
40% of pay for time	—	.9	—	—	—
50% of pay for time	1.5	1.6	—	—	—
Total Percent	100.0	100.0	100.0	100.0	100.0
Total Respondents	954	953	952	951	951

Note: Column spaces are frequently blank for many tradeoff options because questions dealing with different forms of free time did not always have parallel exchange options.

SOURCE: Excerpted from an Aug. 1978 survey conducted by Louis Harris and Associates, as reported in *Exchanging Earnings for Leisure: Findings of an Exploratory National Survey on Work Time Preferences*, R&D Monograph 79 (Washington, D.C.: U.S. Department of Labor, Employment and Training Administration, 1980), 81.

ple's attitudes and values concerning time, and the results confirmed that "We are at a point in history where, to most Americans, the value of time is reaching parity with the value of money."[5] Seventy percent of the respondents who earn over $30,000 or more and 48 percent who earn $20,000 or less said they would gladly give up a day's pay for an extra day off each week.

Reduced work schedules, as we mentioned earlier in discussing regular part-time, may first be tried by an organization on a case-by-case basis. However, once the organization begins to use regular part-time employment more widely, the value of having a program rather than relying on individual accommodation appeals both to many managers and to employees. A program meets management's need to develop an administrative process to deal with the integration of a variety of reduced and full-time schedules as well as to plan the allocation of work time and do so in a way that ensures equity of treatment for the employees involved.

Who Uses V-Time Programs?

Two counties in northern California, Santa Clara and San Mateo, provided the first sites for V-Time programs. From there, the concept spread to state government. A California legislator used the county V-Time model as the basis for legislation entitled the Voluntary Reduced Work Time Act of 1980. It authorized state employees to request a variety of reduced work time options. Once the legislation had passed, the state Department of Personnel Administration drew up guidelines for the establishment of agency-based programs similar to the ones offered by the two counties. In 1984, the program design was used by New York State as the basis for its "Voluntary Reduction in Work Schedule Program." Shaklee Corporation became the first private-sector user in 1983, when it introduced a V-Time program for its employees, and Ford Motor Company piloted a program in 1992–93. To date, however, there has been very little private-sector experimentation with this option, even though use of regular part-time and job sharing has increased.

When Is V-Time Most Appropriate?

From management's perspective, the primary reason for introducing a V-Time program is to reduce labor costs in a way that accommodates employees' needs and reinforces their commitment to the organization. By offering smaller increments of reduction along with job sharing and more traditional forms of regular part-time work, V-Time maximizes the multiplier effect of the payroll reductions. It also provides a formula for prorating the cost of health insurance and other benefits, establishing a policy context that supports the integration of full- and part-time work. As such, it represents the antithesis of the concepts embodied in the idea of contingent or "core-ring" employment.

Within particular departments, V-Time also creates some additional fiscal flexibility for management. The money saved through payroll cutbacks can be applied elsewhere or held for future use. If it is used to hire additional employees, it may be possible to obtain less-experienced personnel at lower salary rates.

Because V-Time programs offer a wider choice of time reductions under formalized conditions, they provide a broader-based and more efficient response to various kinds of need for reduced work schedules within the labor force. As with other forms of part-time, these needs include:

- More time for family responsibilities
- Time to complete or reenter education programs
- The desire to work part-time at the end of a career as a way of phasing retirement
- Health problems that preclude full-time work
- Time to recuperate from burnout

V-Time programs can also be an important component of a *work sharing* strategy during economic downturns. Many companies have found that some employees will volunteer to cut back on a portion of paid hours in order to save jobs. Management's encouragement, coupled with policies that protect overall employment rights, can enable individual employees to use recessionary periods to reenter education or training programs, catch up on domestic responsibilities, or enjoy some leisure time until the economy picks up again. (See Chapter 9 for an in-depth discussion of work sharing and a description of the University of California's T.R.I.P. program, an example of using a voluntary reduced work time program as a means of minimizing or avoiding layoffs.)

Pros and Cons of V-Time Programs

The advantages of introducing a V-Time program have to do with standardizing the use of reduced schedules, making schedule cutbacks attractive to a wider range of employees, and increasing cost savings and fiscal flexibility. The potential disadvantages involve management and union attitudes.

■ *Standardizing the use of reduced schedules.* While in many organizations, employees are permitted to cut back their hours on a case-by-case basis, management can standardize the process of accommodating employees who need reduced schedules by introducing a V-Time program that permits such reductions under specified conditions and for a specified period of time. This eliminates many of the inequities that inevitably result from an ad hoc management response to requests for part-time. The range of schedule reductions is then made available to employees on a largely voluntary basis.

■ *Increasing the attractiveness of part-time options.* Only a relatively small number of employees can contemplate the 20 percent to 50 percent work time reductions of traditional part-time schedules. The smaller time reductions available under a V-Time program put time/income trade-offs within reach of more employees and therefore enhance the organization's opportunities to reduce its payroll through voluntary cutbacks. Because this range of scheduling options accommodates the needs and interests of such a wide variety of employees, it is also a useful recruitment tool.

■ *Increasing cost savings and fiscal flexibility.* Offering voluntary part-time work options results in a variety of cost savings for the organization, as discussed in Chapter 4, "Regular Part-Time Employment." The cost savings associated with more traditional part-time schedules can be multiplied when a company introduces a V-Time program, under which part-time can be used on a more widespread basis. When employees trade income for time, one of the primary cost reductions is a direct savings in payroll expenditures. Indirect savings may also be realized if new employees are hired at the lower end of the salary scale. Savings of this sort increase management's fiscal flexibility by making available extra dollars that can either be used to reduce the budget or be reallocated to more critical areas.

■ *Management attitudes.* A manager whose department has a heavy workload may be reluctant to approve requests for V-Time—particularly if the company has instituted a hiring freeze tied to a head count, which would prohibit extra hires, or if the department is unable to reduce its workload. Hiring temporary employees is sometimes a way to permit the use of V-Time in departments faced with this type of situation.

■ *Union attitudes.* Labor representatives are often concerned about V-Time's impact on full-time employment. They worry that jobs will be lost if schedule reductions that were originally presented as being voluntary and having a limited duration become mandatory and permanent. Union attitudes toward V-Time, however, tend to become more favorable as positive experience with this option grows.

Should Your Organization Try V-Time?

To determine whether it would be advisable to offer a V-Time program, you will have to examine the problems faced by your organization and compare them to the types of problems most effectively solved through the use of V-Time. That's what this section is all about.

The accompanying profiles entitled Organizational Experience with V-Time examine V-Time programs instituted by other organizations. Notice whether, and how, the experience of these organizations parallels your own company's situation.

Table 7-2 is a questionnaire that focuses on organizational conditions pointing to the use of V-Time. Is your company currently concerned about one or more of these issues? If so, the worksheet shown in Figure 7-2 can help you analyze the need for V-Time and weigh the pros and cons of offering this scheduling arrangement.

Introducing V-Time

In the case of V-Time, the standard eight-step process for implementing a new work time arrangement will focus on gaining the support of top and middle-level management, developing a program design that emphasizes parity with full-time work, and encouraging employee participation and support through an active promotion effort, backed by effective resource materials.

Gain Support for the Program
In order to gain widespread support, a cross-functional task force should be formed whose responsibilities will be to develop a policy and program and design orientation activities for all affected parties.

Table 7-2. V-Time questionnaire.

Would V-Time Benefit Your Organization?

	Yes	No
Has the number of employee requests for reduced work schedules been growing?		
Do the demographics of your organization's labor force indicate a potential interest in a V-Time option?		
Have supervisors expressed a need for guidelines for granting requests from full-time employees to voluntarily reduce their work time?		
Does your organization or industry have peaks and valleys of labor force demand that might be smoothed out by using a wider variety of reduced time schedules?		
Is recruitment or turnover a problem that having a V-Time program might help?		

Figure 7-2. V-Time worksheet.

Assessing the Need for V-Time

List the main reasons why you are considering V-Time:

1. _____

   _____

   _____

2. _____

   _____

   _____

3. _____

   _____

   _____

4. _____

   _____

   _____

List what you see as the advantages and disadvantages of V-Time:

Pros: _____

   _____

   _____

   _____

   _____

(Continued)

Figure 7-2.   *(continued)*

_____

_____

Cons: _____

_____

_____

_____

_____

_____

    If all or part of the workforce belongs to a union, then the task force should include balanced labor representation. If there is no union, employee focus groups or surveys can provide input for the program's design.

    Since the concept of a V-Time program is new and relatively untested, gaining top-level management support will be critical if initiative for the program has begun without it. One way to gain executive-level support is through briefings that point to the business and fiscal benefits of V-Time programs and detail the successful use of voluntary regular part-time in peer organizations. Pilot project experience within the organization can be particularly helpful in this regard.

    Middle-level management support is equally important. To obtain it, the organization should involve managers and supervisors in the design of the program so that they can provide input on both policy and procedural decisions.

    A major concern of department heads and supervisors is how V-Time will influence their budgets and staff allocation. Use of a full-time equivalent personnel accounting system rather than a head count system is particularly important. An equally critical question for many managers is whether allowing their employees to reduce work time will be taken as a signal to those who control the budget that their department can get by on less. Senior executives should reassure middle managers on this point and make them aware of their support, through either written communication, briefing sessions, or both. It also is important to assure middle managers that their department's participation in a V-Time program will not adversely affect future budgets—that, on the contrary, V-Time can give them more flexibility because salary savings can be used somewhere else.

Whether managers will be permitted to participate in the program themselves may influence their response to employee requests and their general attitude about the V-Time program. Middle managers are often more supportive if the program is available to them and their peers and they see this option as applicable to all employees, not just to clerical or lower-level classifications.

Set Up the Program's Administration

When introducing a V-Time program, it is important to designate a program administrator—someone to be in charge of the promotional campaign, application process, record keeping, and other responsibilities associated with planning and startup. The program administrator should work with the payroll department to develop a method for handling payroll and time keeping. Computerization of these functions has eliminated much of the complexity associated with this process once the initial format is designed. Experience has shown that most of the time demands of setting up a V-Time program are at the front end; after the program is in operation, much less time is required. For example, the state of California Department of Real Estate's staff services manager estimates that he initially spent approximately sixty-two hours to plan his organization's V-Time program and advise his 360 employees about it. Once it was in operation, he spent about an hour per month on the program.

Design the Program

Once the support of top management is forthcoming, a task force has been established, and an administrator named, program design can begin. The program design phase requires that decisions be made in various areas, as explained in the following subsections.

Scope. The organization must decide whether the V-Time program will be offered first on a pilot project basis, confined to a particular department or division, or made available companywide.

Eligibility. In some V-Time programs, only exempt-level employees are eligible to participate. This is because the program is new and the organization is unionized. The union wants to limit the program's scope until union leaders are certain that V-Time will not be used to reduce the number of full-time jobs available. In other programs, all employees are eligible but must have their supervisor's approval to enroll.

Range of Reductions to Be Offered. In general, the greater the number of choices, the greater the participation in a V-Time program. The number of choices in existing programs ranges from three to twelve. However, the more variety there is, the more work it is to administer the program. It can be helpful for the organization to discover in advance how many and which employees might be interested in a reduced work time option and what kind of reduction(s) would be most popular. A survey of all employees to determine their interest in V-Time can provide solid information on which to base administrative and program decisions. (A model employee survey is shown in Figure 7-3.)

How Reductions Can Be Taken. How time off can be scheduled is particularly important to employees. For example, many would like to accumulate time and take it off in blocks rather than work fewer hours each day or week. Successful programs offer a choice of (1) working a reduced schedule (either a shorter workday or a shorter workweek) or (2) reducing pay but continuing to work full-time and taking full days or blocks of time off at a later date, with the supervisor's approval. Prospective V-Time program participants should be asked to indicate how they wish to take the time off, and supervisors should review this as part of the application. One program makes all accumulated time off available on the starting date of the program. For example, an employee cutting back by 20 percent gets one day per week, or fifty-two days, off. This could conceivably be taken at the start of the program, with the employee working full-time for the rest of the year. Employees cannot carry over unused time beyond the annual termination date of the program, and an employee who withdraws from the program prior to the termination date gets his or her pay adjusted accordingly.

Enrollment Process. The application form, signed by both the employee and the department head, becomes a contract between the employee and the employer. The form contains pertinent employee information (name, classification, the time reduction requested, preference for scheduling work time and time off) and the length of time that the employee wishes the reduction to be in effect (or the program termination date in cases where this is not a variable). See the sample form shown in Figure 7-4; note that this form also incorporates elements of a work sharing program, which will be discussed in Chapter 9.

(Text continues on page 250.)

Figure 7-3. Sample employee survey on interest in reduced work time options.

Reduced Work Time: Employee Survey

Section A: Background and Demographic Information

(If the surveyor wishes to obtain information about which employees, both now and in the future, are likely to want reduced work time, this section should be included. Many surveys have been conducted without collecting this information.)
Please circle the letter of one alternative for each question:

1. SEX

    a. Male
    b. Female

2. AGE

    a. Under 18
    b. 18–24
    c. 25–34
    d. 35–44
    e. 45–54
    f. 55–64
    g. 65 or over

3. MARITAL STATUS

    a. Single, never been married
    b. Married
    c. Separated, divorced, or widowed

4. FAMILY STATUS

    a. No dependents
    b. 1–2 dependents
    c. 3–5 dependents
    d. More than 5 dependents

(Continued)

Figure 7-3. *(continued)*

5. CURRENT DIVISION *(List all of your organization's divisions/departments here.)*

6. LENGTH OF TIME WORKED FOR EMPLOYER

   a. Less than one year
   b. 1–5 years
   c. 6–10 years
   d. More than 10 years

7. PRESENT SCHEDULE

   a. Full-time
   b. Part-time

8. STATUS

   a. Permanent
   b. Temporary or provisional

9. CURRENT POSITION CLASSIFICATION *(List choices or leave blank for employees to fill in.)*

Section B: Work Time Preference

(This section is the heart of the survey. It is designed to provide information on how many people want reduced work time and the kinds of reduction they want. The surveyor may wish to state here that fringe benefits under this program will remain intact, and respondents should bear that in mind when answering the question(s). Alternatively, a question could be included that would assess the importance of benefits in determining the respondents' choice.)

10. Would you be interested, now or in the future, in reducing the amount of time you work with a commensurated reduction in pay? (*Organizations that conducted surveys indicated that there was some drop-off from the number interested to the number who eventually participated.*)

    a. Yes, definitely
    b. Probably
    c. Maybe
    d. No
    If you answered no to this question, please skip all of the remaining questions.

11. Please indicate when you might be interested in reducing your time base.

    a. Immediately
    b. Within the next six months
    c. Within six months to a year
    d. Within one to three years
    e. Not for at least three years

12. Reduced work time schedules can be arranged in various ways. Please indicate which of the following best describes what you might be interested in.

   a. Regular time off. (This means working fewer hours every day, fewer days every week, fewer weeks each month, or fewer months each year.)
   b. Irregular, but planned, time off. (This means working your full-time schedule and taking your time off in the form of occasional days off or blocks of time off—for example, adding your time onto your vacation.)

13. If your answer to question 12 was a, please indicate which schedule appeals to you most.

   a. Working fewer hours each day
   b. Working fewer days each week
   c. Working fewer weeks each month
   d. Working fewer months each year

14. What percentage best reflects how much time you would like to cut back?

   a. 2.5%
   b. 5%
   c. 10%
   d. 15%
   e. 20%
   f. 40%
   g. 50%

Section C: Reasons for Work Time Preference

(This section, like section A, may not be of interest to those conducting the survey and may be omitted.)

15. If you were to exchange some of your income for reduced work time, how important would the following reasons be in your decision? (1 = very important; 2 = somewhat important; 3 = not important. Circle the number that most closely reflects your feeling.)

More time for family life and household activities	1	2	3
More time for leisure activities	1	2	3
More time for volunteer work	1	2	3
More time for furthering my education	1	2	3
More time for income-producing hobby	1	2	3
More time for a second career	1	2	3
Health benefits	1	2	3
Transition to retirement or semiretirement	1	2	3
Relief from tedious or boring nature of my job	1	2	3
Relief from stress and fatigue of my job	1	2	3

(Continued)

Figure 7-3. *(continued)*

16. The following reasons might prevent you from exchanging some of your income for reduced work time. How important would these reasons be in your decision not to reduce your work time? (Again, 1 = very important; 2 = somewhat important; and 3 = not important. Circle the number that most closely reflects your feeling.)

I need a full-time income.	1	2	3
I enjoy working full-time.	1	2	3
My job is not suitable for reduced/alternative work time.	1	2	3
My productivity would decline.	1	2	3
My transportation (car pool, bus, etc.) arrangements would be affected.	1	2	3
My child care arrangements would be affected.	1	2	3
It would take longer to become eligible for promotions.	1	2	3
I feel that management would view reduced working hours negatively; I would lose status in my work group and organization.	1	2	3
I feel that it would reduce my chances for promotion.	1	2	3
I am afraid I would not be able to work full-time again if I needed to.	1	2	3
It would affect my retirement income.	1	2	3

Duration of Enrollment. All V-Time programs require that an employee sign up for a specific period of time (generally six to twelve months) beginning with the first day of a pay period. This allows managers to plan their budgets and work needs accordingly. Programs vary, but there are two general approaches:

1. *A designated enrollment period.* During this time, an employee must decide whether to enroll, and all V-Time participants start their new schedules on the same date.

2. *Year-round enrollment.* Although some managers worry that year-round enrollment could create an administrative nightmare, one V-Time program coordinator maintains that it produces a regular flow of applicants that is more manageable than if they all started at the same time. It also provides both managers and employees with some negotiating flexibility. For example, if an employee wanted to reduce to half-time from January to March and that is a busy period for the employer, the manager could respond by saying, "I just can't afford to do it then, but if you would like to reduce from April to June, I think we could handle it."

Approval Responsibility. Supervisors generally have the responsibility for approving or denying requests for a reduced schedule.

Figure 7-4. Sample V-Time application form for an organization seeking to avoid layoffs.

Voluntary Reduced Workweek Request

I hereby volunteer for a reduced workweek as an alternative to layoff.

Effective the _____ (1st or 16th) of _____, 19___, I volunteer to work not less than 30 hours per week to be scheduled as indicated here:

☐ 1. 30 hour workweek: Four (4) 7½ hour days.

☐ 2. 32 hour workweek: Four (4) 8 hour days.

☐ 3. 33.75 hours (10% reduction): Five (5) 6¾ hour days.

☐ 4. 35 hour workweek: Five (5) 7 hour days.

☐ 5. 67½ hours in two workweeks: 1 scheduled day off every other week.

☐ 6. 1 scheduled day off each month.

I fully understand the effect of a reduced workweek on my salary and benefits. I also understand that in order to withdraw from the reduced workweek program, I must submit a written request to my supervisor at least two weeks in advance of the effective date of the withdrawal.

_____   _____
Employee's Name   Employee's Signature

_____   _____
Department/Division   Date

- -

I agree to the terms described above for this employee's participation in the voluntary reduced workweek program.

_____   _____
Dept. Supervisor's Signature   Date

They should be aware of top management support for the program and be encouraged to give favorable consideration whenever possible. It is important for the success of the program that employee requests for participation be handled fairly and objectively. Decisions that seem arbitrary or based on favoritism will quickly foster resentment and erode morale. To ensure fairness, the organization should:

■ Establish guidelines for approving or denying requests.
■ Establish an appeal process.
■ Provide employees and supervisors with written information covering the guidelines and appeal process. (Examples are presented in the next subsection.)

Program Termination for Individuals.   Participation in the program automatically terminates when the contract period ends. The employees return to their full-time status and schedules unless both parties agree to a renewal.

Additionally, individual participation automatically ends when the employee is transferred, promoted, or demoted. The employee must renegotiate V-Time program participation in terms of his or her new status if the employee still wishes to do so and the supervisor supports the request.

Some programs also allow either party to terminate the arrangement by giving thirty to sixty days' notice. Some require that hardship be demonstrated before permitting the agreement to be renounced prior to the end of the contract period.

Impact on Employee Status and Benefits.   If participation in the V-Time program is detrimental to employee benefits or status, enrollment will suffer and union support will be more difficult to secure.

The following paragraphs detail the various ways in which the major employee status and benefits issues have been dealt with in existing programs.

■ *Health and dental benefits.* The impact of V-Time on health and dental benefits depends on whether current policy provides these benefits to employees working less than full-time. As noted in Chapter 4, all employees need access to group health insurance. Prorating the cost of this kind of benefit is viewed as equitable by most employees and employers.

■ *Holidays.* In some organizations, part-time employees are paid for a proportionate amount of the day, based on their time base. A half-time employee would receive four hours' compensation for each holiday in the pay period. A 19/20 time employee would receive 7.6 hours' compensation for each holiday in the pay period (8 hours × 19/20 = 7.6 hours). In other organizations, employees are compensated as though they worked full-time but at a reduced hourly rate.

■ *Disability*. Generally, these benefits are prorated according to the employee's time base and salary. This may lower premiums as well as benefits.

■ *Life insurance*. Since life insurance coverage is tied to salary, the employer's cost will usually decline somewhat, as will the employee's coverage.

■ *Merit salary increases*. A V-Time program generally has no impact on merit raises.

■ *Overtime*. Employees must work more than forty hours in one workweek to qualify for overtime pay.

■ *Probationary period*. Participation in the V-Time program is generally limited to employees who have completed their probationary period, so there is no impact.

■ *Opportunities for promotion*. In some V-Time programs, qualifying experience is prorated; otherwise there is no impact.

■ *Order of layoff*. The policy on layoffs is one key determinant of whether an employee will feel able to enroll in a V-Time program. The state of California Department of Real Estate's policy states the following provisions for handling layoffs when a V-Time program is in effect:

> If layoff becomes unavoidable, employees who participate in a voluntary reduced work time program pursuant to this article shall not routinely be subject to layoff ahead of full-time employees. Such part-time employees shall be subject to the same seniority and other layoff considerations as full-time employees in determining the order of layoff.[6]

(See also the following discussions of retirement benefits and seniority and service credit.)

■ *Retirement benefits*. Retirement benefits can be based on either (1) contributions (V-Time participants will contribute less because the formula is generally a percentage of the monthly salary) or (2) the employee's full-time equivalent salary, using the same formula as for any other regular employee contributing to the retirement fund. (See also the following discussion of seniority and service credit.)

■ *Seniority and service credit*. In some programs, all participating employees, regardless of their individual time reductions, continue to receive one year of service credit for each twelve months that they are employed. In other programs, seniority and service credit are prorated, based on hours actually worked. For instance, an employee taking a 20 percent work time reduction would earn 80 percent of one year of service credit for the year in which he or she participates in the program.

The following is an example of a method for determining service credit developed by the state of California: A full-time employee earns one-tenth of a credit per qualifying (in this case, monthly) pay period up to one credit per year. An employee on a reduced schedule who works the equivalent of ten qualifying pay periods per year would therefore continue to receive full retirement credit. (Although the state does not have a time base of 10/12, this applies to time bases of 17/20, 9/10, or 19/20—that is, pay reductions of up to 15 percent.) Greater time-base reductions will have a negligible effect on retirement credit. (For example, an 8/10 time base earns .96 retirement service credit per year.) The months selected for a V-Time arrangement may lessen its impact on service credit, because credit is calculated on the basis of service rendered during a state fiscal year, which runs from July 1 through June 30. Thus, a reduced work time employee who works half-time on a V-Time agreement from April in one fiscal year through September in the next (while working full-time during the balance of those fiscal years) would receive full retirement credit for both fiscal years; if the period of the agreement were from June through November, the employee would receive full credit for the first year and .95 retirement service credit for the second year. The net effect of the foregoing method for determining service credit is that retirement benefits will be somewhat less for participants who choose V-Time reductions greater than 15 percent.

If seniority accrual is prorated, V-Time participants will find themselves at the end of one year of participation with less seniority than full-time colleagues whose seniority was previously the same as theirs. Employers should keep in mind that this sort of provision may discourage the use of V-Time as an alternative to layoffs.

■ *Sick leave.* In some programs, sick leave is credited on a prorated basis on the first day of the monthly pay period following completion of a qualifying month. For example, a half-time employee receives four hours' sick leave credit each month; a 19/20 employee receives 7.6 hours' credit each month (8 hours × 19/20 = 7.6). In other programs, the amount of sick leave earned is the same as if the individual were working full-time, but compensation is based on the employee's adjusted hourly rate.

■ *Vacation.* Vacation credits can be earned according to the same formula as for service credit or according to the same formula as for sick leave.

■ *Workers' compensation.* A V-Time program generally has no impact on workers' compensation.

The major program design issues we have just discussed are summarized in Table 7-3. Figure 7-5 is a sample worksheet used to record detailed decisions about program design. A blank copy of this worksheet has also been provided (see Figure 7-6) for use in planning your own V-Time program.

Develop Resource Materials

The organization will need to create resource materials targeted toward managers and supervisors and materials targeted toward

Table 7-3.   Program design checklist: V-Time.

Key Design Issues	Notes
Eliminating current barriers	
☐ Provisions of existing policy on part-time that might hamper V-Time	
Creating new policy	
☐ Scope	
☐ Eligibility	
☐ Range of reductions to be offered	
☐ How reductions can be taken	
☐ Enrollment process	
☐ Duration of enrollment	
☐ Approval responsibility	
☐ Program termination for individuals	
☐ Impact on employee status and benefits	

Figure 7-5.   Sample program design worksheet: V-Time.

■ Range of reductions will include:

   _5_ %, _10_ %, _12.5_ %, _20_ %, _30_ %, _50_ %.

■ Time off may be taken as:

Reduced workday   Additional vacation

Reduced workweek

Personal time off

■ Enrollment will be:

   _X_ Open, all year round. _____ A _____-week period from _____
          to _____.

■ Participants will remain on the reduced schedule for:

   ☐ A fixed period set   two pay   6   12
   by management: _____ periods _____ months _____ months _____ other: _____.
   ☒ Varying periods of time agreed upon between employee and supervisor.

■ Application process tasks:

   1. Form designed   ☑ 3. Termination regulations approved ☑
   2. Criteria for handling requests   4. Approval/denial process
       written   ☑   formulated   ☑
                                  5. Appeals process designed   ☑

■ V-Time's impact on employee status and benefits will be:

   1. Health and dental plans   No impact; retain full coverage.

   2. Holidays   Prorated.

   3. Life insurance   No impact.

   4. Disability insurance   Based on salary; proportionately lower.

   5. Merit salary adjustment   No impact.

   6. Order of layoffs   No impact. However, seniority accrual is
                           prorated (see below).

SOURCE: Adapted from *V-Time: A New Way to Work* (San Francisco: New Ways to Work, 1985), 17.

7. Overtime	Must work more than 40 hours to qualify for overtime.
8. Probationary period	No impact.
9. Promotional opportunities	No impact.
10. Retirement benefits	May be reduced as a result of reduced schedule.
11. Seniority and service credit	Based on hours actually worked.
12. Sick leave	Prorated.
13. Vacation	Prorated.
14. Workers' compensation insurance	No impact on eligibility. Benefits could be reduced.

employees. Some types of resource materials can be used both with managers and supervisors and with employees.

Resource Materials for Managers and Supervisors. These items should include an explanation of the organization's objectives in introducing V-Time, an overview of the program, information on whom to contact with specific questions about implementation of the program, and guidelines for assessing employee requests for a reduced work schedule. Figure 7-7 is an example of a V-Time program description. The type of information presented in it would be useful both to managers and supervisors and to employees. Figure 7-8 is an example of a set of guidelines designed to help supervisors evaluate requests from employees to enroll in the V-Time program.

Managers particularly need to know how V-Time will affect their current and future personnel allotments and budgets. They should be advised whether or not payroll savings can be redirected toward hiring additional permanent or temporary employees or meeting some other critical need. If hiring additional employees is allowed, managers should be reminded that since less-experienced workers can be hired at a lower salary rate to fill the hours no longer worked

Figure 7-6.   Sample program design worksheet: V-Time.

■ Range of reductions will include:

_____%, _____%, _____%, _____%, _____%, _____%.

■ Time off may be taken as:

_____   _____

_____   _____

_____   _____

■ Enrollment will be:

_____ Open, all year round. _____ A _____-week period from _____
        to _____.

■ Participants will remain on the reduced schedule for:

☐ A fixed period set   two pay   6   12
by management: _____ periods _____ months _____ months _____ other: _____.
☐ Varying periods of time agreed upon between employee and supervisor.

■ Application process tasks:

1. Form designed   ☐   3. Termination regulations approved ☐
2. Criteria for handling requests   4. Approval/denial process
   written   ☐   formulated   ☐
                                         5. Appeals process designed   ☐

■ V-Time's impact on employee status and benefits will be:

1. Health and dental plans   _____

2. Holidays   _____

3. Life insurance   _____

4. Disability insurance   _____

5. Merit salary adjustment   _____

6. Order of layoffs   _____

7. Overtime   _____

SOURCE: Adapted from *V-Time: A New Way to Work* (San Francisco: New Ways to Work, 1985), 17.

 8. Probationary period _____

 9. Promotional opportunities _____

10. Retirement benefits _____

11. Seniority and service
    credit _____

12. Sick leave _____

13. Vacation _____

14. Workers' compensation
    insurance _____

by V-Time program participants, they may also be spending less of their budgets for the same number of paid hours.

The guidelines for supervisors should cover such topics as administrative and workload considerations, scheduling of overtime, and maintaining service to the public or clients, if that is appropriate.

Resource Materials for Employees. Employees need overview information that details what kind of effect the program will have on their status and benefits and what the application process is. Potential participants in the program also need resource materials that help them specifically assess the financial impact of V-Time and any effect on their status and conditions of employment as a result of their participation in the program.

As noted above, employees will find it helpful to have a description of the V-Time program, such as that shown in Figure 7-7. Table 7-4 and Figure 7-9 present examples of other types of information that interested employees will need. The table shows the specific effect of various increments of work time reduction on an employee's monthly salary. The figure is a worksheet that employees can use to perform an individualized calculation of their own net pay at various levels of time reduction. Detailed material such as this can

(Text continues on page 269.)

Figure 7-7.   Sample V-Time program description.

Program Guidelines		
date: 5/27/93 _____ supersedes Guidelines issued 9/88	Voluntary Reduction in Work Schedules (Voluntary Furlough) Program Guidelines for Fiscal Years 1993–94 and 1994–95	Page 1

Introduction:

Voluntary Reduction in Work Schedule (VRWS), commonly referred to as Voluntary Furlough, is a program that allows employees to voluntarily trade income for time off. This program is in effect for Fiscal Years 1993–94 and 1994–95. The VRWS program is available to eligible annual-salaried employees in the Professional, Scientific and Technical Services Unit (PS&T) and eligible annual-salaried employees designated Management/Confidential.

1. *Purposes*
   a. VRWS provides agencies with a flexible mechanism for allocating staff resources.
   b. VRWS permits employees to reduce their work schedules to reflect personal needs and interests.

2. *Limitations: Eligibility, Work Schedule Reduction, Term of VRWS*
   a. Eligibility: This program is available only to certain annual-salaried employees in the Professional, Scientific and Technical Services Unit (PS&T) and to certain annual salaried employees designated Management/Confidential.
   (1) Employees are required to have 26 consecutive payroll periods of full-time annual-salaried State service immediately prior to entry into a VRWS program. Payroll periods of VRWS participation, or absences while receiving Sick Leave at Half Pay, Short-Term Disability Leave under the Income Protection Plan or Workers' Compensation Leave under the Leave, Award and Supplement, or Medical Evaluation programs will count as full-time annual-salaried service in computation of the 26 consecutive payroll periods so long as the employee was working on a full-time annual-salaried basis immediately prior to the VRWS participation, Sick Leave at Half Pay, Workers' Compensation, or short-term disability leave under the Income Protection Plan. For example, an employee who had worked twenty-one payroll periods on a full-time annual-salaried basis followed by five payroll periods on Sick Leave at Half Pay and then returned to work would be eligible for VRWS upon return to work.
   (2) For those PS&T unit employees, who were participating in the VRWS program in Fiscal Year 1990–91 and who transitioned to part-time status

SOURCE: Governor's Office of Employee Relations, State of New York. Program guidelines for Voluntary Reduction in Work Schedules program, 1993–1995.

upon termination of such program, the 26 consecutive payroll periods of full-time service requirement, stated in Section 2.a.(1) above, is waived.

(3) Employees, who were eligible for the VRWS program under the 1984–86 Program Guidelines, continue to be eligible to participate in the program even if they never participated in the 1984–86 VRWS program. (Under the Guidelines for the 1984–85 program, VRWS was available to employees who (1) were full-time annual-salaried employees as of April 1, 1984 or (2) first entered the PS&T unit or the M/C group as full-time annual-salaried employees between April 1, 1984 and April 1, 1986.)

b. Work Schedule Reduction: Participating employees may reduce their work schedules (and salaries) a minimum of 5 percent, in 5 percent increments, up to a maximum of 30 percent.

c. Term of VRWS Program: The VRWS program is in effect for Fiscal Years 1993–94 and 1994–95. This program will end at the close of business on the last day of the last payroll period of Fiscal Year 1994–95 unless otherwise extended by the State, or for PS&T employees by agreement between the State and the Public Employees Federation.

3. *Description of an Employee VRWS Program*
    a. Employee develops a plan for a reduced work schedule.
    b. Management reviews and approves plan as long as it is consistent with operating needs.
    c. Jointly agreed plan specifies:
       (1) Duration of VRWS agreement.
       (2) Percentage reduction of work schedule and salary.
       (3) Amount of VR Time earned in exchange for reduced salary.
       (4) Schedule for use of VR Time earned. This may be either a fixed schedule, e.g., every Friday, every Wednesday afternoon, an entire month off, etc. or intermittent time off.
          (i) An employee's fixed schedule VR Time off, once the VRWS schedule has been agreed upon by management, cannot be changed without the consent of the employee except in an emergency. In the event an employee's schedule is changed without the consent of the employee, the employee may appeal this action through an expedited grievance procedure.
          (ii) VR Time used as intermittent time off will be subject to scheduling during the term of the VRWS agreement, and will require advance approval by the employee's supervisor.
    d. While the VRWS agreement is in effect, the employee will earn and accumulate VR credits in accordance with the percentage reduction in workweek, e.g., a 10 percent reduction will result in 7.5 or 8 hours of VR credit earned each payroll period which the employee will charge on his or her scheduled VR absences. If the employee's VRWS schedule calls for one-half day off every Friday afternoon, 3¾ or 4 hours VR credits will be charged for 10 percent reduction and taking an entire month off will work his or her full 37½ or 40 hours each week, accrue 7.5 or 8 hours of VR credit each payroll period, and have the accumulated VR credits to use during that month.
    e. The employee never goes off the payroll. The employee remains in active pay

(Continued)

Figure 7-7. *(continued)*

status for the duration of the agreement and receives pay checks each payroll period at the agreed-upon, temporarily reduced level.

f. The employee will work a pro rata share of his or her normal work schedule over the duration of the agreement period.

g. Participation in the VRWS program will not be a detriment to later career moves within the agency or the State.

h. Scheduled non-work time taken in accordance with a VRWS program shall not be considered to be an absence for the purpose of application of Section 4.5(f) of the Civil Service Rules governing probationary periods.

4. *Time Limits*

The employee and management can establish a VRWS program of any number of payroll periods in duration from one to the number of payroll periods remaining in the term of the VRWS program. The VRWS agreement must begin on the first day of a payroll period and end on the last day of a payroll period. The employee and management may, by agreement, discontinue or modify the VRWS agreement if the employee's needs or circumstances change.

5. *Time Records Maintenance*

a. All VRWS schedules will be based on the crediting and debiting of VR credits on the employee's time card against a regular 37½ or 40 hour workweek.

b. VR credits earned during Fiscal Years 1993–94 and 1994–95 may be carried over on the employee's time card past the end of the individual VRWS agreement and past the end of the VRWS program period but must be liquidated by September 30, 1995. Management and employees should make a concerted effort to make sure accruals will be liquidated by the September 30, 1995 deadline.

Appendix A

VOLUNTARY REDUCTION IN WORK SCHEDULE
Effect on Benefits and Status

Annual Leave—prorate accruals based on the employee's VRWS percentage
Personal Leave—prorate accruals based on the employee's VRWS percentage
Sick Leave at Full Pay—prorate accruals based on the employee's VRWS percentage
Holidays—no change in holiday benefit
Sick Leave at Half Pay—no impact on eligibility or entitlement. Employees who go on Sick Leave at Half Pay for 28 consecutive calendar days will have their VRWS agreement cancelled and be returned to their normal work schedule and pay base.
Workers' Compensation Benefits—no impact on eligibility for entitlement to workers' compensation benefits pursuant to rule or contract. Following 28 consecutive calendar days of absence due to a work-related injury or illness, the VRWS agreement is cancelled and the employee is returned to his or her normal work schedule and pay base. At that point, the employee receives workers' compen-

sation benefits based on the normal full-time salary and no longer earns VR credits.

Disability Under the Income Protection Plan—An employee's VRWS agreement is automatically cancelled on the day the employee begins receiving STD/LTD benefits.

Military Leave—no impact on eligibility or entitlement

Jury-Court Leave—no impact on eligibility or entitlement

Paid Leave Balances on Time Card—There is no requirement that leave credits be exhausted prior to the beginning of the VRWS agreement. Paid leave vacation, sick leave and holiday balances are carried forward without adjustment; personal leave balance is prorated.

Shift Pay—prorate

Inconvenience Pay—prorate

Location Pay—prorate

Geographic Pay—prorate

Pre-Shift Briefing—prorate

Standby Pay—no impact

Salary—normal gross salary earned is reduced by percentage of voluntary reduction in work schedule; no effect on base annual salary rate

Payroll—employee never leaves the payroll; employee remains in full payroll status with partial pay for the duration of the agreement period and receives pay checks each pay period at the agreed upon temporarily reduced level

Return to Normal Work Schedule—employee will return to his or her normal work schedule upon completion of the VRWS agreement period

Banked (Unused) VR Time Upon Return to Normal Work Schedule—VR Time Credits earned during Fiscal Years 1993–94 and 1994–95 program may be carried forward on the employee's time card after completion of the individual VRWS agreement period and past the end of the VRWS program period but must be liquidated by September 30, 1995

Banked (Unused) VR Time Upon Separation—unused VR Time Credits will be paid at the straight time rate upon layoff, resignation from State service, termination, retirement or death

Banked (Unused) VR Time Upon Promotion, Transfer or Reassignment Within an Agency or Within a Facility or Institution—unused VR Time Credits are carried forward on the employee's time card when movement is within an appointing authority. Continuation of the VRWS program is at the discretion of management.

Banked (Unused) VR Time Upon Movement From One Agency to Another or Between Facilities or Institutions Within an Agency—unused VR Time Credits will be paid at the straight time rate by the agency or facility/institution in which the VR Time was earned, unless the employee requests and the new agency or facility/institution accepts the transfer of VR Time on the employee's time card

Health Insurance—no effect; full coverage

Dental Insurance—no effect, full coverage

Employee Benefit Fund—no effect

Survivor's Benefit—no effect

(Continued)

Figure 7-7. *(continued)*

Retirement Benefit Earnings—will reduce final average salary if VRWS period is included in three years earnings used to calculate final average salary
Retirement Service Credit—prorate
Social Security—no change in the contribution rate which is set by Federal Law and is applied to the salary which the employee is paid
Unemployment Insurance—no change; formula set by statute
Performance Advance or Increment Advance—evaluation date is not changed; no change in eligibility
Performance Award or Lump Sum Payment—no impact; no change in eligibility
Longevity Increase—no change in eligibility
Probationary Period—no effect
Traineeship—no effect
Layoff—no impact; seniority date for layoff purposes is not changed
Seniority—no impact; employee never leaves the payroll; seniority date is not changed; full seniority credit is earned
Seniority for Promotion Examinations—no impact; VR Time used shall be counted as time worked in determining seniority credits for promotion exams
Eligibility for Promotion Examinations—no impact; VR Time used shall be counted as time worked in determining eligibility for promotion exams
Eligibility for Open Competitive Examinations—prorate; VR Time used shall not be considered time worked for determining length of service for *open competitive* examinations
Overtime Work—VR Time used shall not be counted as time worked in determining eligibility for overtime payments at premium rates within a workweek

APPLICATION FOR VOLUNTARY REDUCTION IN WORK SCHEDULE

Agency Code: _____   Name: _____

Agency: _____   Title: _____

Division: _____   SG: _____

Office: _____   Line No: _____ NU: _____

Percent Reduction in Work Schedule requested: _____%

Number of pay periods of participation: _____ pay periods

VR Time to be earned during agreement period: _____ days

Beginning 1st day of pay period   #_____, (date) _____, 19_____

Ending last day of pay period   #_____, (date) _____, 19_____

Normal work schedule _____ hours/week; _____ hours/pay period.

Reduced AVG work schedule _____ hours/week; _____ hours/pay period.

VR Time earned _____ hours/week; _____ hours/pay period.

Check type of Proposed Schedule of VR Time use below. Specify schedule for use of VR Time on page 2 of application.

A. ☐ Shorter workday/Normal workweek.

B. ☐ Shorter workweek/Normal workday.

C. ☐ (ALTERNATIVE-WORK-SCHEDULE-TYPE ARRANGEMENT)
    Longer workday/Shorter workweek.
    Note: Copy of this form must be sent to the Division of the Budget, Central Management and Budgeting Unit for employees who receive agency approval to use this scheduling option.

D. ☐ Block(s) of time off.

E. ☐ Intermittent time off. (Specify pattern, if any.)

F. ☐ Combination of above.

Employee Signature	Date

☐ APPROVED   ☐ DISAPPROVED (attach written justification and transmit to Personnel Officer)

Effective Date: _____

I agree to the proposed temporary adjustment in work schedule and understand that this employee will work a pro rata share of his or her normal schedule over the duration of the agreement period.

Supervisor—Date	Section Chief/Office Head—Date

☐ APPROVED   ☐ DISAPPROVED_____
                                    Personnel Officer—Date

AGENCY: KEEP VRWS APPLICATION FORM ON FILE

(Continued)

Figure 7-7. *(continued)*

Schedule for Use of VR Time

Name: _____

Agency Code: _____

Payroll Period _____		Th	Fr	Sa	Su	Mo	Tu	We	Th	Fr	Sa	Su	Mo	Tu	We
No.	Dates Covered														
1															
2															
3															
4															
5															
6															
7															
8															
9															
10															
11															
12															
13															
14															
15															
16															
17															
18															
19															
20															
21															
22															
23															
24															
25															
26															

Instructions

1. In Payroll Period column, indicate beginning and ending dates of each pay period covered by the agreement.
2. For each pay period, indicate all days/time worked (include number of hrs. worked) and days/time not worked, that is indicate all pass days and all VR time off. If you

plan to use other accruals in conjunction with VR schedule, these days/this time should also be included in the schedule. Use the codes listed below to indicate category of days/time.

3. Where the schedule repeats each pay period, fill out the schedule (include number of hrs. worked/not worked) and days off for the first pay period only and indicate "same" for subsequent pay periods.

4. For partial day absences, indicate number of hours worked/off and code for category of leave (for example, 5½-W; 2-VR).

Work/Leave Category Codes

VR—VR Leave   AL—Annual Leave
W—Day Worked   X—Pass Days

VRWS—Examples of VR Time Work Schedule Alternatives

Below are several examples of ways VR Time can be used. They are not intended to be restrictive. Combinations and variations should be considered for an employee's individualized schedule.

A. *Shorter Workday*
   1. A 10 percent reduction on a 37½ hour per week schedule could produce a work week of 5 days at 6¾ hours each.
   2. A 20 percent reduction on a 37½ hour per week schedule could produce a work week of 5 days at 6 hours each.

B. *Shorter Workweek*
   1. A 10 percent reduction could produce a 4½ day work week.
   2. A 10 percent reduction could produce a work week of 3 days at 8½ hours plus a fourth day of 8¼ hours on a 37½ hour work week; or four days of 9 hours each on a 40 hour work week.
   3. A 20 percent reduction could produce a 4 day work week with no change in the length of the work day.
   4. A 20 percent reduction could produce a 3 day work week at 10 hours per day on a 37½ hour work week; or 10⅔ hours per day on a 40 hour work week.

C. *Block of Time (or extended vacation)*
   With a 20 percent reduction for 10 payroll periods, an employee can accumulate VR Time to take off a month. By working the normal full schedule for 8 pay periods and banking VR Time earned, an employee could take off 2 pay periods (a month). The employee would receive a paycheck representing a 20 percent reduction in pay for each of the 10 payroll periods. At the end of the agreement period, employee returns to normal work schedule and salary.
   (earn 2 days VR Time per pay period × 10 = 20 days)
   (20 days + 10 = 2 pay periods or 4 weeks off)

D. *Intermittent Days/Time-Off*
   A 10 percent reduction produces 1 full day of VR Time for each pay period, which could be taken intermittently in the same manner as annual leave.

(Continued)

Figure 7-7. *(continued)*

VRWS—VR Time Earned in Days

# of Pay	Percent Reduction Taken					
	5%	10%	15%	20%	25%	
Periods						
1	½	1	1½	2	2½	3
2	1	2	3	4	5	6
3	1½	3	4½	6	7½	9
4	2	4	6	8	10	12
5	2½	5	7½	10	12½	15
6	3	6	9	12	15	18
7	3½	7	10½	14	17½	21
8	4	8	12	16	20	24
9	4½	9	13½	18	22½	27
10	5	10	15	20	25	30
11	5½	11	16½	22	27½	33
12	6	12	18	24	30	36
13	6½	13	19½	26	32½	39
14	7	14	21	28	35	42
15	7½	15	22½	30	37½	45
16	8	16	24	32	40	48
17	8½	17	25½	34	42½	51
18	9	18	27	36	45	54
19	9½	19	28½	38	47½	57
20	10	20	30	40	50	60
21	10½	21	31½	42	52½	63
22	11	22	33	44	55	66
23	11½	23	34½	46	57½	69
24	12	24	36	48	60	72
25	12½	25	37½	50	62½	75
26	13	26	39	52	65	78

TO CONVERT TO HOURS: Multiply the number of days by the number of hours in a normal workday.

enable employees to determine in advance just where they would stand financially if they were to enroll in the V-Time program.

Announce the Program

Once the program has been designed and the supporting reference materials developed, the availability of this new option should be announced to employees. But as is the case with other part-time alternatives, if the use of a V-Time program is to achieve the organization's objective of greater flexibility, then the program must be an active one rather than just a policy carried on the books. A concerted effort will be required to encourage employees to enroll.

Promote the Program

An employer that introduces V-Time as an alternative to layoffs wants as many workers as possible to enroll in order to achieve the maximum multiplier effect on payroll reduction. Similarly, an employer that plans to use the program to accommodate the needs of

(Text continues on page 278.)

Figure 7-8.   Sample supervisory guidelines for handling V-Time requests.

State of California   Department of Real Estate

GUIDELINES FOR DETERMINING ADMINISTRATIVE
FEASIBILITY OF REDUCED WORK TIME REQUESTS

RE 139 (1/83)

1. *GENERAL NOTES*

State agencies and supervisors are expected to review employee requests for reduced work time positively and, whenever possible, to work out a schedule that will meet both the department's and employee's needs. In meeting this requirement, it may be necessary for supervisors to be more flexible in work scheduling than they have been in the past.

If the supervisor decides that a particular reduced work schedule is not administratively feasible, the employee who made the request for reduced work time should be provided with a written explanation for the decision via the RE 138. Before a proposed schedule is denied, however, all reasonable alternatives for backup coverage or other arrangements should be considered.

SOURCE: State of California Department of Real Estate, reprinted in *V-Time: A New Way to Work* (San Francisco: New Ways to Work, 1985), 30.

(Continued)

Figure 7-8. *(continued)*

2. *SERVICE TO PUBLIC/CLIENTS*

   a. General Coverage

   Adequate scheduling and coordination of reduced work time usually will prevent a significant impact on general service to the public (e.g., public counters, general telephone inquiries, etc.). However, a reduced work time schedule that resulted in an actual disruption of service to the public or an unacceptable decline in its timeliness or quality would not be administratively feasible if the deficiency otherwise could not be corrected.

   b. Special Needs

   Reduced work time may not be feasible where an employee is the *sole* expert in an area requiring coverage during all normal working hours. The same may be the case where employees work on such an intensive one-to-one basis with special clients that assignment sharing would not be appropriate.

3. *ADMINISTRATIVE CONSIDERATIONS*

   Since reduced work-time employees would normally not all be working at the same time, the broadened supervisory span of control resulting from converting one or more full-time positions to part-time should not make a reduced work-time schedule unfeasible. However, where a supervisor already has a wide span of control for the type of work supervised, a reduced work-time schedule that resulted in the transfer of new, untrained staff could be unfeasible. However, before ruling out a reduced work-time schedule on this basis, other possibilities for managing the span of control problem within existing supervisory staffing should be fully explored.

4. *WORK LOAD CONSIDERATIONS*

   In work settings where a heavy, active work load must be accomplished, consideration must be given to high-priority work and the consequences of the effects of reduced work schedules on output before requests for reduced work time are granted.

5. *WORK LOAD AND OVERTIME*

   Participants shall not be assigned work load or mandatory overtime that is excessive in comparison to that assigned to other employees performing similar work.

6. *ADDITIONAL INFORMATION*

   If you have questions not covered by these guidelines or the Reduced Worktime Program Facts (RE 140), contact Personnel.

Table 7-4. Example of the effect of reduced work time on pay.

Associate Analyst Level
Top Step, Gross Salary $2,501

	Married, two exemptions					Single, one exemption				
	Full-Time	Percent reduction				Full-Time	Percent reduction			
		5%	10%	15%	20%		5%	10%	15%	20%
Decrease in net pay		4%	7.5%	11.5%	15.5%		3.5%	7%	10.5%	14%
Gross pay	2,501.00	2,375.95	2,250.90	2,125.85	2,000.80	2,501.00	2,375.95	2,250.90	2,125.85	2,000.80
Net pay	1,697.10	1,633.00	1,568.83	1,504.58	1,432.47	1,454.62	1,404.24	1,353.82	1,303.45	1,252.54
Withholding:										
Federal tax	466.19	427.37	388.62	349.84	317.29	624.20	577.92	531.67	485.39	439.14
State tax	70.74	63.24	55.74	48.36	42.11	155.21	141.45	127.70	113.94	100.19
Social Security	167.57	159.19	150.81	142.43	134.54	167.57	159.19	150.81	142.43	134.54
Retirement	99.40	93.15	86.90	80.64	74.39	99.40	93.15	86.90	80.64	74.39

SOURCE: State of California Employment Development Department, reprinted in *V-Time: A New Way to Work* (San Francisco: New Ways to Work, 1985), 35.

Figure 7-9. Sample worksheet for calculating the financial impact of V-Time.

MANDATORY PAYROLL DEDUCTION WORKSHEET

Employees considering reducing their time base may use this worksheet for computing mandatory deductions (state and federal withholding taxes, Social Security, and retirement) to determine their prospective net monthly salary at the reduced time base.

For easy reference in calculating your deductions, an example showing the mandatory deductions for a married employee with two exemptions and a monthly salary of $1,235.00 is provided.

1. SALARY COMPUTATION

    Example: $1,235.00   ×   85%   = $1,049.75

          Full-time monthly   % of time to   Reduced monthly
          salary rate   be worked   salary

          $ ×   = $

          Full-time monthly   % of time to   Reduced monthly
          salary rate   be worked   salary

- -

2. SOCIAL SECURITY CONTRIBUTION (Omit this step if you are not a member of Social Security system.)

    Example: $1,049.75   ×   6.70%   = $70.33

          Monthly salary   Social Security   Monthly Social
                         contribution rate   Security contribution

          $ ×   6.70%   = $

          Monthly salary   Social Security   Monthly Social
                         contribution rate   Security contribution

- -

3. RETIREMENT CONTRIBUTION (PERS)

    If you have Social Security:

    Example: $1,049.75   − $513.00 = $536.75 × 5% = $26.83

          Monthly salary   Monthly retirement
                                                  contribution

---

The figures in this worksheet were developed in 1985 and serve as an example of what tables should be used.

SOURCE: State of California Employment Development Department, reprinted in *V-Time: A New Way to Work* (San Francisco: New Ways to Work, 1985), 42–46.

$$\underline{\text{\$ \hspace{2cm}}} - \$513.00 = \underline{\text{\$ \hspace{1.5cm}}} \times 5\% = \underline{\text{\$ \hspace{2cm}}}$$

Monthly salary   Monthly retirement
contribution

If you do not have Social Security:

$$\underline{\text{\$1,049.75}} - \$317.00 = \underline{\$732.75} \times 6\% = \underline{\$43.97}$$

Monthly salary   Monthly retirement
contribution

$$\underline{\text{\$ \hspace{2cm}}} - \$317.00 = \underline{\text{\$ \hspace{1.5cm}}} \times 6\% = \underline{\text{\$ \hspace{2cm}}}$$

Monthly salary   Monthly retirement
contribution

---

4. WITHHOLDING TAXES   Your annual salary and annual gross may be applied to both federal and state withholding calculations (Sections A and B which follow). If you are considering changing your number of exemptions when changing to a reduced time base, remember to reflect the change as you work out your withholding.

NOTE: Example computed for married person with two exemptions.

Step 1

Example: $\underline{\text{\$1,049.75}} \times 12 \text{ months} = \underline{\$12,597.00}$ (A)

Monthly salary   Annual salary

$\underline{\text{\$ \hspace{2cm}}} \times 12 \text{ months} = \underline{\text{\$ \hspace{1.5cm}}}$ (A)

Monthly salary   Annual salary

Step 2

Example: $\underline{\$12,597.00}$ (A) $- \underline{\text{\$ \hspace{1cm} 0}} = \underline{\$12,597.00}$ (B)

Annual salary   Annual amount deducted   Annual gross
for deferred compensation

$\underline{\text{\$ \hspace{1.5cm}}}$ (A) $- \underline{\text{\$ \hspace{2cm}}} = \underline{\text{\$ \hspace{1.5cm}}}$ (B)

Annual salary   Annual amount deducted   Annual gross
for deferred compensation

A. FEDERAL WITHHOLDING TAX

Step 1

Example $\underline{\text{\hspace{1cm} 2 \hspace{1cm}}} \times \$1,000.00 = \underline{\$2,000.00}$ (C)

No. exemptions

$\underline{\text{\hspace{2cm}}} \times \underline{\text{\$ \hspace{1cm}}} = \underline{\text{\$ \hspace{1.5cm}}}$ (C)

No. exemptions

(Continued)

Figure 7-9. *(continued)*

<u>Step 2</u>

Example: <u>$12,597.00 (B)</u> − <u>$2,000.00 (C)</u> = <u>$10,597.00 (D)</u>
      Annual gross   Taxable wages

         <u>$ (B)</u> − <u>$ (C)</u> = <u>$ (D)</u>
      Annual gross   Taxable wages

<u>Step 3</u>   Circle the numbers which apply to you in Table A; use them to fill in blanks for Steps 4 and 5.

TABLE A

SINGLE OR HEAD OF HOUSEHOLD

Taxable wages		Amount of tax				
Not over $1,420.00		0				
Over	Not over	(Col. 1)		(Col. 2)		(Col. 3)
$ 1,420.00	$ 3,910.00	$ 0.00	plus	14%	of excess over	$ 1,420.00
$ 3,910.00	$ 5,200.00	4 348.60	plus	16%	of excess over	$ 3,910.00
$ 5,200.00	$ 9,400.00	$ 555.00	plus	19%	of excess over	$ 5,200.00
$ 9,400.00	$14,000.00	$1,353.00	plus	24%	of excess over	$ 9,400.00
$14,000.00	$17,200.00	$2,457.00	plus	29%	of excess over	$14,000.00
$17,200.00	$22,500.00	$3,385.00	plus	32%	of excess over	$17,200.00
$22,500.00	....	$5,081.00	plus	37%	of excess over	$22,500.00

MARRIED

Taxable wages		Amount of tax				
Not over $2,400.00		0				
Over	Not over	(Col. 1)		(Col. 2)		(Col. 3)
$ 2,400.00	$ 7,650.00	$ 0.00	plus	14%	of excess over	$ 2,400.00
$ 7,650.00	$10,900.00	$ 735.00	plus	16%	of excess over	$ 7,650.00
$10,900.00	$15,400.00	$1,255.00	plus	20%	of excess over	$10,900.00
$15,400.00	$23,250.00	$2,155.00	plus	25%	of excess over	$15,400.00
$23,250.00	$28,900.00	$4,117.50	plus	31%	of excess over	$23,250.00
$28,900.00	$34,200.00	$5,869.00	plus	34%	of excess over	$28,900.00
$34,200.00	....	$7,671.00	plus	37%	of excess over	$34,200.00

<u>Step 4</u>

Example: <u>$10,597.00 (D)</u> − <u>$7,650.00</u> = <u>$2,947.00</u> × <u>16%</u> = <u>$471.52 (E)</u>
      Taxable wages   Col. 3,   Col. 2,
                  Table A   Table A

         <u>$ (D)</u> − <u>$ </u> = <u>$ </u> × <u> %</u> = <u>$ (E)</u>
      Taxable wages   Col. 3,   Col. 2,
                  Table A   Table A

<u>Step 5</u>

Example: <u>$471,52 (E)</u> + <u>$735.00</u> = <u>$1,206.52 (F)</u>
                   Col. 1,   Annual tax
                   Table A

$\underline{\$\quad\quad\quad}$ (E) + $\underline{\$\quad\quad\quad}$ = $\underline{\$\quad\quad\quad}$ (F)

Col. 1,   Annual tax
Table A

Step 6

Example: $\underline{\$1,206.52}$ (F) ÷ 12 months = $\underline{\$100.54\quad}$

Annual tax   Monthly tax

$\underline{\$\quad\quad\quad}$ (F) ÷ 12 months = $\underline{\$\quad\quad\quad}$

Annual tax   Monthly tax

B.   STATE WITHHOLDING TAX

Step 1   IF ANNUAL GROSS (SEE #4 WITHHOLDING TAXES, STEP 2 [B]) IS
LESS THAN OR EQUAL TO AMOUNT SHOWN IN TABLE B, <u>NO TAX</u> IS
REQUIRED TO BE WITHHELD.
IF ANNUAL GROSS IS GREATER THAN AMOUNT IN TABLE B, PRO-
CEED TO STEP 2.

TABLE B			
LOW-INCOME EXEMPTION TABLE			
SINGLE	MARRIED		HEAD OF HOUSEHOLD
	"0" or "1" exemption	"2" or more exemptions	
$5,000.00	$5,000.00	$10.000.00	$10,000.00

Step 2   Find your standard deduction in Table C.

TABLE C			
STANDARD DEDUCTION TABLE			
SINGLE	MARRIED		HEAD OF HOUSEHOLD
	"0" or "1" exemption	"2" or more exemptions	
$1,400.00	$1,400.00	$2,800.00	$2,800.00

Step 3

Example: $\underline{\$12,597.00}$ (B) − $\underline{\$2,800\quad\quad}$ = $\underline{\$9,797.00}$ (C)

Annual gross   Standard deduction   Taxable wages
                per Table C

$\underline{\$\quad\quad\quad}$ (B) − $\underline{\$\quad\quad\quad}$ = $\underline{\$\quad\quad\quad}$ (C)

Annual gross   Standard deduction   Taxable wages
                per Table C

(Continued)

Figure 7-9. *(continued)*

Step 4   Circle the numbers which apply to you in Table D; then use them to fill in the blanks on Step 5.

TABLE D

MARRIED

| If the taxable wages are . . . | | Computed tax is . . . | | | | | |
Over	But not over	(Col. 1)		(Col. 2)			(Col. 3)
$ 0	$ 5,700	$ 0.00	plus	1%	of amount over	$ 0
$ 5,700	$ 9,980	$ 57.00	plus	2%	of amount over	$ 5,700
$ 9,980	$14,260	$ 142.60	plus	3%	of amount over	$ 9,980
$14,260	$18,580	$ 271.00	plus	4%	of amount over	$14,260
$18,580	$22,860	$ 443.80	plus	5%	of amount over	$18,580
$22,860	$27,160	$ 657.80	plus	6%	of amount over	$22,860
$27,160	$31,420	$ 915.80	plus	7%	of amount over	$27,160
$31,420	$35,720	$1,214.00	plus	8%	of amount over	$31,420
$35,720	$40,000	$1,558.00	plus	9%	of amount over	$35,720
$40,000	$44,280	$1,943.20	plus	10%	of amount over	$40,000
$44,280	and over . . .	$2,371.20	plus	11%	of amount over	$44,280

SINGLE

| If the taxable wages are . . . | | Computed tax Is . . . | | | | | |
Over	But not over	(Col. 1)		(Col. 2)			(Col. 3)
$ 0	$ 2,850	$ 0.00	plus	1%	of amount over	$ 0
$ 2,850	$ 4,990	$ 28.50	plus	2%	of amount over	$ 2,850
$ 4,990	$ 7,130	$ 71.30	plus	3%	of amount over	$ 4,990
$ 7,130	$ 9,290	$ 135.50	plus	4%	of amount over	$ 7,130
$ 9,290	$11,430	$ 221.90	plus	5%	of amount over	$ 9,290
$11,430	$13,580	$ 328.90	plus	6%	of amount over	$11,430
$13,580	$15,710	$ 457.90	plus	7%	of amount over	$13,580
$15,710	$17,860	$ 607.00	plus	8%	of amount over	$15,710
$17,860	$20,000	$ 779.00	plus	9%	of amount over	$17,860
$20,000	$22,140	$ 971.60	plus	10%	of amount over	$20,000
$22,140	and over . . .	$1,185.60	plus	11%	of amount over	$22,140

UNMARRIED HEAD OF HOUSEHOLD

| If the taxable wages are . . . | | Computed tax is . . . | | | | | |
Over	But not over	(Col. 1)		(Col. 2)			(Col. 3)
$ 0	$ 5,720	$ 0.00	plus	1%	of amount over	$ 0
$ 5,720	$ 8,560	$ 57.20	plus	2%	of amount over	$ 5,720
$ 8,560	$10,710	$ 114.00	plus	3%	of amount over	$ 8,560
$10,710	$12,850	$ 178.50	plus	4%	of amount over	$10,710
$12,850	$15,000	$ 264.10	plus	5%	of amount over	$12,850
$15,000	$17,150	$ 371.60	plus	6%	of amount over	$15,000
$17,150	$19,280	$ 500.60	plus	7%	of amount over	$17,150
$19,280	$21,420	$ 649.70	plus	8%	of amount over	$19,280
$21,420	$23,570	$ 820.90	plus	9%	of amount over	$21,420
$23,570	$25,710	$1,014.40	plus	10%	of amount over	$23,570
$25,710	and over . . .	$1,228.40	plus	11%	of amount over	$25,710

Step 5

Example: $9,797.00 (C) − $5,700.00 = $4,097.00 (D) ×   2% = $81.94 + $57.00 = $138.94 (E)
          Taxable wages   Col. 3,   Col. 2,   Col. 1,
                           Table D   Table D   Table D

          $ (C) − $ = $ (D) ×   % = $ + $ = $ (E)
          Taxable wages   Col. 3,   Col. 2,   Col. 1,
                           Table D   Table D   Table D

Step 6   Circle your tax credit on Table E.

Step 7

Example: $138.94 (E) − $70.00   = $68.94   (F)

                  Tax credit,   Annual tax amount
                  Table E

      $ _____ (E) − $ _____ = $ _____ (F)

                  Tax credit,   Annual tax amount
                  Table E

TABLE E

TAX CREDIT TABLE

MARITAL STATUS	NUMBER OF EXEMPTIONS										
	0	1	2	3	4	5	6	7	8	9	10
SINGLE	$0	$35	$46	$57	$68	$79	$90	$101	$112	$123	$134
MARRIED/ HEAD OF HOUSEHOLD	$0	$35	$70	$81	$92	$103	$114	$125	$136	$147	$158

Step 8

Example: $68.94 (F) ÷ 12 months = $5.75 _____

           Annual tax   Monthly tax
           amount   amount

          $ _____ (F) ÷ 12 months = $ _____

           Annual tax   Monthly tax
           amount   amount

5. NET PAY COMPUTATION

Step 1

Example:

Note: You may have other deductions, such as a credit union payment, association dues, or insurance premium.

$ 70.33 _____ $ _____
Social Security   Social Security

+ $ 26.83 _____   + $ _____
Retirement   Retirement

+ $ 100.54 _____   + $ _____
Federal tax   Federal tax

+ $ 5.75 _____   + $ _____
State tax   State tax

(Continued)

Figure 7-9.   *(continued)*

	+ $ _____	+ $ _____
	Other deductions	Other deductions
	+ $ _____	+ $ _____
	Other deductions	Other deductions
	+ $ _____	+ $ _____
	Other deductions	Other deductions
	$ 203.45	$ _____
	Total deductions	Total deductions

Step 2

Example: $1,049.75   − $ 0   − $203.45   = $846.30

| Monthly salary | Deferred comp. | Total deductions (from Step 1) | Net pay |

$ _____   − $ _____   − $ _____   = $ _____

| Monthly salary | Deferred comp. | Total deductions (from Step 1) | Net pay |

current employees or enhance recruitment will want it to be as attractive as possible. Good program design is essential, but employee interest in working less is influenced by other factors as well, chief among them the impact on the employees' finances and job future. This is where an active promotional campaign comes in.

Promotional materials should present general information about the program, including why it is being initiated, guidelines, some common questions and answers, and how to get answers to other questions. Beyond these topics, promotional materials must deal with financial considerations and the issue of the participating employees' job future if they are to encourage the fullest possible participation in the program. Employees need detailed financial impact worksheets to help them determine whether or not they can afford to work part-time and how much they can afford to reduce their schedule. In addition, they need information to allay their fear of layoffs if cutbacks are required in either the near- or the long-term. Such resource materials will also prove helpful to managers and supervisors in explaining the program and encouraging participation.

Briefing sessions for employees and supervisors are another helpful technique for promoting the use of V-Time programs. Such sessions provide a forum at which management can answer questions and affirm the company's commitment to the program.

Trust between an organization and its employees is an important element. The existing level of trust will determine to a considerable extent the level of participation in the early stages of a V-Time program. A skillful promotional effort, backed by effective resource materials, can go a long way toward establishing and supporting that trust.

Evaluate the Program

The type of evaluation you conduct will depend on management's original objectives in setting up the program. Of general interest, however, will be who applied to participate in the program and how their requests were disposed of, which levels of work-time reduction were requested and which approved, what the supervisory response to the program has been, and how employees feel about V-Time. The program should be examined from a procedural and administrative standpoint as well, in order to identify any problem areas.

Fine-Tune the Program

Once the V-Time program has been evaluated, the organization must address and resolve the problems that have been identified. For example:

Problem	*Solution*
Supervisors complain that the enrollment period for the V-Time program constitutes a disruptive period every twelve months.	Consider changing to a year-round enrollment.
Employee requests for inclusion in the V-Time program remain unprocessed for long periods.	Set a time limit and state that responses to employee requests must occur within that limit.
Supervisors consider the program a drain on their resources.	Hold a workshop for supervisors to discuss ways to improve the allocation of resources—both human and financial—as a result of the greater flexibility made possible by the V-Time program.

Summary

A voluntary reduced work time program offers regular part-time options in a way that overcomes what some employees regard as the disadvantages of more traditional part-time work. There are three main differences between regular part-time and V-Time:

1. While regular part-time work is usually open-ended, an employee enrolls in a V-Time program for a specified time period.

2. While an organization may or may not have an established procedure for a regular part-time employee to return to full-time work, such a provision is an integral part of a V-Time program, since it is expected that unless a continuation of the V-Time schedule is mutually agreed upon by the employee and· his or her supervisor, the employee will resume a full-time schedule once the V-Time agreement expires.

3. While most regular part-time work involves as much as a 20 percent to 50 percent time reduction, V-Time programs provide for a range of reductions from as much as 50 percent to as little as 2.5 percent, making schedule cutbacks feasible for interested employees who could not handle the more substantial time (and salary) reductions of regular part-time.

V-Time programs originated at the county government level, then spread to state government and to the private sector. While experience with V-Time has to date been limited, it is clear that this work time alternative offers a number of features that should make it increasingly attractive to employers in both the public and private sectors.

The net effect of the differences between V-Time programs and regular part-time is that a V-Time program standardizes the option of part-time, eliminating the inequities often associated with ad hoc schedule cutbacks. It also offers a wider range of choice of reduction, which gives it a broader appeal to employees. Hence, it is an especially appropriate choice for an employer that wants to offer a part-time arrangement or multiply the effect of an existing program of part-time options, either to accommodate employee needs or to meet one or more organizational objectives (such as enhancing recruitment, minimizing layoffs, or using payroll cutbacks to generate cost savings that can, if desired, be applied to meet more pressing needs).

A disadvantage of V-Time is that it can provoke concern on the part of managers and labor representatives. The former may worry that a reduced employee time commitment could leave their department unable to cope with a large, fixed workload (particularly if there are restrictions on hiring additional personnel to replace the reduced hours); the latter may worry that V-Time could eventually lead to an involuntary loss of full-time jobs.

Once an organization decides to proceed with the introduction of a V-Time program, it will concentrate on gaining the backing of top and middle-level management, designing a program that will appeal to the widest possible range of employees, and conducting a promotional campaign, backed by solid, detailed resource materials, that will encourage supervisory support and employee participation.

Faced with such problems as the need to accommodate employees seeking a temporarily reduced work schedule, broaden the organization's recruitment effort, generate costs savings, enhance fiscal flexibility, and respond to an economic downturn, an employer would do well to consider a V-Time program.

ORGANIZATIONAL EXPERIENCE WITH V-TIME

New York State

Description: Over 200,000 employees work for the government of New York State.

Reason for Using V-Time: The state of New York has a long history of experimentation with new scheduling arrangements and has a stated objective of creating new forms of part-time work that meet employees' and the organization's needs. In 1984, in response to a survey that indicated employee interest in and need for professional-level reduced work time options, the state of New York added a "Voluntary Furlough Program" to its existing options of regular part-time and job sharing.

Implementation Process: The V-Time option is available to the 55,000 employees represented by the Public Employees Federation and the 14,000 management/confidential employees.

Employees may choose reductions of from 5 to 30 percent in 5 percent increments. A contract is then developed between the employee and the employee's agency that defines the reduced work schedule, salary reduction, and impact on benefits.

Impact to Date: "The state saved about $4 million in reduced salaries during the first two years of the program," said Carol Schlageter, spokesperson for the program. Agency heads have the option of using the realized savings to fill other, sometimes more critical, temporary positions without increasing their budgets.

Employees use the program to phase retirement, pursue artistic interests, travel, or spend more time on family responsibilities. The most popular option, chosen by 32 percent of the employees, is a 10 percent reduction in work time and pay, with another 30 percent choosing to cut back 20 percent.

In 1985, New York State was cited by *Money* magazine in its "Ten Terrific Employers" list for being one of "a handful of employers [that] stand out as leaders in making the unavoidable conflict between job and family easier to bear."

For current guidelines for the program, see Figure 7-7.

SOURCE: *Go Ahead! You've Earned It!* (Albany: New York State Department of Civil Service, Governor's Office of Employee Relations, 1984); "Ten Terrific Employers," *Money* (May 1985), 144; and Governor's Office of Employee Relations, State of New York, 1993–1995.

San Mateo County, California

Description: San Mateo County is located on the San Francisco Bay area peninsula. It employs 4,200 people.

Reason for Using V-Time: The initial reason for offering a Voluntary Time Off (VTO) program was to reduce county costs by a voluntary reduction in full-time employees' salaries in exchange for additional time off. The program proved to be popular and has been an option for all full-time, permanent county employees since 1981.

Implementation Process: Open enrollment is offered twice a year. Employees may request a reduction of 1, 2, 5, 10, or 20 percent to reduce their workday or work week or to take off a block of time. Their department head must approve the request and all VTO time must be taken before the expiration of the fiscal year, or it will be lost to the employee.

Employees are considered to be in a full-time pay status, and enrollment in the program has no effect on most benefits, including accrual of paid time off (vacation, sick leave, etc.). However, all paid time off taken during the program will be compensated at the reduced hourly rate. The reduction in work hours does affect retirement, long-term disability, and overtime.

Impact to Date: At present, 300 to 400 employees enroll in the program each year. Participation has demonstrated savings of as much as a million dollars. Surveyed employees consistently remark that the program has given them important additional time to meet their family needs. This and other work-family programs are often mentioned as primary reasons new employees wish to work for the county.

SOURCE: County informational materials; conversation with Paul Hackleman, Benefits Manager, San Mateo County Human Resources, February 1994.

CHAPTER 8

Leave Time

Leave time is an authorized period of time away from work without loss of employment rights. This absence may be paid or unpaid and is usually extended and taken for such reasons as family responsibilities, health care, education and personal growth, or career breaks. Practically every employer with a staff of at least 100 offers paid vacations and sick leave to its regular employees. Most companies also allow unpaid leave under certain circumstances and commonly permit employees to link paid and unpaid leaves, so that they can be absent from the job for longer periods. Many, if not most, also continue benefits during paid, and in some cases unpaid, leave, although the employee may be asked to pay all or part of the cost of doing so. In the last few years experience with family-related leave time has increased corporate executives' comfort level about how to handle work leaves of more than two weeks. This has encouraged a number of firms to experiment with management-initiated, voluntary unpaid leaves that are designed to support business needs, such as reduction in labor costs and career redirection.[1]

Origins of Expanded Leave Options

As has been the case with other aspects of work time, definitions of leave time and policies regarding it have been undergoing scrutiny and change recently, with the trend being toward creating more flexibility for both the organization and the individual employee.

Since the mid-1980s, particular attention has been focused on policy development relating to two areas: (1) leave time for family responsibilities and (2) paid time off for vacation, holidays, illness or injury, and personal use. A third kind of leave, time off taken for the purpose of a sabbatical or education, has been the subject of less interest since the early 1980s, but its potential for facilitating training and continuing education, as well as alleviating burnout, makes it relevant to the interests of today's managers. Most recently leave time has been initiated by management as a way of reducing labor costs. This chapter provides an overview of current developments relating to each of these kinds of leave policy.

Who Uses Expanded Leave Options?

A 1992 report on corporate sabbaticals notes that "according to various surveys, the current number of policies or programs classified by the respondents as 'sabbaticals' range from 14 to 24 percent. Personal leaves of absence, sometimes also characterized as sabbaticals, are much more common—their prevalence in recent polls ranges from 70 to 90 percent."[2]

In 1991 Louis Harris & Associates surveyed over 400 senior human resources executives in Conference Board member organizations. Sabbaticals or career breaks were offered by 24 percent of the firms, and another 15 percent expected to be offering them within five years.[3]

Because the main categories of leave time involve significantly different considerations and organizational practices differ with respect to each type of leave, this section will discuss the Family and Medical Leave Act, paid and flexible time-off programs, leave banks, extended or enhanced leaves, and sabbatical and educational leaves in separate subsections.

The Family and Medical Leave Act of 1993

The most recent important development related to leave time was the passage of the landmark Family and Medical Leave Act of 1993. On February 5, 1993, it was signed into law and made leave a right, rather than an employer-provided benefit that could be withdrawn at any time.

The Act applies to employers with fifty or more employees who have worked twenty or more workweeks in the current or preceding calendar year. It covers employees who were employed by the employer for at least twelve months who had at least 1,250 hours of service during the past twelve months.

The Family and Medical Leave Act excludes any person employed at a worksite with fewer than fifty employees, if the total number of persons employed by the employer within seventy-five miles of the worksite is also fewer than fifty. An employer may deny job restoration to salaried employees who are among the highest paid 10 percent of the firm's employees if such denial is necessary to prevent substantial economic injury to the employer's operation.

For those employees who are eligible, the law mandates up to twelve weeks' unpaid, job-protected leave per year for the birth or placement for adoption or foster care of a child or a serious health condition of the employee, a child, a parent, or a spouse. Employers or employees may substitute an employee's accrued vacation, personal, or family leave when the employee takes leave because of the birth/adoption/foster care of a child; employees also may use accrued sick leave to care for themselves or sick family members.

Leave taken for birth, adoption, or foster-care placement with the employee expires at the end of a twelve-month period beginning on the date of birth or placement with the employee.

The employer may require that a request for leave be supported by a certification issued by a health care provider as specified in the Act.

The legislation does not supersede any state or local law, collective bargaining agreement, or employment benefit plan providing greater employee family leave rights, nor does it diminish an employer's ability to adopt more generous family leave policies. At the time of its passage, twenty-two states, the District of Columbia, and Dade County, Florida, had family-related leave laws. The states with laws that relate to leave provided by private-sector employers are California, Colorado, Connecticut, Hawaii, Iowa, Kansas, Kentucky, Louisiana, Maine, Massachusetts, Minnesota, Montana, New Hampshire, New Jersey, New York, Oregon, Pennsylvania, Rhode Island, Tennessee, Vermont, Washington, and Wisconsin. Consequently, many employers, particularly those who operate in more than one state, are developing ways to integrate current policy with the new federal mandates.

Key concerns or questions that have been raised by some employers are:

■ How do you integrate some of the state and federal provisions, especially where one is not clearly more beneficial than the other—just different? This is particularly important for employers in states with pregnancy disability leave legislation.

■ Regarding the provision for "intermittent leave" or reduced work schedules when medically necessary: Can benefits be extended beyond twelve weeks under this scenario? Will this provision cause disruption in customer service? What is the relationship with existing short-term paid sick leave programs a company may have? Also, it is unclear how this provision will affect absenteeism counseling.

■ Will this lead to legislation requiring employers to provide paid leave in the future?

■ How difficult will it be to collect benefit contributions from employees who decide not to return to work after having taken leave?

■ Won't the new requirements cause hardship in some areas of the company where there are a large number of employees who could request leave?

■ Will legislation apply to U.S. employees who are working overseas?

■ What if a position is eliminated because of business necessity while an employee is on leave?[4]

Mandating family and medical leave means that employers who already had family leave policies have had to review these policies, coordinate them with any existing state legislation, and ensure their compliance with the federal law. They have also had to formalize processes in more detail than they did before.

Even with relatively straightforward regulations from the Labor Department, there are a number of areas that employers must interpret and define, including:

■ Is the twelve-month period a calendar or a fiscal year? Can employees back up years and take leave the last twelve weeks of one year and the first twelve of the next, ending up with twenty-four weeks' leave?

■ Must employees use up their paid sick leave before taking unpaid family leave?

■ What can a supervisor who suspects that there is insufficient medical reason for the leave do about it? (Note: Company-paid second and third opinions from independent doctors may be required.)

■ What happens to the status of an employee who takes inter-

mittent family/medical leave and, in effect, becomes a part-timer?
■ How will benefit and seniority accruals be handled?[5]

As these questions are answered and policy and practice evolve, other kinds of leave programs will also be affected. Employee interest in leave options will undoubtedly grow. Employers who considered their existing leave programs an important part of gaining a recruitment edge or motivating and retaining good employees may want to consider what kinds of provisions beyond the legal requirements might be appropriate.

Paid Time Off

Separate from leave time, but, as we've already noted, related to it, is policy dealing with the following types of paid absences:

■ Sick leave
■ Holidays
■ Vacation
■ Personal time

Many organizations have been reevaluating their policy in these areas as a result of changes in labor force demographics. There is a growing recognition that a diverse workforce has diverse needs and that the way employees use their sick leave or vacation and holiday time reflects these changed needs. This, in turn, has occasioned changes in policy. In a Conference Board report, *Corporations and Families: Changing Practices and Perspectives,* Helen Axel describes this kind of policy evolution:

> Although personnel executives say that their firms encourage (and, sometimes, require) employees to use their vacations in large pieces of time, many recognize that lifestyles or personal responsibilities do not always make long vacations possible. Most companies now permit employees to take at least some of their vacation time in small increments—days, half-days, or even (in a very limited number of instances) hours. A bank officer relates that, some years ago, her need for one afternoon off each week to care for her infant child precipitated a change in the company's vacation policy to include half-days of vacation. As frequently occurs, practice preceded policy. Until the policy was officially changed, she and her superior agreed that her absences would be shown as full days every other week.[6]

Another issue that has been reevaluated in this benefit area is the use of sick leave for other than employee personal illness. A study conducted for the U.S. Department of Health and Human Services indicates that management practices, in addition to demographics, affect the way sick leave is used. A major conclusion of the study is that:

> [A] significant amount of sick leave cannot be explained by personal illness or injury, care of a family member or preventive medical visit. . . . The researchers posited that there are two additional categories of sick leave use related to occurrences in the workplace—and therefore tractable by management action:

> ■ Time off due to real illness brought about by stress or other events or circumstances in the workplace;
> ■ "Attitudinal" use of sick leave due to conflict with co-workers, resentment of a supervisor, frustration with poor planning, and other management causes.[7]

The report also noted demographic differences in sick leave use: Younger employees were more inclined to use sick leave than were older ones, and there was a tendency toward greater use among less-experienced and less-educated employees, as well as those at lower grade levels.

Flexible Time Off.   In the early 1980s, Hewlett-Packard's reevaluation of its sick leave policy led to changes that many other companies have since followed. They represent a new, individualized, and more flexible approach to policy strategy in the overall area of paid time off. In 1982, Hewlett-Packard began offering a "Flexible Time Off" program, which combined vacation and sick leave time. The impetus for the program was a desire to create a more equitable policy. Previously, the company had realized that only 20 percent of the employees were responsible for using 80 percent of the sick leave time annually. Under the current plan, employees receive from fifteen to thirty days off a year, depending on their length of service. This time can be used at the employees' option as either vacation time or sick leave time. They may carry over a portion of unused time off from year to year (the amount is determined by tenure) and receive a cash payout after twenty years of service. The carried-over block of time can be used for such purposes as extra vacation, temporary illness, personal business appointments, illness in the family, and problems with child care, or it may be saved for later use or a cash benefit. As the company brochure states, "[E]mployees are well able to take responsibility for the important decisions affecting their lives away from the job."[8] (Hewlett-Packard's experience with flexible time off is profiled in a later section of this chapter.)

A California state appeals court ruling (*Boothby v. Atlas Mechanical*) that said that employees have the right to convert vacation to cash has led to a more restrictive policy in other organizations. Employers concerned about the extent of possible future liability are saying "use it or lose it" about vacation time and limiting the amount of time workers can carry over. At SCE Corp., vacation can be deferred for a year. Rohr Inc. limits carryover time to two weeks.[9]

Catalyst suggests offering flexible paid time off as part of a flexible benefits plan and describes two ways to do this: (1) making all kinds of paid time off interchangeable or (2) making paid time off interchangeable with other benefits.[10] (See Figure 8-1.)

Leave Banks. The concept of "leave banks" that enable employees to pool their sick leave is an idea that is gaining acceptance in some areas. Teachers and police officers have pioneered the concept of establishing leave banks to help fellow employees whose sick leave allowance has been depleted by long illness. A special resolution

Figure 8-1.   Two ways to offer flexible paid time off.

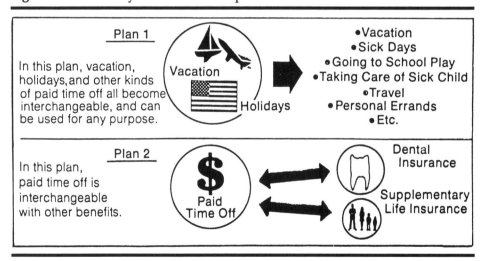

SOURCE: *Flexible Benefits: How to Set Up a Plan When Your Employees Are Complaining, Your Costs Are Rising, and You're Too Busy to Think About It* (New York: Catalyst, 1987), 47. Used by permission of Catalyst, 250 Park Avenue, New York, N.Y. 10003.

allows Florida employees of the Internal Revenue Service to donate up to two years of sick leave and thirty-five weeks of vacation time. This leave bank was established to help a particular couple, both fellow employees, one of whom was very ill.[11]

In 1988 the Federal Employees Leave Sharing Act (PL 100-566) authorized two experiments: leave transfers and leave banks. The transfers program allows employees to donate annual leave (but not sick leave) to a co-worker who has a medical emergency that requires extended absence from work and loss of income because his or her paid leave has been exhausted. The leave banks allow employees to donate annual leave to a pool from which participants can draw for medical emergencies. A 1993 report from the Office of Personnel Management (OPM) indicated that 77 percent of all federal installations surveyed had implemented leave sharing and six agencies had leave banks. Approximately 2,000 employees received almost 500,000 hours of leave from the leave banks. A General Accounting Office employee attitude survey of federal employees showed that the program was widely used and very popular. Almost 20 percent of the respondents said they had donated annual leave to other employees. In September 1993 the House passed the Federal Employees Leave Sharing Amendments Act of 1993 (S.1130) to join the Senate in making leave banks and leave transfers a permanent option.[12]

Extended or Enhanced Leaves

Several large corporations have offered special unpaid leave programs in the last few years. Since 1988 IBM's Personal Leave of Absence program has allowed absences of up to three years with full benefits, service credit, and job security. In the second and third years, employees may be recalled for part-time work if they are needed. And in 1991, IBM announced a Flexible Work Leave of Absence under which employees may work part-time schedules for three years or more with full benefit coverage, service credit, and job security. The company stipulates that these leaves cannot be taken for "profit-making activities" or "extended vacations." Dependent care is the reason that most employees give for requesting this kind of leave.[13]

Since unpaid leave programs clearly reduce labor costs, a few employers have initiated them with this objective in mind. Hallmark Cards offers voluntary leave on a recurring basis in order to even the peaks and valleys of a seasonal business. In 1991, AT&T offered a Special Enhanced Leave of Absence Program. There were two enrollment windows, one immediate and another during the summer. Employees with five years of service were able to apply for unpaid leaves of nine to twenty-four months. There were 1,700 exempt employees who took advantage of the program, which was popular with both employees and the organization. In 1993 the opportunity was again offered, and once again there was an enthusiastic response, with 1,500 employees signing up for the program.

Another innovative use of unpaid time off is Continental Insurance's program that allows employees the option of taking ten days off without pay per year. The policy saves money for the organization and provides employees with additional flexibility in the form of "guilt-free" days off.

Sabbatical and Educational Leaves

In the mid-1970s, there was growing interest in the concept of sabbaticals as an employee benefit and as a way to allow employees to recuperate from burnout. Interest waned in the early 1980s, but a 1986 Bureau of National Affairs phone survey indicated that although few companies have formal programs, "[S]abbaticals in the corporate world . . . are a somewhat rare, but prized, employee benefit, valued by both employers and employees."[14] Unlike vacations, they are not viewed as employee entitlements or earned time but are intended "to encourage future high performance, not to reward the past."[15]

Sabbaticals have been kept alive even in companies facing economic problems, and if current policies related to downsizing and its corollaries, employee stress and "survivor syndrome," continue, they may take on added value.

As Dr. Jack Wood of the Graduate School of Business, Sydney, Australia, noted in a speech on *The Future of Employment*:

> Terms such as "workplace stress," "burnout" and a "decline in the work ethic" have become the core of much of the recent business literature. One strategy that has been implemented in many firms to combat some of these problems in recent years is Sabbatical Leave. Varied models for Sabbatical Leave have been proposed and implemented in both the public and private sectors of industry in OECD [Organization for Economic Cooperation and Development] countries. The major features of some of these schemes are outlined in the following discussion and one prime benefit, the potential to create additional employment, a commonly overlooked dimension, will be emphasized.[16]

Wood goes on to describe several sabbatical programs that are self-funded by the interested employee and that enable him or her to take paid leave of up to a year. Such a program is the "Four Over Five Plan" developed for teachers in the Canadian province of Prince Edward Island. Under this plan, teachers may opt to receive 80 percent of their salary for the first four years of the plan. The deferred 20 percent is accumulated annually with interest and provides the income to finance one year's leave during the fifth year. Fringe benefits are maintained during the leave, and the teacher returns to the same position or a similar one when the leave is completed. Employment opportunities are expanded when the teachers are replaced during their absence.

Rolm Corporation (now a Siemens company) was one of the first high-tech firms to recognize the need for "bounce-back" time and adapt the notion of a sabbatical to the needs of a high-tech company. When that company devised its "Continuous Service Leave" program, under which all full-time employees with seven years' tenure were offered the chance for up to twelve calendar weeks of paid leave in addition to paid vacation, a company objective was the desire to increase productivity by allowing employees to "refresh" themselves. Because long hours are endemic in Silicon Valley, the percentage of firms offering sabbaticals is high. Tandem Computers, another sabbatical pioneer, has a program available after four years of service—the amount of time the company had been operating when it offered its first sabbatical program. And Apple Computer has a sabbatical program aptly titled "Restart" (see page 313).

When Is Leave Time Most Appropriate?

Employers generally offer leave time to facilitate retraining and continuing education, enable employees to cope with stress and burnout and better manage the conflict between work and family responsibilities, and expand employment opportunities.

■ *Retraining and continuing education.* One of the most pressing problems for employers today is how to cope with the ongoing education and training requirements of our highly technical and competitive economy. Encouraging employees to assume some of the responsibilities in this area and providing leave time during which the employee's job is guaranteed are one strategy that deserves consideration.

■ *Stress and burnout.* Work-related stress is beginning to show up as an identifiable cost in the form of increased medical insurance premiums and workers' compensation claims in more and more organizations. A sabbatical or leave time program is one way to combat it.

■ *Conflict between work and family responsibilities.* Leave time is generally discussed in terms of its importance as a means to help working parents adjust to the birth or adoption of a new baby. It can be equally important as an option for senior dependent care or during times of particular family stress or crisis.

■ *Expanding employment opportunities.* Leave programs have been used to spread employment, both by reducing layoffs and by creating short-term employment possibilities. For example, the state of Alaska has an "Approved Leave Without Pay" program designed to minimize layoffs, and the "Four Over Five" sabbatical program available to Prince Edward Island teachers, mentioned earlier, creates new job openings.

Pros and Cons of Leave Time

For an employer, the main advantages of offering a program of leave time options lie in such areas as retaining valued employees, expanding workforce skills, combatting the negative effects of burnout, and reducing labor costs. The disadvantages involve the issue of how to handle the workload during the employee's absence.

■ *Employee retention.* If your organization does not offer certain kinds of leave time—for example, sabbatical leaves if yours is a high-tech company—it may find itself losing valued workers. And when employees leave, the company's investment goes with them.

■ *Expansion of labor force skills.* Broadening your company's educational or training leave policy can encourage employees to expand their current skills or to cross-train. Since training is increasingly expensive for many organizations, particularly those affected by constant technological changes, making it easier for employees to further their own education and training could have considerable cost impact in the future.

■ *Combatting burnout.* Employee burnout can adversely affect both quality and productivity if ways are not developed to periodically reduce its negative effects. A sabbatical or leave program is one proven strategy for revitalizing overly stressed workers.

■ *Managing the workload.* The question of how work will be handled while an employee is on leave is of particular importance to supervisors. The type of options that are available will critically influence their responsiveness, or lack thereof, to employee requests for leave time. In its survey report on the use of leaves, Catalyst listed seven ways that companies handle the responsibilities of employees who are on leave:

1. Work is rerouted to other departmental employees.
2. A replacement from within the company is obtained on a temporary basis.
3. A replacement from outside the company is hired on a temporary basis.
4. Only urgent work is rerouted to other employees, with the remainder of the work held for the leave-taker's attention upon his or her return.
5. Work is forwarded to the leave-taker at his or her home.
6. A permanent replacement is obtained, and the leave-taker is transferred to another job.
7. A permanent new replacement is hired.[17]

Figure 8-2 shows the percentage of companies that opt for each of these solutions in order to cover the responsibilities of leave-takers.

Figure 8-2.   How work is handled for nonmanagerial leave-takers.

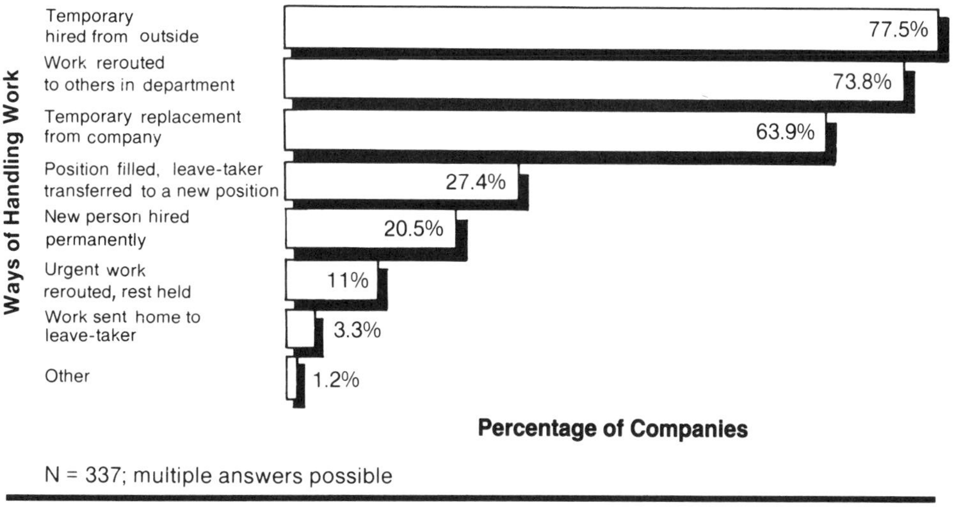

N = 337; multiple answers possible

SOURCE: *The Corporate Guide to Parental Leaves* (New York: Catalyst, 1986), 87. © 1986 by Catalyst. Used by permission of Catalyst, 250 Park Avenue, New York, N.Y. 10003.

With managers, the Catalyst survey found, it is common to reroute only urgent work and, depending on the expected length of the leave, to hold the rest or send it to the leave-taker's home.[18]

Should Your Organization Try Expanding Its Leave Options?

The issue of expanding your organization's leave options involves two decisions: (1) whether or not to expand those options and (2) what types of new options would be appropriate. The tools in this section can help you arrive at these decisions.

Start by referring to Organizational Experience with Leave Time, which profiles the leave programs instituted by four organizations. One deals with flexible time off and two with corporate leave and sabbatical programs. The fourth deals with a leave option not previously mentioned in this chapter: social service leave. While programs that permit leaves for the purpose of serving community needs are seen less often than programs that provide paid time off for a variety of personal purposes and educational or sabbatical leaves, social service leaves are nonetheless an option that should not be overlooked by an employer that wants to encourage its workers to make a meaningful contribution to society. In reviewing the group of organizational profiles, look for parallels between the experience of these employers and the conditions facing your own company.

Table 8-1 is a questionnaire designed to help you examine your company's existing leave program and assess whether its leave options should be expanded and, if so, in what areas. If the questionnaire results indicate that the organization would benefit from offering additional leave options, the worksheet shown in Figure 8-3 can be used to help you further analyze what changes in leave policy would be appropriate.

Introducing Changes in Leave-Time Policy

To expand its present policy on leave time, an organization starts by gaining support for the initiative. The effort involved in gaining support will depend on the extent of the change in leave policy that is being contemplated. The organization then sets up the program's administration, makes major decisions in the area of program de-

Table 8-1. Leave-time questionnaire.

Would Expanding Leave Options Benefit Your Organization?

	Yes	No
Does your organization currently offer the following kinds of leave? • Disability • Sick leave • Personal time off • Sabbatical • Educational/training • Other (social service, loaned employee, etc.):		
Does your organization face any of the following human resources management problems that a redefined or expanded leave policy might address? • A need for skills expansion, continuing education, or training/retraining • Employee stress and burnout • Conflict between work and family responsibilities • A need to expand employment opportunities • The loss of valued employees		
Have employees requested leave time for circumstances that are not covered under current policy?		
Are minimum job protection and employment status guarantees incorporated into present leave policy?		

sign, and develops resource materials. Once the program's design and the supporting resource materials have been finalized, the program is announced and promoted to employees. After a period of operation, the program is assessed and modified as necessary. The rest of this section discusses the foregoing implementation steps in greater detail.

Gain Support for the Program

As we've seen, leave time is an area of human resources management that is undergoing considerable thought and change. Since most companies already have some sort of leave policy, redefining or expanding policy in this area does not entail introducing a new idea. And unlike some other work time arrangements that cannot be introduced except through an all-or-nothing change process, leave policy can be changed either comprehensively or incrementally, with different kinds of leave policy addressed individually.

Figure 8-3. Leave-time worksheet.

Assessing the Need for Expanded Leave Options

List the main reasons why you are considering broadening your organization's current leave program:

1. _____

   _____

   _____

2. _____

   _____

   _____

3. _____

   _____

   _____

4. _____

   _____

   _____

List what you see as the advantages and disadvantages of offering an expanded program of leave options:

Pros: _____

   _____

   _____

   _____

_____

_____

_____

Cons: _____

_____

_____

_____

_____

_____

The degree of difficulty in gaining support for change in an organization's current leave-time policy will depend on the extent and type of change that is being contemplated.

It may, for example, represent a considerable shift in cultural values for a company that now has a more traditional leave policy to consider offering a sabbatical leave that would encourage both male and female employees to take time off in order to renew their energy or take part in an educational or training program that was not directly job-related. To consider replacing a program of paid time off for company-specified purposes with an annual lump-sum amount of paid time off that employees may draw on for purposes of their own choosing is also a significant change. As noted in the Introduction, in cases such as these involving major shifts in policy, gaining broad-based support should be a priority, and a task force can be an effective means of accomplishing this.

If, on the other hand, an incremental change in existing policy is being considered, less-extensive staff commitment in this area may be sufficient.

Set Up the Program's Administration

Whether or not a task force is considered necessary, someone in the human resources management area should be identified as having responsibility for developing background information on what other companies have done in the area of leave policy, drafting a proposal for new policy related to changes in leave time, and acting as a resource for employees and supervisors once the changes are introduced.

Design the Program

When modifying or expanding current leave policy, the first step should be to determine what conditions may be mandated by relevant state and federal law. As we've noted, leave time is a policy area that is evolving rapidly, and new laws are mandating changes in some cases. The 1993 Family and Medical Leave Act is a case in point. Whether determining what legal parameters have been established or defining its own program, the organization should consider the following issues:

■ *Eligibility.* Will a qualifying period of employment be established? Will all leave options be available to all employees, or will some restrictions or qualifications be used to establish eligibility in particular instances? Eligibility requirements might be expressed in terms of seniority level of responsibility and need not be consistent across every aspect of leave policy.

■ *Conditions.* Can the leave be taken at any time, or must the timing be negotiated with a supervisor? Are there restrictions on what leave time may be used for? What are they? What is the maximum duration allowed? Can accrued vacation, sick leave, and compensatory time be added to the allowable leave? Does vacation and/or sick leave have to be used up either as part of any paid portion of the leave or as part of the total leave? If leave is taken for medical or pregnancy reasons, is there the possibility of a part-time transition period before the employee returns to full-time?

■ *Effect on salary and benefits.* Will employer-provided leave time be paid, partially paid, or unpaid? If disability leave will be offered, will regular compensation be continued during the disability period? Will benefits be continued during leave? At whose expense? Will elibigility for vacation time or sabbatical consideration be affected? How will retirement benefits be continued and paid for?

■ *Effect on employment status.* Is reinstatement guaranteed? To the same position, or to a comparable or similar job? Will paid time off and/or sick leave as well as seniority continue to accrue during the leave time? Will the leave time affect possibilities for advancement?

■ *Application procedure.* How does an employee apply for leave time? Who initiates the request? What kind of advance notice is necessary? Who authorizes the leave?

■ *Disposition of workload.* While the employee is on leave, will some or all of the work be rerouted? To whom? Will a replacement be obtained? From within the company or from outside? Will any work be forwarded to the leave-taker? As discussed earlier in the chapter, how an employee's work will be handled during a leave is a critical issue that will significantly affect supervisory responsiveness to requests for leave time. Procedures must be in place, or an agreement must be negotiated in advance, to ensure that the work is performed in a timely manner.

■ *Procedure for returning to work.* Upon completion of the leave, is the employee automatically reinstated to his or her former position? To an equivalent position? How does the employee arrange to return to work? Is there a form to be completed? How far in advance must the employee notify the company of his or her desire to return to work? Is part-time work possible for a transitional step? For how long?

Table 8-2 is a program design checklist that provides an overview of the design issues that are common to any program of expanded leave options. Figures 8-4 through 8-7 are worksheets that you can use to document those design decisions that are peculiar to disability leave, paid time off, education/training leave, or sabbatical leaves.

Develop Resource Materials
The resource materials that an organization creates must meet the needs of supervisory staff as well as employees. Both groups will require detailed information about each type of leave that is available. Beyond that, supervisors must have guidelines for granting requests for leaves of varoius sorts and information on how to arrange for coverage of the workload during the employee's absence. Employees interested in participating in the leave program must have specific information on how taking a particular type of leave will affect them—in terms of such considerations as salary and benefits, employment status, and long-term career prospects.

Table 8-2. Program design checklist: expanded leave options.

Key Design Issues	Notes
☐ Legal requirements	
☐ Eligibility	
☐ Conditions	
☐ Effect on salary and benefits	
☐ Effect on employment status	
☐ Application procedure	
☐ Disposition of workload	
☐ Procedure for returning to work	

Announce the Program

When leave policy has been revised and/or expanded, employees should be notified of the changes through the usual information channels.

Promote the Program

Employees may have to be encouraged to take advantage of the new leave opportunities that have been made available. Historically, certain kinds of leave—for example, sabbaticals to relieve burnout or educational and training leaves to expand the skills of the work-force—have been underutilized even though they are part of company policy. This is often due to employees' fears that the types of responsibilities they are assigned or their future prospects will be harmed if they take leave time. An effective promotional effort can counter this type of concern.

Evaluate the Program

As with other work time alternatives, a leave-time program should be evaluated after it has been in place for several months. Two issues should be particularly scrutinized:

(Text continues on page 306.)

Figure 8-4.   Disability leave worksheet.

Legal requirements

Eligibility

Conditions

Appropriate use:

Duration:

Other:

Effect on salary and benefits

Effect on employment status

Application procedure

Disposition of workload

Procedure for returning to work

Figure 8-5.   Paid time off worksheet.

Structured Time Off
Eligibility
Holiday:
Sick leave:
Vacation:
Conditions
Appropriate use:
Holiday:
Sick leave:
Vacation:
Duration:
Holiday:
Sick leave:
Vacation:
Other:
Holiday
Sick leave:
Vacation:
Application procedure (vacation)
Disposition of workload (sick leave, vacation)

```
                          Flexible Time Off
_____
                             Eligibility
_____


_____
                             Conditions
_____
Appropriate use:
_____
Duration:
_____
Other:


_____
```

Figure 8-6.   Educational/training leave worksheet.

```
_____
                             Eligibility
_____


_____
                             Conditions
_____
Appropriate use:


_____
Duration:


_____
Restrictions:
If paid:
If unpaid:
_____
Reimbursement:
  □ Fees
  □ Supplies
  □ Other:
_____
```

(Continued)

Figure 8-6. *(continued)*

Other:

_____
Effect on salary and benefits
_____

_____
Effect on employment status
_____
Work schedule:

_____

Seniority accrual:

_____

Salary review:

_____

Other:

_____
Application procedure
_____

_____
Disposition of workload
_____

_____
Procedure for returning to work
_____

_____

1. Are employees using the various leave options? If not, why not?
2. Do supervisors feel that the processes established for reapportioning work are successful? If not, and if work coverage is a problem, this issue should be discussed and new strategies devised to deal with it.

Figure 8-7.   Sabbatical leave worksheet.

Eligibility
Conditions
Appropriate use:
Duration:
Restrictions:
If paid:
If unpaid:
Other:
Effect on salary and benefits
Effect on employment status
Application procedure
Disposition of workload
Procedure for returning to work

Fine-Tune the Program

Following the evaluation, the organization should modify those portions of its leave policy that have been identified as problem areas. For example:

Problem	Solution
Significant percentage of maternity leave-takers do not return to their full-time positions.	Pilot-test part-time transition step.
Replacement employees are inadequately trained to assume leave-takers' work.	Assign replacements at least ten days in advance.
Employees are not requesting education or training leaves.	Run feature stories in company newsletter describing career advances of employees who have voluntarily broadened their skills base.
Department heads avoid implementation of leave option.	Tie development of leave program to evaluation.
Evaluation indicates that most first-line supervisors are reluctant to grant requests for leave.	Train/educate first-line supervisors regarding the need for this option. Emphasize "try it, you'll like it."

Summary

While some of the work time alternatives we have discussed in this book would represent a completely new undertaking for many employers, such is not the case with leave time. Most organizations already permit their employees some type of paid or unpaid absence from work during which their jobs are protected.

However, since the mid-1980s, the traditional concept of leave time has been undergoing a variety of changes. Special attention has been focused on two areas: family-related leaves and paid time off for vacation, holidays, illness or injury, and personal use. A third major category of leave time, absence for education or training or for a sabbatical, has received less attention during this period.

Family- and medical-related leaves have now become law. The

area of paid time off for illness or injury, holidays, vacation, and personal reasons has also undergone changes in response to the needs of the workforce for greater flexibility in the use of this time. Whereas absences with pay were once subject to many employer-mandated restrictions on the manner in which they could be taken and the purposes for which they could be used, the trend today is toward permitting employees greater freedom of choice about when and why they use their allotment of paid time off. The restrictions are increasingly on whether and for how long they can "save" this time.

Although the use of sabbatical and educational leaves has not grown appreciably since the early 1980s, employers should not overlook the benefits of providing time off to workers who are suffering from burnout or who want to take advantage of training or educational opportunities. This type of leave can enable an organization to retain the services of a valued but temporarily overstressed employee and to enhance the level of education and training of its workforce.

As noted, leave time is considered an effective strategy for combatting stress and burnout, facilitating employee training and continuing education, helping employees manage conflicts between work and family responsibilities, and, under certain conditions, reducing labor costs. Leaves can also be a means of increasing employment opportunities by creating temporary job openings.

The main concern regarding leaves is how the work will be handled during the employee's absence. This issue will require special attention as a company plans an expansion of its leave options. Provisions must be made to reroute the work, replace the employee temporarily or permanently, forward the work to the leave-taker, or otherwise cover the responsibilities of the position. If this issue is not effectively addressed at the outset, supervisors will be unlikely to support the leave program, and the use of leave time will prove more disruptive than helpful to the organization.

In examining its existing leave policy, a company must start by making sure its policy conforms to the provisions of any applicable state and federal legislation. Beyond that, the employer must consider its own needs in the areas of workforce retention, education/training, and job coverage as well as the needs of its employees for greater flexibility in the use of their time and greater control over their lives. Through careful planning, an organization can structure a program of paid and unpaid leaves that both employer and employees will find beneficial.

ORGANIZATIONAL EXPERIENCE WITH LEAVE TIME

National Westminster Bank PLC

Description: National Westminster Bank, located in London, is Britain's largest bank. It also has U.S. branches located in New York (Manhattan, Long Island, Brooklyn, and Queens); Westchester, Conn.; Los Angeles and San Francisco, Calif.; and Chicago, Ill. The U.S. offices have a similar program available to their employees at the level described.

Reason for Using Leave Time: The leave program is designed to enable members of staff, male or female, who are potential senior management talent to take a break in their career in order to care for young children.

Implementation Process: Applicants must have completed five years' service and expect to return to work with their career commitment undiminished. Selection of participants is at the option of the bank. Throughout the period of absence, which may be up to five years, participants in the career-break scheme are expected to maintain contact with the bank on a regular basis. At a minimum, the bank requires leave-takers to participate in an annual one-day updating program, review regularly issued information packets, and attend occasional social events. Many leave-takers negotiate a regular part-time schedule, an average of six to eight weeks a year, according to Anne Watts, the bank's equal opportunities manager, in order to keep up with changes at the bank. At the end of five years, careers are resumed without loss of pay, seniority, or status.

Impact to Date: Since the program was introduced in 1981, it has attracted considerable attention and been replicated by several other banks and other types of enterprises.

SOURCE: Joann S. Lublin, "Hope for Curse of the Working Mummy," *Wall Street Journal* (Dec. 1987), 35; *Information Service News and Abstracts,* no. 91 (London: Work Research unit, Mar.–Apr. 1988): 10–14.

Hewlett-Packard Company

Description: Hewlett-Packard, an international supplier of computers and instruments for business and medicine, employs 52,000 workers in the United States and another 40,000 in other countries. Its corporate headquarters is in Palo Alto, California. Hewlett-Packard was one of the first American companies to institute a flextime program and also uses job sharing, work sharing, and various forms of contingent employment.

Reason for Using Leave Time: The introduction of the "Flexible Time Off" program was prompted by employee suggestions and by management's perception that the old policy on time off had become inequitable. Hewlett-Packard found that 20 percent of its workforce was responsible for 80 percent of the sick leave use and that employees who would have qualified for a cash payout for good attendance lost out because they left the company before becoming eligible. Management was also interested in offering employees a way to use sick leave to care for ill children or other family members.

Implementation Process: Surveys of employee attitudes and needs were conducted, and a videotape was developed to promote the plan to top management. Designing the plan, getting it approved, and then implementing it took a year and a half. "Flexible Time Off," which is a combined vacation and sick leave benefit, was first offered to all Hewlett-Packard employees in 1982.

Under the previous policy, vacation time ranged from a low of ten days for employees with one year of service to a high of twenty-five days for employees who had been with the company twenty-five years or more. With "Flexible Time Off," the range is from fifteen to thirty days, with employees enjoying the same amount of vacation time as they previously had, plus five additional days. Some unused time may be "banked" and carried over to another year. The amount of time that may be saved is determined by length of service. When employees leave the company, they receive the full cash value, at their current salary level, of the unused portion of banked time.

Impact to Date: Since the program went into operation, the number of sick days that employees take has dropped, and the number of vacation days that employees take has increased proportionately. The company's perception is that employees are now able to be more honest about the reason why they are taking time off.

An employee poll showed an 80 percent positive response to the new program. Employees appreciate the fact that "Flexible Time Off" allows them to accommodate their personal needs in such areas as illness in the family, child-care problems, extra vacation, temporary illness, and personal business appointments or to save the time for later use or for a cash benefit.

Hewlett-Packard management feels that this approach to vacation and sick leave is more consistent with the company's culture than the previous rigid approach. Like the concept of flexible hours, "Flexible Time Off" allows employees discretion over how their paid time off can best be used.

SOURCE: Helen Axel, *Corporations and Families: Changing Practices and Perspectives,* research report no. 868 (New York: The Conference Board, Inc., 1985), 32; New Ways to Work conversations with the corporate human resources staff (Dec. 1993).

Wells Fargo Bank

Description: Wells Fargo is the second largest bank in California. Its corporate offices are located in San Francisco, and it employs almost 30,000 people statewide. The bank offers various other leave options and alternative work time options, including regular part-time and job sharing.

Reasing for Using Leave Time: The "Social Service Leave" program is one of a group of corporate social responsibility programs that were developed as ways for the bank to "respond to the needs of the communities it serves." The program also gives bank employees an opportunity to help solve social problems of personal concern to them.

Implementation Process: Any three-year employee of the bank who is in good standing may submit a proposal for a leave of from one to six months. A selection committee chooses the participants after considering the potential impact of the applicant's goals and efforts toward solving a specific social problem. The committee also evaluates the nonprofit organization that will be the employee's work site during the leave in order to ensure that it meets certain service criteria.

The employee retains full pay and other benefits and continues to earn vacation time during the leave. Salary reviews and increases are given as scheduled. Upon returning, the employee is guaranteed the same position or a comparable one.

Impact to Date: Employees on leave have helped organize and promote recreational programs for disabled people, helped identify foster parents, and accomplished a variety of other socially beneficial objectives. Employees who have participated in the program report both gratification at the opportunity to work with a community agency and a sense of renewal after their break from their regular career.

One leave-taker came back to the bank to find that she had been promoted and made a sales team leader at a new branch bank as a result of her special project. "It was great to know that my efforts at Wells Fargo were recognized, even though I was on leave for six months!" she said.

SOURCE: Wells Fargo employee literature; conversation with Wells Fargo staff (May 1994).

Apple Computer

Description: Apple Computer is a manufacturer of personal computers. It employs 8,000 people in the United States and 12,000 worldwide.

Reason for Using Sabbaticals: The computer industry in Silicon Valley, California, is noted for its high pressure and long work hours. Apple's six-week sabbatical program is aptly called "Restart." It is intended to give a breather to employees who have worked at the company continuously for a minimum of five years; unlike vacation time, it is not considered part of the compensation package. It is meant to be an incentive for continued service. It is also expected that both Apple and its employees will benefit by giving employees an opportunity to expand their skill base by filling in during other employees' absences and learning about other areas of the company.

Implementation Process: The employee's first sabbatical must begin during the year following the employee's fifth year with the company. The employee's manager and HR representative and the benefits department must approve the request. Accrued vacation time may be added to the leave. The leave must be scheduled at least sixty days in advance in order to arrange for sufficient coverage during the Restart period. The six weeks must be used all at once, not incrementally. Employees return to the same position they left, unless business conditions make this impossible. If that is the case, the company will make reasonable efforts to find another suitable position.

Impact to Date: Restart is a very popular program. Employees look forward to their sabbaticals. Some employees travel, others spend time with family, and still others combine the two. It provides Apple a competitive advantage in recruiting and enhances Apple's image as a leading-edge company.

SOURCE: Helen Axel, *Redefining Corporate Sabbaticals for the 1990s* (New York: The Conference Board, 1992), 18; Apple policy and conversations with human resources staff (Dec. 1993).

CHAPTER **9**

Work Sharing

Work sharing is an alternative to layoffs in which all or part of an organization's workforce temporarily reduces hours and salary in order to cut operating costs. In states where work sharing/short-time compensation enabling legislation has been passed, the cutbacks in salary can be partly recompensed by partial payments from the employing company's unemployment insurance account.

In the United States, the most common method of adjusting labor costs during economic downturns has been for employers to lay off workers. Harold Oaklander, professor of management at Pace University in New York City, noted the following in writing about workforce reductions:

> In the United States today, the decision to reduce a company's workforce remains at the discretion of the employer just as it was 100 years ago. The concern of public agencies and employers has taken the form of relieving the financial consequences [to workers] of layoffs rather than of averting layoffs or limiting their duration. The main restrictions derived from collective agreements between unions and employers concern "selection" for layoff rather than layoff avoidance.

An alternative notion, using shorter work hours and spreading available work among more employees to reduce levels of unemployment, has been a subject of debate for some time. It was first articulated in the United States in 1887 by Samuel Gompers, president of the American Federation of Labor, when he declared, "As long as we have one person seeking work who cannot find it, the

315

hours of work are too long."[1] His "share the work" approach was fostered during the Great Depression of the 1930s by the Hoover administration. For many workers, it came to mean "sharing the misery" and was disavowed by workers and their representatives. But by the mid-1970s, the destructive effects of relying on layoffs alone to deal with economic downturns had led to a search for alternative methods.

Origins of Work Sharing

Today, three basic types of work sharing—strategies that temporarily reduce the number of paid hours, rather than the number of paid employees, to adjust labor costs—are beginning to be used by companies in the United States: (1) ad hoc work sharing, (2) work sharing in combination with short-time compensation, and (3) programs that allow or encourage various kinds of voluntary reductions in work time by individual employees.

Ad Hoc Work Sharing

The severity of the 1975 recession caused some employers and policymakers to publicly ask whether there might not be a better way than layoffs to control labor costs during economic downturns. A conference on "Alternatives to Layoffs" held in New York City that year heard testimony from a number of employers, including Hewlett-Packard and Pan American World Airways, Inc., that had elected to reduce work time rather than reduce their workforce as a means of cutting back expenditures. Hewlett-Packard had instituted a companywide four-day workweek, on alternating weeks, for a three-month period. Pan American had developed several different approaches, tailored to specific job classifications, which included voluntary furloughs as well as cutbacks on work time. In the Hewlett-Packard case, layoffs were eliminated, and at Pan American, they were greatly minimized.[2] This kind of ad hoc work sharing has slowly gained adherents and has proved to be a valuable tool for many companies.

Work Sharing with Short-Time Compensation

In Europe, another kind of work sharing strategy was being used. Employers there had a tradition of relying less on layoffs and more on governmental supports and work-spreading strategies than their U.S. counterparts. German representatives at the 1975 "Alternative to Layoffs" conference told of the success of using partial unemployment insurance payments in conjunction with a reduced workweek. This kind of program had first been used in Germany in the 1920s. Its objective was to encourage organizations and workers to temporarily reduce work time with the understanding that the government would reimburse employers for providing partial compensation to employees for lost work. Conceptually, this program combined the two goals of income maintenance and job security. It was financed by a percentage payroll tax dividend equally between employers and employees up to an established earnings ceiling.[3]

Similar programs were used by employers in Belgium, France, Great Britain, the Netherlands, and other Western European countries. As Eleanor Holmes Norton, chair of the New York conference, noted, the approach used unemployment insurance systems in a way that "put a premium on working."[4]

It was interest in the German model that provided the incentive for experimentation with work sharing and a complementary strategy of short-time compensation (STC), or partial unemployment insurance payments, in the United States. In 1978, California became the first state to adapt this concept for use in an American setting. The "Work Sharing Unemployment Insurance" (WSUI) program was a pilot project originally designed to mitigate expected massive layoffs in the public sector. The layoffs never materialized, however, and in 1980 and later, in 1981 and 1982 during a prolonged economic downturn, users of the program were almost entirely private-sector employers. In January 1987, after several revisions and extensions, the California program became a permanent option for that state's employers.

The WSUI program is described in detail in brochures issued by the state of California (excerpts are presented in Figure 9-1). The state's employers use the form shown in Figure 9-2 to submit their work sharing plans initially to the Employment Development Department for review and approval in order that their employees affected by cutbacks may be eligible to receive partial unemployment insurance payments. During the time that the WSUI program is in effect, companies must, on a weekly basis, provide each employee working a reduced schedule with a certification form specifying the percentage by which his or her hours and wages have been cut back during that week. The employee then submits this form to the local Employment Development Department field office to claim WSUI benefits.

In 1980, Rep. Patricia Schroeder introduced federal legislation designed to encourage states to experiment with new ways to

(Text continues on page 326.)

Figure 9-1. Description of California's work sharing unemployment insurance program.

Work Sharing Unemployment Insurance (WSUI)

Senate Bill 1471, passed by the California State Legislature in 1978, authorized the Work Sharing Unemployment Insurance program. This legislation allows payment of work sharing unemployment insurance benefits to persons whose wages and hours are reduced as a temporary alternative to layoffs.

The program helps employers and employees avoid some of the burdens that accompany a layoff situation. For instance, if employees are retained during a temporary slowdown, employers can quickly gear up when business conditions improve. Employers are then spared the expense of recruiting, hiring and training new employees. In turn, employees are spared the hardships of full unemployment. For employers who need to reduce their work force permanently, the program can be used as a phased transition to layoff. Affected employees can continue to work at reduced levels with an opportunity to find other employment before the expected layoff.

THE ADVANTAGES OF WORK SHARING

- **It saves jobs.**
- **Almost any business or industry can participate.**
- **You keep your trained employees.**
- **It's more equitable than layoffs.**

SOURCE: *Work Sharing* (Sacramento: California Health and Welfare Agency, Employment Development Department), DE 8683 Rev. 7 (12–91): 2–8.

Questions and Answers About Work Sharing UI

1. *Who May Participate in WSUI?*

- Any employer who has a reduction in production, services or other condition which causes the employer to seek an alternative to layoffs.

- To participate, an employer must have at least a 10 percent reduction in the work force or in a unit within the work force, and a time and wage reduction of 10 percent.

2. *How Does an Employer Participate in WSUI?*

- Employers may call or write EDD Work Sharing Unit, P.O. Box C-9640, Sacramento, CA 95823-0640. They should ask for a Work Sharing UI Plan.

- The employer sends the completed plan to EDD for approval.

- The plan requires participation of **at least two employees,** a reduction of 10 percent or more of the regular work force or work group unit, and a reduction of 10 percent or more in the wages earned and hours worked of participating employees.

- If collective bargaining agreements cover the employees, a concurrence of **each** union bargaining agent must accompany the application.

3. *How do Employees Qualify for Work Sharing UI?*

- Employees must be regularly employed by an employer whose work sharing plan has been approved by EDD.

- The employee must have qualifying wages in the base quarters used to compute a regular California Unemployment Insurance (UI) claim.

(Continued)

Figure 9-1.   *(continued)*

- At least 10 percent of the employer's regular work force or unit within the work force, who are included in the approved Work Sharing Plan, must participate in each reduced work-week or in **at least** one week of a two-consecutive-week period.

  Example: A work unit includes 100 employees. In the first week, 10 employees (10 percent) are reduced and participate in the program. In the next week, only two employees participate. In **at least** one week of this two-consecutive-week period, 10 percent of the work unit participated. The requirements would not be met if five employees (5 percent) participate in each week.

- The reduction in each participating employee's **normal** workweek schedule and wages must be 10 percent or more.

- New employees hired after the Work Sharing Plan is approved may not participate in the Work Sharing Plan until such time as the employee works one complete, normal workweek (no reduction).

- Employees file initial claims for WSUI by reporting to the local EDD field office to present a certification provided by the employer. After this, transactions are ordinarily handled by mail.

4. *Is WSUI Only for the Private Sector?*

- No. The law originally was intended to help the public sector deal with expected mass layoffs following passage of Proposition 13. Since that time, many private employers have used WSUI as an option to save jobs; hence the WSUI identification with the private sector.

5. *What is the Cost to Employers Participating in WSUI?*

- Workshare benefits paid are charged to the reserve accounts of those employers who are in the claimant's base period in the same manner as any other UI benefit.

- Charges to a reserve account tend to adversely affect the reserve account balance thereby increasing the potential for a higher UI tax rate in future years.

- The Department mails a Notice of Employer Contribution Rates and Statement of Reserve Account, Form DE 2088, in February each year. This notice reflects the status of a reserve account as of the prior June 30. Any employer considering WSUI should review their latest DE 2088 to determine the probable effect on their reserve account. For additional information on reserve accounts or workshare liabilities, contact the Contribution Rate Group at

- **Direct reimbursable account** employers are billed directly for 100 percent of the WSUI costs.

6. *How Much Lead Time is Necessary to Initiate a Plan for WSUI Participation?*

- All Work Sharing Plans begin on a Sunday. An employer may choose the effective date of the plan. However, the earliest a plan may be approved is the Sunday prior to the employer's first contact with the Work Sharing UI Unit.

- If unions are involved, concurring signatures are required from each representative collective bargaining agent.

- The best answer to this question is: allow as much time as possible by starting an application as soon as you know a reduction in the work force is imminent.

(Continued)

Figure 9-1.   *(continued)*

---

7. *What are Some Nonfiscal Merits of WSUI Participation?*

- The outstanding feature of WSUI is: **it saves jobs.** Employees faced with layoff can, instead, work a reduced workweek with minimum salary reduction and continuation of fringe benefits.

- WSUI gives additional time to workers to learn of other work options open to them.

8. *How Flexible is WSUI? Can it be Applied to Most Work Situations?*

- WSUI is **extremely flexible** and can be custom-tailored to a variety of work situations.

- Employers who are potential users of WSUI may call   for specific information regarding individual application of the program.

9. *What is the Duration of a Work Sharing Plan?*

- A Work Sharing Plan is approved for a six-month period. If, at the end of this period, the employer is still experiencing an economic downturn, an application may be submitted for a subsequent WS Plan. Such a plan may be approved immediately after a prior plan expires provided the conditions warrant approval.

10. *Must the Reduced Weeks be Used in Consecutive Order?*

- No. Any sequence of use is allowed. The only restriction is that at least 10 percent of the work force or of a unit within the work force covered in the plan must share in the work and wage reduction in each week, or in at least one week of a two-consecutive-week period.

11. *Can a Percentage of Employees be Rotated so that Different Employees Have Reduced Hours Each Week?*

   • Yes, so long as the 10 percent of the work force criterion is met.

12. *Can Employees be Rotated from Department to Department to Use Different Skills During Slack Periods?*

   • Employees can be rotated to meet individual needs of employers, as long as the 10 percent reduction criterion is observed.

13. *Can an Employer, Operating in Multiple Locations, have more than One Work Sharing Plan?*

   • No. Only **one** WS Plan may be approved under **one** Employer Account Number regardless of the size, structure and/or multiple locations of the employer. However, other units at the same or different location(s) may be added to an existing approved WS Plan (contact the WS Unit at for further information.)

WSUI In Other States

Programs similar to California's WSUI have been adopted by other states. Many additional states and the federal government are now actively considering work sharing legislation. Thousands of California employers have been approved to participate in WSUI.

The work sharing program provides a practical alternative to layoffs. For example, in many other states, if a business with 100 workers faces a temporary lull and must reduce its work force by 20 percent, the employer has no choice but to lay off 20 people, one out of five employees.

(Continued)

Figure 9-1. *(continued)*

Under California's WSUI program, an employer facing the same situation could file a plan with the State Employment Development Department reducing the workweek of all employees from five days to four (20 percent reduction). The employees would be eligible to receive 20 percent of their regular weekly unemployment insurance benefits.

Under this plan, everyone benefits. The employer is able to keep his work force intact during a temporary setback and no employees lose their jobs.

In cases where employers need to reduce their work force permanently, work sharing provides a means to make the transition. Affected workers can continue to work at reduced levels and a more normal income level, with the opportunity to find other employment before the expected layoff.

Several estimates have been made concerning the cost of replacing workers who move to other jobs during temporary layoffs. Some of the factors considered were: average recruitment costs; average cost of screening and selecting new workers; average training costs; and the loss of productivity during the training period. These costs totaled anywhere from $2,500 to $3,000 per employee. By using WSUI and retaining employees, these costs do not occur.

Because of WSUI's built-in flexibility and all possible variations of the program, EDD can make several suggestions concerning a program which will suit most employers' needs.

Let us help you design a program to fit your needs. Phone or write to:

EDD Work Sharing UI Unit
P.O. Box C-9640
Sacramento CA 95823-0640

Figure 9-2. Application for approval of a WSUI plan.

EDD Serving the People of California

First Contact Date _11-2-93 KRob_

WORK SHARING (WS) UNEMPLOYMENT INSURANCE PLAN APPLICATION

For Either: ☐ WS Plan   **OR**   ☐ Expanded WS Coverage

(Complete both sides of this form and submit in duplicate)

ENTER COMPANY INFORMATION AS SHOWN ON MOST RECENT DE 3 QUARTERLY RETURN:

1. A. Name ———————————————————————————————

    B. Mailing Address ————————————————————————————

    C. Phone No. ——————————— D. California Employer Account No. ⎯ ⎯ ⎯ ⎯ ⎯ ⎯ ⎯ ⎯

If name of company/subsidiary or business location where Work Sharing will occur is *different* than above, complete all items in #2, below:

2. A. Name ———————————————————————————————

    B. Mailing Address ————————————————————————————

    C. Phone No. ————————————————

3. Effective date of WS Plan ————————— (Earliest effective date is the Sunday prior to first contact date shown above.)

    OR

    Date of Expanded WS Coverage —————— (Sunday of the week in which first WS reductions have or will occur.)

4. Expected weekly reduction in wages and hours of affected employees ——————— %.

5. Specific type of business ————————————————————————

6. Are any employees who will participate in this plan covered by a collective bargaining agreement? ☐ Yes   ☐ No
(Each applicable collective bargaining agent must complete and sign a collective bargaining concurrence statement–see reverse.)

7. Affected work unit designation (see instructions)

	Bargaining Agent	No. of Employees In Unit	No. of Employees Sharing Work
———————————	———————	———————	———————
———————————	———————	———————	———————
———————————	———————	———————	———————
———————————	———————	———————	———————
TOTALS		=======	=======

8. Your participation in the Work Sharing program is confidential. EDD occasionally receives requests for the names of companies that would be willing to share their experiences in this program. Are you willing to have your name released for this purpose?   ☐ Yes   ☐ No

9. Please describe briefly the circumstances requiring your company's use of the Work Sharing Program to avoid a layoff:

———————————————————————————————————

———————————————————————————————————

10. If additional WS Certification forms are needed, please indicate number: ———————————

11. Is this plan part of a transition to a permanent layoff or company closure?   ☐ Yes   ☐ No

12. Please indicate your payroll week ending day. ————————————————————

FOR DEPARTMENT USE ONLY
13. Eff. Date ———— 14. W/S Ees. ———— 15. % ——— 16. SIC ———— 17. Union (Y or N) ——— 18. Status (T or P) ———

Employment Development Department / State of California

DE 8686 Rev. 8 (1-89)   **(Complete reverse side)**

(Continued)

Figure 9-2. *(continued)*

A. We understand that the reserve account of a participating employer using the tax rate method will be charged in the usual manner for benefits paid under this program. In addition, it is possible that these charges may increase the employer UI contribution rate in future years.

A participating reimbursable employer will be billed quarterly for the cost of benefits in the same manner as they are currently billed for other UI benefits.

We will provide the Employment Development Department with the percentage of hour and wage reduction for each participating employee as a result of this Work Sharing Program. We understand that in order to be eligible, any employee must have worked at least one normal work week (no reduction) prior to issuance of certification forms for benefit payment.

A plan approved by the Department shall expire six months after its effective date. Expanded coverage approved to add other work units shall expire on the same date as the plan. A new plan may be approved immediately following the expiration of the previous plan if the employer finds it necessary to provide employees with continuous coverage under this program.

We have provided the information on this form so that our employees may participate in the shared work unemployment compensation benefit program, in lieu of layoff.

Employer Signature** _____   Contact Person _____

Name (Type or Print) _____   Telephone No. ( ) _____

Title _____   IS THE FORM SIGNED BY A CORPORATE
                                                     OFFICER, SOLE PROPRIETOR OR GENERAL
Date _____   PARTNER? ___ YES ___ NO

Signature must be of a **corporate officer, sole proprietor or general partner.

B.   COLLECTIVE BARGAINING AGENT(S) CONCURRENCE

1.   Union Name: _____   2.   Union Name: _____

      Local Number: _____   Local Number: _____

      Telephone: ( ) _____   Telephone: ( ) _____

      Signature: _____   Signature: _____

      Name (Type or Print): _____   Name (Type or Print): _____

      Title: _____   Title: _____

RETURN TWO COPIES OF THIS APPLICATION TO:

EMPLOYMENT DEVELOPMENT DEPT
SPECIAL CLAIMS OFFICE #850
P.O. BOX 269058
SACRAMENTO CA 95826-9058
(916) 255-1800

minimize layoffs through work sharing and to make the issue a priority for the U.S. Department of Labor (DOL). (See Figure 9-3.) P.L. 97-248 directed the Department of Labor to develop model legislation that can be used by states wishing to establish short-time compensation programs. (See Figure 9-4.) There is no requirement, however, that states adopt this legislation.

(Text continues on page 333.)

Figure 9-3. Text of federal legislation on work sharing supplemented by short-time compensation.

Sec. 194. (a) It is the purpose of this section to assist States which provide partial unemployment benefits to individuals whose workweeks are reduced pursuant to an employer plan under which such reductions are made in lieu of temporary layoffs.

(b)(1) The Secretary of Labor (hereinafter in this section referred to as the "Secretary") shall develop model legislative language which may be used by States in developing and enacting short-time compensation programs, and shall provide technical assistance to States to assist in developing, enacting, and implementing such short-time compensation program.

(2) The Secretary shall conduct a study or studies for purposes of evaluating the operation, costs, effect on the State insured rate of unemployment, and other effects of State short-time compensation programs developed pursuant to this section.

(3) This section shall be a three-year experimental provision, and the provisions of this section regarding guidelines shall terminate 3 years following the date of the enactment of this Act.

(4) States are encouraged to experiment in carrying out the purpose and intent of this section. However, to assure minimum uniformity, States are encouraged to consider requiring the provisions contained in subsections (c) and (d).

(c) For purposes of this section, the term "short-time compensation program" means a program under which—

(1) individuals whose workweeks have been reduced pursuant to a qualified employer plan by at least 10 per centum will be eligible for unemployment compensation;

(2) the amount of unemployment compensation payable to any such individual shall be a pro rata portion of the unemployment compensation which would be payable to the individual if the individual were totally unemployed;

(3) eligible employees may be eligible for short-time compensation or regular unemployment compensation, as needed; except that no employee shall be eligible for more than the maximum entitlement during any benefit year to which he or she would have been entitled for total unemployment, and no employer shall be eligible for short-time compensation for more than twenty-six weeks in any twelve-month period; and

(4) eligible employees will not be expected to meet the availability for work or work search test requirements while collecting short-time compensation benefits, but shall be available for their normal workweek.

(d) For purposes of subsection (c), the term "qualified employer plan" means a plan of an employer or of an employers' association which association is party to a collective bargaining agreement (hereinafter referred to as "employers' association") under which there is a reduction in the number of hours worked by employees rather than temporary layoffs if—

(1) the employer's or employers' association's short-time compensation plan is approved by the State agency;

(2) the employer or employers' association certifies to the State agency that the aggregate reduction in work hours pursuant to such plan is in lieu of temporary

(Continued)

Figure 9-3.   *(continued)*

layoffs which would have affected at least 10 per centum of the employees in the unit or units to which the plan would apply and which would have resulted in an equivalent reduction of work hours;

(3) during the previous four months the work force in the affected unit or units has not been reduced by temporary layoffs of more than 10 per centum;

(4) the employer continues to provide health benefits, and retirement benefits under defined benefit pension plans (as defined in section 3(35) of the Employee Retirement Income Security Act of 1974), to employees whose workweek is reduced under such plan as though their workweek had not been reduced; and

(5) in the case of employees represented by an exclusive bargaining representative, that representative has consented to the plan.

The State agency shall review at least annually any qualified employer plan put into effect to assure that it continues to meet the requirements of this subsection and of any applicable State law.

(e) Short-time compensation shall be charged in a manner consistent with the State law.

(f) For purposes of this section, the term "State" includes the District of Columbia, the Commonwealth of Puerto Rico, and the Virgin Islands.

(g)(1) The Secretary shall conduct a study or studies of State short-time compensation programs consulting with employee and employer representatives in developing criteria and guidelines to measure the following factors:

(A) the impact of the program upon the unemployment trust fund, and a comparison with the estimated impact on the fund of layoffs which would have occurred but for the existence of the program;

(B) the extent to which the program has protected and preserved the jobs of workers, with special emphasis on newly hired employees, minorities, and women;

(C) the extent to which layoffs occur in the unit subsequent to initiation of the program and the impact of the program upon the entitlement to unemployment compensation of the employees;

(D) where feasible, the effect of varying methods of administration;

(E) the effect of short-time compensation on employers' State unemployment tax rates, including both users and nonusers of short-time compenation, on a State-by-State basis;

(F) the effect of various State laws and practices under those laws on the retirement and health benefits of employees who are on short-time compensation programs;

(G) a comparison of costs and benefits to employees, employers, and communities from use of short-time compensation and layoffs;

(H) the cost of administration of the short-time compensation program; and

(1) such other factors as may be appropriate.

(2) Not later than October 1, 1985, the Secretary shall submit to the Congress and to the President a final report on the implementation of this section. Such report shall contain an evaluation of short-time compensation programs and shall contain such recommendations as the Secretary deems advisable, including recommendations as to necessary changes in the statistical practices of the Department of Labor.

Figure 9-4. The U.S. Department of Labor's model legislative language for use by states wanting to implement short-time compensation programs.

A. *Definitions*

1. "Affected Unit" means a specified plant, department, shift, or other definable unit consisting of not less than ___ employees to which an approved short-time compensation plan applies.

2. "Fringe Benefits" include, but are not limited to, such advantages as health insurance (hospital, medical, and dental services, etc.), retirement benefits under defined benefit pension plans (as defined in Section 3(35) of the Employee Retirement Income Security Act of 1974), paid vacation and holidays, sick leave, etc., which are incidents of employment in addition to the cash remuneration earned.

3. "Short-Time Compensation" or "STC" means the unemployment benefits payable to employees in an affected unit under an approved short-time compensation plan as distinguished from the unemployment benefits otherwise payable under the conventional unemployment compensation provisions of a State law.

4. "Short-Time Compensation Plan" means a plan of an employer (or of an employers' association which association is a party to a collective bargaining agreement) under which there is a reduction in the number of hours worked by all employees of an affected unit rather than temporary layoffs of some such employees. The term "temporary layoffs" for this purpose means the separation of workers in the affected unit for an indefinite period expected to last for more than two months but not more than one year.

5. "Usual Weekly Hours of Work" means the normal hours of work for full-time and permanent part-time employees in the affected unit when that unit is operating on its normally full-time basis, not to exceed forty hours and not including overtime.

6. "Unemployment Compensation" means the unemployment benefits payable under this Act other than short-time compensation and includes any amounts payable pursuant to an agreement under any Federal law providing for compensation, assistance, or allowances with respect to unemployment.

7. "Employers' Association" means an association which is a party to a collective bargaining agreement under which the parties may negotiate a short-time compensation plan.

B. *Criteria for Approval of a Short-Time Compensation Plan*

An employer or employers' association wishing to participate in an STC program shall submit a signed written short-time compensation plan to the Director for approval. The Director shall approve an STC plan only if the following criteria are met.

1. The plan applies to and identifies specified affected units.

2. The employees in the affected unit or units are identified by name, social security number and by any other information required by the Director.

3. The usual weekly hours of work for employees in the affected unit or units are reduced by not less than 10 percent and not more than ___ percent.

4. Health benefits and retirement benefits under defined benefit pension

(Continued)

Figure 9-4. *(continued)*

plans (as defined in Section 3(35) of the Employee Retirement Income Security Act of 1974), will continue to be provided to employees in affected units as though their work weeks had not been reduced.

5. The plan certifies that the aggregate reduction in work hours is in lieu of temporary layoffs which would have affected at least 10 percent of the employees in the affected unit or units to which the plan applies and which would have resulted in an equivalent reduction in work hours.

6. During the previous four months the work force in the affected unit has not been reduced by temporary layoffs of more than 10 percent of the workers.

7. The plan applies to at least 10 percent of the employees in the affected unit, and when applicable applies to all employees of the affected unit equally.

8. In the case of employees represented by an exclusive bargaining representative, the plan is approved in writing by the collective bargaining agent; in the absence of such an agent, by representatives of the employees in the affected unit.

9. The plan will not serve as a subsidy of seasonal employment during the off season, nor as a subsidy of temporary part-time or intermittent employment.

10. The employer agrees to furnish reports relating to the proper conduct of the plan and agrees to allow the Director of his/her authorized representatives access to all records necessary to verify the plan prior to approval and, after approval, to monitor and evaluate application of the plan.

In addition to the matters specified above, the Director shall take into account any other factors which may be pertinent to proper implementation of the plan.

C.   *Approval or Rejection of the Plan*

The Director shall approve or reject a plan in writing within ___ days of its receipt. The reasons for rejection shall be final and nonappealable, but the employer shall be allowed to submit another plan for approval not earlier than ___ days from the date of the earlier rejection.

D.   *Effective Date and Duration of Plan*

A plan shall be effective on the date specified in the plan or on a date mutually agreed upon by the employer and the Director. It shall expire at the end of the 12th full calendar month after its effective date or on the date specified in the plan if such date is earlier, provided that the plan is not previously revoked by the Director. If a plan is revoked by the Director, it shall terminate on the date specified in the Director's written order of revocation.

E.   *Revocation of Approval*

The Director may revoke approval of a plan for good cause. The revocation order shall be in writing and shall specify the date the revocation is effective and the reasons therefor.

Good cause shall include, but not be limited to, failure to comply with the assurances given in the plan, unreasonable revision of productivity standards for the affected unit, conduct or occurrences tending to defeat the intent and effective operation of the plan, and violation of any criteria on which approval of the plan was based.

Such action may be taken at any time by the Director on his/her own motion, on the motion of any of the affected unit's employees or on the motion of the appropriate collective bargaining agent(s); provided that the Director shall review the operation of each qualified employer plan at least once during the 12-month period the plan is in effect to assure its compliance with the requirements of these provisions.

F. *Modification of an Approved Plan*

An operational approved STC plan may be modified by the employer with the acquiescence of employee representatives if the modification is not substantial and in conformity with the plan approved by the Director, but the modifications must be reported promptly to the Director. If the hours of work are increased or decreased substantially beyond the level in the original plan, or any other conditions are changed substantially, the Director shall approve or disapprove such modifications, without changing the expiration date of the original plan. If the substantial modifications do not meet the requirements for approval, the Director shall disallow that portion of the plan in writing as specified in section E.

G. *Eligibility for Short-Time Compensation*

1. An individual is eligible to receive STC benefits with respect to any week only if, in addition to monetary entitlement, the Director finds that:

(a) During the week, the individual is employed as a member of an affected unit under an approved short-time compensation plan which was approved prior to that week, and the plan is in effect with respect to the week for which STC is claimed.
(b) The individual is able to work and is available for the normal work week with the short-time employer.
(c) Notwithstanding any other provisions of this Act to the contrary, an individual is deemed unemployed in any week for which remuneration is payable to him/her as an employee in an affected unit for 90 percent or less than his/her normal weekly hours of work as specified under the approved short-time compensation plan in effect for the week.
(d) Notwithstanding any other provisions of this Act to the contrary, an individual shall not be denied STC benefits for any week by reason of the application of provisions relating to availability for work and active search for work with an employer other than the short-time employer.

H. *Benefits*

1. The short-time weekly benefit amount shall be the product of the regular weekly unemployment compensation amount multiplied by the percentage of

(Continued)

Figure 9-4. *(continued)*

reduction of at least 10 percent in the individual's usual weekly hours of work.

2. An individual may be eligible for STC benefits or unemployment compensation, as appropriate, except that no individual shall be eligible for combined benefits in any benefit year in an amount more than the maximum entitlement established for unemployment compensation, nor shall an individual be paid STC benefits for more than 26 weeks (whether or not consecutive) in any benefit year pursuant to a short-time plan.

3. The STC benefits paid an individual shall be deducted from the maximum entitlement amount established for that individual's benefit year.

4. Claims for STC benefits shall be filed in the same manner as claims for unemployment compensation or as prescribed in regulations by the Director.

5. Provisions applicable to unemployment compensation claimants shall apply to STC claimants to the extent that they are not inconsistent with STC provisions. An individual who files an initial claim for STC benefits shall be provided, if eligible therefor, a monetary determination of entitlement to STC benefits and shall serve a waiting week.

6. (a) If an individual works in the same week for an employer other than the short-time employer and his or her combined hours of work for both employers are equal to or greater than the usual hours of work with the short-time employer, he or she shall not be entitled to benefits under these short-time provisions or the unemployment compensation provisions.

   (b) If an individual works in the same week for both the short-time employer and another employer and his or her combined hours of work for both employers are equal to or less than 90 percent of the usual hours of work for the short-time employer, the benefit amount payable for that week shall be the weekly unemployment compensation amount reduced by the same percentage that the combined hours are of the usual hours of work. A week for which benefits are paid under this provision shall count as a week of short-time compensation.

   (c) If an individual did not work during any portion of the work week, other than the reduced portion covered by the shorttime plan, with the approval of the employer, he or she shall not be disqualified for such absence or deemed ineligible for STC benefits for that reason alone.

7. An individual who performs no services during a week for the short-time employer, and is otherwise eligible, shall be paid the full weekly unemployment compensation amount. Such a week shall not be counted as a week with respect to which STC benefits were received.

8. An individual who does not work for the short-time employer during a week, but works for another employer and is otherwise eligible, shall be paid benefits for that week under the partial unemployment compensation provisions of the State law. Such a week shall not be counted as a week with respect to which STC benefits were received.

I. *Charging Shared Work Benefits*

STC benefits shall be charged to employers' experience rating accounts in the same manner as unemployment compensation is charged under the State

(Continued)

law. Employers liable for payments in lieu of contributions shall have STC benefits attributed to service in their employ in the same manner as unemployment compensation is attributed.

J. *Extended Benefits*

An individual who has received all of the STC benefits or combined unemployment compensation and STC benefits available in a benefit year shall be considered an exhaustee for purposes of extended benefits, as provided under the provisions of section ___ , and, if otherwise eligible under those provisions, shall be eligible to receive extended benefits.

An employer's work sharing plan must be agreed to by both employer and union with final approval by the state employment security agency. Highlights of the guidelines developed by DOL are:

- There must be a need for the workweek to be reduced at least 10 percent before a request for STC can be considered.
- STC benefits should be a pro rata of regular unemployment insurance benefits.
- Employees should not be required to make themselves available for other work or conduct a job search as a test of their eligibility to collect STC benefits but are required to be available for their normal workweek.
- The total reduction of hours under STC should be no greater than the reduction in hours would have been had layoffs taken place.
- During the preceding four months, the employer's workforce must not have been reduced more than 10 percent by layoffs.
- The employer must continue to provide health and retirement benefits as though the workweek had not been reduced.
- Where the workforce is unionized, the union must consent to the STC plan.

Voluntary Reduced Work Time

A third work sharing strategy has been to encourage wider use of various kinds of voluntary reduced work time arrangements—unpaid days off, shorter workweeks, sabbaticals. Originally most reduced work time options were introduced in order to accommodate employees' needs. In a growing number of instances, this employee interest has provided a basis for cutting back budgets by allowing employees to voluntarily exchange compensation for more time off. This has been particularly true in the public sector, where cities, counties, school districts, and various state agencies have used voluntary reduced work time as a way to cut labor costs and minimize layoffs. However, as the Charles Schwab & Company example on page 361 illustrates, there is considerable incentive for private-sector employees to use this approach, too.

Who Uses Work Sharing?

This section discusses experience to date with the three main types of work sharing: (1) ad hoc work sharing, (2) work sharing with short-time compensation, and (3) V-Time programs as a means of work sharing.

Ad Hoc Work Sharing

High-technology companies in Silicon Valley, California, have found both ad hoc work sharing and work sharing supplemented by the state's STC program helpful in combatting the up-and-down economic swings that are prevalent in their industry. Hewlett-Packard was a pioneer in the use of ad hoc work sharing, and other employers in the field soon began to follow suit. Here are examples of how some of these Silicon Valley companies employed ad hoc work sharing strategies during the recession of the mid-1980s:

- Hewlett-Packard cut pay for top officials by 10 percent in 1985 and reduced work time by two days a month for everyone else except sales force personnel, who were exempted from the work reduction so that they could keep selling.
- Monolithic Memories, Inc., a semiconductor maker with 1,300 employees, cut hourly workers back to four days' work for four days' pay and salaried workers to five days' work for four days' pay in 1982 and again in 1985. During this period, company officers also took a 10 percent pay cut.
- National Semiconductor Corporation shut down for 34 days in 1985.
- Equitec cut executive salaries from 10 percent to 20 percent, with other employees losing two days of work a month from October 1985 through January 1986.

■ Intel Corporation instituted 4 percent to 8 percent pay cuts and seven days of furlough in 1985.[5]

As you have gathered from the preceding, 1985 was a very bad year for the semiconductor business. However, according to a 1986 report to the state of California's Office of Technology Assessment, a few companies did manage to avoid layoffs completely during that year.[6]

Ad hoc work sharing is not limited to high-tech companies, however. Companies as diverse as Charles Schwab, a discount broker; Humphrey, Inc., a small manufacturer of gyroscopes; and Bell Canada, Canada's largest telephone utility, have minimized or avoided layoffs in this way. A United Auto Workers plan announced in early 1993 was designed to save jobs at a Chrysler assembly plant. It called for workers to alternate shifts—two weeks on, two weeks off—while the plant phased out production of several models. This allowed workers to retain benefits and vacation time and continue to contribute to pension plans.[7] And in September 1993, Bell Canada announced a program that it estimated could save the equivalent of 5,000 jobs by using a combination of shortened work hours, severance incentives, and freezing of management salaries.[8]

Work Sharing with Short-Time Compensation

Since 1982, seventeen states have passed legislation, modeled on California's, that allows employers to use partial payments of unemployment insurance for STC in conjunction with work sharing. States offering STC as of 1993 were Arkansas, Arizona, California, Connecticut, Florida, Iowa, Kansas, Louisiana, Massachusetts, Maryland, Missouri, New York, Oregon, Rhode Island, Texas, Vermont, and Washington. Table 9-1 shows the number of employees

Table 9-1. Work sharing by state: 1990–1992.

	1990	1991	1992
Arkansas	2,247	1,212	9,034
California	24,147	49,912	44,996
Florida	2,916	10,792	7,185
Kansas	5,198	16,434	11,497
Maryland	1,856	2,963	1,108
Washington	4,204	5,373	4,875

SOURCE: New Ways to Work phone survey (Dec. 1993).

in some of these states who participated in work sharing/STC programs between 1990 and 1992.

Motorola, Inc., a major manufacturer of semiconductors, is one of the longest-term large users. (See profile page 364.) Managers there have been very articulate in praising this new alternative. "It doesn't have the disabling effects financially or psychologically that being out of a job does," says Lew Hastings, Motorola legislative counsel. A 1984 study of that company's work-sharing program also showed a savings of $1,800 per worker in new-hiring and training costs.[9]

In most states, use of the STC legislation is not at all widespread. Although there has been much positive experience with this alternative to layoffs, its use has been undercut both by a lack of promotion (its "champions" have moved on to other issues) and because the concepts it represents run counter to the current "downsizing" mindset. Perhaps in the coming decade, interest in employee retention will prevail and work sharing with short-time compensation will provide an important tool once again.

Voluntary Reduced Work Time

Both public- and private-sector employers have used voluntary reduced work time arrangements as part of a work sharing strategy. Corporate users have included Shaklee, Bank of America, and Charles Schwab & Company. (A profile of the Schwab program is on page 361.) Alaska offers a "Reduced Work Week as an Alternative to Layoff" program, and the University of California offers a Time Reduction Incentive Plan (TRIP) (see profile page 361).

In 1979, California passed legislation providing that "[W]henever a reduction equivalent to one percent or more of full-time equivalent jobs is contemplated in the personnel of state agencies or departments, employees in such agencies or departments shall be permitted, under certain circumstances, to voluntarily reduce their work time." (Note: In 1980, recognizing that many employees needed less than full-time schedules for personal reasons, the California state legislature passed the Reduced Work Time Act, which permanently authorizes a variety of voluntary options, including such arrangements as job sharing and four-, five-, and six-hour workdays. It retains language, however, mandating that voluntary work time cuts be offered in cases of projected reductions in force of 1 percent or more. The V-Time programs, which were described in detail in Chapter 7, were designed to comply with this legislation.)

When Is Work Sharing Most Appropriate?

A properly designed program of work sharing is a management strategy that can enable an employer to cut costs during downturns in the economy without the potentially crippling dislocations often caused by widespread layoffs—the loss of trained and experienced employees (which lengthens the company's turnaround time once the economy does pick up and new hires must be recruited and trained), a drop in morale on the part of the remaining employees, and a reversal of affirmative action gains.

■ *Responding to economic fluctuations.* An employer that uses layoffs or downsizing as a strategy for dealing with a faltering economy will indeed cut its payroll costs. This strategy, which prevailed over work sharing in the most recent recession, is not without its price, however. In the short run, the employer incurs such layoff-related expenses as severance pay and retirement incentives. In the long run, the economic outlook will brighten, and the employer will find itself either (1) incurring a variety of hiring and retraining expenses (and associated delays) as it attempts to gear up its operations and regain its competitive momentum or (2) having a vastly restructured workforce composed of fewer core employees and a variety of contingent workers who lack commitment to the organization. On the other hand, the employer that cuts back paid hours and shares the remaining work when faced with a business slump keeps the organization's trained and experienced staff intact, ready for an immediate response to improved conditions.

■ *Turnaround time.* The reduction of turnaround time is probably the most important reason to consider a work sharing program. The time it takes for a company to call back laid-off workers or recruit and train new ones results in productivity losses of various kinds; lost sales, reduced market share, and customer dissatisfaction are just a few of the potential problems.

■ *Employee commitment and morale.* Widespread layoffs take their toll not only on the newly unemployed workers but also on the morale of those who stay with the company. The remaining employees, often termed "survivors," wondering which of them might be next, may experience a drop in both commitment and productivity. A work sharing alternative to layoffs is popular with most employees because it preserves their job security and benefits and distributes the burden of cutbacks more equitably than making a small portion of laid-off workers bear the entire brunt. And combining work sharing with STC can help workers even more by cushioning the impact of their salary loss.

■ *Impact on diversity.* Since women and minorities are often among the most recently hired for certain types of positions, the organization that lays off a portion of its employees in order to cut costs may find itself wiping out hard-won affirmative action gains in the process. One alternative is to use work sharing strategies to keep the workforce intact through an economic downturn, thereby preventing damage to the organization's diversity and avoiding employee lawsuits challenging the layoff procedure.

Downsizing vs. Work Sharing

Two issues that differentiated the 1990–93 recession from previous recessionary periods were (1) the prevalence of organizations that were "downsizing" permanently and (2) the lack of interest in work sharing.

Downsizing differs from traditional layoffs in that the recalling of workers when business improves is not part of the business plan. Downsizing is used to "right size" an organization, not to help it through economic bad times, although business downturns are often cited as the reason for this decision. The end of the 1980s and the early years of the 1990s have been a period of corporate "restructuring" and "reengineering." Begun before the recession, the elimination of staff continued through the course of the economic downturn and beyond. As one business report noted, many firms seemed to be seeking "an irreducible core level of permanent employees."[10] Downsizing has not generally achieved the results that organizations expected. The American Management Association's 1993 survey of downsizing noted that "Fewer than half the firms that have downsized since January 1988 report that profits increased after the cuts were made, and only a third reported increases in worker productivity. Almost invariably, worker morale suffered."[11] A Wyatt Company survey reached many of the same conclusions. As organizations reach the limit of their cutbacks, and understaffing begins to be recognized as a critical issue, the desire to relieve employee stress and retain skills may provide a basis for revived interest in work sharing.

Four-Day Workweek

In Europe, where the idea of spreading work and limiting unemployment is more firmly entrenched, the concept of a four-day workweek has begun to gain adherents. Germany and France in particular have become active advocates owing to growing rates of unemployment. Volkswagen AG's institution of a four-day work-week in 1993 (see page 363) received a great deal of media attention. The adoption of work sharing language in the collective agreements covering the German metalworking industry is another indication that these strategies may rank prominently on many German companies' agendas in the future. They seem to appeal to both employers' associations and trade unions as a means of increasing the number of people who retain a solid labor force attachment.

In France, the government is considering a plan to cut the current five-day, thirty-nine hour workweek to four days and thirty-three hours. And in Canada, the Work Well Network has been established as an umbrella group to coordinate Canadian activities to promote the four-day workweek. Proponents estimate that, combined with controls on overtime and with full employment rights for part-timers, the adoption of a thirty-two hour workweek would create approximately 2 million new jobs in Canada.[12]

Pros and Cons of Work Sharing

When considering the use of work sharing as an alternative to layoffs or downsizing, the major factors that an employer must keep in mind involve the cost implications of both strategies, their effect on productivity, the attitudes of labor and management, the effect of layoffs and work sharing on the company's affirmative action profile, the potential for legal challenges in the wake of layoffs, and the equity of both approaches.

Cost Implications

In this area, we will start by considering the costs that are sometimes reported in connection with the use of work sharing and then examine the savings that can be achieved.

Costs. Work sharing is slightly more expensive on an hourly per capita basis than some of the other reduced work time options because employers continue to pay full fringe benefits even though employees are working less than full-time.

If short-time compensation is used, work sharing may also have a negative effect on employer contributions to the unemployment insurance fund by increasing the organization's experience rating.

Furthermore, if senior as well as junior employees are included in the "work group" that is eligible for STC, the average benefit payout may be raised. On the other hand, layoffs also have the same detrimental effect. Some employers have therefore designed a mixed model approach to work sharing: using STC for nonexempt employees and ad hoc work sharing for top management and some exempt workers.

In addition, some states impose a surcharge on negative-balance employers—that is, those that have contributed fewer dollars to the unemployment insurance fund than their employees have drawn in benefits. California initially had such a policy, but legislation passed in 1988 repealed the surcharge section of the Unemployment Insurance Code. In Arizona employers who have a negative reserve account balance and whose account has been charged for benefits paid under work sharing are assessed an additional rate of tax. In Florida, Missouri, and Oregon any employer participating in a work-sharing program can be assessed a higher rate of contributions than the maximum rate for non-work-sharing employers. In Arkansas, California, Kansas (program does not apply to negative-account-balance employers), Iowa, Louisiana, Maryland, Massachusetts, Rhode Island, Texas, Vermont, and Washington, shared work benefits will be charged to an employer's account in the same manner as regular unemployment benefits. However, in Massachusetts, if an employer's account reserve percentage is negative, the employer will be charged on a dollar-for-dollar basis as if he or she were a reimbursing employer. In New York, shared work benefits are charged to the appropriate account in an amount expressed in dollars rather than effective days.

The labor cost of completing the extensive documentation required in order for a company's employees to receive STC can pose a problem for small to medium-size organizations. This is unfortunate, since in many states, the primary users of STC to date have been smaller companies. In some states, the staff of the administering agency facilitates the paperwork processing in order to reduce the load on participating organizations.

Savings. The most obvious saving associated with a cutback in work time is a reduction in the employer's labor costs. Charles Debow, director of employee relations at Motorola's Phoenix plant, which has used work sharing with STC a number of times, estimates that from 1982 to 1986, this strategy "saved the company $7.7 million in wages."[13] And if the cutbacks take the form of intermittent shutdowns, the employer may also see a reduction in overhead costs.

With respect to unemployment insurance, both the company that lays off workers and the company that cuts back through work sharing in conjunction with STC will face a rise in costs. The difference is that while laid-off workers continue to draw unemployment insurance against their employer's account as long as they remain out of work, employees whose schedules have been reduced through work sharing will immediately stop drawing unemployment insurance once they resume a full-time schedule, thereby lowering the company's unemployment insurance outlay.

Layoff strategies can often require substantial financing in such areas as severance pay and early retirement incentives and can also involve the practice known as "bumping." The work-sharing approach avoids both the up-front expenses of layoffs and the longer-term costs associated with bumping, which can include distorted production scheduling, delayed start-ups, and retraining.[14]

Additional major savings are realized through the retention of trained and experienced employees, which minimizes postrecession turnaround time and avoids the costs of recruitment, training, and so on necessitated by layoff-stimulated turnover. (See also the discussion of productivity in the following subsection.)

Productivity

Because layoffs are so disruptive and painful, both to workers and to the organization, they are usually delayed as long as possible in the face of an economic downturn. Sometimes this sort of delay can be detrimental to an organization's productivity. The various modes of work sharing provide the organization with a range of responses that can be invoked in a more timely fashion, enabling it to take earlier and less-drastic action when business begins to slack off.

Once business starts to pick up again, the organization that has employed a work sharing strategy will find itself in a stronger position than the organization that has dismissed a portion of its workforce. One aspect of the ability to resume normal operations is the retention of employees with company-specific skills, in terms of both technological expertise and experience unique to a particular employer. Clearly, having a trained and committed workforce all ready to go puts a company in a better position to produce goods or services than one that has to recall workers (many of whom may now be employed elsewhere) or recruit and train new employees. In fact, cutting down on the turnaround time needed to get back into a competitive mode following a recession is probably the greatest advantage of work sharing from an organizational standpoint.

Work sharing generally results in improved employee morale. This, in turn, is usually believed to have a positive effect on retention, recruitment, and commitment to the organization, all of which translate into productivity gains.

Labor Attitudes

Although organized labor has negotiated agreements that call for a reduction in hours, or work sharing among employees, before layoffs are permitted, labor has often been skeptical about work sharing, even when STC replaces part of the lost wages. Unions have been concerned about how and when work sharing would be used and about its impact on seniority. Since the mid-1970s, however, there has been a clause in the index of Labor Arbitration Reports on "work sharing to avoid layoff" that indicates growing acceptance of this practice.

In 1981, the executive council of the AFL-CIO endorsed work sharing under certain conditions. The five conditions the council specified were:

1. Adequate financing of unemployment insurance trust funds
2. Approval of the union where there is one
3. A wage replacement level of at least two-thirds of the lost pay and workweek reductions limited to 40 percent
4. Retention of fringe benefits
5. Prohibition of discrimination against recently hired workers, especially minorities and women[15]

According to AFL-CIO spokesperson John Zalusky, about 20 percent of union contracts provide for some form of work sharing.[16]

As Ramelle MaCoy and Martin Morand note, in their book *Short-Time Compensation*:

Layoffs threaten the union not only with short-range losses in dues income but with the demoralizing and disunifying effects on a work force in which some have lost their jobs and the rest feel threatened. Instead of focusing its energies on the causes of this affliction to the collective it represents, the union must devote its energies and resources to the impact on individuals. Its members are not all together at the workplace; they are harder to find, organize and defend.[17]

Management Attitudes

Studies done on work sharing indicate that managers in firms that have used work sharing like this arrangement, partly because it is less disruptive than layoffs and partly because managers generally want to avoid having theirs become known as a "hire-and-fire" company. They also want to retain trained employees.

Motorola executives, looking back on their work sharing experience, offered the following comments:

> Productivity remained high during last year's cutbacks . . . because most [workers] stayed on the same job.

> The big saving for Motorola came when semiconductor orders picked up earlier this year. . . . Recalling workers would have taken a lot longer. . . . You do a lot of wheelspinning to get [laid-off] people back to work.[18]

Diversity

Preserving affirmative action gains was one of the original objectives of advocates of work sharing. Since layoffs generally follow a "last hired, first fired" pattern, they are perceived as affecting female and minority employees disproportionately. Caught between seniority issues and the desire to preserve their hard-won affirmative action profile, many employers have found work sharing, particularly when accompanied by short-time compensation, a middle ground that allows them to achieve a number of objectives.

Legal Incentives

Increasingly, employees, either individually or en masse, are challenging the legality of layoffs and dismissals. The $13 million Atari Corporation workers' class action suit, brought by employees abruptly dismissed in 1983, was one of the most dramatic legal initiatives, but it is not unique. Trying to conduct layoffs that do not discriminate in some way against some group is an increasingly difficult process. Work sharing avoids the problems of legal challenges to the layoff procedure.

The Plant-Closing Law that became effective February 4, 1989, could prove to be an incentive to use work sharing if it were enforced. It has a mass layoff provision that calls for giving employees sixty days' notice if a company dismisses at least fifty people who comprise one-third of the workforce or if the employer terminates 500 people. To date, however, it has not been well enforced.[19]

Equity

As Martin Nemirow, a social science adviser to the U.S. Department of Labor, has noted, "Equity is the major benefit of STC. The economic and social costs of full-time unemployment are distributed more evenly across all workers in a plant (or plant unit) rather than among a small minority of workers."[20]

Concurring, Morand and MaCoy note that equity can also be cost-effective:

Few firms confronted with the necessity of laying off production workers find it feasible to lay off proportionate numbers of clerical, managerial, and supervisory personnel. In a plant of 200 employees, for example, the layoff of 40 production workers will not reduce the need for a foreman or payroll clerk. If the firm opts for STC, however, particularly if the hours reduction should take the form of a four-day week—it would be entirely possible for the firm's supervisory, managerial, and executive employees to share the reduction with the production workers and thus effect additional savings. Such a procedure would also eliminate the bitterness frequently felt by production workers because they are so frequently forced to bear the entire burden of the need for a reduction in labor costs.[21]

Should Your Organization Try Work Sharing?

We have included in this section several tools to help you determine whether or not work sharing would be an effective strategy for your own organization as it confronts periodic fluctuations in the business climate.

First, refer to the accompanying profiles entitled Organizational Experience with Work Sharing/STC. As you read these profiles, take note of factors that might apply to your company's situation.

Table 9-2 is a questionnaire that will focus your attention on the conditions and the climate that usually exist in an organization for which work sharing would be an appropriate option. If your questionnaire results would seem to point toward work sharing, use the worksheet in Figure 9-5 to further assess this alternative.

Introducing Work Sharing

The process of introducing work sharing in an organization as an alternative to layoffs during a business slowdown consists of the

Table 9-2. Work sharing questionnaire.

Would Work Sharing Benefit Your Organization?

	Yes	No
Does your organization's management have a cooperative working relationship with its labor force?		
Would top management fully support using work sharing as an alternative to layoffs?		
Are top managers and professional staff willing to take a pay cut to help the company during a downturn in the economy?		
Can work sharing be presented to employees as a positive, supportive measure that will save jobs?		
Or rather, will work sharing be perceived by employees as a way of exploiting them?		
Would some of your organization's employees like to volunteer to reduce their work time temporarily in order to spend more time with their families, take a training course, return to school, phase into retirement, and so on?		
Is the downturn your company faces expected to be of a short-term nature?		
Or does the downturn instead represent a more difficult, long-term problem that your company or your industry must address?		
If a prolonged downturn is anticipated, is work sharing expected to be a transition phase before layoffs?		
Does your state have legislation allowing employers to use short-time compensation under certain conditions?		

following steps: Gain support from all levels of management and from labor. Set up the program's administration, which should comprise both a task force and an administrator. Design the program, assessing the entire range of relevant issues. Develop resource materials, both for managers and for employees. Announce the program and then promote it to employees so that work sharing will be seen as being of mutual benefit to labor and to the organization. Assess the effect of the program and make appropriate improvements. We will now take a closer look at each of these steps in the program implementation process.

Gain Support for the Program

For a work sharing strategy to be effective, it must have the support of all segments of your company's workforce: top management,

Figure 9-5.   Work sharing worksheet.

Assessing the Need for Work Sharing

List the main reasons why you are considering work sharing:

1. _____

   _____

   _____

2. _____

   _____

   _____

3. _____

   _____

   _____

4. _____

   _____

   _____

List what you see as the advantages and disadvantages of work sharing:

Pros: _____

_____

_____

_____

_____

Cons: _____

_____

_____

_____

_____

_____

_____

_____

middle management, labor representatives, and employees. Top management's leadership is particularly important, because top management must help the organization's employees see work sharing for what it is: a way to preserve jobs during an economic downturn. In a unionized workplace, labor's support is equally important. A joint union-management task force, with balanced representation, can be critical to its success.

In companies that have had a history of commitment to employment security, work sharing will probably be perceived as a natural outgrowth of traditional policy and culture. In companies that have generally used layoffs to control labor costs, it may take more effort to gain general support for work sharing, particularly from those segments of the workforce who felt they were relatively secure from being laid off.

Set Up the Program's Administration

Work sharing is a relatively new concept. It often affects different departments and job classifications unevenly, so it is particularly important to use a task force when developing a work sharing plan for the first time. Once top management and labor representatives are committed to using work sharing, broadening companywide understanding and support will be the task force's next objective.

The task force should also be charged with gathering background information necessary for decision making and soliciting input about the design of the work sharing program. (See the following subsection for a discussion of the major program design issues that must be addressed.)

An administrator should be appointed to provide staff support to the task force and, once the program's design is agreed upon, to administer the work sharing plan.

Design the Program

Before beginning to design the work sharing program, the task force will have to compile certain background information and address several key questions. For example:

- Have other companies in your area tried work sharing? What kind of program did they use, and what was its effect?
- How long is the business slump expected to last?
- By how much will the organization need to reduce its expenditures during this period?
- What activities have to continue, and to what extent, in order to maintain the company's viability?

Once these questions have been considered, determinations can be made about the following program design issues.

Duration. Although it is impossible to predict at the outset just how long a recessionary period will last, management should establish a time period for the work sharing plan and announce it to employees in order to reinforce the fact that this is a temporary measure. At the end of the specified period, the current plan can be evaluated and a decision made about whether conditions warrant a return to normal operating capacity or whether work sharing, perhaps in a modified form, should be continued.

In states that currently have short-time compensation legislation, variations in allowable program duration exist: It is limited to twenty weeks in California and in New York (exclusive of the waiting week); twenty-six weeks in Arizona (but may be extended if the insured unemployment rate for a thirteen-week period is equal to at least 4 percent), Arkansas, Florida, Iowa, Kansas, Louisiana, Maryland, Missouri, Oregon, Rhode Island, Texas, Vermont, and Washington; and thirty weeks in Massachusetts in any twelve-month period.

Scope. Since work sharing must often be targeted, affecting particular areas of a company differently, a decision must be made about whether work sharing will be used companywide, only in designated departments or divisions, or only in designated job classifications.

Form. One key decision that must be made is what form, or combination of forms, of work sharing would effectively address the situation presently facing your organization. The task force's assessment of the probable duration of the recessionary period will be the most important factor in determining what kind of degree of work sharing will be most appropriate initially: ad hoc mandated strategies, work sharing combined with partial unemployment insurance payments (assuming that your state has passed enabling legislation making short-time compensation available through the unemployment insurance system), voluntary reduced work time options, or some combination of the three.

The following are components of a work sharing strategy that can be applied either singly or in combination:

■ *Promoting existing voluntary reduced work time options.* These options include such strategies as a V-Time program, job sharing or regular part-time employment, unpaid leave with a guarantee of a job upon return, and phased or partial retirement.

■ *Introducing ad hoc work sharing tactics.* These may include a wage and/or hiring freeze, furlough days, mandatory use of paid time off, elimination of banking or carryover of paid time off, one or more short plant shutdowns (for instance, between Christmas and New Year's, in the summer, or periodically).

■ *Instituting salary reductions.* Some companies have coped with business downturns by cutting salaries for a defined duration. These reductions, which are usually confined to company officers, top management, and highly paid professional staff, sometimes take the form of "five days' work for four days' pay" but have also taken the form of percentage cutbacks.

■ *Reassigning employees.* Reassignments enhance other work sharing tactics by allocating existing human resources more efficiently. They have the added benefit of cross-training the employees involved, which broadens both the employees' and the organization's options not only during the recessionary period but also during the following economic recovery.

■ *Using short-time compensation.* If, in conjunction with a work sharing strategy, it is possible to replace a portion of the lost wages through partial unemployment insurance payments, cost-reduction measures will become more palatable, particularly to employees in lower-paid job classifications. In those states that permit partial unemployment insurance payments to workers whose hours have been cut back, STC is usually available only for a specified period of time (see section on Duration above).

Because of the paperwork demands occasioned by the use of STC and the potentially negative effect on future unemployment insurance ratings, employers generally target the application of STC rather than making it available companywide at all levels of responsibility. In designing a work sharing program, management and labor must carefully consider which departments or job classifications should be designated as recipients of partial unemployment insurance payments and for how long.

Although work sharing is still in its infancy as a human resources management strategy in the United States, what is known about the experience of various organizations to date suggests the following rules of thumb for determining the form that a work sharing program should take:

■ If your company is facing a small, short-term cutback, the situation might best be dealt with through expanded use of voluntary reduced work time arrangements such as those mentioned earlier in this section.

■ If voluntary reductions are insufficient but the cutback is perceived as being short-term and involves no more than a 20 percent reduction, then ad hoc work sharing should be considered. (It is generally felt that ad hoc work sharing can be used successfully only for reductions of 20 percent or less, and then only for a short period of time.)

■ If cutbacks of 20 to 40 percent are projected for more than a few weeks, then short-time compensation is necessary in order for employees to continue receiving a living wage. (Employers in those states that do not have STC enabling legislation might consider bringing the need for this option to the attention of their state legislature.)

The major program design issues we have just discussed are summarized in Table 9-3, which can be used to keep track of where you stand in addressing each of these issues. Table 9-4 is a sample

Table 9-3. Program design checklist: work sharing.

Key Design Issues	Notes
☐ Duration	
☐ Scope	
☐ Form	
☐ Existing V-Time options	
☐ Ad hoc work sharing approaches	
☐ Salary reductions in selected positions	
☐ Employee reassignments	
☐ Short-time compensation	

work sharing matrix that illustrates how one organization planned a series of targeted reductions of various types and for various durations; it compares the savings that could be achieved over a twenty-week period and over the course of a year. Table 9-5 is a blank copy of this matrix that you may wish to use as an aid to planning cutbacks within your own organization.

Develop Resource Materials

A company that plans to institute a work sharing plan will be faced with a variety of questions and concerns on the part of management and employees. Effectively designed resource materials can do a great deal to foster understanding and acceptance of the cost-cutting measures.

Resource Materials for Managers. The topics of most interest to managers will be:

- How the work sharing schedule will affect their department in terms of both finances and staffing—that is, in terms of the bottom line and the production line

(Text continues on page 356.)

Table 9-4. Sample work sharing matrix.

Activity	Exempt			Nonexempt			Total Savings: 20 wks.	Total Savings: 1 yr.
	No. Emp.	For	Savings	No. Emp.	For	Savings		
Voluntary Reductions								
V-Time								
Job sharing								
• Technical writers (50%)	4	1 yr.	$50,000				$ 19,231	$ 50,000
• Assemblers (50%)	8	1 yr.	$52,912				$ 20,351	$ 52,912
Regular part-time								
Unpaid leave								
Phased/partial retirement								
Ad Hoc Work Sharing								
Hiring freeze								
Wage freeze								
Furlough days								
Mandatory use of paid time off								
Elimination of banking or carryover of paid time off								
Plant shutdown:								
—Christmas–New Year's								
—Summer								
• Division II (100%)	24	1 wk.	$21,000	150	1 wk.	$ 74,508	$ 95,508	$ 95,508
—Periodic								

Salary reductions:
- —Officers
- —Top mgt/professional
  - • Mgt Division III (20%)   20   20 wks. $50,000 $ 50,000 $ 50,000
- —Other

Short-Time Compensation
(if provided for under existing state legislation)
Companywide
Defined work groups:
- —Headquarters staff
- —Division
- —Office
Job classifications:
- —Clerical
- —Production
  - • Division III (20%)   150   20 wks. $765,000 $765,000 $ 765,000
- —Other

TOTAL SAVINGS $950,090 $1,013,420

Table 9-5. Work sharing matrix worksheet.

Activity	Exempt			Nonexempt			Total Savings: ___ wks.	Total Savings: 1 yr.
	No. Emp.	For	Savings	No. Emp.	For	Savings		
Voluntary Reductions								
V-Time								
Job sharing								
Regular part-time								
Unpaid leave								
Phased/partial retirement								
Ad Hoc Work Sharing								
Hiring freeze								
Wage freeze								
Furlough days								
Mandatory use of paid time off								
Elimination of banking or carryover of paid time off								
Plant shutdown:								
—Christmas–New Year's								
—Summer								
—Periodic								

Salary reductions:
—Officers
—Top mgt./professional
—Other

Short-Time Compensation
(if provided for under existing
   state legislation)
Companywide
Defined work groups:
—Headquarters staff
—Division
—Office
Job classifications:
—Clerical
—Production
—Other

TOTAL SAVINGS

■ How to encourage the use of available voluntary reduced work time options in their departments and how to support employees who voluntarily reduce their work time beyond the mandated cuts

■ How the short-time compensation process works and what their responsibilities are in this area (assuming that STC is available in your state)

■ How long this phase of work sharing is expected to last

Resource Materials for Employees. The topics of most interest to employees will be:

■ How the various work sharing strategies will affect them individually. For example: Will performance or salary reviews be rescheduled as a result of wage freezes? What, if any, impact will the work sharing program have on pension fund payments?

■ The projected duration of the cutbacks.

■ The process for receiving partial unemployment-insurance payments (if appropriate).

■ The expected long-range benefits of this strategy, both to themselves and to the company.

Announce the Program

When an economic downturn threatens, rumors about layoffs and job cuts abound. In such an atmosphere of widespread concern, the work sharing program announcement will play a critical role in determining how this cost-reduction measure will be perceived by the organization's employees. Good communication with all levels of the labor force, starting with the program announcement, is a must if work sharing is to succeed.

Information about company plans for work sharing should be imparted as soon as possible. If the organization is using this alternative to layoffs for the first time, a companywide meeting can be scheduled at which top management and members of the task force can explain the purpose of work sharing and answer employee questions from the floor about the mechanics of the program and how it will affect their unit and their own status. Employee resource materials can be distributed at this time and an announcement made about how more detailed questions will be handled. A briefing session such as this establishes an air of candor that will be helpful in the weeks to come.

Promote the Program

Although user organizations report that work sharing is very popular among employees, it is still important to promote the concept. Three points should be emphasized:

1. Work sharing is a way of providing some employment security.
2. It is more equitable and less disruptive than layoffs by order of seniority.
3. It will leave the company in a better competitive position when the economy recovers than it would be if layoffs had been used.

Instilling a sense of working together to get through a difficult time will create a positive dynamic that will have a carryover effect when the downturn ends.

Evaluate the Program

Unless the business slump is of very short duration, the design of the initial work sharing program should be evaluated within six or eight weeks of the time the program is put into effect. This evaluation should focus on two areas:

1. Did the kind of cutbacks that were used achieve the desired results in the targeted areas (for example, a reduction in total wages or in hiring or training costs)? If not, what changes in type or degree of work sharing can be made to improve the program's effectiveness?
2. Did the use of work sharing have a positive impact on the organization's ability to resume its operations at normal capacity once economic conditions improved?

Fine-Tune the Program

Based on the results of the evaluation, the organization should take whatever measures are warranted to improve the program's effectiveness, in terms of both achieving the targeted cutbacks while the program is in effect and enhancing the organization's competitive position once the program had ended. For example:

Problem	*Solution*
Managers complain that employees must take too much time off work to deal with the registration and reporting forms required to receive Short Time Compensation.	Ask the State Employment Security Office if it will arrange to send someone on-site to handle the paperwork for your firm's employees.
The marketing department reports that the reduced schedule inhibits its ability to keep up with orders requests.	Review the situation to see if the marketing staff should resume full schedules.
Employees cannot receive Short Time Compensation because enabling legislation has not been introduced in your state.	Assign staff responsibility for developing an industry initiative to introduce STC legislation.

Summary

Work sharing is a cost-reduction strategy that a company can use to avoid laying off a portion of its workforce in the face of an economic slowdown. It involves cutting back the hours and salary of some or all of the organization's staff.

There are three basic approaches to work sharing, which can be used singly or combined in a variety of ways. The first is ad hoc work sharing, in which the involved members of the labor force reduce hours and salary by a specified amount. When work sharing is combined with short-time compensation, employees receive partial unemployment insurance payments to make up for a portion of the lost wages. (This second approach is possible only in states that have passed short-time compensation enabling legislation.) And finally, the company's employees can be encouraged to reduce their hours on a voluntary basis. Ad hoc work sharing is used by many organizations whose industries are affected by periodic swings in the economy, such as high-technology companies in the computer field. During a business slowdown, some organizations elect to use ad hoc work sharing for more highly paid employees while reserving STC for lower-paid workers, thereby reducing both their companies' experience rating and future payments to the unemployment insurance fund. Seventeen states currently allow partial unemployment insurance payments to employees whose hours have been reduced as part of a work sharing program.

Although experience with work sharing/STC has been limited, and was minimal during the most recent recession, we do know that this approach has thus far been used most extensively in the manufacturing sector. V-Time options have been used in both the public and private sectors as a means of reducing expenditures without reducing the workforce.

Work sharing is most appropriate when a company wants to respond to economic fluctuations in a way that keeps both its workforce and employee morale intact, so that affirmative action and diversity gains will not be jeopardized and turnaround time will be minimal.

The costs that have been reported in connection with work sharing involve such things as the continuation of full fringe benefits for employees on a reduced schedule, a rise in the employer's experience rating if STC is used, and the paperwork burden imposed on the company in order for its employees to receive STC.

On the other hand, the organization that chooses work sharing in lieu of layoffs reduces its labor costs while avoiding such expenditures as severance pay, early retirement incentives, and the dislocations that can come when bumping occurs in conjunction with labor force reductions. Work sharing with STC offers an additional advantage, in that employees are dropped from the unemployment insurance rolls the minute they resume a full-time schedule, so the company is spared the specter of laid-off workers drawing benefits for a potentially prolonged period of time.

The organization also realizes both savings and productivity gains by retaining its trained and experienced staff, thanks to the fact that work sharing minimizes damage to employee morale and gives the company a competitive advantage once the economy picks up and normal operations must resume.

Before downsizing became so prevalent, work sharing received a positive reception from managers, who preferred not to lose their trained staff or have their company get a reputation for layoffs that could damage future recruitment prospects. It is increasingly being accepted by unions as well, provided certain safeguards are instituted.

In addition to the advantage, mentioned above, of preserving affirmative action gains, work sharing enables the organization to cut costs in a way that does not provoke legal challenges from laid-off workers and does not unfairly impose the entire burden of the reduction on a selected few employees.

To introduce a work sharing option, especially for the first time, an organization should focus on making sure that the program will accomplish the desired reductions in a way that does not damage the company's viability. To do this, the organization must see that work sharing is fully understood and supported by all segments of its workforce, target the types of work sharing to be used, and periodically monitor the program's effectiveness in achieving its objectives.

In short, if your company is looking for a way to weather a recession with minimal disruption to its operations, a carefully selected mix of work sharing strategies might be the way to go.

ORGANIZATIONAL EXPERIENCE WITH WORK SHARING

Charles Schwab & Company

Description: Charles Schwab & Company, the nation's largest discount broker, with approximately 6,526 employees, is based in San Francisco, California.

Reason for Using Voluntary Work Sharing: The work sharing plan was devised in June 1988 as a means of cutting operating costs. This was necessary because of a downturn in the brokerage industry. The objective was to achieve a 10 percent reduction in expenses such as compensation, promotion, printing, and telecommunication while, at the same time, retaining highly trained staff.

Implementation Process: Salaries of approximately 200 managers, including the president and the chairman of the board, were temporarily reduced by 5 percent to 20 percent. In addition, employees were offered the opportunity to take sabbaticals at 25 percent of their normal pay or to temporarily cut their workweeks, take unpaid days off, or opt for early vacations. Employee requests for sabbaticals or shortened workweeks had to be approved by two supervisors.

Impact to Date: By November of 1988, Jim Wiggett, senior vice president of human resources, estimated that "almost 100 percent" of Schwab's employees were participating in the program. He projected that the firm would save approximately $3.5 million by the end of the year as a result of the voluntary cutbacks. In May of 1994, responding to a stock market slowdown, Schwab again instituted some of these work sharing procedures.

SOURCE: *Schwab Plans to Implement Further Cost Reductions,* Charles Schwab news release, San Francisco, CA, June 2, 1988; Lloyd Watson, "People in Business," *San Francisco Chronicle* (Nov. 11, 1988), B3; "Schwab to Cut Costs," *San Francisco Chronicle* (May 27, 1994).

University of California at Berkeley

Description: The Time Reduction Incentive Plan (TRIP), which was developed by systemwide administrators, has been offered for the past two years to staff employees on all nine campuses of the University of California system. The Berkeley campus has approximately 6,000 career nonacademic staff.

Reasons for Using V-Time as a Work Sharing Strategy: Offering nonacademic staff employees an opportunity to voluntarily reduce their time in exchange for certain benefits and protections is one of many approaches the University of California has taken in response to the state's unprecedented budget crisis. The intent is to retain valued employees through the crisis period, avoiding the extensive reductions in force or deep salary cuts that might otherwise have been necessary.

Implementation Process: In exchange for volunteering to reduce time by a fixed percent (ranging from 10 percent to 45 percent) for a designated period (twelve or eighteen months), employees are given:

- Exemption from salary cuts for the duration of the TRIP.
- Bonus paid leave upon completion of the TRIP (ranging from forty hours to ninety-six hours).
- Service credit toward University retirement benefits as though the employee had remained at 100 percent (provided time is not reduced below 75 percent).

Other key features are the following:

- Although both full- and part-time employees are eligible, the resulting appointment must be at least 50 percent time in order to maintain career status.
- Time worked may vary from month to month provided the average over the period of the TRIP equates to the agreed-upon percentage reduction.
- Vacation leave and sick leave are prorated, just as they are for other part-timers; however, the reduced leave accruals are more than compensated for by the bonus leave.
- Bonus leave is payable only upon completion of the TRIP.
- Changes to the agreed-upon schedule, or withdrawals from TRIP, must be by mutual agreement of employee and supervisor.

Managers retained the right to decline employee requests for TRIP based on operational needs. This discretion was essential because many departments were short-staffed as a consequence of early retirements resulting from the retirement incentive program. However, campus administrators urged departments to approve TRIP requests whenever feasible as a means of meeting budget targets. Departments were also motivated to approve requests in order to protect employees from possible involuntary pay cuts or even layoff.

Impact to Date: More than 400 Berkeley campus employees (of a career nonacademic staff of approximately 6,000 employees) took TRIP in 1992. Estimated salary savings for the campus were in excess of $2 million.

SOURCE: Greg Kramp, Director, Personnel Programs, Dec. 1993; Margo Wesley, Manager, Policy Communications and Grievance Coordination, UC Berkeley, "UC Berkeley Offers a TRIP"; WORKTIMES (San Francisco: New Ways to Work) 11, no. 4 (1993): 1.

Volkswagen, AG

*Description:*Volkswagen is Germany's largest automobile manufacturer. It employs 100,000 people.

Reasons for Using Work Sharing: VW faced a problem of serious overstaffing as a result of a combination of improved worker productivity and low demand for cars. In order to avoid having to reduce the company's workforce by almost a third, VW's management suggested, and the trade unions agreed to, the institution of a four-day workweek.

Implementation: As of January 1994, standard working time was reduced from thirty-six hours to 28.8, and the monthly income of employees was maintained at the same level as before. In order to cover the costs of this strategy, a variety of fiscal strategies were introduced: a 3.5 percent collective pay rise was postponed from November 1, 1993; a 3 percent pay effect of the thirty-five hour week with full wage compensation was pulled forward from October 1, 1995; one percent, part of the collective pay rise, was pulled forward from August 1, 1994; 2 percent general compensation—for example, the extra holidays for shift workers—was cancelled; 6.5 percent of the monthly payment of the annual bonus and 4 percent of the monthly payment of two-thirds of the extra holiday pay of 70 percent of the monthly pay was used.

Impact to Date: Employees in 1994 will earn approximately 10.5 percent less than their gross annual income in 1993. The company had reduced its personnel capacity by 20 percent as of January 1, 1994; hourly wage costs rose by approximately 10 percent.

SOURCE: Dr. Andreas Hoff, Hoff, Weidinger und Partner, Berlin, Germany, paper delivered at International Society for Work Options meeting, Amersfoort, The Netherlands (April 1994).

Motorola, Inc.

Description: Motorola is a major manufacturer of semiconductor products. The corporate offices are in Schaumberg, Illinois, but the semiconductor production is concentrated in the Phoenix area, where 20,000 are employed. It is this facility that was the site for Motorola's initial work sharing program.

Reason for Using Work Sharing/STC: Motorola used this option in order to retain trained employees during an economic downturn. The devastating layoffs that the company had experienced in the course of the 1975 recession prompted it to investigate how the California model of work sharing with short-time compensation might be introduced in Arizona, where Motorola is the state's largest employer. In 1981, work sharing legislation was passed in that state, and during the 1982 recession, Motorola enrolled in the new program.

Implementation Process: The company determined the extent of the cutback that was needed and the work groups that would be affected. It presented its plan to the state's work sharing office and, once the plan was approved, enrolled in the program. Typical cutbacks for production-line workers were half a day's work and wages per week, with a portion of the loss being made up by partial unemployment insurance payments.

Impact to Date: Motorola estimates that it saved over 1,000 jobs and $1.5 million in the fourth quarter of 1982, when the use of work sharing peaked.

Once orders picked up, the company turnaround time was greatly enhanced because it had retained its workforce, which put it in a better competitive position than companies that had used layoffs.

SOURCE: Heywood Klein, "Interest Grows in Worksharing, Which Lets Concerns Cut Workweeks to Avoid Layoffs," *Wall Street Journal* (Apr. 7, 1983), 33; correspondence with the vice president and director of personnel administration, Motorola (June 1988).

Conclusion:
On to the Future—
Major Trends Affecting
The Need for Flexibility

Back to Basics

In 1989, when the first edition of *Creating a Flexible Workplace* was published, corporate America's attention was riveted on the coming century. Of particular concern were questions of demographics: Would there be enough workers, who would they be, what skills would they have, what kinds of new practices would be necessary to incorporate them into the emerging service industry?

But other revolutionary forces—the globalization of markets, the spread of information technology, the dismantling of organizational hierarchy—coupled with a recession, overrode concerns about labor shortages.[1]

Conventional wisdom in the United States maintains that downturns, either real or projected, are best countered by eliminating organizational "fat." And fat is almost always defined as people. With the slowing of the global economy, management strategy focused on "downsizing" as companies struggled to find their "right" size. In many cases, the results of these efforts have been to create a situation where companies are seriously understaffed or staffed by people who are overstressed and undercommitted.[2]

As this revised edition is being written, each day seems to bring more evidence that it is time for a new approach, or perhaps a variant of the old standards that worked so well for this country's economic growth in the past—specifically, a recommitment to, and investment in, employees. The Wyatt Company report referenced in the Introduction is only one of a growing number of experts who point to the failed objectives of the pervasive downsizing that has been going on.[3] Other research reminds us of the competitive advantage of a committed, participative workforce. Like an echo from the past, Jerome Rosow, president of Work in America Institute, tells attendees at the Productivity Forum: "People—not capital or technology—are the keystone of the high-performance workplace." But the date is 1993, and he is citing current industry research to prove his point.[4]

Two new management books—one by Jeffrey Pfeffer of Stanford Business School, the other by Robert Waterman, co-author with Tom Peters of *In Search of Excellence*[5]—also assert that "worker-friendly employees are outperforming more profit-minded rivals" and that "such firms are going to pull still farther ahead in the future, as easier access to capital and technology makes other competitive strategies ever simpler to imitate."[6] These are ideas that have not been heard in a while but may gain adherents as faith in "lean and mean" fades.

Unfinished Business

Two unresolved issues that continue to have ramifications for the workplace of the future are: (1) the relationship between demographic changes and employees' needs to be able to integrate work with other aspects of their lives and (2) the role of education and training in the increasingly sophisticated labor market.

Balancing Work and Life

Women, minorities, and immigrants—the majority in their child-bearing years—are still expected to account for more than 80 percent of the new additions to the labor force between now and the year 2000. The pool of younger workers is still shrinking and older workers with training and experience are still retiring earlier than they did twenty years ago. As a recent article on workplace flexibility and diversity notes: "It follows, then, that the companies that can attract, retain, motivate, and engage the most talented within these groups will be most likely to succeed, while those that do not may not even survive."[7]

As for helping these workers integrate work with other aspects of their lives so that they can function better, although more firms have flexible work options that make this theoretically possible, a very small number of employees (2 percent, according to the survey cited earlier) feel able to avail themselves of these arrangements. Too many feel overburdened by work, burned out by their jobs, but fearful that they will be among the next group of employees to be let go if they show any interest in flexible work arrangements.

Revitalizing their workers will present a major challenge for employers during the next few years because, as *Fortune* magazine noted, "Survivors become risk-averse . . . unlikely to produce the new, creative ideas that companies will need to prevail in competitive markets."[8] The same article goes on to observe that:

> For the transformation of the workplace to establish a new equilibrium, employers and employees must somehow find ways for workers to lead balanced lives. Empowerment and shared responsibility are undeniably good—but paradoxically, they increase the burdens of people who are already stressed. Workers who lack the time and emotional energy to lead balanced lives risk burnout, and the companies that depend on them will lose.

One of the findings of a national study of 3,400 U.S. workers, conducted by the Families and Work Institute and released in 1993, supports that observation and points to the payoffs employers could expect if corporate value systems really supported workers' needs for more flexibility. According to the report:

> Workers with more job autonomy and control of their work schedules are less burned out by their work, are more satisfied with their jobs, and take more initiative at work. In addition, workers with greater job autonomy are more committed to doing their jobs well, are more loyal to their employers, and plan to remain with their current employers longer than other workers.[9]

As Gil Gordon commented, when reviewing the results of the study in his newsletter,

> The good news is that the solutions to the problems cited don't require huge investments, and are quite consistent with other workplace initiatives underway, such as employee empowerment, total quality management, and work-family balance programs. . . . [The findings] put the keys to enhance employee effectiveness, loyalty, and retention in the hands of the smart employers who choose to take them.[10]

However, although it may be cost-effective, it is increasingly evident that changing corporate policy, systems, and culture in ways that allow employees to balance work and their personal lives is a very necessary but complex task—one that will require both time and significant changes in societal cultural values as well. Lotte Bailyn of MIT's Sloan School of Management notes that:

> Some companies have attempted to respond to these changes by providing child care, family leave, and flexible work arrangements. . . . Presented as solutions at the margin, they are not always successful. Men prove to be unwilling to take advantage of flexible arrangements when offered and reluctant to take time off when it is labeled paternity leave. Women continue to have primary responsibility for the "second-shift"— the work of the home—even when fully engaged in paid employment. Managers, moreover, continue to find it difficult to relinquish continuous visual oversight of their employees.[11]

She defines the problem as one of "organizing work in this new world" and calls for a reconsideration of management practices that foster both the persisting "gendered construction" of the separation of spheres [private and public] and "this separation of public and private lives." Bailyn designates the changes in the organization of work that such rethinking requires as "lying at the core of the challenges facing American industry." She goes on to observe: "There is no escape from these problems; companies *must* include— explicitly, imaginatively, and effectively—the private needs of employees when reengineering their work. Only if they do so can they gain a competitive edge."[12]

Keeping Up: Education and Training in the Year 2000

The problems of skills shortages is not new. Three of the eight trends that the Hudson Institute report *Workforce 2000* highlighted involved projected skills shortages, in addition to labor shortages, because of the shift to a service- and information-based economy and the demand for higher skill levels.[13] Since the report was issued, growing deficiencies in U.S. public education systems have exacerbated the mismatch between skills needed and skills available. At the same time as some employers are projecting that more than 50 percent of the new jobs created by the year 2000 will require some postsecondary training and one-third a college degree, the dropout rate in the United States is over 25 percent nationally and 50 percent in the inner cities.[14]

Today technology is constantly upgrading work content, requiring both people and organizations to accommodate to ongoing change. Learning on the job has taken on a new urgency. Somehow a commitment to work with learning must become an integral part of the work/life process early in life. Programs that help young people combine work with education, such as New Ways to Work's New Ways Workers program, can lead to an understanding of how work and education interact. Flexible work arrangements that facilitate skills expansion and encourage the possibility of combining work with recurrent education and training will be an important aspect of both helping workers succeed in the global marketplace and ensuring an organization's ongoing competitiveness. McKesson Corporation's Work Experience Program (see Chapter 5, "Job Sharing," page 165) and leave and sabbatical programs that encourage cross-training are good models to replicate and expand on.

Flexible Scheduling: Managing the Process of Change

One aspect of the workplace of the future is likely to be ongoing change as companies adapt to new technologies and fluctuating markets. As we've noted throughout this book, the ability to manage change as a process, rather than as a one-time event, will necessitate organizational structures, systems, and cultures that can support the processes of transformation. The term *flexibility* is often used to describe this capability, and for many, creating a flexible workplace starts with introducing a framework of scheduling flexibility.

In his paper *Controlling Hours of Work*, R. A. Lee, of the Department of Management Studies at the University of Loughborough in Great Britain, notes:

> [T]he accepted norm of "fixed hours" is giving way to the development of appropriate hours for different situations. A number of factors have stimulated progress. . . . [T]he strongest pressure of all comes from the need for productive performance in a time of economic stringency.[15]

The paper concludes with the following comments:

> In the longer term it is tempting to foresee a society whose organizations operate a complex variety of hours patterns, these being designed to accommodate developing technologies,

changing family life styles and leisure activities and to share work equitably. It is the intervening processes of change which make this optimistic future seem far away.[16]

As part of the "intervening processes of change," one of the more interesting strategies that organizations have tried is the annual hours contract.

Annual Hours Programs

The idea of an annual hours contract was first articulated in the mid-1970s[17] in Scandinavia as a result of the organizational need for a more efficient way to balance labor supply and labor demand. The system was pioneered in Swedish and later in Finnish pulp and paper industry plants; it then spread, in 1983, to the British paper and board industry.

The annual hours concept is relatively simple: Management and labor agree on the number of hours of work that will be needed during a given year and then design a scheduling format by which those hours will be provided. The schedule may be fixed or variable. All the hours may be scheduled at the outset, or some may be held in reserve to be used when the employer and employees decide they are needed. The result is what British management consultant Philip Lynch has termed an "essential framework around which worktime can be arranged in whatever units or form the business requires and employees will agree to."[18] Lynch notes that the annual hours approach offers four types of benefits:

1. It separates employee hours from production hours.
2. It enables the organization to schedule more employee hours during peak periods of activity and extend operations where needed.
3. It forces a redefinition of overtime and eliminates overtime as a means of production.
4. This new scheduling strategy can be used as a change agent—that is, as a means of creating change—within the organization.[19]

This latter point, Lynch believes, is:

the most powerful advantage of the [annual hours] concept. . . . The major changes that annual hours can help produce include:

■ a stable earnings pattern and progress towards salaried status;

- improved work organisation and more productive work practices;
- more efficient planning and improved use of capital and labour;
- better and less costly training programmes;
- improved versatility and flexibility.[20]

Initially most of the annual hours programs were used in continuous-process production facilities. However, a 1993 study of the use of annual hours in the United Kingdom indicates that the use of these programs is not only growing but spreading to service organizations in both the public and the private sector, such as finance, health services, retail, and broadcasting organizations.[21] The annual hours concept has a broad potential application, offering a structure within which a wide variety of full- and part-time schedules and off-site options can be applied. Its implementation in U.K. service-sector organizations appears to be "demand-led," with employers introducing it in response to workers' needs for more flexibility.

As with the other new flexible scheduling options that have been described in previous chapters, considerable thinking and planning should go into changing an organization's work-hours system. Proponents of annual hours programs recommend conducting a feasibility study that focuses on the following issues:

- The compensation system—particularly the use of overtime—to determine whether the current pay system can be adapted to new work schedules and practices.
- Work time usage—to see what kinds of changes might improve scheduling efficiency.
- Production processes—to determine whether production can be increased with the same amount of labor and capital and what impact any changes might have on labor force needs.
- Work organization—in terms of normal and minimum staffing levels, transferable skills, arrangements to cover for other employees, and so on.

Once the feasibility of adopting an annual hours approach has been determined and a decision has been made to use this strategy, the implementation steps are as follows:

- *Design the schedule.* The most critical task in implementing an annual hours program is calculating the annual hours and then designing the schedule. There are three main steps to this process:

(1) calculating annual output or operating hours (see Figure 10-1), (2) calculating annual available employee hours (see Figure 10-2), and (3) calculating the staffing levels required (see Figure 10-3). The challenge for many employers is to correctly assess the number of hours needed in a year. Where demand is unpredictable, the estimated hours may be too high, and the company is then committed to paying for hours that are not needed; if the estimate is too low, additional costs may be incurred (Figure 10-1). The issues of keeping some employee hours in reserve, unrostered, and rostering holidays are ones to be carefully thought out. Unrostered, or "owed," hours can provide extra flexibility for the employer, but if they are overused, they can be a subject of employee dissatisfaction. Keeping them at a minimum, or eliminating them altogether, is recommended by most users of annual hours.

Annual employee hours available are computed by multiplying the weeks per year by the hours per week and subtracting holidays. Figure 10-2 is a sample annual employee hours calculation. It is based on a thirty-nine hour workweek with five weeks annual holiday entitlement.

The difference between the estimated operating hours and the available employee hours is the reserve, or "owed," hours. Figure 10-3 provides several suggested ways of reconciling the two sets of numbers.

Figure 10-1. Calculation of annual output or operating hours.

The basic formula is:

Annual operating hours = Available operating hours per year minus 'shut' hours (nonoperating hours) per year

Example: Assuming a continuous operation of 7 days per week, 24 hours per day with a minimum shut requirement of 7 days per annum then:

Available weeks per year = 52.179*

$$\text{Total available operating hours per year} = (52.179 \times 7 \times 24) - (7 \times 24)$$
$$= 8{,}766 - 168$$
$$= 8{,}598$$

*The figure of 52.179 is arrived at after taking into account a leap year—365.25 ÷ 7

SOURCE: Excerpted from Sue Hutchinson, *Issues in People Management, No. 5: Annual Hours Working in the UK* (London: Institute of Personnel Management, May 1993), 81–84.

Figure 10-2.   Calculation of annual employee hours.

There are many different formulas for calculating the annual number of employee hours although the principle remains the same—to establish the available number of hours per year after taking into account holiday entitlement. This can be translated into the basic formula of:

Annual employee hours = Weeks per year × hours per week minus holiday entitlement

Example: Assuming five weeks annual holiday entitlement and an average 39-hour basic week

Total holiday entitlement   • Annual = 5 weeks
                            • Public = 1.6 weeks (8 days ÷ 5)
                            ———————————————————————————
                              Total   = 6.6 weeks

Available working weeks per year = Total weeks minus holiday entitlement
                                  = 52.179 − 6.6
                                  = 45.579

Available working hours per year = Available working weeks ×
                                    average weekly hours
                                  = 45.579 × 39
                                  = 1,778

Note: The figure of 1,778 has been arrived at after taking holidays into account and all hours outside the annual hours commitment are therefore leisure time. In theory this means that there is no need to distinguish between holidays and rest days.

SOURCE: Excerpted from Sue Hutchinson, *Issues in People Management, No. 5: Annual Hours Working in the UK* (London: Institute of Personnel Management, May 1993), 81–84.

■ *Redesign the compensation system.* Eliminating the overtime culture is an objective for many employers. In order to gain employee support for a change to the new system, the potential loss of earnings when overtime is reduced must be balanced out by other gains—more stability in pay, better pension or sick pay, more time off. In one company, the new salary structure compensated for the loss of bonuses and overtime pay by maintaining contractual earnings, increasing salaries, and adding 25 percent of the previous year's overtime earnings for all shift employees.

■ *Develop control systems.* The organization will need some sort of system for monitoring the schedule to ensure that the actual worked and paid hours conform to the annual hours plan. Some proponents of the annual hours approach suggest that an individual

Figure 10-3.   Calculation of crewing levels required.

Assuming no overtime is to be worked the basic formula is:

$$\text{Theoretical number of crews required} = \frac{\text{Annual operating hours}}{\text{Annual employee hours}}$$

Example: Using results of calculations in Figures 10-1 and 10-2

$$\text{Theoretical number of crews required} = \frac{8{,}598}{1{,}778}$$

$$= 4.8$$

However, in practice 4.8 crews are not possible, and the options will be:

1) 4 crews

With four crews each employee will be required to work:

$$\frac{\text{Annual operating hours}}{\text{Number of crews}}$$

$$\frac{8{,}598}{4}$$

$$= 2{,}149.5 \text{ hours}$$

If the contractual hours remain at 1,778, then 371.5 hours (2,149.5 − 1,778) extra will need to be worked by each employee (as overtime or banked hours).

2) 4.5 crews

$$\text{With 4.5 crews each employee will be required to work: } \frac{8{,}598 \text{ hours}}{4.5}$$

$$= 1{,}910.7$$

If the contractual hours remain at 1,778, then 132.7 hours (1,910.7 − 1,778) extra will need to be worked by each employee. Again these will be overtime or banked hours.

3) 5 crews

$$\text{With five crews each employee will be required to work: } \frac{8{,}598 \text{ hours}}{5}$$

$$= 1{,}719.6$$

SOURCE: Excerpted from Sue Hutchinson, *Issues in People Management, No. 5: Annual Hours Working in the UK* (London: Institute of Personnel Management, May 1993), 81–84.

If the contractual hours remain at 1,778, then each employee will owe 58.4 hours per year (1,778 − 1,719.6). These owed hours are commonly called reserve, committed, or payback hours.

Therefore, the decision is whether to have overtime or reserve hours built into the contractual hours. Each of these options has a different impact on earnings and total costs.

Note: Variations on the formula may occur for the following reasons:
1) Counting the annual length of the year as 52 weeks or as 52.2 weeks.
2) Variations in the number of hours in the basic working week (for example, 37 rather than 39).
3) Using days rather than 'weeks' in the calculations (for example, 365 days rather than 52 weeks).
4) Rounding up or down the annual hours to the nearest complete shift—for example, with 8-hour shifts, 1,778 could be rounded to 1,776 (222 shifts).
5) Other known absences are taken into account in the calculation of available employee hours per year—for example, a 5 percent level of sickness absence.

work-time account be established for each employee. Such an account starts with the employee's total targeted hours for the year, which are then debited throughout the year until the account totals zero at the end of twelve months.

■ *Redesign jobs.* One aspect of the implementation of an annual hours program is redesigning jobs in order to improve the processes for organizing work and achieve greater flexibility.

■ *Train employees and supervisors.* It is important that workers and their supervisors be trained, both in terms of any skills required to perform the redesigned jobs and in terms of handling the new scheduling arrangements.

The steps outlined above would, for most organizations, represent a radical overhaul of the existing work-hours system. In the companies in which such a program has thus far been implemented, the benefits appear to be substantial. The research to date indicates that from the organization's perspective, these benefits include:

■ Improvement in unit costs and productivity
■ Elimination of overtime as a means of production and of the "overtime culture"
■ Enhanced ability to adapt to future technological changes and business requirements
■ Increased flexibility with respect to both skills and hours, thanks to changed attitudes and practices

■ Better planning and use of available time and resources
■ Simplified and stable pay structures
■ Better-organized and less-costly training
■ Reduced vulnerability to strikes
■ Improved motivation
■ Improved administration[22]

On the employee side, the reported benefits are:

■ Improved basic pay
■ Increased leisure time
■ Structured opportunities for personal development
■ Increased job satisfaction
■ Improved mutual support and cooperation among employees
■ Progress toward salaried status[23]

In the 1993 U.K. study, "nearly all the organisations surveyed were extremely satisfied with their schemes and had no wish to return to their old system of working." One personnel manager echoed Philip Lynch when he commented that "its most powerful benefit has been as a vehicle for change."[24]

As management, labor, and government policymakers begin to review the ramifications of the Fair Labor Standards Act in terms of today's workers' and workplace needs for both flexibility and protection from exploitation, they might find direction in the work of the European Community. The Working Time Directive, adopted by a qualified majority vote of the Social Affairs Council of the European Union Employment Ministers on November 23, 1993 (to be implemented by November 1996), contains the following provisions for all workers:

■ A maximum forty-eight hour week (including overtime) on an average over four months.

■ Eleven consecutive hours of rest per day.

■ Thirty-five consecutive hours of rest per week, in principle including Sundays, although this would not be mandatory. The weekly rest periods could be averaged out over two weeks. The thirty-five hours could be reduced to twenty-four for objective technical or work organization reasons.

■ Rest break during the day for all workers working over six hours and terms to be fixed by collective agreement or national legislation/practice.

■ Four weeks' paid annual leave, subject to the conditions of entitlement laid down by national law/practice. Three weeks would be permitted for the first three years after implementation of the directive (that is, until 1999).

Leave entitlement could not be cashed in (except for outstanding leave on termination of contract).

■ Work organization to take into account health and safety and workers' needs.

The directive also includes special provisions for night workers and modifications to the general rule for certain industries/circumstances to allow them to deviate under specified circumstances—for example, some kinds of seasonal work or activities where a permanent presence is required or continuity of production services is necessary. The details of these modifications would be defined by national law or by collective agreements at national, regional, or local levels as appropriate.[25]

In the future the concepts embodied in annual hours systems would appear to be a promising area for employers seeking to move beyond the programmatic use of flexibility towards more strategic applications.

Equiflex

In the first edition of *Creating a Flexible Workplace*, we introduced the term *equiflex*. An amalgamation of two words, *equitable* and *flexibility*, it seemed an appropriate concept to strive for. The crux of equiflex is providing reduced and restructured work-time and work-site options at wage and prorated benefit levels that make these alternative modes truly comparable to full-time, on-site work. It is the basis of win-win strategies, which in turn can help build stronger, more viable organizations. The principles of equiflex are built into the descriptions of best practices in the preceding chapters. Hallmarks include:

■ The company's culture and its systems reflect flexibility throughout.
■ All employees feel fully enfranchised.
■ Policies are not punitive.
■ Scheduling options are available.
■ Layoffs are considered a last resort.
■ Cross-training, multi-skilling, and lateral mobility are encouraged.

■ A balance is sought between the needs of the firm and its employees.

As companies move towards using a wider variety of work-time and work-site options, one catalytic strategy would be to use the annual hours process (which, as noted earlier in the chapter, allows for scheduling in "whatever units or form the business requires and employees will agree to") in combination with a voluntary reduced work time (V-Time) program (which is designed to respond to employees' needs for less than full-time schedules in order to balance work with other aspects of their lives). Both the annual hours and V-Time programs can be examples of equitable flexibility, or Equiflex, and consequently represent "win-win" situations. Together, they could provide a framework for alternative work-time and work-site options.

As we move on to the future, organizations will find that their potential for profitability is significantly affected by how skillfully they can integrate a variety of work-time and work-site options to create a climate of equitable flexibility.

Notes

Introduction: Win-Lose or Win-Win?

1. *Best Practices in Corporate Restructuring* (Chicago: The Wyatt Company, 1993), 146.
2. Walter Kiechel III, "How We Will Work in the Year 2000," *Fortune* (May 17, 1993): 38.
3. Douglas T. Hall and Victoria A. Parker, *Organizational Dynamics* (Summer 1993).
4. Stanley D. Nollen, *New Work Schedules in Practice*, Work in America Institute Series (New York: Van Nostrand Reinhold, 1982), 1.
5. Mary Holt, "Changing Organizational Culture," *Work Times* (Oct. 1993): 3.
6. Ibid.
7. Gil Gordon, remarks at *Reinventing the Workplace* conference, sponsored by New Ways to Work and The Conference Board, New York City (June 1993).
8. Ibid.
9. David Jamieson and Julie O'Mara, *Managing Workforce 2000* (San Francisco: Jossey-Bass, 1991).
10. Ibid., 178.
11. *New Skills Needed by Managers in Restructured Firms*, Work in America Productivity Forum press release (Scarsdale, N.Y.: May 6, 1987), 2.
12. Press release for *Flexible Work Arrangements II: Succeeding with Part-Time Options* (New York: Catalyst, Inc., 1993).
13. "Flexible Career Paths?" *Sacramento BEE* (Sept. 12, 1993), Section D.
14. Stanley Nollen, *New Work Schedules in Practice*, Work in America Institute Series (New York: Van Nostrand Reinhold, 1982), vii.

Part I: Flexible, Restructured, and Off-Site Work

1. Paul Dickson, *The Future of the Workplace* (New York: Weybright and Talley, 1975), 209.

Chapter 1: Flextime

1. *Monthly Labor Review* 109, no. 11 (Washington, D.C.: U.S. Department of Labor, Bureau of Labor Statistics, Nov. 1986): 18.

2. *Current Population Survey*, special supplement (May 1991).
3. Ibid.
4. Kathleen Christensen, *Flexible Staffing and Scheduling in U.S. Corporations*, Research Bulletin No. 240 (New York: The Conference Board, 1989): 14.
5. Louis Harris & Associates, *Laborforce 2000* survey summary report (1991).
6. Quoted in "Improving Your Workforce through Flextime," *Small Business News* (Cleveland, Ohio).
7. Hewitt Associates survey as reported in *Work in America* 18, no. 12 (New York: Work in America Institute, Dec. 1993): 6.
8. Stanley D. Nollen, "Does Flextime Improve Productivity?" *Harvard Business Review* 57 (Sept.–Oct. 1979): 12–22.
9. J. Carroll Swart, "Clerical Workers on Flextime: A Survey of Three Industries," *Personnel* 62 (Apr. 1985): 41.
10. Ibid., 40–44.
11. Administrative Management Society, *Flexible Work Survey* (Trevose, Pa.: AMS, 1987): 4.
12. Simcha Ronen, *Flexible Working Hours* (New York: McGraw-Hill, 1981), 223.

Chapter 2: Compressed Workweek

1. Herman Gadon and Allan R. Cohen, *Alternative Work Schedules: Integrating Individual Organizational Needs* (Reading, Mass.: Addison-Wesley, 1978), 50.
2. Shirley J. Smith, "The Growing Diversity of Work Schedules," *Monthly Labor Review* 109, no. 11 (Washington, D.C.: U.S. Department of Labor, Bureau of Labor Statistics, Nov. 1986): 10.
3. *The Changing American Workplace: Work Alternatives in the 80's* (New York: AMACOM, 1985), 20.
4. Kathleen Christensen, *Flexible Staffing and Scheduling in U.S. Corporations*, Research Bulletin No. 240 (New York: The Conference Board, 1989), 13.
5. Hewitt Associates survey as reported in *Work in America* 18, no. 12 (New York: Work in America Institute, Dec. 1993): 6.
6. Stanley D. Nollen and Virginia H. Martin, *Alternative Work Schedules*, Parts 2 and 3 (New York: AMACOM, 1978), 57.
7. Stanley D. Nollen, *New Work Schedules in Practice*, Work in America Institute Series (New York: Van Nostrand Reinhold, 1982), 68.
8. Ibid.
9. Nollen and Martin, *Alternative Work Schedules*, 55.
10. Ibid., 57.

Chapter 3: Flexplace

1. *Telecommuting: The State of the Art and Market Trends* (New York: Electronic Services Unlimited, 1984), 1.
2. Frank Schiff, *Flexplace: An Idea Whose Time Has Come*, speech to the Engineering Management Society Institute of Electrical and Electronics Engineers (New York: Engineering Management Society, 1981), 5.
3. *Telecommuting Review: The Gordon Report* (Monmouth Junction, N.J.: Gil Gordon Associates, June and July 1993): 11.

4. *Telecommuting Review: The Gordon Report* (Monmouth Junction, N.J.: Gil Gordon Associates, June 1993): 8.
5. Joanne H. Pratt, "Myths and Realities of Working at Home: Characteristics of Homebased Business Owners and Telecommuters," by *Telecommuting Review: The Gordon Report* (Monmouth Junction, N.J.: Gil Gordon Associates, July 1993): 10.
6. *Runzheimer Reports on Transportation* (Rochester, Wis.: Runzheimer International).
7. *Financial Times* (Oct. 26, 1993).
8. *Telecommuting Review: The Gordon Report* (Monmouth Junction, N.J.: Gil Gordon Associates, Jan. and Aug. 1993): 7, 6.
9. Sue Shellenbarger, "Refusing In-Home Work Costs Him His Job," *Wall Street Journal* (April 8, 1994): B1.
10. *Telecommuting Review: The Gordon Report* (Monmouth Junction, N.J.: Gil Gordon Associates, Oct. 1987): 8.
11. "Labor Letter," *Wall Street Journal* (Jan. 6, 1987), 1.
12. *Telecommuting Review: The Gordon Report* (Monmouth Junction, N.J.: Gil Gordon Associates, Nov. 1, 1992): 2.
13. Adapted with permission from Gil E. Gordon and Marcia M. Kelley, *Telecommuting* (Englewood Cliffs, N.J.: Prentice Hall, 1986), 166.
14. Ibid., 178.
15. "VDT Monitoring Sparks Work Privacy Debate," *Work in America* 12, no. 11 (Nov. 1987): 1.
16. Ibid.
17. Gordon and Kelly, *Telecommuting*, 75.
18. Ibid., 78.

Part II: Reduced Work Time

1. *Part-Time Employment in America: Highlights of the First National Conference on Part-Time Employment* (McLean, Va.: Association of Part-Time Proefessionals, Oct. 1983), 36.
2. *The Changing Workplace: New Directions in Staffing and Scheduling* (Washington, D.C.: Bureau of National Affairs, 1986), 43.

Chapter 4: Regular Part-Time Employment

1. U.S. Department of Labor, Bureau of Labor Statistics, as quoted in Polly Callaghan and Heidi Hartmann, *Contingent Work: A Chart Book on Part-Time and Temporary Employment* (Washington, D.C.: Economic Policy Institute, 1991), 3.
2. *New Work Schedules for a Changing Society* (Scarsdale, N.Y.: Work in America Institute, 1981), 31.
3. Hudson Institute, *Workforce 2000* (Washington, D.C.: U.S. Department of Labor, Employment and Training Administration, May 1987), 4.
4. *Part-Time Employment in America: Highlights of the First National Conference on Part-Time Employment* (McLean, Va.: Association of Part-Time Professionals, Oct. 1983), 36.

5. Chris Tilly, *Short Hours, Short Shrift: Causes and Consequences of Part-time Work* (Washington, D.C.: Economic Policy Institute, 1990), 2.

6. Kathleen Christensen, *Flexible Staffing and Scheduling in U.S. Corporations*, Research Bulletin No. 240 (New York: The Conference Board, 1989), 13.

7. Louis Harris and Associates, *Laborforce 2000* survey summary report (1991). Also quoted in Douglas T. Hall and Victoria A. Parker, "The Role of Workplace Flexibility in Managing Diversity," *Organizational Dynamics* (Summer 1993): 4.

8. Hewitt Associates survey as reported in *Work in America* 18, no. 12 (New York: Work in America Institute, Dec. 1993): 6.

9. *Survey on Work Time Options in the Legal Profession: San Francisco and Alameda Counties* (San Francisco: New Ways to Work, 1986), 19.

10. "News Briefs," *HR Executive* (July 1993): 5.

11. Sherry Herchenroether, "Retain or Replace? Not So Rhetorical a Question," *Looking Ahead* XIII, nos. 1/2, Washington, D.C.: National Planning Association (1991): 39.

12. Ibid., 40.

13. *Operations Report: Keeping a First-Rate but Flexible Work Force* (New York: Research Institute of America, 1986), 7.

14. Department of Labor, Bureau of Labor Statistics survey conducted in 1991 and released May 1993.

15. Mark Manin, "Flexible Benefits for Part-Time Employees," *Benefits News Analysis* 9, no. 3 (1987): 11–12.

16. "Financial Strategies," *Inc. Magazine* (July 1992): 128.

17. Manin, "Flexible Benefits," 12.

18. Ibid.

19. Stanley Nollen, B. Eddy, and V. Martin, *Permanent Part-Time Employment: The Manager's Perspective* (New York: Praeger Publishers, 1978), 70.

20. Stanley Nollen, *New Work Schedules in Practice*, Work in America Institute Series (New York: Van Nostrand Reinhold, 1982), 17.

21. Priscilla H. Claman, *It Works—Part-Time Employment in State Agencies* (Boston: Commonwealth of Massachusetts, Division of Personnel Administration, 1980), 4 and 6.

22. *Part-Time Employment: Implications for Families and the Workplace* (Albany: New York State Council on Children and Families, 1983), 53.

23. Ibid., 19.

24. *Exchanging Earnings for Leisure: Findings of an Exploratory National Survey on Work Time Preferences*, R&D Monograph 79 (Washington, D.C.: U.S. Department of Labor, Employment and Training Administration, 1980), 2.

25. Claman, *It Works*, 2.

26. *Detailed Summary: Forum for Personnel Managers—Part-Time Employment: Implications for NYS Agencies*, Part-Time/Shared Job Project (Albany: New York State Department of Civil Service, 1983), 1.

Chapter 5: Job Sharing

1. *1987 Flexible Work Survey*, AMS Business Trend Survey Series (Trevose, Pa.: Administrative Management Society, 1987), 6; *The Changing American Workplace: Work Alternatives in the 80's*, AMA Survey Report (New York: AMACOM, 1985), 20; *The Changing Workplace: New Directions in Staffing and Scheduling* (Washing-

ton, D.C.: Bureau of National Affairs, 1986), 7; *Survey of Private Sector Work and Family Policy: San Francisco and Alameda Counties* (San Francisco: New Ways to Work, 1986), 12.

2. Kathleen Christensen, *Flexible Staffing and Scheduling in U.S. Corporations*, Research Report No. 240 (New York: The Conference Board, 1989), 15.

3. Louis Harris and Associates, *Laborforce 2000* survey summary report (1991). Also quoted in Douglas T. Hall and Victoria A. Parker, "The Role of Workplace Flexibility in Managing Diversity," *Organizational Dynamics* (Summer 1993): 4.

4. Hewitt Associates survey of 1,034 major employers as reported in *Work in America* 18, no. 12 (New York: Work in America Institute, Dec. 1993): 6.

5. *Job Sharing in Health Care* (San Francisco: New Ways to Work, 1984), 42; *Survey of Work Time Options in the Legal Profession: San Francisco and Alameda Counties* (San Francisco: New Ways to Work, 1986), 20.

6. *Work Times* 5, no. 2 (San Francisco: New Ways to Work, Winter 1987): 1.

7. *Trend Report* (Minnetonka, Minn.: Work Family Connections, Dec. 1993): 1.

8. *Part-Time Schedules: A Guide for NYS Supervisors and Managers*, Part-Time/Shared Job Project (Albany: New York State Department of Civil Service, 1985).

Chapter 6: Phased and Partial Retirement

1. "Flexible Age Retirement: Social Issue of the Decade," *Industry Week* 197, no. 4 (Cleveland: Penton/IPC, Inc., 1978): 66.

2. *Issue Brief*, no. 68 (Washington, D.C.: Employee Benefit and Research Institute, July 1987): 8.

3. *The Travelers Pre-Retirement Opinion Survey: Report of Results* (Hartford: Travelers Insurance Company, 1981), i.

4. *AARP Bulletin* 33, no. 6 (Washington, D.C.: American Association of Retired Persons, June 1992): 2.

5. *Issue Brief*, 8.

6. "Shift of Retirement Age to 67 Should Be Speeded Up, Bentzen Suggests," *San Francisco Chronicle* (Dec. 20, 1993), 1.

7. *The Reduced Work Load Program in the State Teachers' Retirement System* (Sacramento, Calif.: Office of the Legislative Analyst, Sept. 1980).

8. *Looking to the Future* (AT&T, July 1992), 1–10.

9. "Exxon's Retirement Offers Cut Its Staff of Spill Experts," *New York Times* (Mar. 30, 1989).

10. Milo Geyelin, "Age Bias Cases Found to Bring Big Jury Awards," *Wall Street Journal* (Dec. 17, 1993). Legal Beat.

11. "Retiree Benefits Cast a Shadow," *New York Times* (July 21, 1987), Business Day section, D2.

12. *Wall Street Journal* (Jan. 6, 1987), Labor Letter, 1.

13. *Partial Service Retirement* (Sacramento: California Public Employees' Retirement System, June 1984).

Chapter 7: Voluntary Reduced Work Time Programs

1. *Exchanging Earnings for Leisure: Findings of an Exploratory National Survey on Work Time Preferences*, R&D Monograph 79 (Washington, D.C.: U.S. Department of Labor, Employment and Training Administration, 1980), 2.

2. George Gallup poll conducted in conjunction with the White House Conference on Families, 1980; *Families at Work*, General Mills, 1981; *Better Homes and Gardens* readers' polls, 1982 and 1988.
3. *Better Homes and Gardens* (Nov. 1988): 44.
4. *The Travelers' Pre-Retirement Opinion Survey: Report of Results* (Hartford: Travelers Insurance Company, 1981), 13.
5. Quote from Dr. John Robinson, Director of the University of Maryland's "Americans' Use of Time Project" and director of the Hilton survey, 1991.
6. Barney Olmsted and Barbara Moorman, "V Time: A New Way to Work" (San Francisco: New Ways to Work, 1985): 39.

Chapter 8: Leave Time

1. Helen Axel, *Redefining Corporate Sabbaticals for the 1990s*, Report No. 1005 (New York: The Conference Board, 1992), 9.
2. Ibid., 10.
3. Louis Harris and Associates, *Laborforce 2000* survey summary report (1991). Also quoted in Douglas T. Hall and Victoria A. Parker, "The Role of Workplace Flexibility in Managing Diversity," *Organizational Dynamics* (Summer 1993): 4.
4. From a survey of San Francisco Bay Area employers conducted by One Small Step, a United Way–sponsored membership association dedicated to promoting the development of work/family policies and programs in San Francisco Bay Area workplaces.
5. Barbara Presley Noble, "At Work: Interpreting the Family Leave Act," *New York Times* (Aug. 1, 1993): 24.
6. Helen Axel, *Corporations and Families: Changing Practices and Perspectives*, Report No. 868 (New York: The Conference Board, 1985), 32.
7. Work in America Institute, *World of Work Report* 11, no. 8 (Elmsford, N.Y.: Pergamon Press, Aug. 1986): 7.
8. Axel, *Corporations and Families*, 32.
9. Labor Letter, *Wall Street Journal* (June 29, 1993): 1.
10. Flexible Benefits (New York: Catalyst, 1987), 47.
11. *Work in America* 12, no. 4 (Washington, D.C.: Buraff Publications, Apr. 1987): 8.
12. *Reauthorization of the Federal Employees Leave Sharing Act of 1988* (Washington, D.C.: General Accounting Office, May 13, 1993).
13. Helen Axel, *Redefining Corporate Sabbaticals for the 1990's*, Report No. 1005 (New York: The Conference Board, 1992), 28.
14. "Daily Report for Executives" (Washington, D.C.: Bureau of National Affairs, 1986), L-1.
15. Axel, *Corporate Sabbaticals*, 15.
16. Jack Wood, *The Future of Employment*, keynote address at Australian Democrats National Conference (Cremorne, Australia: Jan. 24, 1987).
17. *Report on a National Study of Parental Leaves* (New York: Catalyst, 1986), 87.
18. Ibid., 48.

Chapter 9: Work Sharing

1. Quoted in Fred Best, *Work Sharing: Issues, Policy Opinions, and Prospects* (Kalamazoo, Mich.: W. E. Upjohn Institute, 1981), 3.

2. Edith F. Lynton, *Alternatives to Layoffs*, conference report (New York: Commission on Human Rights, Apr. 1975), 39, 41.

3. Ibid., 3.

4. Quoted in *Alternatives to Layoffs*, 57.

5. "HP Will Extend Cut in Work Hours," *San Francisco Chronicle* (Sept. 24, 1985), 22; Michael Malone, "MMI Outduels the Big Boys," *San Francisco Chronicle* (May 5, 1986), 25; John Eckhouse, "National Semi Plans Furlough; LSI Sees Loss," *San Francisco Chronicle* (1985), 29; Gail E. Shares, "Equitec Cuts Costs to Halt Profit Slump," *San Francisco Chronicle* (Oct. 8, 1985), 25.

6. Unpublished report to the state of California's Office of Technology Assessment (1986).

7. *Employee Relations Weekly* (Washington, D.C.: Bureau of National Affairs, Jan. 18, 1993).

8. Christopher J. Chipello, "Bell Canada to Cut Personnel Costs, Capital Outlays," *Wall Street Journal* (Sept. 29, 1993).

9. Bennett Burgoon and Robert D. St. Louis, *The Impact of Work Sharing on Selected Motorola Units*, technical report 84-12 (Tempe: Arizona State University, Oct. 1984), 16.

10. American Management Association, *Survey on Downsizing: Summary of Key Findings* (New York: AMA, 1992), 1.

11. American Management Association, *Survey on Downsizing: Summary of Key Findings* (New York: AMA, 1993), 4.

12. Bruce O'Hara, "The Future Isn't What It Used to Be," unpublished paper for meeting of International Society for Work Options, Amersfoort, The Netherlands, April 1994, 8.

13. "Shorter Workweeks: An Alternative to Layoffs," *Business Week* (Apr. 14, 1986), 77.

14. *New Work Schedules for a Changing Society* (Scarsdale, N.Y.: Work in America Institute, 1981), 89.

15. John Zalusky, "Short-Time Compensation," remarks to the Interstate Conference of Employment Security Agencies (Sept. 23, 1982), quoted in Ramelle MaCoy and Martin J. Morand, *Short-Time Compensation: A Formula for Work Sharing*, Work in America Institute Series (Elmsford, N.Y.: Pergamon Press, 1984), 45.

16. MaCoy and Morand, *Short-Time Compensation*, 44.

17. Ibid., 48.

18. Burgoon and St. Louis, *The Impact of Work Sharing on Selected Motorola Units*, 4.

19. Alison Leigh Cowan, "The Plant-Closing Law Reaches Into Wall Street," *New York Times* (Oct. 27, 1988), C1.

20. Quoted in MaCoy and Morand, *Short-Time Compensation*, 166.

21. MaCoy and Morand, *Short-Time Compensation*, 26.

Conclusion: On to the Future—
Major Trends Affecting the Need for Flexibility

1. Thomas A. Stewart, "Welcome to the Revolution," *Fortune* (Dec. 13, 1993), 66.

2. In 1992 the Olsten Corporation reported that 40 percent of the 427 companies surveyed regarding their current staffing strategies were understaffed. *New*

Staffing Strategies for the 90s (Westbury, N.Y.: The Olsten Corporation, 1992). In a 1993 follow-up, 47 percent reported understaffing as a problem.

3. In addition to the Wyatt report cited in the Introduction, other reports on this subject have been Kenneth P. De Meuse, Paul A. Vanderheiden, and Thomas J. Bergmann, "Is Lean and Mean Really Better Than Fat and Happy?" paper presented at the Human Resource Planning Society Symposium, Cornell University, New York (June 17, 1993); American Management Association, *Survey on Downsizing* (1993); Helen Axel, *HR Executive Review: Downsizing* (New York: The Conference Board, 1993).

4. Jerome M. Rosow, *Work in America* 18, no. 12 (New York: Work in America Institute, 1993): 1.

5. Jeffrey Pfeffer, *Competitive Advantage through People* (Boston: Harvard Business School, 1994); Robert Waterman, *What America Does Right* (New York: Norton, 1994).

6. *The Economist* (March 19, 1994): 84.

7. "The Role of Workplace Flexibility in Managing Diversity," *Organizational Dynamics* (Summer 1993): 5.

8. "A Brave New Darwinian Workplace," *Fortune* (Jan. 25, 1993).

9. Ellen Galinsky, Jane T. Bond, and Dana E. Friedman, "The Changing Workforce: Highlights of the National Study" (New York: Families and Work Institute, 1993).

10. *Telecommuting Review: The Gordon Report* 10, no. 10 (Monmouth Junction, N.J.: Gil Gordon Associates, Oct. 1993), 12.

11. Lotte Bailyn, *Breaking the Mold: Women, Men and Time in the New Corporate World* (New York: The Free Press, 1993): xi.

12. Ibid., 11.

13. Hudson Institute, *Workforce 2000* (Washington, D.C.: Department of Labor Employment and Training Administration, May 1987).

14. "Looking to the Future: An Environmental Scan," AT&T internal corporate white paper, July 1992.

15. R. A. Lee, "Controlling Hours of Work," *Personnel Review* 14, no. 3 (1985): 3.

16. Ibid., 11.

17. Bernhard Teriet, "Flexiyear Schedules—Only a Matter of Time?" *Monthly Labor Review* (Dec. 1977): 62–65.

18. Philip Lynch, "Annual Hours: An Idea Whose Time Has Come," *Personnel Management* (Nov. 1985): 46. Most of the detailed information about annual hours programs in this chapter was drawn from Mr. Lynch's article.

19. Ibid., 46 and 47.

20. Ibid., 47.

21. Sue Hutchinson, "The Changing Face of Annual Labour," *Personnel Management* (April 1993): 42.

22. Ibid., 49.

23. Ibid.

24. Ibid., 47.

25. Sue Hutchinson, *Issues in People Management, No. 5: Annual Hours Working in the UK* (London: Institute of Personnel Management, May 1993), 86–87.

Suggested Reading List

General Reading

Bailyn, Lotte. *Breaking the Mold: Women, Men and Time in the New Corporate World.* New York: The Free Press, 1993.
Addresses the need for radically rethinking basic assumptions about career paths, management strategies, and the time clock.

Change at the Top: Working Flexibly at Senior and Managerial Levels in Organizations. London: New Ways to Work/London, 1993.

Christensen, Kathleen. "Flexible Staffing and Scheduling in U.S. Corporations," Research Bulletin No. 240. New York: The Conference Board, 1989.

Conditions of Work Digest 9, no. 2. "The Hours We Work: New Work Schedules in Policy and Practice." Geneva: International Labour Office, 1990.

Flexibility: Compelling Strategies for a Competitive Workplace. New Ways to Work staff in conjunction with Du Pont Co. San Francisco: New Ways to Work, 1991.

Hall, Douglas T., and Victoria A. Parker. "The Role of Workplace Flexibility in Managing Diversity." *Organizational Dynamics*, summer 1993.

Hinrichs, Karl, William Roche, and Carmen Sirianni. "Working Time in Transition: The Political Economy of Working Hours in Industrial Nations." Philadelphia: Temple University Press, 1991.

Jamieson, David, and Julie O'Mara. *Managing Workforce 2000.* San Francisco: Jossey-Bass, 1991.

Discusses how to go beyond "one size fits all" management and gain the diversity advantage. Proposes a six-step Flex-Management process.

Johnson, Arlene. *Work-Family Roundtable: Flexibility* 1, no. 1. New York: The Conference Board, 1991.

Society of Management Accountants of Canada, The. *Implementing Workplace Flexibility*. Hamilton, Ontario: The Society of Management Accountants of Canada, 1994.

Chapters 1 and 2:
Flextime and Compressed Workweek

Nollen, Stanley D., and Virginia H. Martin. *Alternative Work Schedules, parts 1, 2, and 3,* AMA Survey Reports. New York: AMA-COM, 1978.

Ronen, Simcha. *Flexible Working Hours: An Innovation in the Quality of Work Life*. New York: McGraw-Hill, 1981.

Extensive study of the implications of flextime, its results in a variety of organizations, and its effects on both the labor force and transportation.

Swart, J. Carrol. "Clerical Workers on Flextime: A Survey of Three Industries." *Personnel* (Apr. 1985): 40–44.

A survey of the effects of flextime on clerical workers in banking, insurance, and utilities. It indicates that flexible schedules improve productivity and morale.

Chapter 3:   Flexplace

Christensen, Kathleen E. *Impacts of Computer-Mediated Work on Women and Their Families*. New York: City College of New York, June 1985.

Discusses the role of technology in home-based work, the necessary safeguards, and the differences between being an entrepreneur and being an employee. The work was sponsored by the U.S. Office of Technology Assessment.

Fleming, Lis. *The One Minute Commuter: How to Keep Your Job and Stay at Home Telecommuting*. Davis, Calif.: Lis Fleming, Ltd., 1988.

Gordon, Gil. *Telecommuting Review: The Gordon Report*. Monmouth Junction, N.J.: Gil Gordon Associates.

Monthly newsletter presenting information on a variety of issues related to telecommuting and flexplace. It is an excellent resource for employers interested in telecommuting or those who already have a program up and running and want to keep abreast of new resources in this rapidly changing field.

Gordon, Gil, and Marcia M. Kelly. *Telecommuting: How to Make It Work for You and Your Company*. Englewood Cliffs, N.J.: Prentice Hall, 1986.

Provides evaluation guidelines for the full range of remote work locations, with special attention to the pros and cons of the home as a work site. Explains remote supervision options, discusses how to determine when on-site supervision is needed, and provides a job-selection profile that helps determine which jobs will best fit into a telecommuting program.

Gordon, Gil, Mike Gray, and Noel Hodson. *Teleworking Explained*. New York: Wiley, 1993.

Midwest Institute for Telecommuting Education (MITE). *Telecommuting Implementation Manual*. Minneapolis, Minn., 1993.

Treasury Board of Canada. *Telework Pilot Program in the Public Service*. Ottawa: Treasury Board of Canada, 1993.

U.S. Dept. of Labor and Local 12, AFGE, AFL-CIO. *Flexplace Pilot Guidelines*. Washington, D.C.: Dept. of Labor, 1994.

Wheeler, Michael, and Dana Zackin. *Work-Family Roundtable: Telecommuting*. New York: The Conference Board, 1994.

Chapter 4:   Regular Part-Time Employment

Flexible Work Arrangements: Establishing Options for Managers and Professionals. Catalyst staff. New York: Catalyst, 1989.

Report on a study of the use of part-time, job sharing, and telecommuting in managerial and professional levels in U.S. companies.

Flexible Working Arrangements II: Succeeding with Part-Time Options. Catalyst staff. New York: Catalyst, 1993.

Longitudinal follow-up on the study initiated in 1989. Focuses on the impact on employees rather than on the human resources aspect of flexible work arrangements.

Herchenroether, Sherry. "Retain or Replace? Not So Rhetorical a Question." *Looking Ahead* XIII, nos. 1/2. Washington, D.C.: National Planning Association, 39.

Describes the process Aetna Life & Casualty went through in assessing the cost of losing a significant number of employees who did not return from maternity leave.

International Labour Office. *Part-Time Work,* Report V (2). Geneva, Switzerland: ILO, 1993.

Report on the ILO's 1993 International Labor Conference, which laid the groundwork for adopting new standards to reinforce the protection of part-time work and recognize the growing importance of part-time work for employment growth and economic prosperity.

Jallade, Jean-Pierre. *Towards a Policy of Part-Time Employment.* Maastricht, Netherlands: European Centre for Work and Society, 1984.

Studies the extent and nature of part-time employment in Europe and recommends a policy to create more part-time jobs.

Kahne, Hilda. *Reconceiving Part-Time Work: New Perspectives for Older Workers and Women.* Totowa, N.J.: Rowman and Allanheld, 1985.

Describes programs that permit shorter hours and more leisure in later life and a reduced schedule for women during the child-rearing years.

Manin, Mark B. "Flexible Benefits for Part-Time Employees." *Benefits News Analysis* 9, no. 3 (1987): 12.

Nollen, Stanley D., Brenda Broz Eddy, and Virginia H. Martin. *Permanent Part-Time Employment: The Manager's Perspective.* New York: Praeger, 1978.

Schor, Juliet B. *The Overworked American: The Unexpected Decline of Leisure.* New York: Basic Books, 1991.

Documents the unanticipated decline in leisure both at work and in the home.

Tilly, Chris. *Short Hours, Short Shrift: Causes and Consequences of Part-Time Work.* WDC Economic Policy Institute, 1990.

Examines the growth in involuntary part-time employment and the resistance to developing regular part-time opportunities within the framework of core employment.

Chapter 5:   Job Sharing

McGuire, Nan, et al. *Job Sharing in Health Care*. San Francisco: New Ways to Work, 1984.
A guide for administrators and job sharers, with case studies, cost analyses, and sample proposals.

New York State Department of Civil Service. *Part-Time Schedules: A Guide for NYS Supervisors and Managers*. Albany, N.Y.: New York State, Oct. 1985.

Olmsted, Barney. "Job Sharing: An Emerging Work Style." *International Labour Review* 118, no. 3 (May–June 1979): 283–297.
Explains the mechanics of job sharing and discusses its broader implications for society.

Olmsted, Barney, and Suzanne Smith. *The Job Sharing Handbook*. San Francisco: New Ways to Work, revised edition 1994.
An essential guide to sharing the responsibilities and rewards of one full-time job. Contains checklists, questionnaires, case histories, and practical suggestions.

Zackin, Dana. *Work-Family Roundtable: Job Sharing*. New York: The Conference Board, 1994.

Chapter 6:   Phased and Partial Retirement

Axel, Helen. *Job Banks for Retirees*. Research Bulletin No. 929. New York: The Conference Board, 1989.

Barocas, Victor S., et al. "Employee, Retiree Options for an Aging Work Force." *Business and Health* (Apr. 1985): 25–29.
Includes a discussion of retirement-oriented work options.

Carlson, Elliot. "Longer Work Life? A Look at the Future of Retirement." *Modern Maturity* (June–July 1985): 22–28.
Presents arrangements for retirees to work part-time, in special programs, or as job sharers.

Christensen, Kathleen. *Flexible Work Arrangements and Older Workers: Older Workers' Experiences with Part-Time, Temporary, Off-the-Books Jobs and Self-Employment.* New York City Center for Human Environments, Graduate School, City University of New York, May 27, 1988.

Foulkes, Fred K., and Robert D. Paul. "Company Liabilities Are Soaring." *New York Times* (Nov. 29, 1987): B2.

Looks at the cost of some companies' early retirement programs. Discusses the efforts of some organizations to contain retiree health care expenses.

Honig, Marjorie, and Gloria Hanoch. "Partial Retirement as a Separate Mode of Retirement Behavior." *Journal of Human Resources* (winter 1985): 21–46.

A study of the various forms of partial retirement, with many detailed tables.

State of California, Legislative Analyst. *The Reduced Work Load Program in the State Teachers' Retirement System.* Sacramento, Calif.: Sept. 1980.

Explains the regulations for the program and its costs. Indicates a net saving to the school system.

Swank, Constance. *Phased Retirement: The European Experience.* Washington, D.C.: National Council for Alternative Work Patterns, 1982. (available from New Ways to Work, San Francisco)

Discusses the operation, costs, and benefits of phased retirement programs in six European countries. Includes case studies and company profiles.

Chapter 7:   Voluntary Reduced Work Time Programs

Best, Fred. *Exchanging Earnings for Leisure: Findings of an Exploratory National Survey on Work Time Preferences.* R&D Monograph 79. Washington, D.C.: U.S. Department of Labor, Employment and Training Administration, 1980.

Moorman, Barbara, and Barney Olmsted. *V-Time—A New Way to Work: A Resource Manual for Employers and Employees.* San Francisco: New Ways to Work, 1985.

A unique book that contains detailed case histories, sample legislation, useful forms, and much more.

Chapter 8: Leave Time

Axel, Helen. *Redefining Corporate Sabbaticals for the 1990's.* Research
Bulletin no. 1005. New York: The Conference Board, 1989.

Best, Fred. *Flexible Life Scheduling: Breaking the Education-Work-Retirement Lockstep.* New York: Praeger, 1980.

Considers the appropriate allocation of work, income, and leisure throughout the life span.

FlexPulse: Time Away from Work. New York: Towers Perrin, 1993.

Reports on a survey of 162 employers, many of whom have
programs that give employees more flexibility in deciding when
to take time off and for what purposes.

Friedman, Dana E., Ellen Galinsky, and Veronica Plowden, eds.
Parental Leave and Productivity: Current Research. New York: Families and Work Institute, 1992.

Compilation of papers from researchers and policy experts on
the impact of employees taking leaves.

Milofsky, David. "The Baby vs. the Corporation." *Working Woman*
(June 1985): 133–134.

Discusses paternity leave as a benefit required by laws against
discrimination and also expresses what such leave means to the
author's feelings as a parent.

O'Malley, I. K. "Paid Educational Leave in Australia, Canada,
Ireland, and the United Kingdom." *International Labour Review*
(Mar.–Apr. 1982): 169–183.

Examines the policies of the four countries following the adoption of International Labor Organization Convention 140.

"So You Think You're Ready for the FMLA." Society of Human Resource
Management. Alexandria, Va.: SHRM, 1993.

A reformatted version of the proposed FMLA regulations. Includes a sample poster and sample medical certification form.

"Survey Results: Family and Medical Leave Act." Berkeley, Calif.: William M. Mercer, Inc. and University of California, Berkeley, Jan.
1994.

Survey of 980 employers in several western states on what
actions employers are taking in response to the law, how they

are interpreting the law, and administrative, financial, and human resource impacts they have identified.

Wood, Jack M. *Educational Leave and the Balance of Skills: An Australian Perspective*. Paris: Organization for Economic Cooperation and Development, Jan. 1993.
Maintains that Australia will fall behind the world "balance of skills" if more is not done to provide leave for continuing education and describes the extent of public- and private-sector schemes.

Chapter 9: Work Sharing

Batz, Julie, and the staff of New Ways to Work. *Work Sharing: An Alternative to Layoffs*. San Francisco: New Ways to Work, 1988.

Best, Fred. *Reducing Workweeks to Prevent Layoffs: The Economic and Social Impacts of Unemployment Insurance-Supported Work Sharing*. Philadelphia: Temple University Press, 1988.

————. "Short-time Compensation in North America: Trends and Prospects." *Personnel* (Jan. 1985): 34–41.
Examines short-time compensation experience (which includes partial unemployment insurance benefits) in California, Canada, and West Germany and its impact on companies, workers, and governments.

————. *Work Sharing Issues, Policy Options and Prospects*. Kalamazoo, Mich.: The W. E. Upjohn Institute for Employment Research, 1981.
Principal topics include the variety of ways in which work can be shared to reduce unemployment, the economic effects of work sharing, and how work sharing can be made more attractice to workers and employers.

De Meuse, Kenneth P., Paul Al Vanderheiden, and Thomas J. Bergmann. *Is Lean and Mean Really Better Than Fat and Happy?* Eau Clair, Wis.: University of Wisconsin, 1993.
Paper delivered to Human Resource Planning Society Research Symposium, Cornell University, New York. Challenges the conventional wisdom of cutting the size of the organization to reduce fat and waste when sales are lagging and costs are rising.

MaCoy, Ramelle, and Martin J. Morand, eds. *Short-time Compensation: A Formula for Work Sharing*. New York: Pergamon Press, 1984.

A Work in America Institute-sponsored study of alternatives to layoffs in Canada and West Germany and in the states of California, Oregon, and Arizona. Includes management and union viewpoints.

Meltz, Noah, Frank Reid, and Gerald S. Swartz. *Sharing the Work: An Analysis of the Issues of Worksharing and Job Sharing*. Toronto, Ontario, Canada: University of Toronto Press, 1981.

Presents a theoretical model to assess the feasibility of shared employment in the Canadian labor market, with costs and implications for workers and government. Has a good analysis of job sharing.

O'Hara, Bruce. *Jobs 4 ALL!* Courtenay, B.C.: Work Well Publications, 1993.

Conclusion: On to the Future—Major Trends Affecting The Need for Flexibility

"Changing Times: A Guide to Flexible Work Patterns for Human Resource Managers." London: New Ways to Work, November 1993.

A practical manual that will help managers implement a range of flexible working arrangements. Contains case histories from National Westminster Bank, Boots the Chemists, The Inland Revenue, and others.

"Flexible Working Practices." Stockton-on-Tees, United Kingdom: Jim Conway Memorial Foundation. Trade Union Report 7, no. 2 (Mar. 1986): 8–17.

Hutchinson, Sue. *Annual Hours Working in the UK, Issues in People Management*, no. 5. Institute of Personnel Management, May 1993.

Reports on the trends and variations of annual hours arrangements in the UK. Includes case studies.

Income Data Services. *Part-Time Work*. Study no. 495. July 1991.

Looks at the reasons why employers introduce annual hours programs and examines how the schemes operate.

Lee, R. A. "Controlling Hours of Work." *Personnel Review* 14, no. 3 (1985): 3.

Provides an overview of the various innovations that have been introduced in the management of hours systems and some of the related reserarch initiatives that have been undertaken. The author, a member of the department of management studies at the University of Loughborough, Great Britain, notes that "It is surprising how little attention has been focused on [organizational hours systems] relative to other influence mechanisms, such as pay, job design, appraisal systems, budgets, and so on."

Lynch, Philip. "Annual Hours: An Idea Whose Time Has Come." *Personnel Management* (Nov. 1985): 46–50.

An overview of annual hours contracts, a new way to organize work time that is attracting increasing interest in some industries in Great Britain.

Woodcock, Gerry. "Achieving Annual Hours." *Industrial Society* 68 (June 1986): 12–14.

A report on how Thames Board, Workington Division, a part of Thames Group, a wholly owned subisdiary of Unilever in Great Britain, achieved an annual hours contract over an eighteen-month period.

Index